The Books of HAGGAI and MALACHI

PIETER A. VERHOEF

WILLIAM B. EERDMANS PUBLISHING COMPANY
GRAND RAPIDS, MICHIGAN

255 Jefferson Ave. S.E., Grand Rapids, Michigan 49503

Printed in the United States of America

00 9 8 7 6 5

Library of Congress Cataloging in Publication Data

Verhoef, Pieter A.
The books of Haggai and Malachi.
(The New international commentary on the Old Testament)
Bibliography: p. xv.
Includes indexes.
1. Bible. O.T. Haggai—Commentaries. 2. Bible.
O.T. Malachi—Commentaries. I. Title. II. Series.
BS1655.3.V47 1986 224′.97077 86-19830
ISBN 0-8028-2533-8

This book is dedicated to the memory of
my parents:
Lodewijk Henricus Wilhelm Verhoef (1880–1955)
Antje Maria Verhoef-Poletiek (1883–1956)

AUTHOR'S PREFACE

Many years ago I was invited to write this volume, but its speedy completion was prevented by my involvement with the New Afrikaans Translation. In fact, I completed this manuscript just about the time that the New Afrikaans Translation was published on December 3, 1983. Professor R. K. Harrison, the general editor of NICOT, had to apply both the carrot and the stick in order to expedite the completion of the commentary.

The books of Haggai and Malachi belong to the Minor Prophets, so-called—according to Augustine—not because they are of less importance than the Major Prophets (Isaiah, Jeremiah, and Ezekiel) but because "their messages are comparatively short."

The significance of both prophets has been variously assessed. In his important commentary on Haggai, W. Rudolph concludes that the message of this prophet has no relevance whatsoever for the Christian faith. This verdict is in accordance with a widely held view that the OT must be interpreted entirely on its own, without a perspective on the realities of the NT dispensation. This kind of approach ignores a major hermeneutical key to the understanding of the OT. In the Introduction and throughout the Commentary I have tried to stress the relevance of the prophet's message in terms of continuity and discontinuity for the Christian church.

The same negative evaluation has been given to Malachi. According to B. Duhm, for example, the book of Malachi reflects the intellectual poverty of its time, and the prophet's message cannot be compared with that of the "classical" prophets of preexilic times. These and similar views are subjective and do not comply with the real significance of Malachi's message. The book of Malachi contains a number of high points in the history of the divine revelation in the OT, such as the stress on God's enduring love for his covenant people (1:2–5) and the surprising emphasis on the importance of the priesthood's teaching function that is unsurpassed elsewhere in the OT (2:1–9). Nowhere else do we find such an elevated view of marriage or such an explicit condemnation of divorce (2:10–16), and nowhere else is the antithesis between the righteous and the wicked explicated in such an eschatological perspective (3:13–21 [Eng. 4:3]).

It had been my privilege to write a commentary on Malachi for the Dutch series *Commentaar op het Oude Testament* (Kampen: Kok, 1972). The present commentary deviates from its Dutch counterpart in two major respects: it introduces structural analysis as an exegetical method, and it emphasizes the message rather than technical detail.

In conclusion, I would like to thank all those who have shared with me the exhilarating experience of writing, typing, and editing this commentary. A special word of thanks and appreciation goes to Professor R. K. Harrison for the invitation to participate in this NICOT venture and for his subsequent scrutiny and editing of the manuscript. A word of thanks also to Mr. Gary Lee for his professional handling of the manuscript and for his major and minor corrections. Special thanks also to my daughter-in-law Elza not only for typing the manuscript but also for her keen interest in the project itself,* and to my wife Rita for her constant support and encouragement. The librarians and staff of the libraries both of the Faculty of Theology and of the University of Stellenbosch have rendered invaluable assistance in finding the relevant literature.

Both my parents were keen students of the Bible; they taught me to love the Scriptures, and I shared with them a conservative and evangelical approach to the Bible as the Word of God. Especially my mother stirred in me an interest in the prophecies of the OT. That is why I am dedicating the commentary to their esteemed memory.

PIETER A. VERHOEF

*Unfortunately, Elza died prior to publication.

CONTENTS

ABBREVIATIONS

AfO	*Archiv für Orientforschung*
ANEP	*Ancient Near Eastern Pictures*. 2nd ed. Edited by J. B. Pritchard. Princeton: Princeton University, 1969
ANET	*Ancient Near Eastern Texts*. 3rd ed. Edited by J. B. Pritchard. Princeton: Princeton University, 1969
AOB	H. Gressmann, *Altorientalische Bilder zum Alten Testament*. Berlin-Leipzig: 1927
AT	Ancien/Altes Testament
ATD	Das Alte Testament Deutsch
ATANT	Abhandlungen zur Theologie des Alten und Neuen Testaments
AV	Authorized (King James) Version
BA	*The Biblical Archaeologist*
BASOR	*Bulletin of the American Schools of Oriental Research*
BAT	Die Botschaft des Alten Testaments
BDB	F. Brown, S. R. Driver, and C. Briggs. *A Hebrew and English Lexicon of the Old Testament*. Oxford: Clarendon Press, 1907, repr. 1959
BeO	*Bibbia e oriente*
BHK	Biblia Hebraica. 3rd ed. Edited by R. Kittel. Stuttgart: Deutsche Bibelgesellschaft, 1937
BHS	*Biblia Hebraica Stuttgartensia*. Edited by K. Elliger and W. Rudolph. Stuttgart: Deutsche Bibelstiftung, 1968–1977
BHT	Beiträge zur historischen Theologie
Bib	*Biblica*
BibLeb	*Bibel und Leben*
BJRL	*Bulletin of the John Rylands Library*
BK	Biblischer Kommentar
BOT	Boeken van het Oude Testament
BT	*Bible Translator*
BTB	*Biblical Theology Bulletin*
BV	The Berkeley Version
BWANT	Beiträge zur Wissenschaft vom Alten und Neuen Testament
BZ	*Biblische Zeitschrift*
BZAW	Beiheft *ZAW*

CBQ	*Catholic Biblical Quarterly*
COT	Commentar op het Oude Testament
CurTM	*Currents in Theology and Mission*
DJD	*Discoveries in the Judaean Desert (of Jordan).* Oxford
ed.	edition, editor
ETR	*Etudes théologiques et religieuses*
EvQ	*Evangelical Quarterly*
EvT	*Evangelische Theologie*
ExpTim	*Expository Times*
FRLANT	Forschungen zur Religion und Literatur des Alten und Neuen Testaments
Fest.	Festschrift
GB	W. Gesenius and F. Buhl. *Hebräisches und aramäisches Handwörterbuch über das Alte Testament.* Leipzig: 1921
GKC	W. Gesenius, E. Kautzsch, and A. E. Cowley. *Hebrew Grammar.* Oxford: Clarendon Press, 1910, repr. 1946, 1949
GN	Die Gute Nachricht (Die Bibel in heutigem Deutsch), 1982
Groot NB	Groot Nieuws Bijbel, 1983
GTT	*Gereformeerd Theologisch Tijdschrift*
HAT	Handbuch zum Alten Testament
HKAT	Handkommentar zum Alten Testament
HSAT	Die Heilige Schrift des Alten Testaments
HTR	*Harvard Theological Review*
HUCA	*Hebrew Union College Annual*
IB	*Interpreter's Bible.* 12 vols. Edited by G. Buttrick. Nashville: Abingdon Press, 1952–1957
ICC	International Critical Commentary
IDB	*Interpreter's Dictionary of the Bible.* 4 vols. Edited by G. Buttrick. Nashville: Abingdon Press, 1962. Supplementary volume edited by K. Crim, 1976
IEJ	*Israel Exploration Journal*
Int	*Interpretation*
ISBE	*International Standard Bible Encyclopedia.* 4 vols. Rev. ed. Edited by G. W. Bromiley, et al. Grand Rapids: Eerdmans, 1979–1987
JB	Jerusalem Bible, 1966
JBL	*Journal of Biblical Literature*
JBR	*Journal of Bible and Religion*
JJS	*Journal of Jewish Studies*
JNES	*Journal of Near Eastern Studies*
JPSV	Jewish Publication Society Version
JQR	*Jewish Quarterly Review*
JSS	*Journal of Semitic Studies*
JTS	*Journal of Theological Studies*

KAI	H. Donner and W. Röllig. *Kanaanäische und aramäische Inschriften.* 3 vols. Wiesbaden: Harrassowitz, 1962–64
KAT	Kommentar zum Alten Testament
KB	L. Koehler and W. Baumgartner. *Lexicon in Veteris Testamenti Libros.* Leiden: Brill, 1953
KEH	Kurzgefasstes Exegetisches Handbuch zum Alten Testament
KHC	Kurzer Handkommentar zum Alten Testament
KV	Korte Verklaring der heilige Schrift
LB	Die Lewende Bybel, 1982
lit.	literally
LXX	Septuagint
Moffatt	J. Moffatt, *A New Translation of the Bible,* 1926
MPG	J. P. Migne. *Patrologiae cursus completus.* Series Graeca. 162 vols. 1857–1866
MPL	J. P. Migne. *Patrologiae cursus completus.* Series Latina. 221 vols. 1844–1864
ms(s).	manuscript(s)
MT	Masoretic (Hebrew) Text
Murabba'at	The Scroll of the XII Prophets from the Wadi Murabba'at. See *DJD* II:181–205
NAV(B)	Nuwe Afrikaanse Vertaling (Bybel), 1983
NBC	*The New Bible Commentary.* Edited by D. Guthrie, et al. 3rd ed. London: Inter-Varsity, Grand Rapids: Eerdmans, 1970
NBD	*The New Bible Dictionary.* Edited by J. D. Douglas. London: Inter-Varsity, Grand Rapids: Eerdmans, 1962
NBG	Dutch Version of the Nederlands Bijbelgenootschap, 1951
NEB	New English Bible. Cambridge: 1970
NGTT	*Nederduitse Gereformeerde Teologiese Tydskrif*
NIV	New International Version, 1978
NT	New Testament
NTT	*Nederlands Theologisch Tijdschrift*
OT	Old Testament
OTL	Old Testament Library
OTS	*Oudtestamentische Studiën*
OTWSA	*Ou-Testamentiese Werkgemeenskap van Suid-Afrika*
par.	parallel
part.	participle
PEQ	*Palestine Exploration Quarterly*
Pesh.	Peshitta
POT	De Prediking van het Oude Testament
RB	*Revue Biblique*
RGG	*Religion in Geschichte und Gegenwart.* 6 vols. Edited by K. Galling. 3rd ed. Tübingen: Mohr/Siebeck, 1957–62

RHPR	*Revue d'histoire et de philosophie religieuses*
RSV	Revised Standard Version, 1952
RTR	*Reformed Theological Review*
RV	Revised Version, 1885
SAT	Die Schriften des Alten Testaments im Auswahl. . . .
ST	*Studia Theologica*
Syr.	Syriac
Targ.	Targum
TBT	*The Bible Today*
TEV	Today's English Version (Good News Bible), 1976
TDNT	*Theological Dictionary of the New Testament*. 10 vols. Edited by G. Kittel and G. Friedrich. Translated by G. W. Bromiley. Grand Rapids: Eerdmans, 1964–1976
TDOT	*Theological Dictionary of the Old Testament*. Edited by G. Botterweck and H. Ringgren. Translated by D. Green, et al. Grand Rapids: Eerdmans, 1974–
THAT	*Theologisches Handwörterbuch zum Alten Testament*. 2 vols. Edited by E. Jenni and C. Westermann. München: Chr. Kaiser, 1971–76
TLZ	*Theologische Literaturzeitung*
TRu	*Theologische Rundschau*
TU	Texte und Untersuchungen
TZ	*Theologische Zeitschrift*
UT	C. H. Gordon, *Ugaritic Textbook*. Analecta Orientalia 38. Rome: Pontifical Biblical Institute, 1965
Vulg.	Vulgate
VT	*Vetus Testamentum*
VTSup	*Vetus Testamentum,* Supplements
WMANT	Wissenschaftliche Monographien zum Alten und Neuen Testament
WZKM	*Wiener Zeitschrift für die Kunde des Morgenlandes*
ZAW	*Zeitschrift für die alttestamentliche Wissenschaft*
ZDMG	*Zeitschrift der Deutschen Palästina-Vereins*
ZDPV	*Zeitschrift des deutschen Palästina-Vereins*
ZPEB	*Zondervan Pictorial Encyclopedia of the Bible*. 5 vols. Edited by M. C. Tenney. Grand Rapids: Zondervan, 1975
ZTK	*Zeitschrift für Theologie und Kirche*

BIBLIOGRAPHY

Ackroyd, P. R. "The Book of Haggai and Zechariah I–VIII." *JJS* 3 (1952) 151–56.

______. *Exile and Restoration.* OTL. 2nd ed. London: SCM, Philadelphia: Westminster, 1972.

______. "Haggai." In *Peake's Commentary on the Bible.* Rev. ed. Edited by M. Black, et al. London: Nelson, 1962. Pp. 643–45.

______. "The History of Israel in the Exilic and Post-Exilic Periods." In *Tradition and Interpretation.* Edited by G. W. Anderson. Oxford: Clarendon Press, 1979. Pp. 320–50.

______. "Some Interpretative Glosses in the Book of Haggai." *JJS* 7 (1956) 163–67.

______. "Studies in the Book of Haggai." *JJS* 2 (1951) 163–76; 3 (1952) 1–13.

______. "Two Old Testament Problems of the Early Persian Period." *JNES* 17 (1958) 13–37.

Adamson, J. T. H. "Malachi." In *The New Bible Commentary.* 3rd ed. Edited by D. Guthrie, et al. London: Inter-Varsity, Grand Rapids: Eerdmans, 1970.

Albright, W. F. *The Biblical Period from Abraham to Ezra: An Historical Survey.* New York: Harper & Row, 1963.

Allison, Dale C., Jr. "Elijah Must Come First." *JBL* 103 (1984) 256–58.

Allrik, H. L. "The Lists of Zerubbabel (Neh. 7 and Ezra 2) and the Hebrew Numeral Notation." *BASOR* 136 (1954) 21–27.

Amsler, S. *Aggēe-Zecharie 1–8.* Commentaire de l'Ancien Testament 11. Neuchatel: Delachaux & Niestlé, 1981.

Andersen, F. I. "Who Built the Second Temple?" *Australian Biblical Review* 6 (1958) 1–25.

André, T. *Le prophète Aggée.* Paris: Fischbacher, 1895.

Baldwin, J. G. *Haggai-Zechariah-Malachi.* Tyndale Old Testament Commentaries. London: Tyndale, Downers Grove: Inter-Varsity, 1972.

Bauer, H. and P. Leander, *Historische Grammatik der hebräischen Sprache des Alten Testamentes.* Repr. Hildesheim: Olms, 1965.

Bentzen, A. "Quelques remarques sur le mouvement messianique parmi les Juifs aux environs de l'an 520 avant Jesus-Christ." *RHPR* 10 (1930) 493–503.

Beuken, W. A. M. *Haggai-Sacharja 1–8: Studien zur Überlieferungsgeschichte der frühnachexilischen Prophetie*. Assen: Van Gorcum, 1967.

Bewer, J. A. *The Book of the Twelve Prophets*. Vol. 2. Harper Bible. New York: Harper and Brothers, 1949.

Beyse, K. M. *Serubbabel und die Königserwartungen der Propheten Haggai und Sacharja*. Stuttgart: Calwer, 1972.

Blenkinsopp, J. *A History of Prophecy in Israel*. London: SPCK, Philadelphia: Westminster, 1984.

Bloomhardt, P. F. "The Poems of Haggai." *HUCA* 5 (1928) 153–95.

Boecker, H. J. "Bemerkungen zur formgeschichtlichen Terminologie des Buches Maleachi." *ZAW* 78 (1966) 78–80.

Böhme, W. "Zu Maleachi und Haggai." *ZAW* 7 (1887) 215–16.

Bonnandière, A. M. *Les douze petits prophètes*. Bibl. Augustiana. Paris: 1963.

Botterweck, G. J. "Jakob habe ich lieb—Esau hasse ich," *BibLeb* 1 (1960) 28–38.

———. "Ideal und Wirklichkeit der Jerusalemer Priester, Auslegung von Mal. 1:6–10; 2:1–9," *BibLeb* 1 (1960) 100–109.

———. "Schelt- und Mahnrede gegen Mischehe und Ehescheidung, Auslegung von Mal. 2:2, 10–16," *BibLeb* 1 (1960) 179–85.

———. "Die Sonne der Gerechtigkeit am Tage Jahwes, Auslegung von Mal. 3:13–21," *BibLeb* 1 (1960) 253–60.

Brandenburg, H. *Die kleinen Propheten*. Vol. 2. Das Lebendige Wort, 10. Basel/Giessen: Brunnen, 1963.

Braun, R. L. "Malachi: A Catechism for Times of Disappointment." *CurTM* 4 (1977) 297–303.

Bright, J. "Aggée: Un exercice en herméneutique," *ETR* 44 (1969) 3–25 (tr. D. Lys).

———. "Haggai among the Prophets: Reflections on Preaching from the Old Testament." In *From Faith to Faith*. Fest. D. G. Miller. Edited by D. Hadidian. Pittsburgh Theological Monograph Series, 31. Pittsburgh: Penwick, 1979. Pp. 219–34.

———. *A History of Israel*. 3rd ed. Philadelphia: Westminster, 1981.

Brockelmann, C. *Hebräische Syntax*. Neukirchen: Kreis Moers, 1956.

Brockington, L. H. "Malachi." In *Peake's Commentary on the Bible*. Rev. ed. Edited by M. Black, et al. London: Nelson, 1962. Pp. 656–58.

Buccellatti, G. "Gli Israeliti di Palestina al tempo dell'esilio." *BeO* 2 (1960) 199–210.

Budde, K. "Zum Text der drei letzten kleinen Propheten." *ZAW* 26 (1906) 1–28.

Bulmerincq, A. von. *Der Prophet Maleachi*. Vol. 1 (Dorpat: Matthieseus, 1926). Vol. 2 (Tartu: 1932).

Bunsen, C. C. J. *Die Propheten*. Die Bibel oder die Schriften des Alte und Neue Bundes. Leipzig: Brockhaus, 1860.

Calvin, J. *Praelectiones in XII Prophetes*. Amsterdam: 1667. Eng. tr.: *Commentaries on the Twelve Minor Prophets*. Vols. 4 and 5. Translated by John Owen. Grand Rapids: Eerdmans, 1950.
Cappellus, L. *Commentarii et Notae Criticae in Vetus Testamentum*. Amstelodami: 1689.
Caquot, A. "Brève explication du livre de Malachie." *Positions Luthériennes* 17 (1969) 187–201; 18 (1970) 4–16.
Cashdan, E., et al. *The Twelve Prophets*. Edited by A. Cohen. Soncino Bible. London: Soncino, 1948.
Chary, T. *Aggée-Zacharie-Malachie*. Sources Bibliques. Paris: Gabalda, 1969.
______. *Les prophètes et le culte à partir de l'exil*. Paris: Desclée, 1955.
Clark, David J. "Problems in Haggai 2:15–19." *BT* 1 (1983) 432–39.
Clark, D. G. *Elijah as Eschatological High Priest: An Examination of the Elijah Tradition in Mal. 3:22–24*. Notre Dame, Ind.: University of Notre Dame, 1975.
Clement of Alexandria. *Stromata* 5, col. 133–36.
Collins, John J. "The Message of Malachi." *TBT* 22 (1984) 209–15.
Coppens, J. *Les douze petits prophètes*. Paris: Bruges, 1950.
Cyrillus of Alexandria. In MPG 71, col. 327–1062; 72, col. 11–364 (see also the edition of P. E. Pusey [Oxford: 1868, 1964]).
Dalman, G. *Arbeit und Sitte in Palästina*. 7 vols. Repr. Hildesheim: Olms, 1964.
Deddens, K. *Maleachi's Dialogen*. Goes: Oosterbaan & Le Cointre, 1970.
Deden, D. *De kleine profeten*. BOT. Roermond-Maaseik: Romen & Zonen, 1953–1956.
Deissler, A. *Zwölf Propheten*. Die Neue Echter Bibel 4. Stuttgart: Echter, 1981.
Deissler, A. and M. Delcor. *Les petits prophètes*. Vol. 2. La Sainte Bible, Pirot-Clamer 8. Paris: Letouzey & Ané, 1964.
Deist, F. E. *Die dag sal brand*. Cape Town: N. G. Kerk Uitgewers, 1976.
Dentan, R. C. "The Book of Malachi." In *IB* 6. Nashville: Abingdon, 1956. Pp. 1115–44.
De Vaux, R. "The Decrees of Cyrus and Darius on the Rebuilding of the Temple." In *The Bible and the Ancient Near East*. Translated by D. McHugh. London: Darton, Longman & Todd, Garden City: Doubleday, 1972. Pp. 61–96. (Originally published in *RB* 46 [1937] 29–57.)
Devescovi, U. "L'alleanza di Jahwe con Levi." *BeO* 4 (1962) 205–18.
De Villiers, D. "Maleagi." In *Bybel met verklarende aantekeninge*. Vol. 2. Cape Town: Verenigde Protestantse Uitgewers, 1958.
Driver, S. R. *The Minor Prophets*. Century Bible. 2 vols. New York: Oxford, 1906.
______. *A Treatise on the Use of Tenses in Hebrew*. Oxford: Clarendon, 1874.
Drusius. *Commentarius in Prophetas Minores XII*. 1627.

Duhm, B. *Anmerkungen zu den zwölf Propheten*. Sonderndruck aus der ZAW. Giessen: Rickei'sche, 1911.

Dumbrell, W. J. "Kingship and Temple in the Post-Exilic Period." *RTR* 37 (1979) 33–42.

Dummelow, J. R., ed. *A Commentary on the Holy Bible*. London: Macmillan, 1944.

Edelkoort, A. H. *De Christusverwachting en het OT*. Wageningen: Veenman & Zonen, 1941.

Edgar, S. L. *The Minor Prophets*. Epworth Preacher's Commentaries. London: Epworth, 1962.

Ehrlich, A. B. *Randglossen zur hebräischen Bibel*. Repr. Hildesheim: Olms, 1969.

Elliger, K. *Das Buch der zwölf kleinen Propheten*. Vol. 2. ATD 25/2. 7th ed. Göttingen: Vandenhoeck & Ruprecht, 1975.

______. "Maleachi und die kirchliche Tradition." In *Tradition und Situation: Studien zur alttestamentlichen Prophetie*. Fest. A. Weiser. Edited by E. Würthwein and O. Kaiser. Göttingen: Vandenhoeck & Ruprecht, 1963. Pp. 43–48.

Ewald, H. *Die Propheten des Alten Bundes*. 2nd ed. Göttingen: Vandenhoeck & Ruprecht, 1867.

Eybers, I. H. "Haggai, the Mouthpiece of the Lord." *Theologia Evangelica* 1 (1968) 62–71.

______. "Malachi: The Messenger of the Lord." *Theologia Evangelica* 3 (1970) 12–20.

______. "The Rebuilding of the Temple according to Haggai and Zechariah." In *Studies in Old Testament Prophecy. OTWSA*. Edited by W. C. van Wyk. Potchefstroom: Pro Rege, 1975. Pp. 15–26.

Fischer, J. A. "Notes on the Literary Form and Message of Malachi." *CBQ* 34 (1972) 315–20.

Fleming, J. "Thoughts on Haggai and Zechariah." *JBL* 53 (1934) 229–35.

Fourie, L. C. H. "Die betekenis van die verbond as sleutel vir Maleagi." M.Th. thesis. University of Stellenbosch, 1982.

Freedman, D. N. "Divine Commitment and Human Obligation." *Int* 18 (1964) 419–31.

Freeman, H. E. *An Introduction to the Old Testament Prophets*. Chicago: Moody, 1969.

Frey, H. *Das Buch der Kirche in der Weltwende: Die kleinen nachexilischen Propheten*. BAT 24. 5th ed. Stuttgart: Calwer, 1963.

Gailey, J. H. *Micah to Malachi*. Layman's Bible Commentaries. London: SCM, 1962.

Galling, K. *Studien zur Geschichte Israels im persischen Zeitalter*. Tübingen: Mohr, 1964.

______. "Serubbabel und die Wiederaufbau des Tempels in Jerusalem." In *Verbannung und Heimkehr*. Fest. W. Rudolph. Edited by A. Kuschke. Tübingen: Mohr, 1961. Pp. 67–96.

Gelin, A. *Aggée, Zacharie, Malachie*. Bible de Jerusalem. Paris: Cerf, 1973. Pp. 1385–1401.

______. "Message aux prêtres (Mal. 2:1–9)." *Bible et Vie Chrétienne* 30 (1959) 14–20.

Gelston, A. "The Foundation of the Second Temple." *VT* 16 (1966) 232–35.

Gemser, B. *Hebreeuse Spraakkuns*. Pretoria: J. L. van Schaik, 1953.

Goddard, B. L. "Malachi." In *The Biblical Expositor* 2. Edited by C. F. H. Henry. Philadelphia: Holman, 1960.

Grosheide, H. H. *Israel na de Babylonische ballingschap*. Verkenning en Bezinning 13. Kampen: Kok, 1979.

______. *De terugkeer uit de ballingschap*. Exegetica 2/4. The Hague: Uitgeverij van Keulen, 1957.

______. "Zerubbabel." *GTT* 48 (1948) 65ff.

Guglielmo, A. de. *Dissertatio exegetica de reditu Eliae (Mal. 3,22–24)*. Jerusalem: 1938.

Halevy, J. "Le prophète Malachie." *Revue sémitique* 17 (1909) 1–44.

Haller, M. "Das Judentum." In SAT 2/3. Göttingen: Vandenhoeck & Ruprecht, 1925.

Hammershaimb, E. *Some Aspects of Old Testament Prophecy from Isaiah to Malachi*. Copenhagen: Rosenskilde & Bagger, 1966.

Heigel, M. P. *Mal'ak Habb^{e}rit sive de Angelo Foederis*. Jena: Literis Samuelis Krebsii, 1660.

Herranz, A. "Dilexi Jacob, Esau autem odio habui." *Estudios Biblicos* 1 (1941) 559–83.

Hesse, F. "Haggai." In *Verbannung und Heimkehr*. Fest. W. Rudolph. Edited by A. Kuschke. Tübingen: Mohr, 1961. Pp. 109–34.

Hitzig, F. *Die prophetischer Bücher des Alten Testaments*. 3rd ed. Leipzig: Hirzel, 1863.

Hitzig, F., and H. Steiner. *Die zwölf kleinen Propheten*. KEH. Leipzig: Herzel, 1881.

Hoeke, P. van. *Ontledende Uytlegging over de drie laatste Propheten, Haggai, Zacharia en Maleachi*. 2nd ed. Amsterdam: Leyden, 1731.

Holladay, W. L. *A Concise Hebrew and Aramaic Lexicon of the Old Testament*. Leiden: Brill, Grand Rapids: Eerdmans, 1971.

Holtzmann, O. "Der Prophet Maleachi und der Ursprung des Pharisaerbundes." *Archiv für Religionswissenschaft* 19 (1931) 1–21.

Hoonacker, A. van. *Les douze petits prophètes*. Etudes Bibliques. Paris: Gabalda, 1908.

Horst, F. *Die zwölf kleinen Propheten*. Vol. 2. HAT 1/14. Tübingen: Mohr/Siebeck, 1964.

Ibn Ezra. See *Miqra'ot Gedalot*.

Jagersma, H. "The Tithes in the Old Testament." In *Remembering all the way. . . . OTS* 21. Leiden: Brill, 1981. Pp. 116–28.

Jamieson, R., Fausset, A., and Brown, D. *Commentary Practical and*

Explanatory on the Whole Bible. Repr. Grand Rapids: Zondervan, 1961.

Jepsen, A. *Das Zwölfprophetenbuch*. Bibelhilfe für die Gemeinde. Leipzig: Schloessmanns, 1937.

Jeremias, J. J. "*Hēl(e)ías*." In *TDNT* 2 (1964) 931–33.

Jerome. In MPL col. 855–1654.

Jones, D. R. *Haggai, Zechariah and Malachi*. Torch Bible Commentaries. London: SCM, 1962.

Joüon, P. *Grammaire de l'hébreu biblique*. Rome: Pontifical Biblical Institute, 1923, repr. 1965.

Junker, H. *Die zwölf kleinen Propheten II*. HSAT 8/3/2. Bonn: Hanstein, 1938.

Kaiser, W. C. *Malachi: God's Unchanging Love*. Grand Rapids: Baker, 1984.

Keil, C. F. and F. Delitzsch. *Commentary on the Old Testament 10: Minor Prophets*. Translated by J. Martin. Repr. Grand Rapids: Eerdmans, 1978.

Kimchi. See *Miqra'ot Gedalot*.

Koch, K. "Haggais unreines Volk." *ZAW* 79 (1967) 52–66.

Köhler, A. *Die Weissagungen Maleachis*. Erlangen: Deichert, 1865.

König, E. *Historisch-Comparative Syntax der hebräischen Sprache*. Leipzig: Dieterich, 1897.

Koole, J. L. *Haggai*. COT. Kampen: Kok, 1967.

Krause, G. "'Aller Heiden Trost,' Haggai 2:7." In *Solange es "Heute" heisst*. Fest. R. Herrmann. Berlin: 1957. Pp. 170–78.

______. *Studien zu Luthers Auslegung der kleinen Propheten*. Tübingen: Mohr/Siebeck, 1962.

Kroon, J. "De wederkomst van Elias." *Studiën* 131 (1939) 1–11.

Kruse-Blinkenberg, L. "The Book of Malachi according to Codex Syro-Hexaplaris Ambrosianus." *ST* 21 (1967) 62–82.

______. "The Peshitta of the Book of Malachi." *ST* 20 (1966) 95–119.

Laetsch, T. *The Minor Prophets*. Bible Commentary. St. Louis: Concordia, 1956.

Lagrange, J. M. "Notes sur les prophéties messianiques des derniers prophètes." *RB* 25 (1906) 79–83.

Lange, J. P. *A Commentary on the Holy Scripture, Vol. 14: The Minor Prophets*. Translated and edited by P. Schaff. New York: Scribner, 1874.

Lapide, Cornelius à. *Commentaria in XII Prophetas*. Antwerp: 1625.

Lattey, C. *The Book of Malachi*. London: Longmans, Green, 1935.

Luther, M. *Luther's Works*. Vol. 20. Translated by J. Pelikan. St. Louis: Concordia, 1974. (See also G. Krause, *Studien*.)

Mackenzie, S. L. and H. H. Wallace. "Covenant Themes in Malachi." *CBQ* 45 (1983) 549–63.

Malchow, Bruce V. "The Messenger of the Covenant in Mal. 3:1." *JBL* 103 (1984) 252–55.

Marck, J. *Haggaeum, Zacharjam et Malachiam*. Lugduni Batavorum: J. Luchtmans, 1702.

Marshall, J. T. "The Theology of Malachi." *ExpTim* 7 (1896) 16–19, 73–75, 125–27.

Marti, K. *Das Dodekapropheton*. KHC 13. Tübingen: Mohr, 1904.

Mason, R. A. *The Books of Haggai, Zechariah and Malachi*. Cambridge Bible Commentary. Cambridge: University Press, 1977.

______. "The Purpose of the 'Editorial Framework' of the Book of Haggai." *VT* 27 (1977) 413–21.

May, H. G. "'This People' and 'This Nation' in Haggai." *VT* 18 (1968) 190–97.

Michel, W. J. "I Will Send You Elijah." *TBT* 22 (1984) 217–22.

Migne, J. P. *Patrologiae cursus completus*. Series Graeca (MPG) et Latina (MPL).

Miklik, J. "Textkritische und exegetische Bemerkungen zu Mal. 3:6." *BZ* 17 (1925/26) 225–37.

Miller, J. H. "Haggai-Zechariah: Prophets of the Now and Future." *CurTM* 6 (1979) 99–104.

Miqra'ot Gedalot. New York: Pardes, 1950–51.

Mitchell, H. G. *A Critical and Exegetical Commentary on Haggai and Zechariah*. ICC. Edinburgh: T. & T. Clark, 1912, repr. 1961.

Moor, J. C. de. *De profeet Maleachi*. Amsterdam: Kirberger & Kesper, 1903.

Moore, T. V. *A Commentary on Haggai and Malachi*. Geneva Series Commentary. London: Banner of Truth Trust, 1960. Repr. of *Prophets of the Restoration*. 1856.

Morgan, F. C. *Haggai: A Prophet of Correction and Comfort*. London: Marshall, Morgan & Scott, 1935.

Nikel, J. *Die Wiederherstellung des judischen Gemeinwesens nach dem babylonischen Exil*. Biblische Studien 5/2.3. Freiburg im Breisgau: Herder, 1900.

Noordbeek, E. *Verklaringe der Prophetie van Maleachi*. Workum: 1716.

North, F. S. "Critical Analysis of the Book of Haggai." *ZAW* 68 (1956) 25–46.

Nötscher, F. *Zwölfprophetenbuch*. Echter Bibel. 2nd ed. Wurzburg: Echter, 1957.

Nowack, W. *Die kleinen Propheten*. HKAT 3/4. 3rd ed. Göttingen: Vandenhoeck & Ruprecht, 1922.

Orelli, C. von. *The Twelve Minor Prophets*. Translated by J. S. Banks. Edinburgh: T. & T. Clark, 1897.

Ostervald, J. F. *La Sainte Bible*. Bruscelles: Societé Biblique Brittannique et Étrangère, 1891.

Perowne, T. T. *Haggai, Zechariah, and Malachi*. Cambridge Bible for Schools and Colleges. 2nd ed. Cambridge: University Press, 1901.

Petersen, D. L. "Israelite Prophecy and Prophetic Traditions in the Exilic and Post-Exilic Periods." Ph.D. diss. Yale University, 1972.

———. *Late Israelite Prophecy*. Missoula, Mont.: Scholars Press, 1977.

———. "Zerubbabel and Jerusalem Temple Reconstruction." *CBQ* 36 (1974) 366–72.

Pfeiffer, E. "Die Disputationsworte im Buche Maleachi." *EvT* 19 (1959) 546–68.

Pocock, Ed. *Commentary on Malachi*. Oxford: 1677.

Pressel, W. *Commentar zu den Schriften der Propheten Haggai, Sacharja und Maleachi*. Gotha: Schloessmann, 1870.

Procksch, O. *Die kleinen prophetischen Schriften nach dem Exil*. Erlauterungen zum AT. Stuttgart: Calwer, 1929.

Pusey, E. B. *The Minor Prophets*. Vol. 2. London: Parker, Deighton, Bell, & Co., 1860.

Rashi. See *Miqra' ot Gedalot*.

Reinke, L. *Der Prophet Maleachi*. Giessen: Ferber'sche Universitätsbuchhandlung, 1856.

Renker, A. *Die Tora bei Maleachi: Ein Beitrag zur Bedeutungsgeschichte von tora im Alten Testament*. Freiburg: Herder, 1979.

Reuss, Ed. *La Bible, traduction nouvelle avec introductions et commentaires*. 3 vols. Paris: 1879.

Ridderbos, J. *De kleine propheten III*. KV. Kampen: Kok, 1952.

Ridderbos, N. H. "Maleachi." In *De Bijbel . . . van verklarende aantekeningen voorzien* 2. Kampen: Kok, 1954.

Riessler, P. *Die kleinen Propheten oder das Zwölfprophetenbuch*. Rottenburg: Badaer, 1911.

Rinaldi, G. and F. Luciani. *I profeti minori*. Vol. 3. La Sacra Bibbia. Rome: Marietti, 1969.

Robinson, G. L. *The Twelve Minor Prophets*. Grand Rapids: Baker, 1952.

Rothstein, J. W. *Juden und Samaritaner: Die grundlegende Scheidung von Judentum und Heidentum*. BWANT 3. Leipzig: J. C. Hinrichs, 1908.

Rudolph, W. *Haggai, Sacharja 1–8, Sacharja 9–14, Maleachi*. KAT 13/4. Gütersloh: Mohn, 1976.

Sänger, M. "Maleachi: Eine exegetische Studie über die Eigenthumlichkeiten seiner Redeweise." Diss. Jena, 1867.

Sauer, G. "Serubbabel in der Sicht Haggais und Sacharjas." In *Das ferne und nahe Wort*. Fest. L. Rost. Edited by F. Maass. BZAW 105. Berlin: Töpelmann, 1967. Pp. 199–207.

Schep, J. A. *De Profeet Maleachi*. De Bijbel toegelicht voor het Nederlandse Volk. Kampen: Kok, n.d.

Schumpp, P. M. *Das Buch der zwölf Propheten*. Herders Bibelkommentar 10/2. Freiburg: Herder, 1950.

Sellin, E. *Serubbabel: Ein Beitrag zur Geschichte der messianischen Erwartung und der Entstehung des Judentums*. Leipzig: A. Deichert, 1898.

______. *Studien zur Entstehungsgeschichte der jüdischen Gemeinde nach dem babylonischen Exil*. 2 vols. Leipzig: Deichert, 1900–01.

______. *Das Zwölfprophetenbuch*. KAT 12. 2nd and 3rd ed. Leipzig: Deichert, 1929–30.

Seybold, K. "Die Königserwartung bei den Propheten Haggai und Sacharja." *Judaica* 28 (1972) 69–78.

Siebeneck, R. T. "The Messianism of Aggeus and Proto-Zacharias." *CBQ* 19 (1957) 312–28.

Skrinjar, A. "Angelus Testamenti." *Verbum Domini* 14 (1934) 40–48.

Smit, G. *De kleine profeten III: Habakuk, Haggai, Zacharia, Maleachi*. TU. The Hague: Wolters, 1934.

Smith, G. A. *The Book of the Twelve Prophets*. 2 vols. The Expositor's Bible. Repr. Grand Rapids: Baker, 1943.

Smith, J. M. P. *A Critical and Exegetical Commentary on the Book of Malachi*. ICC. Edinburgh: T. & T. Clark, 1912, repr. 1961.

Smith, R. L. *Micah–Malachi*. The Word Biblical Commentary 32. Waco: Word, 1984.

Snyman, S. D. "Antiteses in die boek Maleagi." Ph.D. diss. University of Pretoria, 1985.

______. "Chiasmes in Mal. 1:2–5." *Skrif en Kerk* (Jan. 1984) 17–22.

______. "Haat Jahwe vir Esau? ('n Verkenning van Mal. 1:3a)." *NGTT* 25 (1984) 358–62.

Spoer, H. H. "Some New Considerations towards the Dating of the Book of Malachi." *JQR* 20 (1908) 167–86.

Steck, O. H. "Zu Haggai I 2–11." *ZAW* 3 (1971) 355–79.

Steinmann, J. *Le livre de la consolation d'Israel et les prophètes du retour de l'exil*. Lectio Divina 28. Paris: Cerf, 1960.

Stendebach, F. J. *Prophetie und Tempel: Haggai-Sacharja-Maleachi-Joel*. Stuttgarter Kleinen Kommentar. Stuttgart: Katholisches Bibelwerk, 1977.

Stenzel, M. "Das Dodekapropheton in Überzetsungswerken lateinischer Schriftsteller des Altertums." *TZ* 9 (1953) 81–92.

Stiassny, M. J. "Le prophète Élie dans le Judaïsme." In *Élie, le Prophète*. By G. Bardy, et al. Bruges: Desclée de Brouwer, 1956. Pp. 199-255.

Stock, R. and S. Torshell. *Malachi*. Nichol's Series of Commentaries. Edinburgh: Nichol, 1865.

Stuhlmueller, Carroll. "Sacrifice among the Nations." *TBT* 22 (1984) 223–25.

Theodore of Mopsuestia. MPG 66, col. 105–652.
Theodoret. MPG 81, col. 1545–1988.
Thomas, D. Winton. "The Book of Haggai." In *IB* 6. Nashville: Abingdon, 1956. Pp. 1035–49.
Til, S. van. *Malachias Illustratis*. Lugduni Batavorum: 1701.
Torrey, C. C. "The Edomites in Southern Judah." *JBL* 17 (1898) 16–20.
———. "The Prophecy of Malachi." *JBL* 17 (1898) 1–15.
Townsend, T. N. "Additional Comments on Haggai II 10–19." *VT* 18 (1968) 559–60.
Umbreit, E. W. C. *Praktischer Commentar über die kleinen Propheten*. Hamburg: Perthes, 1846.
Valeton, J. J. P. "Maleachi's Prediking." In *Oud-Testamentische Voordrachten*. Nijmegen: H. ten Hoet, 1909. Pp. 221–60.
Van Andel, J. *De kleine profeten*. 2nd ed. Kampen: Bos, 1905.
Van Selms, A. "The Inner Cohesion of the Book of Malachi." In *Studies in Old Testament Prophecy*. *OTWSA*. Edited by W. C. van Wyk. Potchefstroom: Pro Rege, 1975. Pp. 27–40.
Venema, H. *Uitverkiezen en uitverkiezing in het NT*. Kampen: Kok, 1965.
Verhoef, P. A. *Maleachi*. COT. Kampen: Kok, 1972.
Vitringa, C. "Dissertatio de Malachias." In *Observationes Sacrae* 6, cap. 7.
Vriezen, Th. C. *De verkiezing van Israel volgens het Oude Testament*. Exegetica, n.s. 2. Amsterdam: Ton Bolland, 1974.
Vuilleumier, R. *Malachie*. Commentaire de l'Ancien Testament 9. Neuchatel: Delachaux & Niestlé, 1981.
Waldman, N. M. "Some Notes on Malachi 3:6, 3:13 and Ps. 42:11." *JBL* 93 (1974) 543–45.
Wallis, G. "Wesen und Struktur der Botschaft Maleachis." In *Das ferne und nahe Wort*. Fest. L. Rost. Edited by F. Maass. BZAW 105. Berlin: Töpelmann, 1967. Pp. 229–37.
Waterman, L. "The Camouflaged Purge of Three Messianic Conspirators." *JNES* 13 (1954) 73–78.
Wellhausen, J. *Die kleinen Propheten übersetz und erklärt*. 4th ed. Berlin: De Gruyter, 1963.
Wendland, E. "Linear and Concentric Patterns in Malachi." *BT* 36 (1985) 108–21.
Whedbee, J. W. "A Question-Answer-Schema in Haggai 1: The Form and Function of Haggai 1:9–11." In *Biblical and Near Eastern Studies*. Fest. W. S. LaSor. Edited by G. A. Tuttle. Grand Rapids: Eerdmans, 1978. Pp. 184–94.
Wiseman, D. J. "Haggai." In *NBC*. 3rd ed. London: Inter-Varsity, Grand Rapids: Eerdmans, 1970. Pp. 781–85.
Wolf, H. "Desire of All the Nations in Haggai 2:7: Messianic or Not?" *Journal of the Evangelical Theological Society* 19 (1976) 97–102.
Wolff, H. W. *Haggai*. Biblische Studien 1. Neukirchen: Buchhandlung des Erziehungsvereins, 1951.

Wolmarans, H. P. "What Does Malachi Say about Divorce?" *Hervormde teologiese studies* 22 (1967) 46–47.
Woude, A. S. van der. "Der Engel des Bundes." In *Die Botschaft und die Boten*. Fest. H. W. Wolff. Edited by Jorg Jeremias and L. Perlitt. Neukirchen-Vluyn: Neukirchener, 1981. Pp. 289–300.
______. *Haggai, Maleachi*. POT. Nijkerk: Callenbach, 1982.
Wright, J. S. *The Building of the Second Temple*. London: 1958.
Zorrell, F. *Lexicon Hebraicum et Aramaicum Veteris Testamenti*. Rome: Pontifical Biblical Institute, 1947.

The Book of
HAGGAI

INTRODUCTION

I. THE PROPHET

The postexilic community, consisting of the returned exiles from the Babylonian captivity and the people who remained in the promised land,[1] were not without civil and religious leaders, but they had not heard the word of a prophet since the time of the Exile. Now it happened. On the first day of the sixth month in the year 520 B.C., God again fulfilled his promise to raise up for his people a prophet who would convey to them everything he commands (Deut. 18:15, 18). Haggai had the privilege and the responsibility of being the first prophet of the postexilic era.[2]

Haggai's prophetic office and function are well attested. He is called "the prophet" in seven out of eleven occurrences of his name in the Bible (cf. Hag. 1:1, 3, 12; 2:1, 10; Ezra 5:1; 6:14). He apparently needed neither introduction nor identification. It seems that he was well known in the small postexilic community in and around Jerusalem. As a "messenger of the Lord" (1:13), he is represented in his book as an authoritative instrument of the word of God, whose main task it was to admonish and inspire leaders and people to rebuild the temple. That the people responded favorably to his message (1:12–15a) is a further indication of his authority as a true prophet of the Lord.

1. K.-M. Beyse, *Serubbabel und die Königserwartungen der Propheten Haggai und Sacharja* (Stuttgart: Calwer, 1972), p. 34, agrees that the people addressed by Haggai were essentially the returned exiles, but with the inclusion of the sedentary population. According to K. Galling, *Studien zur Geschichte Israels im persischen Zeitalter* (Tübingen: Mohr, 1964), p. 136, Haggai addressed himself to the returned exiles only.

2. The identity and date of the so-called Trito-Isaiah are disputed. According to C. Westermann, *Isaiah 40–66*, OTL, tr. D. M. G. Stalker (Philadelphia: Westminster, 1969), pp. 295–96, Trito-Isaiah's ministry must have been somewhere between 537 and 521 B.C. In this case, he would have been an older contemporary of Haggai. See also W. A. M. Beuken, *Haggai-Sacharja 1–8: Studien zur Überlieferungsgeschichte der frühnachexilischen Prophetie* (Assen: Van Gorcum, 1967), pp. 222–29, for the relationship between Haggai and Trito-Isaiah.

Apart from being a prophet, nothing else is known of him with certainty, and indeed we have no means of establishing his biography. As is the case with Obadiah and Habakkuk, nothing is mentioned about his ancestors or circumstances of birth, life, and death.

Haggai's name is one of several in the OT derived from the root *ḥag*, "festival." Haggi is the name of one of the clans of the tribe of Gad (Gen. 46:16; Num. 26:15), the feminine Haggit was the name of one of David's wives (2 Sam. 3:4), and Haggiah was a descendant of Merari (1 Chr. 6:30). The more common form of the name is evidently Haggai, or more correctly Haggay. The Masoretic vocalization is supported by the Greek *Aggaios* and the Latin *Haggaeus* or *Aggaeus*.[3] Jerome and most modern scholars take the termination *ay* as adjectival, as in the case of the names Barzellai, Kelubbai, etc. The meaning of the name Haggai would then be "festal," perhaps because he was born on a feast day. A parallel to his name is Shabbethai (Ezra 10:15), probably so-called because he was born on a sabbath (cf. Dominicus, "a Sunday's child"). The name Haggai is also found in Aramaic letters, for example, on an ostracon from Elephantine that contains a greeting from a pagan to a Jew: "To my brother Haggai, your brother Yarho."[4] It is also found on Hebrew seals and in Phoenician and South Arabic sources.[5]

There are a number of improbable theories about the derivation and significance of the name Haggai. Köhler, Wellhausen, Frey, et al. see in Haggai a probable contraction for Hagariah, "YHWH has girded," as Zaccai, the original of Zacchaeus, is a contraction of Zechariah.[6] The difficulty with this hypothesis is that Hagariah is not attested either in the OT or outside it.[7]

The paucity of the biographical evidence and the peculiarity of the name Haggai, meaning "my feasts," led T. André to the conclusion that Haggai, like Malachi, is in reality a symbolic title, given by a later hand to the anonymous writer of the book, because of the coincidence that the prophecies it contained were all dated on feast days: 1:1 on the New Moon's

3. For the doubling of the *gimel* and the ending *-ay*, see M. Noth, *Die israelitischen Personennamen im Rahmen der gemeinsemitischen Namengebung* (repr. Hildesheim: Olms, 1980), pp. 36ff.

4. See *ANET*, p. 491.

5. Cf. F. Vattioni, "I sigilli ebraici," *Bib* 50 (1969) 360, sub 2; F. Benz, *Personal Names in the Phoenician and Punic Inscriptions*, Studia Pohl 8 (Rome: Pontifical Biblical Institute, 1972), p. 307; W. W. Müller, *ZAW* 75 (1963) 308; *ANET*, pp. 492, 548–49.

6. A. Köhler, *Die nachexilischen Propheten erklärt, I: Die Weissagung Haggais* (Erlangen: 1860–65). Cf. Derenbourg, *Histoire de la Palestine*, pp. 95, 150, quoted by G. A. Smith.

7. Cf. Van der Woude, p. 9.

day, 2:1 on the seventh day of the Feast of Tabernacles, and 2:18 on the day when the "foundation" of the temple was laid.[8] This theory is unlikely, however. The comparison with the name Malachi presupposes an unacceptable interpretation of its meaning (cf. the Introduction to Malachi below), and the historical data provided in the book constitute "as good a ground for accepting the historical reality of Haggai as that, for example, of Habakkuk" (so G. A. Smith). That the name Haggai is well attested as a personal name makes it unlikely that it could have been a nickname (contra Baldwin).

The time of Haggai's activities as a prophet poses no problem, because all his prophecies are dated precisely. It is evident that his ministry was of short duration. All his messages were delivered within the space of fifteen weeks during the second year of Darius I (521–486 B.C.), that is, in the year 520 B.C.[9] With the help of evidence from a vast number of Babylonian texts and from new moon tables calculated from astronomical data, it has proved possible to synchronize the old lunar calendar with the Julian calendar with accurate results.[10] Baldwin provides an appropriate table with the dates given in Haggai and Zechariah, with their equivalents. In Haggai's case it amounts to the following:

The first day of the sixth month (1:1) = 29 Aug. 520
The twenty-fourth day of the same month (1:15) = 21 Sept. 520
The twenty-first day of the seventh month (2:1) = 17 Oct. 520
The twenty-fourth day of the ninth month (2:10, 20) = 18 Dec. 520

We agree with the view that there are no reasons to doubt the historicity of the dates, which were attached to the prophecies of Haggai probably from the very beginning.[11]

An interesting question concerning the time of Haggai's ministry is whether it could be extended both ways: prior to 29 August and after 18 December 520 B.C. Rudolph answers this question in the affirmative. The first date mentioned in the book is the prophecy addressed to Zerubbabel and

8. T. André, *Le prophète Aggée* (Paris: Fischbacher, 1895).

9. It concerns the "regnal year," not the "accession year"; cf. P. R. Ackroyd, *JNES* 17 (1958) 13ff.; Beyse, op. cit., p. 10.

10. Cf. R. A. Parker and W. H. Dubberstein, *Babylonian Chronology 626 BC–AD 75* (Providence: Brown University, 1956). Cf. also H. H. Grosheide, *Ezra-Nehemia I*, COT (Kampen: Kok, 1963), pp. 112–13; J. van Goudoever, *Biblical Calendars* (Leiden: Brill, 1959).

11. So Van der Woude. See also Beuken, op. cit., pp. 25–26, whose investigation into the dates of the prophetic literature led him to the conclusion that there are no reasons for denying the authenticity of the dates in Haggai (and Zechariah). The only exception among the scholars in this regard is Ackroyd, "Studies in the Book of Haggai," *JJS* 2 (1951) 171–73.

Joshua. According to Rudolph this was only the report of the people's reaction to Haggai's message to them, which was given an unspecified period of time before. To enhance this conclusion Rudolph alters the text of 1:3, and asserts that the prophecy of 1:1–11 was addressed solely to the leaders. Both assumptions are unlikely (see the commentary). According to Rudolph, Haggai's prophetic activities extended to the time of the completion of the temple in the spring of 515 B.C.[12] This conclusion is deduced from Ezra 6:14: "So the elders of the Jews continued to build and prosper under the preaching of Haggai *[binᵉḇû'aṯ ḥaggay]* the prophet and Zechariah, a descendant of Iddo" (NIV). The expression *binᵉḇû'aṯ ḥaggay* is rather vague and does not allow for a specific conclusion regarding the scope of Haggai's (and Zechariah's) ministry. We agree with the point of view that the task of the rebuilding of the temple was finished, not so much during Haggai's ministry but as a result of his (and Zechariah's) prophecies (so NEB; cf. Van der Woude). Baldwin, therefore, correctly asserts that there is no means of knowing what happened to Haggai after 18 December 520.

We may assume that he died soon after he had delivered his last message, or else that he vanished from the scene, because Zechariah adequately continued his mission.[13] The assumption that Haggai died shortly after 520 B.C. is an additional argument in favor of the theory that he was a man of old age when he delivered his messages. According to Jewish tradition he had lived the greater part of his life in the Babylonian captivity. Partly on this tradition and partly on inference from Hag. 2:3, some scholars hypothesize that he was one of the elderly people who had seen the former temple, had subsequently gone into exile, and was now a very old man.[14] We agree with G. A. Smith, Van der Woude, et al. that this theory may be probable, but it is not conclusive. We simply do not know where and when

12. So Albright, *The Biblical Period from Abraham to Ezra* (New York: Harper & Row, 1963), p. 88; and J. Bright, *The History of Israel,* 3rd ed. (Philadelphia: Westminster, 1981), p. 372. According to J. Morgenstern the temple was completed in September 516 B.C., *HUCA* 22 (1951) 365ff.; 27 (1956) 159ff.; *VT* 5 (1955) 63 note. So also Baldwin.

13. Cf. Beyse, op. cit., p. 37: Haggai's religious-political expectations especially with regard to the Davidic dynasty were not generally accepted. Zechariah changed it accordingly, and so supersedes Haggai, who subsequently vanished from the scene.

14. H. Ewald, *Die Propheten des Alten Bundes,* vol. 3 (Göttingen: Vandenhoeck & Ruprecht, 1867), p. 178, is of the opinion that Haggai had seen the first temple, as are Van Hoonacker, Mitchell, Elliger, Ackroyd (in *Peake's Commentary on the Bible*). Others deny this possibility: Von Orelli, André, Marti, G. A. Smith, Sellin, Junker, Deissler, Sellin-Fohrer (*Introduction to the Old Testament,* tr. D. Green [New York: Abingdon, 1968]), Deden, et al. Beuken, op. cit., p. 219, considers this possibility not entirely without support.

Haggai was born, where he lived, and at what age he was called as the "messenger of the Lord."[15]

This conclusion is also applicable to the thesis defended by W. A. M. Beuken, according to which Haggai was originally one of the Judean farmers who were left behind in Palestine.[16] The motivation for this theory is that his name does not appear on the lists of returned exiles (Ezra 2; Neh. 7 and 12), that he obviously had an intimate knowledge of the agricultural circumstances of his time, and that he referred to "the people of the land" (2:4), assuming that they belonged to the sedentary population. These and similar arguments, however, are not convincing. If Haggai was a child at the time of the return, the omission of his name from the list in Ezra 2 would be understandable (so Baldwin). The references to the adverse agricultural circumstances must be seen in the context of the curse and blessing formulas of the covenant (cf. Lev. 26; Deut. 28; and the commentary below on 1:6, 9; 2:6–7). The expression "the people of the land" does not distinguish the sedentary population from the returned exiles (cf. the commentary on 2:4). Thus we really have no convincing evidence about Haggai's former life and must acknowledge that we simply do not know.

According to an ancient Christian tradition Haggai belonged to a priestly family. He was born in Babylon and came to Jerusalem while he was still a youngster. He was an eyewitness of the rebuilding of the temple and after his death was buried with honor near the sepulchres of the priests (cf. Mitchell, who quotes Dorotheus and Hesychius in this regard). Some scholars draw attention to the fact that in the versions certain Psalms are attributed to Haggai and Zechariah, a fact which seems to add support to Haggai's priestly descent. With Zechariah, Haggai appears on the titles of Pss. 137, 145–148 in the LXX, of 111, 145, and 146 in the Vulgate, and of 125, 126, and 145–148 in the Peshitta. The assumption that Haggai and Zechariah perhaps were responsible for the recension from which the Greek translation was being made (so Baldwin) would suggest that they also were responsible for the recensions of the Hebrew text from which the Vulgate and the Peshitta were being made, which of course would be unlikely, especially in the case of Pss. 111, 125, and 126.

Some scholars infer from Hag. 2:12–14 that Haggai must have been a priest because he showed interest in the cultic procedures. But this is hardly conclusive. On the contrary, that Haggai was directed to acquire an official ruling from the priests (2:12–14) distinguishes him from the priests. This

15. Cf. Beyse, op. cit., p. 37.

16. See esp. the section in his book, op. cit., pp. 216–29, concerning Haggai's milieu. Beyse, op. cit., pp. 50–51, contradicts Beuken's point of view. According to him Haggai returned with Zerubbabel from exile.

conclusion is substantiated by the Hebrew tradition, which did not reckon Haggai among the priests, and by modern scholars like Marti. Haggai is deliberately and emphatically called "the prophet," and nowhere is it even suggested that he had a priestly affiliation.[17]

An alternate view advocated by some scholars is that Haggai must have been a cultic prophet, i.e., one whose work was closely associated with the sanctuary.[18] This hypothesis is unacceptable, however. If Haggai really was associated with the temple, why had he allowed the house of God to remain a ruin? We have no evidence whatsoever that Haggai had a function in the cult. He naturally was very much concerned about the cult,[19] but this does not imply that he was a cultic prophet. Rudolph rightly distinguishes between the two possibilities.[20]

We agree with Van der Woude's evaluation of Haggai's prophetic ministry. In spite of the short duration of his ministry and the fact that his book is the second smallest in the OT, he may be considered one of the great figures in Israel.[21] In a time of deep decline and discouragement, his single-minded and ardent preaching again gave the people of God new perspectives on their relationship with God and on the promised blessings. In encouraging the people to rebuild the temple, Haggai gave them a new spiritual center, without which they would have perished as the people of God in the vortex of history.

17. Cf. Beyse, op. cit., pp. 50–51.

18. Cf. Jones, et al. Cf. also G. Sauer, "Serubbabel in der Sicht Haggais und Sacharjas," in *Das ferne und nahe Wort,* Fest. L. Rost, ed. F. Maass, BZAW 105 (Berlin: Töpelmann, 1967), p. 206; and now also J. Blenkinsopp, *A History of Prophecy in Israel* (London: SPCK, Philadelphia: Westminster, 1984), p. 232: "Haggai was himself in all probability a cult prophet."

19. Contra Sauer, op. cit., p. 206, who regards Haggai as the first (and only) court prophet of postexilic times.

20. For a thorough discussion of the various traditions and legends surrounding Haggai, see T. André, *Le Prophète Aggée,* pp. 13–18.

21. Beyse, op. cit., p. 65, agrees with J. Lindblom, *Prophecy in Ancient Israel* (Oxford: Blackwell, Philadelphia: Fortress, 1963), p. 421, that the postexilic prophets (Haggai and Zechariah) may not unfairly be described as epigones, against the evaluation of W. Nowack, *Die kleinen Propheten,* HKAT 3/4, 3rd ed. (Göttingen: Vandenhoeck & Ruprecht, 1922), p. 311, that with them we have the signs of declining prophecy.

II. AUTHORSHIP

Scholars of every persuasion agree on one point with regard to the authorship: the series of four comparatively brief prophecies were delivered by the prophet Haggai.[1] This conclusion is incontestable in view of the precise dates and the remarkable way in which Haggai was accredited as the mediator *(b^eyad)* of the divine revelation.

Scholars also seem to agree that only the essentials of the prophet's four messages have been recorded in the book. With this point a distinction is made between the orally delivered messages and their written record in the book itself.[2] In addition some scholars are inclined to distinguish between the actual prophecies and the editorial framework in which they are set.[3] Elements of this framework include the dated introductions (1:1; 2:1, 10, 20), the narrative (1:12), and the abbreviated introductions (2:13, 14), because all of them refer to Haggai in the third person. The real issue is whether Haggai was responsible, apart from his oral messages, also for the written book as we have it.

Haggai's authorship is generally denied on the following grounds:

(a) Most scholars stress that the historical character of its contents shows clearly that Haggai could not have been the book's author. The book of Haggai differs from most other prophetical books in the OT in that while the others are mainly collections of prophetical utterances, the book of Haggai is more in the nature of a report on the prophet's utterances and on the effect they produced upon the hearers. This view is endorsed by the fact that Haggai is frequently referred to in the third person. This would suggest that the prophet himself could not have been the author of the book in its present form. This view is also endorsed by other features of the book:

1. Cf. Von Orelli, Driver, Junker, Nötscher, Gelin, Van Hoonacker, Keil, D. Winton Thomas, et al.

2. Cf. Nowack, Marti, Mitchell, Sellin, Horst, Deden, Elliger, Deissler, Birkeland, Ackroyd ("Studies in the Book of Haggai," *JJS* 2 [1951] 163–76), Van der Woude, et al.

3. An important contribution to this approach was made by A. Klostermann, *Geschichte des Volkes Israel* (München: Beck, 1896), pp. 212ff. According to him the books of Haggai and Zechariah originally were part of a Temple Chronicle, interspersed with words of the Lord. Zechariah was responsible for the final edition. J. W. Rothstein, *Juden und Samaritaner: Die grundlegende Scheidung von Judentum und Heidentum,* BWANT 3 (Leipzig: Hinrichs, 1908), pp. 34–41, regards the book of Haggai as a chronicle, written by a person other than Haggai himself. Subsequently most scholars have agreed that the book of Haggai is mainly a historical narrative which comprises the framework for the prophecies. See Ackroyd, *JJS* 2 (1951) 166–73; 3 (1952) 2, 12, 152; and Beuken, *Haggai-Sacharja 1–8,* pp. 14–15.

(1) The addition of the title "the prophet" to the name Haggai (1:1, 3, 12; 2:10) is more easily explicable on the supposition that the prophet himself was not responsible for it.[4]

(2) The point of view that the prophet had been the instrument of the divine revelation, as is evident from the use of *b^eyaḏ* (1:1; 2:1, 10), instead of the obvious *'el,* shows that the narrator belonged to those who had received the word of God *through (b^eyaḏ)* the prophet.

(3) The manner in which the prophecies are presented suggests that somebody other than the prophet was the author of the book (cf. Keil, D. Winton Thomas, et al.), especially in the arrangement of the material, so that those oracles which refer to the future come last (D. R. Jones, et al.).

Most scholars would agree with D. Winton Thomas, Keil, and others that though Haggai cannot be regarded as the author of the book in its present form, there can be no doubt that the book contains genuine utterances of the prophet. It may well be that the editor who drew up the report had in his possession some of the prophet's personal notes. From these he may have obtained his information as to the dates in which Haggai's utterances were delivered.

Scholars are also agreed that the "editor" could not have presented the contents of the prophecies long after the demise of the prophet.[5] It is obvious that he had no knowledge of Darius II, and that he was well acquainted with the dates of the prophecies. He recounted without any remark the divine promise that Zerubbabel would be a messianic king (2:20–23). Especially the last considerations led to the conclusion that the book in its present form was completed either during the rebuilding of the temple or soon afterward, in any case before Zerubbabel (figuratively) vanished from the scene.

A few specific theories concerning the authorship of the book are those of W. Rudolph, P. R. Ackroyd, A. Klostermann, and W. A. M. Beuken. According to Rudolph, Haggai is a *Flugblatt des Freundeskreises,* that is, an apology by Haggai's friends or disciples, with the purpose of proclaiming Haggai's priority over Zechariah with regard to the rebuilding

4. This was already pointed out by Rothstein as one of the three main arguments why Haggai could not have been the author of "his" book, the other two being that the reference to the prophet is consistently in the third person and that the messenger formula characterizes the position of the narrator: the prophet is the instrument *(b^eyaḏ)* of the divine revelation, and the narrator belonged to those who received the word. See also Beuken, op. cit., pp. 11–12.

5. Marti was the first to make this point. According to him the contents of the book were committed to writing shortly after Haggai delivered his messages. This point of view is shared by Mitchell, Sellin, Horst, Deden, Deissler, et al. Elliger refrains from giving a precise date.

of the temple, because they were afraid that Zechariah's ministry would eclipse that of Haggai.

This hypothesis is unconvincing, however. That Haggai did not refer to Zechariah in his third prophecy (2:10–19), notwithstanding that Zechariah had already started with his ministry,[6] belongs to the general mystery in the OT of people not referring to their predecessors or compatriots,[7] and is a precarious *argumentum e silentio*. Nowhere in the book of Haggai is there any reference or suggestion that these two prophets acted as rivals or that the one needed to be vindicated over against the other.

P. R. Ackroyd regards the compiler of Haggai as responsible for the dating and arrangement of the oracles, possibly one century or even two centuries after the time of Haggai. "In the case of Haggai, we may assume that the oracles were transmitted for a period, probably orally, though possibly committed to writing, before they came into their present form. The length of that period cannot be determined, but in view of the similarities already indicated between the dates in Haggai and those of the Chronicler, we can estimate that it was not much less than a century, and possibly as much as two centuries."[8]

Ackroyd's theory is too speculative to be acceptable. The essence of his argument rests on the identification of similarities between Haggai and the Chronicler. This point of view, shared by some scholars,[9] is contested by others. According to Van der Woude, the style especially of the "editorial

6. Zech. 1:1: "In the eighth month, in the second year of Darius," i.e., Oct./Nov. 520 B.C.

7. There are no cross references among the contemporaries Isaiah, Hosea, and Micah, nor between Jeremiah and Ezekiel. J. Bright calls Jeremiah's precise attitude toward the great reform of Josiah, which took place some five years after he began his ministry, a "mystery" (*The Kingdom of God* [Nashville: Abingdon, 1953], p. 106). C. J. Goslinga wrote an interesting article on "the mystery of the expectation of David's kingship" ("Het geheim der verwachting van Davids koningschap," *GTT* 57 [1957] 6–21).

8. Ackroyd, who translated O. Eissfeldt's massive *Introduction*, has written extensively on Haggai: "Studies in the Book of Haggai," *JJS* 2 (1951) 163–76; 3 (1952) 1–13; "The Book of Haggai and Zechariah I–VIII," *JJS* 3 (1952) 151–56; "Haggai," in *Peake's Commentary on the Bible*, rev. ed., ed. M. Black, et al. (London: Nelson, 1962), pp. 643–45; he also devotes a chapter to Haggai in *Exile and Restoration*, OTL (London: SCM, Philadelphia: Westminster, 1968), pp. 153–70.

9. Cf. D. N. Freedman, "The Chronicler's Purpose," *CBQ* 23 (1961) 436–42; P. F. Bloomhardt, "The Poems of Haggai," *HUCA* 5 (1928) 153–95, esp. p. 156; F. S. North, "Critical Analysis of the Book of Haggai," *ZAW* 68 (1956) 25–46; Beuken, op. cit., pp. 10–15, and passim; Beyse, op. cit., p. 12: the work of the Chronicler is of a later date but contains older material.

framework" is more Deuteronomistic than Chronistic.[10] If, therefore, the very base of an argument is susceptible to doubt, then the theory itself cannot be convincing.

The same criticism applies to the view of A. Klostermann, shared and revised by other scholars, that the book of Haggai and Zech. 1–8 originally belonged to an account of the rebuilding of the temple in the reign of Darius, chronologically arranged and probably edited by Zechariah.[11]

Koole rightly raised two main objections against this theory: We know very little about this supposed "temple-chronicle," because all evidence, with the exception of Haggai (!), seems to have been lost; the book of Haggai itself provides insufficient evidence about the actual rebuilding of the temple, and therefore could not have been considered to be a summary of such a chronicle. With the exception of Hag. 1:15a, all dates concern the oracles of the prophet rather than the history of the rebuilding of the temple (cf. also Van der Woude).

The theory that Haggai and Zech. 1–8 were edited "in a Chronistic milieu" was proposed by W. A. M. Beuken in his doctoral thesis.[12] His argument is that the same major interest in the temple, its ritual, and the continuity of the Davidic line dominates both these prophets and the books of Chronicles.[13]

We have already commented on the argument based upon the assumed similarities between Haggai (and Zech. 1–8) and Chronicles, and may add with Baldwin that it seems both more likely and more logical that Haggai was edited early, and that he and Zechariah together molded the thinking of those who edited the books of Chronicles.[14]

A few conservative scholars either concede to the possibility that Haggai himself could have been the author of his book[15] or are adamant that he actually was the author.[16] In this company of conservative theologians we

10. Beuken, op. cit., pp. 28, 35, etc., concedes that the Chronicler often "inherited" Deuteronomistic language.

11. Klostermann, *Geschichte des Volkes Israels,* pp. 212ff.

12. Beuken, *Haggai-Sacharja 1–8*.

13. See esp. his conclusion, op. cit., pp. 331–36.

14. Cf. Van der Woude's criticism and that of R. A. Mason, *VT* 27 (1977) 416–17.

15. E.g., G. Ch. Aalders, *Oud-Testamentische Kanoniek* (Kampen: Kok, 1952), pp. 274–75; R. K. Harrison, *Introduction to the Old Testament,* pp. 944–48; I. H. Eybers, *Die boeke van die Wet en die Profete,* Studieboekreeks 6 (Pretoria: University of South Africa Press, 1977), pp. 213–16. See also n. 1 above.

16. E.g., J. Ridderbos, *De Kleine Propheten Haggai, Zacharia, Maleachi,* KV (Kampen: Kok, 1935); E. J. Young, *An Introduction to the Old Testament* (Grand Rapids: Eerdmans, 1949), pp. 267–69; G. L. Archer, Jr., *A Survey of Old*

also find O. Eissfeldt.[17] He deems it unnecessary to assume a secondary authorship, in the sense that an editor or compiler was responsible for the written record of the prophet's utterances. He thinks rather that Haggai himself could have been the author, deliberately choosing the third person in order to enhance the impression of the complete objectivity of his report. The third-person account of Haggai is quite similar in purpose and intent to the first-person accounts in the prophecies of Amos, Hosea, Isaiah, Jeremiah, Ezekiel, and Zechariah.

An important contribution to the solution of the problem of authorship is made by J. L. Koole.[18] His point of departure is the intent of the specified dates with regard to the prophecies in general, and specifically in Haggai. His conclusion is that it served as a warranty for the authenticity of the word of God and especially for his promises concerning the rebuilding of the temple. Therefore, the importance of the book of Haggai is that it stated irrefutably that the rebuilding of the temple of the Lord was not humanly inspired but a product of God's own initiative. It is conceivable, therefore, that Haggai could have been the author of this very important piece of propaganda on behalf of the rebuilding of the temple. Koole then compares the way other prophetic books originated, and concludes that Haggai, like Jeremiah, probably dictated his own notes to one or two of his disciples. This procedure would account for the third person, the brevity of the record, and the peculiar use of the formula of revelation.[19]

In the light of all the arguments pro and contra Haggai's authorship, we may stress first the important consideration, which is conceded by most scholars, that the prophecies in this book were originally delivered by Haggai himself, and, second, that there seems to be some doubt that he was responsible for the written record in its present form. The argumentation of scholars like Eissfeldt and Koole seems convincing in this regard. Weiser's remark endorses this stand. According to him the book of Haggai gives the impression of being close to the events and of going back to reliable sources.

Testament Introduction (Chicago: Moody, 1966), pp. 407–408; H. E. Freeman, *An Introduction to the Old Testament Prophets* (Chicago: Moody, 1968), pp. 326–32.

17. O. Eissfeldt, *The Old Testament: An Introduction*, tr. P. Ackroyd (Oxford: Blackwell, New York: Harper and Row, 1965), pp. 426–29.

18. J. L. Koole, *Haggai*, COT (Kampen: Kok, 1967), pp. 5–10. See Beuken, op. cit., pp. 21–26, on the dates in the prophetic literature.

19. Koole, op. cit., p. 9.

III. UNITY

"The book Haggai is so brief that it seems almost ridiculous to suspect its unity" (so Mitchell). As a matter of fact no one has doubted the authenticity of all four sections of the book until relatively recently, when W. Böhme, besides pointing out some useless repetitions of single words and phrases, cast suspicion on 1:13 and questioned the whole of the fourth section, 2:20–23.[1] Subsequently criticism was posed against some passages, especially by T. André, who claims to have shown that 2:10–19 is an interpolation, being in fact a prophecy delivered by an unknown person on the twenty-fourth of the ninth month, not of the second but of the first year of the reign of Darius. Mitchell summarizes André's arguments and observes: "In fact, in every instance either the allegation or the inference from it is mistaken." André's hypothesis has met with little favor from biblical scholars.[2]

The main "objections" (Eissfeldt) against the unity of the book concern the structure of 1:1–11, the assumed textual dislocation of 2:15–19 (allegedly caused by a confusion of dates in 1:15 and 2:18), and a number of glosses.[3] According to Eissfeldt 1:1–11 seems not to be in order. Especially vv. 5–11 seem to be overloaded, because vv. 5–6 are parallel to vv. 7, 9–11. His proposed solution is that elements of two separate collections were joined together, i.e., from Haggai's memoirs (= 1:1–6, 8) and from a collection of his utterances (= 1:7, 9–11). Odil H. Steck endorses Eissfeldt's point of view. According to him two sayings of the prophet Haggai have been redactionally linked: 1:2, 4–8, a "discussion saying" which reaches its climax in a promise of salvation; and 1:9–11, a fragment of a "discussion saying" which was to lead up to a demand parallel to v. 8a but is no longer preserved. Both sayings belong to the same situation in the year 520; they aim to stimulate the inhabitants of Judah to rebuild the temple but are addressed to different elements in the population: 1:2, 4–8 to the Judeans who had remained in the land, and to their theological doubts about an immediate rebuilding of the temple; and vv. 9–11 to those who had just returned from the Babylonian Exile, who gave priority to the building of their own houses over the rebuilding of the temple of God.[4]

1. W. Böhme, "Zum Maleachi und Haggai," *ZAW* 7 (1887) 215–16; see also G. A. Smith.

2. Except for André's argument that 2:10–19 disrupts two parallel sections (2:6–8 and 2:20–23), which was subsequently endorsed by many scholars. Cf. also G. A. Smith.

3. Cf. P. R. Ackroyd, "Some Interpretative Glosses in the Book of Haggai," *JJS* 7 (1956) 163–67. See esp. the thorough discussion by Beuken, op. cit., pp. 27–83, on the final form of the book.

4. Cf. O. H. Steck, "Zu Haggai 1:2–11," *ZAW* 83 (1971) 355–79; cf. also

It is true that this section of the book seems "overcrowded" because of the repetition of thoughts and phrases, as in 1:5 and 1:7. The problem is solved, however, not by emending the text or by assuming a combination of various sayings, but by applying a structural analysis to this section and by recognizing the difference in intent, especially of vv. 5–7 and 9–11. For both aspects of our solution, we may refer to the introductory remarks in the commentary, both of the section as a whole and of v. 7.

The genuineness of 1:13 has been seriously questioned, first by Böhme and subsequently by the majority of scholars,[5] because (1) it disturbs the narrative; (2) it offers a mere repetition of the promise: "I am with you," compared with 2:4; (3) the terminology used for the prophet and his message is a substantial reiteration of v. 12; and (4) Haggai is here called not "the prophet" but "the messenger of the Lord."

This criticism of the authenticity of v. 13 cannot be maintained, however. Verse 13 contains an indispensable element in the response of leaders and people to the word of the Lord. They must substitute trust and consolation for their fear (v. 12). It is quite natural that the same word of encouragement should be repeated in 2:4, where leaders and people are admonished to be strong and work. The argument that the terminology used for the prophet and his message is identical with that in v. 12 rests on the assumption that v. 12b refers to the mission of the prophet instead of to his message.[6] The designation of the prophet as "messenger of the Lord" is not without precedent (cf. 2 Chr. 36:15, 16; Isa. 44:26), and is here applied to emphasize the authenticity of the messenger and his message.

Scholars have traditionally regarded 1:15 as a unit and combined it with the following passage to form the first verse of ch. 2 (so LXX, Vetus Latina, Vulg., Pesh.). The consensus of modern opinion, however, is that the double dating suggests a division between v. 15a and vv. 15b–2:1, and that the usual order of year-month-day when reference is made to the kingship of Darius endorses this division. When this division is effected, another major problem arises: the date of 1:15a requires a context, which has been lost or must be provided by relocating 2:15–19 at this place. A solution to this twofold problem is to afford the phrase "in the second year of King Darius" a

---

Horst, who was the first to draw attention to the compound character of 1:2–11; Deden, Elliger, Deissler, Beuken, op. cit., pp. 27–30.

5. Cf. Böhme, op. cit.; also G. A. Smith, Nowack, Marti, Mitchell, Horst, Deissler, Sellin, Deden, who transposed it after 1:15. According to Beuken, op. cit., p. 45, there is no reason whatsoever to regard v. 13 secondary. Structurally it fits the context.

6. Van der Woude stresses this point.

double function: it concerns the dates in both 1:15a and 1:15b. The unity of v. 15 could then be maintained, with v. 15b constituting the beginning of ch. 2. Thus 1:15–2:1 could be rendered as follows: "(It happened) on the twenty-fourth day of the sixth month in the second year of King Darius. (In the second year of King Darius), on the twenty-first day of the seventh month" (cf. TEV, NIV, the Dutch Groot NB).

The literary unity of 2:10–14 with 2:15–19 was denied, especially by J. W. Rothstein.[7] His point of departure is that the events described in Ezra 3:8–4:3 did not occur in 536 B.C. and that the expression "this people" in 2:14 does not refer to the remnant of Israel but to the Samaritans. As a matter of fact, the purpose of 2:14 was to thwart the Samaritans from participating in the rebuilding of the temple, and that is why the twenty-fourth day of the ninth month, in the second year of Darius, is considered "the day of the birth of pure Judaism." The suggestion that 2:15–19 should follow 1:15a also originated with Rothstein, with the additional comment that this prophecy was delivered on the twenty-fourth day of the sixth month!

This hypothesis of Rothstein found wide acceptance, especially among European scholars, with minor or major variations in the rearranging and interpretation of details. The introduction to 2:10–19 will deal with Rothstein's hypothesis and the modifications of scholars like Sellin, Deden, Elliger, Horst, Deissler, and others,[8] and will offer our main objections against this theory. It has rightly been pointed out that a form-critical analysis favors the literary unity of 2:10–19 (cf. Van der Woude). There are no indisputable arguments against the unity and authenticity of this section. We agree with Baldwin that the proposed dislocation of sections radically alters the book and is quite unsupported by any known text or version.

A last category of material that is considered to be secondary is the assumed presence of glosses on the text (cf. 1:15a, "in the sixth [month]"; 2:5a, 6, 16, 17, 18, 19, and 22a). We have dealt with these "glosses" in the commentary, and we are inclined to endorse Harrison's general solution to

7. Rothstein, *Juden und Samaritaner*.

8. Cf. I. H. Eybers, "The Rebuilding of the Temple according to Haggai and Zechariah," *Studies in Old Testament Prophecy, OTWSA* 1970/71, ed. W. C. van Wyk (Potchefstroom: Pro Rege, 1975), pp. 15–26. He transposes the whole of 2:15–23 to the end of ch. 1—the date in 2:20 (where the month is not mentioned) then referring to the sixth (1:15) rather than the ninth month (2:20) (p. 19). This means that the book of Haggai originally ended with 2:14, and the reason for the transposition became clear: 2:14 ended with the statement that the people as well as their actions and offerings were unclean. This may later have been regarded as a very unsuitable ending and so the promise of blessing which we find in 2:15–23 may have been placed after the original end of the book. Cf. also C. Kuhl, *Die Entstehung des Alten Testaments* (Bern: Francke, 1960), p. 218.

this problem: "the stylistic clumsiness (of the author) is predominantly responsible for awkward passages in the Hebrew text."[9]

IV. STYLE

The evaluation of Haggai's style has led scholars to conflicting conclusions. According to Mitchell it has long been the fashion to disparage the book of Haggai. One aspect of this disparagement is to belittle the significance of the prophet (cf. Marti) and to evaluate his style as "the most colorless prose" (so Reuss). The other extreme is to regard Haggai's style as poetic. According to Engnell the words of the prophet "can and ought to be arranged metrically."[1] Bentzen has applied this assertion to the text and agrees with Engnell.

We agree with Rudolph and others that a "metrical" pattern can be established only by means of a drastic emendation of the text that is not supported by any internal or external evidence. Elliger attempted to arrange the stichs of the book in accentuation patterns, but clearly without success. Especially in ch. 1 it is not feasible to impose a rhythmic pattern on the text. My own attempts, without emending the text, are as follows:

1:3 = 3 + 4 (Elliger deletes)
4 = 3 + 3 + 3 (Elliger ditto)
5 = 4 + 4 (Elliger: 3 [4])
6 = 4 + 3; 3 + 3 (4); 3 (2) + 2 (Elliger: 2 + 2, 3, 3, 3, 3 + 2)
7 = 3 + 4 (Elliger deletes)
8 = 2 + 2 + 2; 2 + 2 + 2 (Elliger ditto)
9 = 4 + 4; 4 + 4 + 4 (3) (Elliger: 4 + 4; 4; 4 + 4)
10 = 5 (2 + 3) + 3 (Elliger: 4 + 3)
11 = 3 + 4; 4 + 4; 4 + 3 (Elliger: 4 + 4; 4 + 4; 4 + 3)

We may agree with Wiseman, Rudolph, and others that Haggai employed a rhythmic prose style rather than the common poetic form often characteristic of the prophets. This does not mean that the book is without poetic significance. Parallelism, a poetic feature, is often employed. Four

9. Harrison, *Introduction,* p. 947. See A. van Selms's introductory remarks to his article, "The Inner Cohesion of the Book of Malachi," *Studies in Old Testament Prophecy, OTWSA* 1970/71, pp. 27–40, concerning the tendency to "Westernize" biblical literature.

1. I. Engnell, *Svenskt Bibliskt Uppslagwerk* (Stockholm: Norstedt & Söner, n.d.), quoted by A. Bentzen, *Introduction to the Old Testament,* 2 vols. (Copenhagen: G. E. C. Gads, 1958), 1:156n.3.

times the prophet resorts to a chiastic construction to emphasize his point (1:4, 9, 10; 2:23). Grammatical devices, for example, in the form of a series of infinitives absolute, are employed in order to bring out the verbal idea in a clear and more expressive manner (cf. 1:6, 9). Another feature of Haggai's "rhythmic prose" is his style of dialogue, which is similar to that of Malachi (cf. 1:4, 5, 9; 2:11–13; etc.).[2] Remarkable is the play on words, with a literary and intentional effect: because the people left the temple in *ruin (ḥārēḇ),* God will command a *drought (ḥōrēḇ)* on the land (vv. 1–9, 11).

Extremes in the evaluation of Haggai's style are not warranted. We may agree with the assertion of Baldwin: "Whether he used poetry or prose, Haggai was forthright and uncompromising. . . . No-one could fail to grasp his meaning, for he constantly repeated his favourite imperatives: 'consider' (1:5, 7; 2:15, 18), 'take courage', 'work' (2:4). He made frequent reference to the words of earlier prophets (e.g. 1:6, cf. Hos. 4:10; Mic. 6:15; and 1:11, cf. Hos. 2:9, etc.) and could introduce an apt metaphor (1:6e)." Baldwin also emphasizes the very free use of the "messenger formula" as a characteristic of Haggai's style. We have no evidence either to support or to contradict the assumption that Haggai may have put his prophetic oracles into poetic form when he first delivered his messages but that the written record was cast in prose. Our evaluation must evidently rest on the present form of the text.

V. TEXT

I want to begin this section on a personal note. My fifteen-year experience in Bible translation has strengthened the conviction that the majority of proposed alterations to the text (cf., e.g., *BHK/S*) are really unnecessary. This conclusion also applies to the text of Haggai (and Malachi). Mitchell's list of additions, omissions, and errors, for example, is impressive, but most of the items are arbitrary (e.g., in 1:2, 3, 4, 6, 9, 10, 11, 12, 15; 2:2, 5, 7, 15–16, 17, 18, 19, 22, 23). In the commentary we have pointed out that the "defectiveness" of the text need not be interpreted as corruption, but rather as the result—as Harrison puts it—of "stylistic clumsiness." In most cases the meaning of the text is clear. The Hebrew text of Haggai is generally supported by the fragments from the caves of Murabba'at, especially with regard to the order of the verses. The extant material (289 words out of a total of 600) differs in only two minor points from the MT of Haggai: in 2:1 *('el* instead of *bᵉyaḏ),* and 2:3 *('ittô* instead of *'ōṯô).*

2. C. Westermann, *Vergleiche und Gleichnisse im Alten und Neuen Testament,* Calwer Theologische Monographien 14 (Stuttgart: Calwer, 1984), p. 75, draws attention to 2:10–14 as the beginning in the OT of a new kind of comparison.

The four main witnesses to the text (the LXX, Vulg., Pesh., and Targ.) are essentially in agreement with the MT. In assessing their relevance as witnesses to the text, we must consider both their own peculiarities and the rules which apply in establishing the original reading, especially to prefer the reading which is more difficult from the point of view of language and subject matter.[1]

The LXX corresponds generally with the MT. A significant feature of the LXX text is the manner in which verses are rearranged: 1:9 and 10 are linked together; 1:15 is joined with the following verses (MT 2:1–2), and indicated as 2:1, which affects the numeration of the whole of ch. 2. The final clause of 2:15 (MT 14) is added to the beginning of 2:16 (MT 15). The LXX has some smaller or larger additions to the text, underscoring its inclination for "verbal expansion."[2] Differences in rendering are "out of the tribe of Judah" instead of "the governor of Judah" (1:1, 14; 2:2 [LXX 3]), "and cut" instead of "and bring" (1:8), as well as many other passages.[3] It is important to note that the LXX does not support some proposals to emend the text, for example, in 1:4, 10, 13, the dislocation of 2:15–19 (MT 16–20), and 2:4 (MT 5).

The Vulgate supports the proposed alterations in the text in the following instances: 1:2 *(nondum venit),* 1:4 *(in domibus),* 1:12 (the addition of *ad eos* = *'ᵃlêhem,* "to them"). On the other hand, it supports the MT in the other instances where *BHS* proposes an alteration to the text. This is the case in 1:9 (*et ecce,* "and look"), 1:10 (*super vos* = *ʿᵃlêḵem,* and *ne darent rorem* = *miṭṭāl*), 1:11 (*et super oleum,* "and on the oil"), etc. But the Vulgate is predominantly in accord with the MT.

In the Peshitta we must take into account the influence of both the LXX and the Targum, and also the translator's own peculiarities of style and interpretation. Its rendering mainly corresponds with the MT; some interesting deviations are 1:1, 14; 2:2, 21: *rb,* "the great one," "the leader" of Judah, instead of "the governor of Judah." In this aspect the Peshitta corresponds with the Targum. In 2:10 the Peshitta again is in accord with the LXX and the Targum in rendering *byd ḥgy* "through Haggai" instead of "to *['el]* Haggai."

1. Cf. E. Würthwein, *The Text of the Old Testament,* 4th ed., tr. E. Rhodes (Grand Rapids: Eerdmans, 1979), p. 116. F. E. Deist, *Towards the Text of the Old Testament* (Pretoria: D. R. Church Booksellers, 1978), pp. 244–45, stresses this basic rule in the evaluation of the text, but on one condition: "This more difficult reading must be a reading which we are able to *understand.*" On the other hand: "Giving preference to the easier reading is always an 'emergency measure' or an interim solution" (p. 245).

2. See J. M. P. Smith; cf. 1:1, 11, 12; and esp. 2:9, 14, 21 (LXX 10, 15, 22).

3. E.g., 1:9, 11, 13, 14; 2:1, 3, 5, 6, 7, 9, 14, 15, 17, 18 (LXX 2, 4, 6, 7, 8, 10, 15, 16, 18, 19).

Compare also 1:2, 4, 6, 9, 10, 12; 2:2, 6, 7, 16, 17. The Peshitta does not have the major LXX additions mentioned above.

The harsh verdict of A. Sperber on the text of the Targum to the Latter Prophets, viz., that it "has come down to us in a most deplorable state of corruption,"[4] is but partly true of the text of Haggai. There is a basic correspondence between the Targum and the MT. The Targum, for instance, supports the MT against many of *BHS*'s proposed alterations (e.g., 1:6, 7, 10a, 11, 12, 15; 2:2, 4, 5, 15, 16, 17a, 18, 19, 22, 23). In a few cases the Targum supports the proposed alterations of *BHS,* viz., in 1:2 ("the time has not yet come"), 1:4 ("in the houses"), 1:9 (probably "and it was"), 1:12 (with the addition of *ʿalêhem,* "to them"), 1:13 ("the prophet" instead of "the messenger"), and 2:17 ("a *return* to me"). In 2:23 the Targum reads "I have received you with pleasure" instead of "I have chosen you."

On the whole we agree with many scholars that the text of Haggai is well preserved.

VI. STRUCTURAL ANALYSIS

Because of Haggai's predominantly prose character, the literary unit in the book is not the stich or colon but the sentence. Our analysis is in broad outline only, with deliberate exclusion of technical jargon and detail.

A. FIRST SECTION

The first section can be divided into two related subsections: the command to rebuild the temple (vv. 1–11), and the people's favorable response (vv. 12–15).

1. The Command to Rebuild the Temple (1:1–11)

The structural analysis of 1:1–11 amounts to the following. Verses 1 and 2 serve a double purpose: they both form a general introduction to the following section (1:3–11) and have a specific application. They are addressed to the leaders but refer to the people and concern specifically the time and instrument of the reception of the word of the Lord.

Verse 1 consists of (a) the messenger formula, "the word of the Lord came"; (b) the adverbial definition of time, "in the second year of King Darius"; (c) the adverbial definition of the addressed, "to Zerubbabel"; and

4. A. Sperber, *The Bible in Aramaic III: The Latter Prophets according to Targum Jonathan* (Leiden: Brill, 1962), p. xi.

(d) the indication of the instrument through whom the word of the Lord was communicated, "through the prophet Haggai."

Verse 2 forms a separate sentence with embedded clauses and a marked antithesis in the parallel clauses: (a) Thus said the Lord: (b) these people say: (c) the time is not ripe to rebuild the temple.

Verses 3 and 4 are an extended parallel to v. 2, but at the same time they introduce a new message from the Lord. Note again the parallel clauses in vv. 2–4: "Thus said the Lord" and "the word of the Lord came through the prophet Haggai"; "The time has not yet come" and "Is it a time for you (yourselves)"; "these people" contra "this house"; "the time for rebuilding" and "a time to dwell"; "Thus said the Lord" contra "these people say"; "paneled houses" versus "this house a ruin." Verses 3 and 4 constitute a separate sentence with embedded clauses: (a) The Lord spoke through Haggai: (b) Is it a time to dwell in paneled houses, (c) while this house remains a ruin.

Verses 5 and 6 are closely linked with the preceding verses in that they constitute the connection between the ruined temple (v. 4) and the people's adverse circumstances (v. 6): (a) Thus said the Lord: (b) Consider your experiences. (c) Your primary occupation and needs were frustrated: (i) you have sown, (ii) you have eaten, (iii) you drank, (iv) you clothed yourselves, (v) you have hired yourselves out for wages—but all in vain.

Verses 7 and 9–11 form a literary unit and are an extended parallel to vv. 5–6. The connection between cause and effect with regard to the people's adverse circumstances is spelled out explicitly. Verses 10 and 11 reflect the relationship between a general and a specific statement, while the description of the effect of the drought in v. 11 moves from the general to the specific areas. See the commentary below for more detail.

Structurally v. 8 stands apart, and thus forms the parenetic focal point of the whole section. In positive terms the message of the Lord through his prophet is spelled out: "Go up into the mountains, get timber, and rebuild the house." The purpose and significance of this exercise is the pleasure and honor of God.

The section 1:1–11 abounds with interesting structural features: contrasting and synonymous parallelism; chiastic constructions (vv. 4, 9, 10); the series of infinitives absolute in vv. 6 and 9; the dialogue, similar to that of Malachi (vv. 4, 5, 9); the play on words, with a different meaning (vv. 4, 9, 11); and the recurrence of key words, "say," "word," "time" (vv. 2, 4), "house" (vv. 2, 4, 8, 9), "build" (vv. 2, 8), etc. It is important to note that the situation with regard to the temple is expressed in three parallel statements in vv. 2, 4, and 9d and e: the temple remained a ruin while the people lived in adorned houses.

2. The People's Favorable Response (1:12–15a)

This section forms a literary unit and recounts the fact that Haggai's sermon (1:1–11) was not in vain. Through his word and Spirit the Lord had stirred up the spirits of leaders and people to begin work on the temple. This was on the twenty-fourth day of the sixth month in the second year of King Darius.

Sentences 1 and 2 (v. 12) belong together and describe the twofold reaction to the word (voice) of the Lord. Leaders and people (1) obeyed and (2) feared the Lord. This reaction presupposes the preceding message of the prophet (1:1–11).

Sentence 3 (v. 13) forms a unit: it concerns the word of God and its content. Haggai's function as mediator of the divine revelation is emphasized in a remarkable manner: he "speaks" *('āmar)* as "messenger" *(mal'āḵ)*, according to the "commission" *(b^e^mal'^a^ḵûṯ)* of the Lord, and his "word" is identical with the word of the Lord himself *(n^e^um)*.

Sentences 4 and 5 (vv. 14, 15a) belong together. After the Lord had moved the hearts of leaders and people, they began work *(m^e^l'āḵâ)* on the temple. The date when the work was started is mentioned (v. 15a).

Several points should be noted. The subjects of sentences 1 and 2 embrace both leaders and people; the correlation between the word of God and the response of leaders and people is striking. God took the initiative. It concerns his *voice*, the words which Haggai has spoken according to his *command*, and the *inspiration* of his Spirit. The people reacted in a threefold manner: they *listened, feared, and worked*. Note the striking use of the Hebrew words *mal'āḵ*, "messenger," *mal'^a^ḵûṯ*, "message," and *m^e^lā'ḵâ*, "work" (vv. 13, 14).

B. SECOND SECTION

The second section can be divided into three consecutive subsections: 1:15b–2:9; 2:10–19; 2:20–23.

1. The Promised Glory of the New Temple (1:15b–2:9)

Sentence 1 (vv. 1:15b–2:4) consists of a number of subclauses: (a) The word of the Lord came: (b) on a precise date, (c) through the prophet Haggai, (d) addressed to leaders and people, (e) with a specific message: (i) Who had seen the previous glory of the temple? (ii) How does it look now? (iii) Is it not like nothing in your eyes?

Note that subclauses (a)–(d) are nearly a verbal parallel to 1:1; subclauses (e) (i) and (ii) constitute a contrasting parallelism: the former is contrasted with the present, and in both cases it concerns the seeing (Heb.

rā'â) of the house. The comparison is not in favor of the present appearance of the new temple-to-be.

Sentence 2 (v. 4a–d) stands apart and conveys the command to leaders and people to be strong, to take heart, and to do (the work). The function of *w*e*ʿattâ,* "and now," is the same as in 1:5, to recapitulate and to introduce a new statement. The exhortation to be strong, repeated three times, corresponds with the assertion in 1:4 that the Lord has stirred up *(yāʿar)* the spirit of leaders and people.

Sentence 3 (vv. 4e–5) comprises a number of subclauses: God's promise, underlying *(kî)* his command to leaders and people, consists of: (a) the assurance of his divine presence (v. 4e); (b) the motivation of his intervention on behalf of the people in the past (v. 5a, b); and (c) the appeal to them not to fear (v. 5e).

Note the emphasis in this unit on the prepositions with the suffix of the second person plural: "with you" (twice, Heb. *'itt*e*ḵem*), and "among you" (Heb. *b*e*ṯôḵ*e*ḵem*), and the key words "the word" *(haddāḇār),* in the sense of the covenant promise, and "remains" (*ʿōmeḏeṯ,* Qal active participle).

Sentence 4 (vv. 6 and 7) describes in terms of a number of embedded clauses what the Lord is on the point of doing in the interest of the rebuilding of the temple: (a) Thus says the Lord: (b) In a little while he will shake the universe; (c) he will shake all nations; (d) he will cause the desired things of the nations to come in; (e) he will fill this house with glory. Note the emphasis that is being laid on God's initiatives, expressed in terms of the suffix of the first person singular, *I,* and on the key word "shake" (Heb. Hiphil of *rāʿaš*).

Sentence 5 (v. 8) provides the ground for God's initiatives on behalf of the temple: all the material wealth is his.

Sentences 6 and 7 (v. 9) describe the result of God's actions: The temple's subsequent and future glory and splendor will be greater than that of the former (sentence 6), and God will grant "peace" in "this place" (sentence 7).

This section emphasizes God's word, promise, and actions. The reference to his "saying" (Heb. *'āmar* and *n*e*um*) occurs eight times. Note also the comparison between the three stages of the temple: the former, present, and future states.

2. Blessings for a Defiled People (2:10–19)

In broad outline the structural analysis of this section is as follows:

Sentence 1 (v. 10) stands apart and provides the date and messenger formula.

Sentence 2 (vv. 11–13) consists of a number of subclauses and constitutes a unity. (a) It introduces the word of the Lord, (b) with the request to the priests for (c–e) an official ruling on a matter of ritual concerning the distinction between purity and impurity.

Sentence 3 (v. 14) provides the application: as a defiled nation the people have defiled everything they have touched.

Sentences 4–7 (vv. 15–17) form a literary unit. The people are reminded of what they have experienced in the past because of their uncleanliness. The connection with the preceding sentence is evident: because of their impurity they must consider their past experiences as a token of God's displeasure with them.

Sentences 8–10 (vv. 18–19) are closely connected with the preceding sentence but open a perspective on the people's subsequent experiences "from this day on." The central theme of this section as a whole is found in sentence 10 (v. 19b): "From this day on I will bless (you)."

Several points should also be noted here. (a) The word of the Lord came *to ('el)* Haggai (cf. also 2:20), instead of *through (b^eyaḏ)* the prophet (cf. 1:1, 3; 2:1). The difference in meaning is negligible. Haggai remains the mediator of God's word. (b) The request to the priests presupposes their authority and emphasizes their teaching ministry (cf. Mal. 2:5–7). (c) Sentence 2 (vv. 11–13) presupposes the written (and oral?) ritual law. (d) The reference to the people in sentence 3 (v. 14) is remarkable: "This people," "this nation." See the commentary. (e) The people are encouraged to consider two different experiences: *before* and *after* the rebuilding of the temple has started. We have here the same connection between temple-ruin and the people's experiences as in 1:1–11. (f) The "house" of 1:2–11 is here called the "temple" (Heb. *hêḵal,* sentence 4, v. 15). (g) The style of dialogue between the prophet and the priests is apparent.

3. Zerubbabel, the Lord's Chosen Signet Ring (2:20–23)

Sentence 1 (v. 20) comprises the messenger formula and date.

Sentence 2 (vv. 21–22) consists of a number of subclauses: (a) The message of the Lord is addressed to Zerubbabel. (b) Its contents are: The Lord will perform remarkable feats on behalf of Zerubbabel. He will: (i) shake the universe; (ii) overthrow royal thrones; (iii) shatter the power of foreign kingdoms; (iv) overthrow chariots and their drivers; (v) cause horses and their riders to fall in deadly combat. See the commentary for a more detailed analysis of this sentence.

Sentence 3 (v. 23) also has a few subclauses: (a) The Lord Almighty declares that he will do the following on that day: (b) he will adopt his servant Zerubbabel; (c) he will appoint him to be a signet ring; (d) he has chosen him for that reason. See the commentary for a number of additional observations.

One of the four chiastic constructions in the book of Haggai (cf. 1:4, 9, 10) is found in subclauses 3c and d:

I will set you . . . as a signet ring
For you . . . I have chosen

Structural analysis as an exegetical method is in dispute. The present writer deems it one of several methods to establish the meaning of a passage. It concentrates attention upon salient points in the exegesis, and is in itself a significant antidote for deliberately dismembering a literary unit.[1]

VII. HISTORICAL BACKGROUND

The historical setting of the prophecies of Haggai is the restoration of the Jewish community in Palestine.[1] This period began in 539 B.C. when Cyrus, after twenty years of conquest, established himself as the king of a new world empire by entering Babylon as victor (see Baldwin).

The situation as it affected the people of God immediately afterward is recorded in Ezra 1:1–4:5; 6:3–5.[2] The latter (Ezra 6:3–5) is in the form of a *diḵrônâ,* i.e., a memorandum of an oral decision of the king filed in the royal archives. It provides that the temple should be rebuilt as a place to present sacrifices, that the costs are to be paid by the royal treasury, and that the gold and silver articles of the temple taken by Nebuchadnezzar should be restored to their rightful place. The other report (Ezra 1:2–4), the authenticity of

1. Structural analysis as a predominantly synchronic approach to the text must be distinguished from the diachronic approach, including a variety of form-critical, traditio-historical, and redaction-historical approaches. Cf. my *Metodiek van die Eksegese,* 2nd ed. (Cape Town: N. G. Kerk Uitgewers, 1981), pp. 52–80. For a traditio-historical approach to Haggai (and Zech. 1–8), see the doctoral thesis of Beuken, op. cit.

1. See J. Bright, *History of Israel,* 3rd ed. (Philadelphia: Westminster, 1981), pp. 360–72. See also Beyse, *Serubbabel und die Königserwartungen der Propheten Haggai und Sacharja* (Stuttgart: 1972), pp. 14–28; *New Atlas of the Bible: Judah as Part of the Persian Empire* (London: Collins, 1969), pp. 105–11; and now also J. Blenkinsopp, *A History of Prophecy in Israel* (London: SPCK, Philadelphia: Westminster, 1984), pp. 225–80.

2. Cf. Beuken, *Haggai-Sacharja 1–8: Studien zur Überlieferungsgeschichte der frühnachexilischen Prophetie* (Assen: 1967), p. 14.

which need not be doubted,[3] states that Cyrus not only ordered the rebuilding of the temple but also permitted Jews to return to Palestine, while others, who preferred to stay behind,[4] were besought to provide the necessary contributions. Ezra 1:7–11 also reports the return of the sacred vessels taken by Nebuchadnezzar, and recounts that the charge of this venture was placed in the hands of Sheshbazzar, the prince of Judah, a member of the royal house.[5]

The biblical account is supplemented by the "Cyrus Cylinder,"[6] in which the king records how, after his victorious entry into Babylon, he rebuilt temples and restored gods to their places. In allowing the Jews to return to Palestine, in helping to reestablish their cult in Jerusalem, and in entrusting the venture to a member of their royal house, Cyrus thus acted strictly in accord with his policy.[7]

Under the charge of Sheshbazzar the returned exiles proceeded at once with work on the temple and actually began the laying of its foundations (Ezra 5:16; cf. 3:6–11; Zech. 4:9). The altar of burnt offerings was also rebuilt (Ezra 3:2–6).

A minor historical problem concerns the relationship between the two civil leaders of the returned exiles, Sheshbazzar and Zerubbabel.[8] The laying of the temple's foundations is credited to Zerubbabel in Ezra 3:6–11

3. Bright, op. cit., p. 361n.43, refers to C. C. Torrey, *The Chronicler's History of Israel* (New Haven: Yale, 1954); and R. H. Pfeiffer, *Introduction to the Old Testament* (New York: Harper & Brothers, 1941), pp. 823–24, in this regard.

4. Cf. Albright, *Biblical Period,* p. 87. According to Beyse, op. cit., p. 34, the elderly people of Hag. 2:3 belonged to the sedentary population, because there could not have been old people among the returned exiles. The sedentary population were addressed in Hag. 1:15b–2:5, according to him.

5. Cf. Bright, op. cit., p. 361.

6. Cf. *ANET,* p. 316; K. Galling, *Textbuch zur Geschichte Israels* (Tübingen: Mohr, 1968), p. 84; E. J. Bickermann, "The Edict of Cyrus in Ezra 1," *JBL* 64 (1946) 249–75; and L. Rost, "Erwagungen zum Kyroserlass," in *Verbannung und Heimkehr,* Fest. W. Rudolph, ed. A. Kuschke (Tübingen: Mohr, 1961), pp. 301–307.

7. Cf. Bright, op. cit., p. 362.

8. They must not be identified, contra Josephus *Ant.* 11.1.3 (11–14); T. V. Moore, *A Commentary on Haggai and Malachi,* Geneva Series Commentary (repr. London: Banner of Truth Trust, 1960), p. 56; etc. Modern scholars distinguish between them, with Sheshbazzar the official governor appointed by the Persian government and Zerubbabel the representative of the Jewish community, he being heir to the throne of David; cf. Grosheide, *Ezra-Nehemiah,* COT (Kampen: Kok, 1963), 1:78–79; idem, "Zerubbabel," *GTT* 48 (1948) 65ff.; idem, *De terugkeer uit de ballingschap,* Exegetica 2/4 (The Hague: Uitgeverij van Keulen, 1957). Probably Zerubbabel succeeded Sheshbazzar as governor of Judah. See also Beyse, op. cit., pp. 23–28.

(cf. Zech. 4:9), but to Sheshbazzar in Ezra 5:16. Bright's solution to this problem is that the Chronicler (Ezra 3:6–11) appears to have telescoped the work of the two men. "Since we do not know precisely when Zerubbabel arrived, it is possible that their labors overlapped so that it was possible to credit the laying of the foundation to either." He deems it equally possible that although Sheshbazzar began the work, he got so little done that, when it was later resumed, the whole of it could be credited to his successor.[9] Although a new beginning was made, the progress really was short-lived. The early years and experiences of the restored community provide the historical setting of Haggai's prophecies.

The world situation between 538 and 522 B.C. was not encouraging.[10] Cyrus was succeeded by his son Cambyses (530–522), whose outstanding achievement was to add Egypt to the Persian empire. On his way back from Ethiopia Cambyses died, probably by his own hand,[11] in July, 522 B.C. In the absence of a direct successor, Darius, son of the satrap Hystaspes, an officer in Cambyses entourage and a member of the royal family by a collateral line, claimed the throne.[12]

The death of Cambyses sparked off rebellions in many parts of the empire. A disputed point is how long it took Darius to quell this universal revolt. According to Bright it was probably not until late in 520 that his position was actually secure.[13] Darius himself recounts that he had crushed his opponents within one year's time, the last of the opponents being the so-called Nebuchadnezzar IV, who started a revolt in Babylon.[14] At this stage Darius concluded his Behistun inscription with an epilogue stating that he had established himself on the throne. It is true that Darius recorded in an added column the revolt in Elam and the revolt by the Scythians, which occurred respectively in 520 and 519 B.C.[15] The fact remains, however, that Haggai (and Zechariah) could not have envisaged a breakdown of the Persian empire when they started to prophesy. Like their predecessors they

9. Bright, op. cit., p. 363.

10. Under the heading "The Early Years of the Restoration Community," Bright discusses (a) "The World Situation: 538–522"; (b) "The Jewish Community: Years of Hardship and Frustration"; (c) "The Spiritual Emergency of the Community" (op. cit., pp. 364–68). See also Koole, pp. 15–18; Beyse, op. cit., pp. 14–28.

11. Cf. Bright, op. cit., p. 369: "Cambyses thereupon, under circumstances that are obscure, took his own life."

12. So Bright, op. cit., p. 369.

13. Bright quotes additional literature to confirm his statement that the precise chronology of these rebellions in Babylon "is obscure and disputed," p. 369n.66.

14. See the Behistun inscription, col. 4, lines 4–5, 60; R. T. Hallock, "The 'one year' of Darius I," *JNES* 19 (1960) 36ff.

15. So Koole, p. 16.

surely were given their message at a critical time, but if political revolt against Persia had been in their minds, as Elliger suggests, they were too late.[16] We agree with Van der Woude that it is incorrect to explain Haggai's prophecies, especially those with a universal and cosmological intent (2:6, 7, 21–22), against the background of the contemporaneous political and international situation.[17] Haggai's point of departure is not so much the world events of his time but the covenant curse because of the people's negligence in rebuilding the temple, and the traditio-historical conceptions of the holy war on the Day of the Lord, connected with the Davidic dynasty.[18] In Haggai's prophecies there was no evidence of a fighting spirit among those whom he addressed (Baldwin),[19] and no highly strung messianic expectations (Van der Woude). Therefore we may grant that world events helped to give urgency to the prophetic message,[20] but the message itself was rooted in divine revelation, as it was received by Haggai, in accordance with the messages and themes of his great predecessors.

The subsequent circumstances among the Jewish community are aptly described as "years of hardship and frustration."[21] The response of the

16. So, correctly, Baldwin, Koole, Van der Woude, et al. According to Beyse, op. cit., p. 35, Darius's victory over the last two rebellions occurred on 7 April 520, nearly four months prior to Haggai's first prophecy. All hope for a breakdown of the Persian empire was thus frustrated.

17. See the commentary on 2:6–7 and 2:21–22; also Beyse, op. cit., pp. 35, 54, and 103.

18. So Van der Woude and Koole, correctly.

19. See also Beyse, op. cit., p. 35, and esp. p. 56. Haggai's point of reference is the adverse economical circumstances and the need to rebuild the temple. This malaise in Palestine and in the Persian empire reminded him of God as the Lord over nature and of world history (cf. Isa. 40:21–26; 41:2–4; 43:14–21). It is not either/or—either the international turmoil (Ackroyd, Elliger, Sellin) or the prophetic tradition concerning the theophany (Mitchell)—but both/and.

20. The intimate relationship between prophecy and history cannot be denied. In his Dutch edition, *Hoofdlijnen der Theologie van het Oude Testament*, 4th ed. (Wageningen: H. Veenman, 1974), p. 206 (Eng. p. 190), Th. C. Vriezen defines the relationship between revelation and history adequately: "God's revelation in history is every time anew accompanied by the proclaimed word of God." See his discussion, with literature, on pp. 204–208 (cf. *An Outline of Old Testament Theology*, tr. S. Neuijen, rev. ed. [Oxford: Blackwell, Newton, Mass.: Branford, 1970], pp. 188–92). See also P. R. Ackroyd, *JNES* 17 (1958) 13n.4: "Such a statement of the relationship does not involve the conclusion that the prophets were mere politicians, but simply indicates that the 'word of the Lord' came to them in real historical situations." Cf. R. T. Siebeneck, "The Messianism of Aggeus and Proto-Zacharias," *CBQ* 19 (1957) 312–28, esp. p. 313: "As always in prophetic borrowing there is the exploiting of the message to continue its value in contemporary and concrete circumstances."

21. Bright, op. cit., p. 365.

Jews in Babylon to Cyrus's edict had been disappointing. Only a minute proportion of them returned, probably in successive groups, so that by 522 the total population of Judah, including those who remained behind, can scarcely have been much above 20,000.[22] Jerusalem itself, still thinly populated seventy-five years later (Neh. 7:4), remained largely a ruin.[23]

The returned exiles faced years of hardship, privation, and insecurity. Bright aptly describes their plight. They had to make a fresh start in a strange land. They were dogged by a succession of poor seasons and partial crop failures (Hag. 1:9–11; 2:15–17). Their neighbors, especially the aristocracy of Samaria, were openly hostile. Tensions between the returned exiles and the resident members of the community were ever present. The Jews resident in the land regarded it as theirs (Ezek. 33:24) and were reluctant to share it with the newcomers. Bright seems to share the view that Hag. 2:10–14 was addressed to the contamination caused by contact with the native population, which comprised both the Samaritans and the exiles' less orthodox brethren.[24] We do not agree with this point of view, but grant the tension and bitterness which prevailed between the different groups of people.[25]

The right of the Jews to rebuild the temple was challenged by the pro-Persian governors of Trans-Euphrates, who applied to Darius in writing for confirmation that Cyrus had authorized the project. In an official memorandum discovered at Ecbatana, Darius forbade Tattenai[26] and his fellow officials to interfere with the work on the temple and decreed that the expenses for the work must be fully paid out of the royal treasury (Ezra 5:6–6:12). Whatever may have happened later, the rebuilding of the temple appears to have proceeded peacefully until its completion in March of 515 B.C. The biblical records are silent about the Jews of Jerusalem once the temple was completed (see Baldwin).

Two relevant points of the historical background of Haggai's prophecies must be highlighted: the history and role of both Zerubbabel and Joshua,[27] and the date that Judah became a consular province.

22. See Albright, *Biblical Period,* pp. 87, 110–11n.180.

23. See Bright, op. cit., p. 365.

24. Bright, op. cit., pp. 366, 368.

25. See the commentary on 2:10–14. Beuken, op. cit., elaborates on this "tension." See also H. H. Grosheide, *Israel na die Babylonische ballingschap,* Verkenning en Bezinning 13 (Kampen: Kok, 1979), concerning religious currents in the first centuries after the Exile.

26. See Bright, op. cit., p. 372, and esp. Beyse, op. cit., pp. 42–45.

27. Cf. Beyse, op. cit., 1–49; H. H. Grosheide, "Zerubbabel," *GTT* 48 (1948) 65ff. Zerubbabel is mentioned in Hag. 1:1, 12, 14; 2:2, 4, 21, 22; Zech. 4:6, 7, 9, 10; Ezra 2:2; 3:2, 8; 4:2, 3; 5:2; Neh. 7:7; 12:1, 47; 1 Chr. 3:19; 1 Esd. 4:13; 5:5,

We agree with the point of view that Zerubbabel and Joshua came to Jerusalem with the first caravan to return in the reign of Cyrus (cf. Ezra 3:1-13).[28] The lists in Ezra 2 and Neh. 7 (cf. 1 Esd. 5:7-45) may be the aggregate of several groups of names, representing several repatriations, but even so the fact that the names of both Zerubbabel and Joshua head the list

---

8, 48, 56, 68, 70; 6:2, 18, 27, 29; Sir. 49:11, 12. He was a member of "the royal line after the exile" (1 Chr. 3:17–24). He is generally indicated as "son of Shealtiel" (Hag. 1:1, 12, 14; 2:2, 23; Ezra 3:2, 8; 5:2; Neh. 12:1), but according to the genealogy in 1 Chr. 3:19 he seems to have been the son of Padaiah, the third son of Jehoiachin, whereas Shealtiel, the eldest, appears to have been childless. A probable solution is that 1 Chr. 3 indeed presents a list of the royal heads of families, with their respective sons. After Jehoiachin the next head of families was Padaiah, and he again was followed by Zerubbabel. In this sense he was called "the son of Padaiah," because he succeeded his uncle as head of the royal family. See Grosheide, *Ezra-Nehemiah,* COT, p. 84; idem, *GTT* 48 (1948) 51–62; idem, *Terugkeer,* pp. 25–26. For an alternative explanation see W. Rudolph, *Chronikbücher,* HAT (Tübingen: Mohr, 1955); and Baldwin. See esp. Beyse, op. cit., pp. 28–30.

Joshua (Heb. *yᵉhôšūaʿ*, in Ezra-Nehemiah *yēšûaʿ*, LXX *Iesous*) is mentioned eleven times in the OT as "son of Jehozadak" (Hag. 1:1, 12, 14; 2:2, 4; Zech. 6:11; Ezra 3:2, 8; 5:2; 10:18; Neh. 12:26; cf. also Zech. 3:1–9; Neh. 7:7). According to 1 Chr. 5:41 (Eng. 6:15) Jehozadak was deported when the Lord sent Judah and the citizens of Jerusalem into exile. At that time his father was chief priest (cf. 2 K. 25:18; 1 Chr. 5:40, 41 [Eng. 6:14, 15]). We may assume that Joshua was born during the Exile between 585 and 560 B.C. He was a descendant of Zadok and of Aaron (1 Chr. 5:29–41 [Eng. 6:3–15]; 2 Chr. 31:10). In Haggai and Zechariah Joshua is introduced as "high priest," the man responsible for ecclesiastical affairs in the postexilic community. Probably because of the importance of the high priestly office in this critical stage of Israel's history, the first of the four families of priests who returned from exile were called "sons of Joshua" (Ezra 2:36–39; 10:18–22). Beyse, op. cit., p. 33n.1, deems the title "high priest" premature, because it was—according to him, with reference to K. Galling, *Studien zur Geschichte Israels im persischen Zeitalter* (Tübingen: Mohr, 1964), p. 135—only after the completion of the temple that the title was instituted.

28. See Albright, *Biblical Period,* p. 87. Similarly, Bright, op. cit., p. 367, suffices with a broad statement: "All we can say is that Zerubbabel arrived between 538 and 522, and very possibly early in that period during the reign of Cyrus." He is a little more specific on p. 366: "who . . . apparently arrived in the interim at the head of a further group of returning exiles." H. H. Grosheide, in several writings, maintains that Zerubbabel (and Joshua) were among the first group to return to Palestine. Also in several works K. Galling argued that Zerubbabel returned to Palestine shortly before 520 B.C. ("Syrien in der Politik der Achaemeneden," *AfO* 36 [1937] 7ff.; "Von Naboned zu Darius," *ZDPV* 70 [1954] 4–32; "Serubbabel und der Wiederaufbau des Tempels in Jerusalem," in *Verbannung und Heimkehr,* Fest. W. Rudolph, ed. A. Kuschke [Tübingen: Mohr, 1961], pp. 67ff.). Beyse's contention is that Zerubbabel (and Joshua) returned with a major group of exiles between 525 and 523 B.C. (op. cit., pp. 22, 31–32).

should suggest that they were the first two to lead such a return.[29] Therefore, they came to Jerusalem in 537 B.C. At that time neither of them bore a title.[30]

The relationship between Zerubbabel and Joshua has a bearing upon our interpretation of passages like Hag. 2:10–14 and 2:20–23. In both passages some scholars detect a derogatory attitude of the prophet toward Joshua,[31] but we do not agree with this interpretation. It is true that Joshua is mentioned in the second place after Zerubbabel in Haggai, but this was probably due to the transitory status of the high priest at that point of time (so Koole). But Joshua is introduced, both in Haggai and in Zechariah, as high priest, the man responsible for the ecclesiastical affairs in the postexilic community. In Ezra 3:2 he is mentioned before Zerubbabel in connection with the rebuilding of the altar of God, this project being a specifically religious activity.[32]

What happened to Zerubbabel after 520 is a mystery.[33] The lack of information about his fate and the fact that he does not seem to have had a successor have led to the conjecture that the Persians objected to the claims made for him (Hag. 2:21–23; Zech. 4:6, 7), removed him from office, and stripped the Davidic house of its prerogatives.[34] It seems that Judah afterward continued as a sort of theocratic community under the authority of the high priest Joshua and his successors until the time of Nehemiah (Neh. 12:26).

29. So Baldwin; cf. H. H. Grosheide, *Ezra-Nehemia,* pp. 81ff.; H. L. Allrik, "The Lists of Zerubbabel (Neh. 7 and Ezra 2) and the Hebrew Numeral Notation," *BASOR* 136 (1954) 21–27.

30. Cf. Ezra 3:63; Grosheide, op. cit., p. 85.

31. Cf. Horst, Nötscher, Sellin, and esp. K. H. Bernhardt, *Das Problem der altorientalischen Königsideologie im Alten Testament unter besonderer Berücksichtigung der Geschichte der Psalmenexegese dargestellt und kritisch gewürdigt,* VTSup VIII (Leiden: Brill, 1961), p. 129. Beyse, op. cit., p. 66, deems the fact that Zechariah mentions Joshua along with Zerubbabel an element of his criticism of Haggai.

32. Cf. Van Selms, Bowman, et al., quoted by Grosheide, op. cit., p. 113.

33. Albright, *Biblical Period,* p. 88: "Whether Zerubbabel died a natural death or was removed, we cannot say; there is not the slightest reason to suppose that he committed any overt act of disloyalty to the crown." See also Bright, op. cit., p. 372. According to A. T. Olmstead, *History of the Persian Empire* (Chicago: University of Chicago Press, 1948), p. 142, he was executed. Bright rejects this assertion as being without evidence, op. cit., p. 372. Cf. also Koole, p. 17. Beyse's conclusion, op. cit., p. 49, is that Zerubbabel died shortly after the completion but before the dedication of the temple in the first days of April 515 B.C. See also G. Hölscher, *Geschichte der israelitischen und jüdischen Religion* (Giessen: A. Töpelmann, 1922), p. 124.

34. Cf. Bright, op. cit., p. 372, who deems this probable but emphasizes that we do not know with certainty.

The second problem of some historical relevance is the meaning of the loanword *peḥâ,* "governor," applied to Zerubbabel (Hag. 1:1; etc.).[35] In other words, what was the character and extent of Zerubbabel's authority as "governor" of Judah, or when did Judah become a consular province?[36] According to A. Alt, whose view is endorsed by most modern scholars, Judah became a separate subprovince of the Persian empire only in the time of Nehemiah.[37] The contention is that the relationship between Samaria and Judah as centers of government was, as late as the time of Nehemiah, not clearly defined, and that we do not know whether there was a succession of governors in Jerusalem between Zerubbabel and Nehemiah (cf. Baldwin). Therefore Koole, Chary, and others explain *peḥâ* to mean a representative official, because Judah at that time was part of Samaria, and Zerubbabel himself was subordinate to the governor of Samaria.

Others, like Grosheide, convincingly argued that Judah had been a separate subprovince even in the days of Sheshbazzar and Zerubbabel.[38] The fact that Haggai repeatedly called Zerubbabel "the governor of Judah" (1:1, 14; 2:2, 21; without the title in 1:12; 2:4, 23) seems to point to a status of real authority.[39]

To these leaders and this postexilic community, with their throes and disappointments, their lack of material goods and of fervor in the service of the Lord, with their frustrated hopes and expectations, the prophet Haggai was called to address himself, conveying to them the message of the Lord.

VIII. MESSAGE

The three major themes of Haggai's "theology" concern God, the temple, and the anointed one of the future.

35. See the commentary below, esp. on Mal. 1:8, and Grosheide, *Ezra-Nehemia,* COT, p. 160; *GTT* 48 (1948) 65ff.; Beyse, op. cit., p. 24n.8. Beyse stresses that *peḥâ* does not of itself denote the specific function of a person. It could refer to a vice-governor (Ezra 5:3, 6; 6:13, Tattenai), or a *Regierungskommissar,* a state commissioner (Ezra 5:14; Hag. 1:1; etc.). See also F. C. Fensham, "*Peḥā* in the Old Testament and the Ancient Near East," in *Studies in the Chronicler, OTWSA* 19, pp. 44–52.

36. Cf. M. Avi-Yonah, *IEJ* 23/4 (1973) 209–13.

37. Alt, "Die Rolle Samarias bei der Entstehung des Judentums," in *Festschrift Otto Procksch* (Leipzig: Deichert and Hinrichs, 1934), pp. 5–28 (repr. in *Kleine Schriften* [München: Beck'she, 1953], II:316–37).

38. Grosheide, *Ezra-Nehemia,* COT, pp. 79, 82–83.

39. According to Blenkinsopp, op. cit., p. 227, Jerusalem and the surrounding area of Judah (Yehud) formed one of several provinces, together with Syria, Samaria, Megiddo, and others, under the jurisdiction of the local satrap, probably resident in Damascus.

A. GOD

In full accord with the preexilic prophets, Haggai's message is predominantly characterized by its God-centeredness. This is evident throughout the book, especially in connection with the word and the acts of God.

The *message* of the prophet is essentially equal to the *word* of the Lord. In the book of Haggai the formula of revelation, in its various forms, occurs not less than twenty-nine times.[1] The specific indication that the word of the Lord *came* (Heb. *hāyâ*) occurs four times (1:1; 2:1, 10b, 20), which is also characteristic of the formula introduced in Jeremiah, Ezekiel, and Zechariah.[2] It is important to note that the formula of revelation obtained an objective and real character; the word did not originate in the mind of the prophet, but occurred, manifested itself, and thus was received *('el)* and communicated *(bᵉyaḏ)* by the prophet. The objective quality of this word was demonstrated by the fact that its occurrence could be dated (so Koole, correctly).

In Haggai the *word* of the Lord is synonymous with what he *said* *('āmar* and *nᵉum),* and with his *voice* (1:12). The prophet was "the messenger" who mediated and communicated the word of God which he had received. There is no disparity between the word of God and the message of the prophet.

Haggai also presented God as the source of all power, the controller of all armies on earth and in heaven, the Lord Almighty,[3] whose initiatives pervaded the whole fabric of the revelation in this book. He rebuked leaders and people because of their sinful negligence in rebuilding the temple (1:2–11; 2:15–17). The drought and crop failure were due to his judgment, because the people disregarded the priorities consistent with the covenant relationship between God and his people.

The claim to obey unconditionally the command of the Lord presupposes an act of faith, a venture in the firm belief and trust that God will comply to their material needs if only they would first seek his kingdom (Matt. 6:33).

In the paragraphs 1:12–14; 2:6–8; and 2:20–23 the full emphasis of Haggai's message is on God's initiatives. He spoke to the people through his messenger, the prophet. He promised leaders and people his gracious and abiding presence, counteracting their sense of fear and guilt (1:13; 2:4). He

1. Hag. 1:1, 3, 5, 7, 8, 9, 12, 13; 2:1, 4a, 4c, 4d, 6, 7b, 8, 9a, 9b, 10b, 11, 13, 14b, 15, 17c, 18a, 18c, 20, 23a, 23b, 23c.

2. Jer. 1:2, 4, 11, 13; 2:1; 7:1; 11:14; 12:1, 17, 21, 26; etc.; Ezek. 1:3; 3:16; 6:1; 7:1; 11:14; 12:1, 17, 21, 26; etc.; Zech. 1:1, 7; 4:8; 6:9; 7:1, 4, 8; 8:1; etc.

3. Cf. Baldwin's "Additional Note on 'the Lord of Hosts,'" pp. 44–45, and the commentary below on Mal. 1:4.

activated them to engage themselves to work on his temple, thereby endorsing the word of the apostle: "For it is God who works in you to will and to act according to his good purpose" (Phil. 2:13, NIV).

In 2:6–8 Haggai depicts what the Lord intends doing in the interest of the temple: he will shake nature and nations; he will cause the desired things of the nations to come in, and he will fill the house with glory, because all material goods are at his disposal.

The same emphasis on God's initiatives is found in 2:20–23. On behalf of his chosen signet ring, Zerubbabel, he will shake the universe; he will overthrow royal thrones; he will shatter the power of foreign kingdoms; he will overthrow chariots and their drivers; he will cause horses and their riders to fall in deadly combat.

This God-centerdness of Haggai's message is also endorsed by the people's reaction: they obeyed the word of the Lord, they humbled themselves under his mighty hand, and they acted according to his good purpose (1:12–14).

B. THE TEMPLE

The second major theme of Haggai's message concerns the rebuilding of the temple. The parenetic focal point of this pervading theme is expressed in 1:8 with a series of commands, leading up to their climax: "and build the house." To appreciate the importance of this message, we will have to consider the theological significance of the temple.

In the history of Israel the tabernacle and subsequently the temple were the places of the *praesentia Dei realis* among his people (Exod. 25:8). In Hebrew this is expressed by two verbs: *yāšaḇ*, "sit," "dwell," and *šāḵan*, "settle," "live in." It is important to note that the "dwelling"[4] of God in the temple must not be interpreted as permanent or static, but rather as an aspect of his self-disclosure, his communion with his people. Von Rad's distinction between "dwelling-temple" and a "theophany-temple" is contrary to the Near Eastern conception of a temple, and does not comply with the temple of Solomon.[5] Both interpretations are applicable in establishing the real meaning of the temple: God's divine presence in the temple was real, but at the

4. Cf. R. E. Clements, *God and Temple* (Oxford: Blackwell, 1965), pp. 58, 92, and 116ff.

5. G. von Rad, "The Tent and the Ark," in *The Problem of the Hexateuch and Other Essays*, tr. E. W. Trueman Dicken (London: Oliver & Boyd, New York: McGraw-Hill, 1966; repr. London: SCM, 1984), pp. 103–24; idem, *Old Testament Theology*, tr. D. M. G. Stalker (London: SCM, New York: Harper & Row, 1962), 1:234ff. (German ed., 1:233–40). Cf. Clements, op. cit., pp. 37ff.

same time it was the consequence of his dynamic, living presence in all the cultic events, of his self-disclosure to his people.[6]

In 1 K. 8:10–13 we have both the "theophany" and the "dwelling." The priests, we are told, withdrew from the holy place because of the cloud, "for the glory of the Lord filled his temple" (vv. 10, 11). Then Solomon said: "The Lord has said that he would dwell *[šāḵan]* in a dark cloud; I have indeed built a magnificent temple for you, a place for you to dwell *[yāšaḇ]* forever" (vv. 12, 13).

Of course, God's "dwelling" in the temple does not mean that he was confined to that structure or—especially—that his presence was an automatic fact. Neither was the case. In Solomon's prayer of dedication he poses the rhetorical question, "But will God really dwell *[yāšaḇ]* on earth?" The answer is obvious: "The heavens, even the highest heaven, cannot contain you. How much less this temple I have built" (1 K. 8:27, NIV). Scholars are inclined to account for this dual conception of God's dwelling in the temple (cf. Josh. 1:12) and his being in heaven (cf. Isa. 18:4) by attributing to the Deuteronomic school the notion of God's dwelling through his "name" (Deut. 12:5, 11), and to the priestly theology the idea of his "glory" which filled the tabernacle (Exod. 40:34–38).[7] These hypotheses are, however, without clear evidence.

The second proviso to the idea of God's *praesentia* in the temple is that it presupposes the covenant relationship between God and his people, which entails, on their part, faith, obedience, dedication, worship, etc. There is no automatic warranty that God will dwell in the temple among his people when they break the covenant and do not turn from their evil ways and evil practices (Zech. 1:1–6). The prophets were adamant about that. "Do not trust in deceptive words and say, 'This is the temple of the Lord, the temple of the Lord, the temple of the Lord'" (Jer. 7:4, NIV; cf. 26:6, 18). Ezekiel was a witness to the fact that the "glory" of the Lord indeed departed from the temple (Ezek. 10:1–22). The catastrophe of 587 endorses the undeniable fact that God can and will indeed abandon his temple. The priorities in God's relationship with his people are not the temple and temple worship as such, but God himself and his covenant, and only in this context of a living faith and genuine obedience to the word of God can the temple

6. Cf. Vriezen, *An Outline of Old Testament Theology*, p. 240 (Dutch ed., pp. 268–69): "The priest could mediate in the intercourse between God and people because Israel had received a *sanctuary* from God where He would reveal Himself in a particular manner, and because that sanctuary contained symbols He would make use of to maintain the relationship with His people."

7. Cf. Vriezen, op. cit., pp. 207–209 (Dutch ed., pp. 225–26).

again become the veritable house of the Lord, the place of God's divine and gracious presence.

Haggai's message concerning the rebuilding of the temple must be viewed in this light. He does not deny the spiritual realities of the people's relationship with God. These are evidently implied when he rebuked the people because of their wrong priorities (1:2, 4, 9), when he reminded them of God's pleasure and honor as the very essence and purpose of his presence among them (1:8), when he recounted the people's reaction to the word of God in terms of obedience, fear, and dedication (1:12–14), when he conveyed to them God's promises (1:13; 2:4, 5, etc.). The real danger for the postexilic community, however, was that they could have become accustomed to being without a temple and thus could have "spiritualized" their religion. Against this background Haggai delivered his messages and urged the people to combine the spiritual realities of their covenantal relationship with the institutional reality of a rebuilt temple. M. Schmidt rightly called Haggai a champion against false transcendental ideas.[8] By referring to God's dwelling in his "house," Haggai has vindicated God's accountableness, his actual presence among, and his living communion with, his people (so Koole, correctly). The consequence and relevance of the rebuilt temple is spelled out: "Then I will again take pleasure in it and will reveal my glory" (1:8). This is the significant perspective on the function and purpose of the temple. It concerns God's pleasure and honor. The result of God's intervention on behalf of the temple is the perspective on its future glory and "peace" (2:9).

In trying to assess the theological significance of Haggai's message concerning the temple for us, we must allow for both a continuity and a discontinuity in the interpretation and application of the material.[9] Both aspects are linked with the history of the prophecy's fulfillment. In this connection we must allow for a fulfillment in stages.[10]

(a) The temple was completed after four years, also due to "the precious things" decreed by Cyrus, endorsed by Darius (Ezra 6), and pre-

8. M. Schmidt, *Prophet und Tempel* (Zürich: Evangelischer Verlag, 1948), pp. 192ff.

9. For the concept of continuity and discontinuity, see J. Bright, *The Authority of the Old Testament* (Nashville: Abingdon, 1967), pp. 201–12; and my essay, "The Relationship between the Old and the New Testaments," in *New Perspectives on the Old Testament*, ed. J. Barton Payne (Waco: Word, 1970), pp. 280–303.

10. Cf. K. Frör, *Wege zur Schriftauslegung* . . . (Düsseldorf: Patmos, 1968), pp. 146–55. Concerning eschatological fulfillment, the NT witnesses to the fact that the promises and expectations of the old covenant are being fulfilled in Christ, and that they still will be fulfilled in the end, with reference to 2 Cor. 1:20 (p. 147).

sented by Artaxerxes (Ezra 7:15). This temple, expanded and adorned by Herod, was indeed of greater splendor than the contemporaries of Haggai could have imagined (Mark 13:1).[11]

(b) The terms of the promise will, however, be fully realized when Christ comes again. Then we will receive a kingdom that cannot be shaken (Heb. 12:26–28). Then the glory and honor of the nations will be brought into it (Rev. 21:24, 26). It is true that the temple as a separate sanctuary will disappear (Rev. 21:22), but the essence of this promise will be fulfilled in the New Jerusalem, where the "dwelling" of God is with people (Rev. 21:3).[12]

(c) Although the terms of the prophecy do not allow their application to the first coming of Christ and to the Church, this application may be implied.[13] In Christ the very essence and purpose of the OT temple is fulfilled, "For God was pleased to have all his fullness *dwell* in him, and through him to reconcile to himself all things" (Col. 1:19–20). In and through Christ, the Church and believers became the temple of God (1 Cor. 3:16; 6:19; 2 Cor. 6:16; Eph. 2:21, 22).[14]

C. ESCHATOLOGY

The third major theme, intimately connected with the theme of the restored temple, is the promise of a chosen signet ring, an anointed one in the lineage of David (Hag. 2:20–23). In the commentary we reject the purely historical explanation of Zerubbabel's role and stress the eschatological context and perspective in terms of the promise made to David (2 Sam. 7, 23).

Traditio-historically Haggai's prophecy is embedded in the intimate connection between king and temple in Jerusalem. The background of this theology is God's election of Mount Zion as his earthly abode, and his eternal covenant with David and his descendants (cf. 2 Sam. 7:1–17; Pss. 2, 18, 20, 67–72, 78, 89, 132, etc.; also 46, 48, 76).[15]

The problem with this prophecy of Haggai is that scholars are agreed that the prophet was mistaken about the person of the anointed one. According to Bright it is obvious that the hopes voiced by Haggai (and Zechariah) did not materialize. "David's throne was not reestablished, and the age of

11. See the commentary below on Hag. 2:9. Van der Woude concedes this point of view, but regards it as irrelevant for the interpretation of this text (p. 52).

12. Van der Woude stresses the importance of the prophecies of Haggai for the second advent of Christ, rather than that of his first coming (p. 75). Cf. my article, "Eschatological Preaching," *NGTT* 21 (1980) 80–86.

13. Cf. K. Frör, op. cit., pp. 136–43.

14. See esp. Chary.

15. Cf. Bright, "Aggée: un exercice en herméneutique," *ETR* 44 (1969) 13.

promise did not dawn."[16] Indeed, Zerubbabel vanished from the scene soon after Haggai's prophecy was announced. We agree with Van der Woude and others, however, that with this evaluation not everything has been said. The prophecy concerning Zerubbabel was inspired by the quest for the legitimate king of the future. This expectation remained, even after the demise of Zerubbabel; it is the perspective on the chosen "Son of God," to whom will be given dominion over all the nations of the earth (Pss. 2, 110; Matt. 28:18; Phil. 2:9–11; Heb. 1).

We also agree with Van der Woude that the prophecy concerning Zerubbabel does not justify a typological exegesis, according to which Zerubbabel is interpreted as a foreshadowing of Jesus of Nazareth. If the prophecy is to be interpreted christologically, then the emphasis, according to him, is more on the second advent of Christ than on the first. We may concede to this interpretation, but we would like to add that this perspective is indeed according to the very nature of prophecy: its content is projected on the ultimate and final stage of God's intervention in history. The history of the fulfillment, however, reveals a salvation-historical dimension, which can only be ascertained in the light of Christ's vicarious work on the cross (cf. Rom. 1:1–4; Matt. 1:6–16; John 7:42).

The question whether Haggai had identified Zerubbabel with the promised Messiah may be left open. In Zech. 3:8 and 6:9–15 there seems to be a distinction. But the promises concerning Zerubbabel were an actualization of the promise that the Messiah would be a descendant from the house of David (cf. Matt. 1:6–16; Luke 3:27).

Koole rightly compares the theological significance of the temple with a crystal, of which every facet contains a messianic expectation. This is the case with the prophecy concerning Zerubbabel (2:20–23). The same applies to the theme of the pilgrimage of the nations, who come to present their wealth to the temple (2:7–9).

Haggai's reference to blessings and curses (1:5–11; 2:15–19) must not be regarded as obsolete,[17] but as the announcement of the time of salvation, of which the rebuilt temple would be the guarantee.

Messianic associations are to be found in the promise "I am with you" (1:13; 2:4), compared with Immanuel, "God-with-us," in Isa. 7:14–16; the "peace" which will be granted in "this place" (2:9) reminds one of the "Prince of Peace" in Isa. 9:5 (Eng. 6), and the reference to the "Spirit" in 2:5 may be associated with the one in Isa. 11:2 on whom the Spirit of the Lord will rest (so Koole; cf. also Chary).

16. Bright, *History,* p. 372.

17. Contra F. Hesse, "Haggai," in *Verbannung und Heimkehr,* Fest. W. Rudolph, ed. A. Kuschke (Tübingen: Mohr, 1961), pp. 109–34.

In Haggai's "eschatology" two new elements, apart from the *Naherwartung* as the characteristic structure of OT expectation,[18] occur, viz., the pilgrimage of the nations is joined with the eschatological motif of the holy war, and the gifts of the nations are intended, not for Israel, but for the temple (so Koole, correctly).

For an account of Haggai's message in more detail, see the summaries at the end of each section in the commentary. Of course, we do not agree with scholars like Rudolph, Hesse, and others, according to whom Haggai's prophecies have no relevance whatsoever for the Christian faith.

IX. ANALYSIS OF CONTENTS

The book of Haggai, the tenth among the Twelve[1] both in the Hebrew and in the Greek Bibles, with its thirty-eight verses and two chapters, comprises four short oracles given by the prophet himself, written in the third person singular and connected mainly with the rebuilding of the temple. Each of the prophecies commences with the messenger formula and is precisely dated.

The book can be outlined as follows:

A. The command to rebuild the temple (1:1–11), and the people's favorable response (1:12–15a)

B. The promised glory of the new temple (1:15b–2:9)

C. Blessings for a defiled people (2:10–19)

D. Zerubbabel, the Lord's chosen signet ring (2:20–23)

The structural analysis of the book (see above) sets forth its contents in more detail. In broad outline it amounts to the following. At a New Moon festival the prophet enlightened Zerubbabel and Joshua, the civil and religious leaders of the postexilic community, about the attitude of the people toward the Lord's temple, which remained a ruin, and admonished both leaders and people to rebuild the temple. He accused the populace as a whole of regarding their own material comforts, slight as they were, as having priority, instead of exerting themselves to rebuild the house of the Lord. The neglect of the past sixteen years caused the Lord to punish them by means of natural disasters in order to remind them of the required priorities in the

18. Cf. Frör, op. cit., p. 151.

1. The canonicity of Haggai and its place among the Twelve were never questioned. Cf. R. K. Harrison, *Introduction to the Old Testament* (Grand Rapids: Eerdmans, 1969), pp. 260–88; R. Laird Harris, *Inspiration and Canonicity of the Bible*, rev. ed. (Grand Rapids: Zondervan, 1969), esp. pp. 180–95; A. H. van Zyl, *Net een Boek* (Pretoria: N. G. Boekhandel, 1974), esp. pp. 116–21.

kingdom of God (cf. Matt. 6:33). After an interlude of twenty-four days, leaders and people responded favorably to the prophet's exhortation (Hag. 1:12–15).

About seven weeks after Haggai's first prophecy (1:1–11), and nearly four weeks after the preliminary work actually began (1:12–15a), Haggai was given his second oracle (1:15b–2:9), in order to encourage leaders and people to dedicate themselves again to restoring the temple, with the assurance that the Lord himself would provide the required material and adornment. Contrary to appearances, the temple's future splendor would be greater than that of the temple of Solomon. The warranty of that rests in the promise of God's divine and gracious presence among his people, and in the manner in which he will intervene in the interest of the temple, causing Gentile peoples to present gifts of "precious things" (2:7) in order to beautify and adorn the house of the Lord.

The third oracle (2:10–19) presents the word of the Lord to Haggai, commanding him to obtain answers from the priests on a twofold question pertaining to ritual purity and impurity. The answers are applied to the people: because of their impurity, being in direct and prolonged contact with the "dead body" of the ruined temple, they have defiled whatever they have done and whatever they have offered (2:10–14). In 2:15–19 Haggai promised that the future would be better than the past, with the assurance as central theme of this section: "From this day on I will bless (you)."[2]

Haggai's last recorded word (2:20–23) was addressed to one of the community's leaders, Zerubbabel, on the same day on which he had pronounced the previous prophecy (2:10–19), the twenty-fourth day of the (ninth) month. In an eschatological context, in terms of what he had said before concerning the shaking of the universe and of the nations (2:6–9), Haggai again combined the cosmological with the military-political upheaval on the Lord's Day as a prelude to the ushering in of a new dispensation, in which Zerubbabel will become God's chosen man of the hour. As the vice-regent of God upon earth (cf. Zech. 3:8; 6:12–13), Zerubbabel was to bear the stamp of divine authority, and it was as a "signet ring upon the right hand" that he was remembered by Ben Sira (Sir. 49:11).[3]

2. Endorsed by Elliger and Beuken, *Haggai-Sacharja 1–8*.

3. Cf. Harrison, op. cit., p. 946. Since Rothstein the argument has prevailed that Hag. 2:20–23 was uttered to encourage Zerubbabel, because of the general disagreement with his firm stand against the participation of the Samaritans in the rebuilding of the temple. Cf. Beuken, op. cit., pp. 78–79; Beyse, op. cit., pp. 35–36, 52–53. According to Beyse, op. cit., p. 53, Haggai addressed this prophecy in Zerubbabel's absence.

TEXT AND COMMENTARY

I. REBUILDING THE RUINED TEMPLE (1:1–15a)

Haggai's single objective was to encourage the leaders and the people to complete an unfinished task, the rebuilding of the temple. In ch. 1 it is evident that the word of God did not return to him empty (cf. Isa. 55:11). The people responded favorably to the message of the Lord (Hag. 1:12–15).

This chapter can be subdivided into two related sections: A. The command to rebuild the temple (1:1–11), and B. The people's favorable response (1:12–15). For the structural analysis of this section see the Introduction.

A. THE COMMAND TO REBUILD THE TEMPLE (1:1–11)

1 *In the second year of King Darius, in the sixth month, on the first day of the month, the word of the Lord came through the prophet Haggai to Zerubbabel son of Shealtiel, the governor of Judah, and to Joshua son of Jehozadak, the high priest:*
2 *Thus said the Lord Almighty:*[1] *These people say, "The time has not yet come, the time*[2] *for rebuilding the house of the Lord."*
3 *The word of the Lord came (again) through the prophet Haggai:*
4 *"Is it a time for you to dwell in your paneled houses,*[3] *while this house remains a ruin?"*

1. The Hebrew phrase includes the infinitive construct of *'āmar,* "saying." In this and similar contexts it serves to denote the pause before the direct speech, and therefore can be rendered by a colon. Cf. KB, pp. 63–64.

2. Lit. "It is not time for the coming of the time." See the commentary.

3. The expression *b^{e}ḇāttêḵem s^{e}p̱ûnîm* (lit. "your houses being paneled") poses a few syntactical problems. When a substantive is determined, in this case by a suffix, the attribute should be determined by means of an article (GKC, § 126y). That *s^{e}p̱ûnîm* is not determined may be a good instance of a Hebrew adjective in the stative form (cf. Ezek. 34:12, and Wellhausen), but it is probably to be explained not as in apposition but as an attribute expressing a state, and is consequently less closely

5 *And now this is what the Lord Almighty says: Consider your ways!*
6 *You have sowed much and brought in little; you eat without being satisfied; you drink without getting your fill; you clothe yourselves, but no one gets warm; and he who earns anything earns it to be put in a purse with holes.*
7 *This is what the Lord Almighty says: Consider your ways!*
8 *Go up into the hills, get*[4] *timber, and rebuild the house!*
Then I will again take pleasure in it and will reveal my glory, says the Lord.
9 *(Consider your ways): You have been expecting much, but look, it turned out to be little; and when you brought it home, I blew on it! Why? asks the Lord Almighty.*
Because of my house which lies in ruins, while you are all running each on behalf of his own house!
10 *That is why because of you*[5] *the skies have withheld their moisture*[6] *and the earth has withheld its yield.*
11 *I have summoned a drought*[7] *upon the fields and upon the mountains, upon the grain, the new wine, the oil, and upon all that the ground produces, upon man and beast, and upon all the fruits of labor.*[8]

---

attached to the preceding substantive (GKC, §§ 118p, 126z, 131hn.1; E. König, *Historisch-Comparative Syntax der hebräischen Sprache* [Leipzig: Hinrichs, 1897], § 332g; C. Brockelmann, *Hebräische Syntax* [Neukirchen: Kreis Moers, 1956], §§ 81–82). See also Rudolph. This construction provides for a certain emphasis: "in your houses, the well-built ones." The suffix attached to "houses" is necessary because it emphasizes the contrast with "this house." *BHS* and *BHK* propose to delete this suffix on the basis of the ancient versions (LXX, Vulg., Targ.), but the absence of the suffix in those versions may be explained as a problem inherent to all translations into a foreign language (so Koole).

4. The LXX has a variant reading which does not affect the meaning of the command to "bring" timber. It reads *kaí kópsate*, probably a rendering of Heb. *wᵉhikkîṯem*, Hiphil perfect of *nāḵâ*, "to strike down." See K. Budde, *ZAW* 26 (1906) 11–12. We agree with Rudolph that the reading of the LXX is a paraphrase rather than the rendering of another Hebrew word.

5. Lit. "Therefore, on your behalf, because of you." In Pesh. *ʿal-kēn* is deleted; in LXX *ʿᵃlêḵem* is omitted. Because *ʿᵃlêḵem* is also applicable to vv. 10b and 11, the local meaning "above you" (so Van Hoonacker, et al.) is impossible, as Rudolph pointed out. Targ. renders *ʿᵃlêḵem* "because of your sins," thus explicating the Hebrew text.

6. Lit. "without dew, so that there is no dew." Cf. Vulg. and König, *Syntax*, § 406p, for the meaning of *min* in this construction. See the commentary.

7. The LXX and Pesh. read, incorrectly, "the sword" (Heb. *ḥereḇ*). Because both meanings can occur in Aramaic, the Targ. specifies the meaning with *yûḇᵉšâ*, "dryness."

8. Lit. "produce of the hands." The LXX and Pesh. insert suffixes of the third person plural instead of the second person plural.

1:1–11 THE COMMAND TO REBUILD THE TEMPLE

The prophecy of Haggai is without the customary heading. In this way it corresponds with the prophecies of Ezekiel, Jonah, and Zechariah. The opening verse is merely an introduction to the first of a brief series of prophecies contained in the two chapters of the book.[9]

1 Verse 1 consists of the following components: the formula of revelation, the most significant phrase: "The word of the Lord came"; the adverbial definition of time in connection with the coming of the word: "In the second year of King Darius, on the first day of the sixth month"; the adverbial definition of destination: "To Zerubbabel . . . and Joshua"; and the instrument through whom the word of the Lord was conveyed: "Through the prophet Haggai."

That the word of the Lord *came* (Heb. *hāyâ)* is of momentous importance, both in the historical circumstances of the postexilic era and in the book of Haggai. For the first time after the Exile the people of God could again listen to the authentic voice of prophecy. In the book of Haggai the formula of revelation, in its various forms, occurs not less than twenty-seven times.[10] The specific indication that the word of the Lord *came* occurs four times (1:1; 2:1, 10b, 20) and is characteristic of the formula introduced in Jeremiah and Ezekiel,[11] and also, in a stereotyped sense (so Koole), in Zechariah (1:1, 7; 4:8; 6:9; etc.). In this way the formula of revelation obtained an objective and real character; the word did not originate in the mind of the prophet, but occurred, manifested itself, and thus was received and communicated by the prophet. The objective quality of this word was demonstrated by the fact that its occurrence could be dated.

In Haggai *the word of the Lord* is synonymous with what he *said ('āmar* and *n*^{e}*'um)* and his *voice (qôl).*[12] This formula of revelation is used as an indication of a direct message or is implied in the context of a discussion. The dialogue[13] in Haggai differs from that in Malachi in the sense that in

9. According to Jones the opening verse of the book of Haggai is part of an editorial framework (cf. 2:1, 10, 20), which has the effect of making the book a report on the prophetic activity of Haggai and on the response of his hearers. This point of view is shared by other scholars. According to Beuken, op. cit., pp. 27ff., 184ff., the editorial framework in ch. 1 consists of vv. 1–2, 12b, and 13–15. Haggai's message is found in 1:4–11 and 1:12a. The editor provided 1:3 as an introduction to the prophet's message in conjunction with 1:1.

10. Cf. n.1 to Section VIII in the Introduction above.

11. Cf. n.2 to Section VIII in the Introduction above.

12. Cf. O. Grether, "Name und Wort Gottes im AT," *ZAW* 64 (1934) 59ff., 150ff.

13. Cf. J. W. Whedbee, "A Question-Answer Schema in Haggai 1," in *Biblical and Near Eastern Studies,* Fest. W. S. LaSor, ed. G. Tuttle (Grand Rapids: Eerdmans, 1978), pp. 184–94.

Haggai God is mostly answering his own questions (1:4, 5, 9; 2:3, 11–14, 19). For a fuller definition of the phrase "word of the Lord," see the commentary on Mal. 1:1.

in the second year of King Darius, in the sixth month, on the first day of the month. This comprehensive manner of dating also occurs in 1:15b–2:1a, and with the inverted sequence of year-month-day in 2:10. Twice reference is made to day and month only (1:15a; 2:20). In the OT the sequence of year-month-day is the most frequent, while the inverted sequence is found in Num. 1:1; Ezra 6:15; Zech. 1:7. Alternative datings are: year-day-month (Zech. 7:1), month-year-day (Exod. 40:17), and month-day-year (2 K. 25:8; Jer. 52:12). By far the most common manner of dating is the reference to the day and the month (45 instances), followed by the reversed indication of the month and the day (19 instances). In a number of instances the explanation for the specific sequence is apparent: when a month is introduced for the first time, the general order is month and day, but the opposite order is followed when the narrative is continued (see Exod. 12:18; Lev. 23:5, 6; 23:24, 27–39; Num. 28:16, 17–25; etc.). This obvious rule is not consistently applied.

The sequence day-month-year is generally used in decrees which required a precise chronology, for instance: "On the twentieth of Markeshvan, year seventeen of King Darius (II)."[14] The other main chronology of year-month-day[15] is found when historic events need a precise date, for example: "In the year of (the eponym) Daian-Ashur, in the month Aiaru, the fourteenth day, I departed from Nineveh."[16] In the Assyrian-Babylonian literature the more comprehensive dating is generally restricted to the period of the Neo-Babylonian and Persian empires.[17]

The use of a precise date to introduce a specific prophecy is common in postexilic writings.[18] Thus it occurs in Ezekiel (8:1), in Daniel (7:1; 8:1; 9:1, 2), and in Zechariah, the contemporary of Haggai (Zech. 1:1, 7).

14. See *ANET*, pp. 491–92.

15. Beuken, op. cit., p. 22, calls this a "calendar date," and deems it typical for Ezekiel.

16. See *ANET*, p. 278.

17. See *ANET*, pp. 301–303, 305–306.

18. So D. J. Wiseman, "Haggai," in *NBC*, 3rd ed. (London: Inter-Varsity, Grand Rapids: Eerdmans, 1970), p. 782. In general the dates in the prophetic literature are confined to the superscriptions to collections of prophecies; cf. Isa. 1:1; Jer. 1:1, 3; Hos. 1:1; Amos 1:1; Mic. 1:1; Zeph. 1:1; cf. also Isa. 24:1; 27:1; 32:1; 33:1; 34:1; etc. For a thorough discussion of the dates in the prophetic literature, see Beuken, op. cit., pp. 21–26. He asserts that the older preexilic prophets are without dates for separate prophecies. This form of dating really started with the autobiographical call narrative of Isa. 6:1. Cf. N. Habel, "The Form and Significance of the Call Narratives," *ZAW* 77 (1965) 297–324.

1:1–11 The Command to Rebuild the Temple

In the historical narratives of the OT the dating of events serves both to clarify their sequence and to emphasize their reality in time and space.[19] In the prophetic literature the purpose of a precise date is not only to establish the historical reality of the occasion on which the prophecy was pronounced but especially to emphasize the authenticity of the prophetic message.

Although the first purpose of precise dating—to establish the historicity of the occasion—is valid, it must not be overestimated. The real purpose of a precise date is overemphasized when some scholars consider the book of Haggai to be originally part of a major chronological narrative concerning the rebuilding of the temple, accompanied by the messages of the prophet.[20] This point of view does not take into account that the factual data in the book of Haggai are insufficient to be regarded as an abstract of an original work, and that nothing is known about the so-called chronicle of the building of the temple.[21]

The second purpose of precise dating—to establish the authenticity of a prophecy—is of paramount importance for evaluating the significance of the precise dates. (See Section II in the Introduction.) Apart from the relative relationship between the dated event and the accompanying word of the prophet (cf. Isa. 6:1; 7:1–14; 14:28; 20:1), the emphasis is on the authenticity of the proclaimed message, for present as well as future reference (cf. Isa. 8:1–4; 30:8). Koole rightly pointed out that such prophetic utterances, in the form of a written record, not only required witnesses but also a precise date to enhance the validity of the prophetic word.[22] The same applies to the dates in Haggai. The historical data concerning the rebuilding of the temple are important but secondary. Rather, the dates concern the guaranteed character of the messages and promises that were expressed with regard to

19. So, correctly, J. B. Payne in *ZPEB*, ed. Merrill C. Tenney (Grand Rapids: Zondervan, 1975), I:829. According to Beuken, op. cit., p. 25n.1, the dates in the work of the Chronicler can either precede or follow the indication of the event. Thus date-event: 2 Chr. 7:10; 16:1; 29:17a; etc.; event-date: 2 Chr. 15:10; 29:17a; 30:14; 35:1; etc. The formula in Ezekiel is usually *wayyᵉhî*-date-event. The same formula is found in the NT, esp. in Luke.

20. So A. Klostermann, *Geschichte des Volkes Israel* (München: Beck, 1896), pp. 212ff., and scholars like J. W. Rothstein, *Die Genealogie des Königs Jojachin und seiner Nachkommen in 1 Chr. 3:17–24* (Berlin: Reuther und Reichard, 1902), pp. 33ff.; cf. Sellin, Deden, Dhorme, Smit, Elliger, et al.

21. So, correctly, Koole, p. 6. The reference in 1:15a to a precise date surely has a bearing on the events described in 1:14. But this is the only instance in Haggai where the event is emphasized by a reference to a date. Elsewhere in Haggai the dates serve rather to stress the message of the prophet, e.g., 2:15, 18.

22. Cf. also J. Hempel, *Die althebräische Literatur* (Berlin: De Gruyter, 1930), p. 68; and W. Zimmerli, *Ezekiel*, Hermeneia, tr. R. Clements (Philadelphia: Fortress, 1979), 1:27–28.

the rebuilding of the temple. The rebuilding of the temple was the object of God's command (1:1–11), with the promise of his cooperation (1:14) and of his own assistance (2:1–9). The significance of the precise dates was to affirm beyond any doubt that the rebuilding of the temple was not humanly inspired but was a "work" which originated with God. The rebuilt temple, therefore, must be considered a "gift" from God to his people.[23]

The date of the first prophecy is *the second year of King Darius,* in the sixth month, on the first day of the month. All Haggai's prophecies were delivered in the second year of Darius, respectively on the first day of the sixth month (1:1), on the twenty-fourth day of the sixth month (1:15a), on the twenty-first day of the seventh month (1:15b–2:1a), and twice on the twenty-fourth day of the ninth month (2:10 and 2:20). Thus all of them were given within a period of four months.

The king to whom reference is here made is Darius Hystaspes, who reigned from 521 until 486 B.C. Therefore his second year is 520 B.C. The OT knew of two kings by the name of Darius. The first one is described as "Darius, the son of Ahasuerus, a Mede by descent" (Dan. 9:1); he was introduced as a predecessor of "Kores (Cyrus), the Persian" (Dan. 6:29 [Eng. 28]). The extrabiblical literature does not refer to this king, which of course is no reason to deny his existence.[24] The most famous Darius is the one mentioned in Haggai (1:1, 15b; 2:10), Zechariah (1:1, 7; 7:1), Ezra (4:5, 24; 5:1–6:22), and Nehemiah (12:22). He is called "the king of Persia" (Ezra 4:5, 24; Neh. 12:22), and "King Darius" (Hag. 1:1, 15b; Ezra 5:6, 7; 6:15). In the Uruk King List from Kandalanu to Seleucus II, he is mentioned after Cyrus and Cambyses.[25] A number of representations of King Darius have also survived.[26] A "Receipt of Feudal Dues" concluded with the words: "Babylon, the month of Nisan, the eleventh day, the twenty-seventh year of Darius, the king of Babylon, the king of the lands."[27] In an Akkadian version of a foundation tablet from Persepolis, concerning Xerxes (485–465 B.C.), this king called himself: "The son of king Darius, the Achaemenian, a Persian, son of a Persian, an Aryan of Aryan descent (lit.: seed)," with

23. So Koole, p. 7, Jones, et al. Beuken, op. cit., p. 26, defines the dating in Haggai (and Zechariah) as "annals," describing the ministry of the two prophets on behalf of the rebuilding of the temple. See the Introduction above on this point of view.

24. Cf. J. C. Whitcomb, "Darius the Mede," in *ZPEB,* II:29; D. J. A. Clines, "Darius," in *ISBE,* ed. G. Bromiley, et al. (Grand Rapids: Eerdmans, 1979), I:867.

25. See *ANET,* p. 566.

26. See *ANEP,* nos. 249, 250, 462, 463, 766, 769.

27. See *ANET,* p. 221.

reference to the countries over which he (Xerxes) reigned as king "under the 'shadow' of Ahuramazda."[28] A number of Aramaic Letters mention King Darius; for example, in "The Passover Papyrus" the festival of unleavened bread for the Jewish garrison was authorized by Darius. This was in "the fifth year of King Darius."[29]

In extrabiblical literature the name Darius was attached to two subsequent rulers, Darius II, Notus (423–404 B.C.), and Darius III, Codomannus (338–330 B.C.).

In Haggai, Darius Hystaspes is designated as "the king" (1:1, 15b). Other OT references add "of Persia" (Ezra 1:1; Dan. 1:10). The extensive and superfluous titles that extrabiblical sources usually give to the kings of world empires are deliberately omitted in the OT,[30] which ascribed these titles only to the Lord. The simple reference to Darius, the king, was significant enough for the postexilic community, not merely as a means of identification but also as a means of reassurance that he will act favorably on their behalf (cf. Ezra 9:9; cf. also Koole).

in the sixth month. In Haggai the Hebrew word for "month" is *ḥōḏeš,* from a root *ḥāḏaš,* meaning "new." *Ḥōḏeš,* denoting the "new" appearance or the crescent of the moon, is translated respectively as *month* and *New Moon.*

The consensus of scholarly opinion regarding the thorny problem of the ancient Near Eastern and OT calendars suggests the following stages in the historical development. In preexilic times the Hebrew year was reckoned from autumn to autumn, and the months were indicated by the Old Hebrew or Canaanite names, which were related to the seasons, such as Abib, the month of the ears of grain (Exod. 13:4; 23:15; 34:18; Deut. 16:1); Ziv, the month of the bright flowers (1 K. 6:1, 37); Ethanim, the month in which only the ever-flowing rivers have water left (1 K. 8:2). During the Exile the Jews adopted the Babylonian calendar, according to which, at that time, the year began in spring. This development was enhanced by the Persian conquerors of Babylon, who first adopted the Babylonian calendar for themselves, and subsequently imposed it upon every part of their empire.[31]

In the official calendar in Israel the Old Hebrew names of the months were eventually dropped, and in early exilic days numbers were substituted

28. See *ANET*, p. 316.

29. See *ANET*, pp. 491–92.

30. The exception being Ezek. 26:7, where Nebuchadnezzar of Babylon is introduced as "king of kings."

31. Cf. J. Lilley, "Calendar," in *ZPEB*, I:687, with special reference to E. J. Bickermann, *Chronology of the Ancient World* (Ithaca, N.Y.: Cornell University Press, 1968), p. 24.

for the names. This system really dated from early times, but according to De Vaux it was not introduced in Israel before the fall of Jerusalem (with reference to 2 K. 25–Jer. 52).[32] Thus this change in the system coincided with the adoption of the Babylonian calendar during the Exile.[33] Later the Babylonian names of the months were introduced. At first there seems to have been a reluctance to adopt the Babylonian names, because they were associated with heathen worship, but eventually, by the fifth century B.C., the heathen connections seem to have been forgotten.[34]

The *sixth* month in the lunar calendar, commencing in spring, is elsewhere (Neh. 6:15) called Elul, a name derived from the Babylonian Ululu. This month coincides with our August/September, the time of year when grapes, figs, and pomegranates were being harvested.[35]

on the first day of the month. This was the day of the New Moon in the lunar calendar, and as such has been observed as a festival occasion. "On the first of every month" a burnt offering was presented to the Lord (Num. 28:11). At Israel's appointed feasts and New Moon festivals they had to sound the trumpets over their offerings, since these were times of rejoicing (Num. 10:10; Ps. 81:4 [Eng. 3]). The New Moon festivals were associated with the sabbaths in a number of texts (2 K. 4:23; Isa. 66:23; Ezek. 45:17; 46:1, 3; Ps. 81:4 [Eng. 3]; Neh. 10:34 [Eng. 33]; 1 Chr. 2:3 [Eng. 4]; 8:13; 31:3; cf. also Num. 28:14; Ezek. 46:6; Ezra 3:5). "The gate of the inner court facing east is to be shut on the six working days, but on the Sabbath day and on the day of the New Moon it is to be opened" (Ezek. 46:1, NIV). "On the Sabbaths and New Moons the people of the land are to worship in the presence of the Lord" (Ezek. 46:3, NIV).

On this significant day, a day of worship and rejoicing (Num. 10:10), the word of the Lord came *to Zerubbabel and Joshua,* the civil and religious leaders of the postexilic congregation. For a discussion of the identity of and the problems concerning both leaders, see the Introduction.

We may assume that the word of the Lord did not come to them separately, but to both of them, perhaps during an appointment in Zerubbabel's home. This was not a social call but a solemn and official visit. These

32. R. de Vaux, *Ancient Israel: Its Life and Institutions,* tr. J. McHugh (London: Darton, Longman & Todd, New York: McGraw-Hill, 1961), p. 185.

33. Cf. Beuken, op. cit., p. 25n.3.

34. The problem is that such names also occur in Zech. 1:7 and 7:1. The assumption is that either Zechariah was younger than Haggai and less conservative, or that his book was edited later; cf. De Vaux, op. cit., p. 185; D. Winton Thomas; Baldwin; et al.

35. So Baldwin, and the dating in Ezek. 8:1; 20:1; 24:1; 26:1; 29:1, 17; 30:20; 31:1; 32:1, 17; 33:21.

two leaders were the official representatives of God's people, and, therefore, the word to them very much concerned the people as well.

through the prophet Haggai. The Hebrew idiom, literally "by the hand of," is frequently used to denote the human instrument of the word of the Lord. In the Pentateuch the instrument of God's word or command is usually Moses (Exod. 9:35; 35:29; etc.), and this is the case even in the historical books (cf. Josh. 14:2; 20:2; 21:2, 8; 22:9; Judg. 3:4; 1 K. 8:53; Ps. 77:21; Neh. 8:14; etc.). Elsewhere individual prophets are mentioned in this respect (cf. 2 Sam. 12:25; 1 K. 2:25; etc.), and also the prophets in general (1 Sam. 28:15; 2 K. 17:13; etc.). In Haggai *b^e^yaḏ,* "by the hand of" (1:1, 3; 2:1, 10) is elsewhere (2:20) replaced by the ordinary preposition in this context, *'el,* "to." In the scroll from Murabba'at one of the two deviations in the extant fragments from the MT is the reading *'el* instead of *b^e^yaḏ* in 2:1.[36] Both prepositions indicate the prophet as being the receiver *('el)* and mediator *(b^e^yaḏ)* of the special revelation. "It is therefore unlikely that any doubt is cast on the degree of inspiration of the prophet Haggai" (Baldwin).[37]

For the name and person of the prophet Haggai see the Introduction. Apart from the fact that Haggai was called *the prophet,* nothing else is known about his person or the circumstances of his life. The suggestions that he, like Zechariah, was from priestly origin (cf. 2:12), and that he must have been old, with reference to 2:3, are most unlikely. The main facts concerning Haggai are that he was the first prophet after the Exile, that he was an authoritative instrument of the word of God as his "messenger" (1:13), and that his primary task was to encourage and inspire leaders and people to rebuild the temple. That both leaders and people responded favorably to his message is a further indication of his authority as prophet.

The LXX's addition to the Hebrew text, viz., *légōn Eipón,* "saying: Speak to," does not presuppose a variant reading, but is a paraphrase in terms of 2:1.

2 Verse 2 commences with the "messenger formula": *Thus said the Lord Almighty.* The "messenger" is the prophet Haggai (1:1, 13), and his authority to speak on behalf of his sender is unmistakable. This is emphasized by the favorable response of both leaders and people (1:12–15a). The

36. Cf. P. Benoit, J. T. Milik, and R. de Vaux, *DJD II: Les Grottes de Murabba'at,* A. *Planches* (Oxford: Oxford University Press, 1961), pp. lxxi–lxxii; B. *Texte,* pp. 202–205.

37. According to Budde the use of the two prepositions, *b^e^yaḏ* and *'el,* suggests two separate *Gattungen.* He is justly criticized by Beuken, op. cit., p. 28, who states that the construction *b^e^yaḏ*-name-prophet is commonly used by the Deuteronomist and the Chronicler; he considers this usage a Deuteronomical-Chronistic element.

"message" is identified with "the word of the Lord" that came through the medium of the prophet. A. H. van Zyl argued that the phrase *kō 'āmar YHWH* must be translated in the past tense: "thus the Lord has said."[38] There is an element of truth in this point of view, when we consider the two acts in connection with the communication of God's word: the act of receiving the word and that of communicating it. When the "messenger" delivers the message, he already knows its content. This point of view emphasizes the prophet's personal and intimate involvement with the message which he has received and is obliged to convey to specific addressees. The problem with the past tense, however, is that an undue stress is being placed upon the historical sequence of the double act of receiving and communicating the word of God, thus allowing for a certain discrepancy between the word received and the word conveyed. The prophet's word is represented, here and now, as the actual word of the Lord, irrespective of the presupposed time lapse between its reception and communication.[39]

The subject of the message is *YHWH ṣᵉḇā'ôṯ*. The Hebrew word *ṣᵉḇā'ôṯ*, "hosts," has the primary meaning "army" (hence the Latin *Dominus Exercituum*, "Lord of armies"). The rendering of the expression in most of the older modern versions by "the Lord of hosts" is based upon this interpretation. Indeed, in a few contexts the Lord is spoken of as God of Israel's armies (1 Sam. 17:45; Ps. 24:7–10). The problem is that this title for God occurs predominantly in the prophetic books (247 times out of a total of nearly 300), and that it is particularly frequent in Haggai (14), Zechariah (53), and Malachi (24). In the prophetic literature other "powers" are at the Lord's disposal when he executes judgment upon the enemies of his people. Therefore we agree with the view that *ṣᵉḇā'ôṯ* must be explained not as a genitive but as an apposition to the name of the Lord, with the intensive plural denoting the comprehensive scope of God's might. He is "Lord Almighty" who has all powers in heaven and on earth at his disposal.[40]

The momentous significance of this title must be evaluated against the historical background. The emperor of Persia had at that time sovereign sway over his vast empire, including the minor province of Jerusalem-

38. A. H. van Zyl, "The Message Formula in the Book of Judges," *OTWSA*, Papers read at the second meeting (Potchefstroom: Pro Rege, 1959), pp. 61–64.

39. Cf. N. H. Ridderbos, "Einige Bemerkungen über den Propheten als Boten von Jahwe," in *Travels in the World of the Old Testament*, Fest. M. A. Beek, ed. M. S. H. G. van Voss, et al. (Assen: Van Gorcum, 1974), pp. 211–16.

40. Cf. O. Eissfeldt, "Jahwe Zebaoth," *Miscellanea Academia Berolinensia* II/2 (1950), pp. 128ff.; the commentary below on Mal. 1:1, 4; and Baldwin, pp. 44–45.

Judah. The emperor's word was law, even to the Jewish community. Now, however, another word was conveyed to them, the word of the Lord Almighty, he being the highest and the most absolute Potentate in the whole universe, including the Persian empire!

The message of the Lord was addressed to Zerubbabel and Joshua, in conjunction with v. 1. The problem is that the "message" seems to be abbreviated. It concerns only what "this people" were contemplating about the inconvenient time for rebuilding the temple. This "message" could not have claimed the authority of a divine revelation. The words and thoughts of the people were empirically defined facts and need not be presented as the content of revelation. Accordingly, most scholars are of the opinion that Haggai's message to Zerubbabel and Joshua is continued in vv. 4–11, with various suggestions concerning the secondary nature of either v. 2 or v. 3.[41]

The subject matter in both v. 2b and vv. 4–11 is admittedly the same, because both concern the rebuilding of the temple. The parallelism of vv. 2 and 3–4 suggests the structural unity of the pericope. On the other hand, the addressees of the two messages are different. Verses 1 and 2 concern Zerubbabel and Joshua, while vv. 4–11 address the people. This distinction is evident from the following. In v. 2b the reference to the people is in the third person and uses an expression which usually implies an absent category: "these people" (so Koole). In vv. 1 and 2 the prophet addresses the two leaders with an eye on the people.[42] In vv. 4–11 the addressees were the people. They were busy each with his own house (v. 9e), and they were experiencing failure of crops, on account of the drought (v. 11). This could not have applied to the leaders in the first instance, because they were not

41. Cf. esp. Elliger's suggestions concerning the relationship between vv. 2 and 3 (ATD, p. 86). This relationship, he asserts, presupposes a basic literary form, which consisted of three metrically structured oracles. The editor was responsible for the hiatus between vv. 2 and 3. If v. 2 had belonged to the original text, then v. 3 could be deleted as secondary. But then we do not know how the insertion came about. It is different when we may assume that v. 3 originally introduced the discourse which started with v. 4, and that an editor inserted v. 2 along with v. 1. The editor probably found this arrangement in the original and copied it in an arbitrary way.

Mitchell, Sellin, Horst, Chary, et al., deem v. 3 (Chary, v. 3a) a later addition. According to Beuken, op. cit., p. 30, the author of the Chronicle framework must have found it at the beginning of Haggai's message. He retains it, and accommodates it in the context of v. 1 by adding the introductory clause "through the prophet Haggai."

We agree with Jones, Koole, et al., that the attempts to rearrange these verses are unfounded. They are not supported by the history and tradition of the text.

42. So also Beuken, op. cit., p. 29.

directly dependent upon crops for their own sustenance. Furthermore we may assume a different venue for the two messages: the one for the leaders in the privacy of Zerubbabel's house, and the other for the people somewhere on the temple plain, because Haggai is referring to "this house."

These people say. The prophet addresses the leaders and in the name of the Lord contradicts a current argument among the people. "These people" represent the opposite party in a lawsuit, and the reference is judicially valid even though the party itself is absent. With the expression "these people" the Lord indicates his displeasure with them. Their sentiment was contrary to the will of God and to the best interests of his people. The use of the perfect tense indicates that what they have said in the past was still in vogue at that time.[43] Their point of view has had its own history. It was not a casual observation but a consistent argument, which they were sharing among themselves. What they said is represented in an abridged form. The prophet refers only to the very essence of the argument. It may be considered a summary of the prophet's case in court.[44]

The time has not yet come, the time for rebuilding the house of the Lord. In Hebrew the structuring of the phrase is terse and uncommon. Literally: "It is not time for the coming of the time of the house of the Lord to be rebuilt." The ancient versions seem to have rendered Heb. *ʿēṯ*, "time," only once. The LXX and Peshitta have "The time has not yet come to build the house of the Lord." The Targum adds *ʿaḏ keʿan*, "'until now' the time has not yet come (for) the house of the sanctuary of the Lord to be built." The Vulgate has *nondum venit tempus domus domini aedificandae*, "The time has not yet come for the house of the Lord to be built."

With the exception of the deletion of one *ʿēṯ*, "time," and the rendering of the Hebrew verb as a perfect or infinitive absolute, the versions presuppose the Hebrew text. The generally accepted alteration of the text to read *ʿattâ bāʾ*, "(the time) has now not come," is probable but not absolutely necessary. The word *ʿēṯ*, "time," preceding the verb is also found in Gen. 24:11: "the time to go out," 29:7: "it is not time . . . to be gathered" (cf., e.g., 2 Sam. 11:1).[45] The construction with the preposition *le* and the infinitive is also found in v. 4, and in Ps. 102:14 (Eng. 13); 119:126; Eccl. 3:2–8.

43. Cf. GKC, § 106g-l.

44. For the lack of literary finesse in Haggai's style, cf. Section IV in the Introduction, and esp. Beuken, op. cit., pp. 202–205. It reflects the spoken word. The narrative is hurried, abrupt, without introductions and transitions. It is not a literary composition—with reference to Wolff's remarks concerning the prophecies of Hosea in *Hosea*, Hermeneia, tr. G. Stansell (Philadelphia: Fortress, 1974), pp. 95–96; cf. pp. xxiii–xxiv, 75–76, 110–11.

45. Cf. KB, p. 746.

Koole's remark that the Hebrew verb *bô'*, "come," is never used with "time" is incorrect.[46] We have the combination of these two words in Isa. 13:22: "her time is coming near"; Jer. 46:21: "the time of disaster is coming upon them"; Jer. 50:31 (cf. 51:33; Ezek. 7:7, 12; 16:8; 23:3; etc.): "the time has come" (so Rudolph, correctly). The only difference from our text is that the verb precedes the subject in all the texts mentioned.

The conjecture of Ehrlich to rearrange the words at the end of the phrase to read "the time to build the house of the Lord," instead of "the time for the house of the Lord to be built," is superfluous. The same applies to Koole's observation that the word of the Lord concerns itself with the (favorable) time of building, not with the time of the temple. Allowing for the exceptional order of the Hebrew words, the meaning is evidently the same: it concerns the time for the rebuilding of the house of the Lord. "The time of the temple" in itself and without the appropriate verb does not make sense. We may, therefore, agree with Koole, with reference to Ibn Ezra, that the statement of our text must be considered as a popular saying, although we do not deem it necessary to confine the saying primarily to the words "the time of the house has not (yet) come" with the later addition of the words "the Lord to be built."

According to *these people* the time for rebuilding the temple was inconvenient. They do not doubt the necessity of rebuilding the temple or their obligation to rebuild it. Their argument concerns the aspect of timing only. According to them—and on this they were all agreed—this momentous task must be postponed a little. The present circumstances prevent them from doing what surely has to be done. The time is just not ripe. We must concede to the validity of their argument. The circumstances were indeed not favorable for such a task.

Cyrus, the Persian king, had ordered the rebuilding of the temple initially (Ezra 1:2, 3; 4:4), but according to Ezra 4:5 it seems that he had refrained from interfering when the Samaritans and other groups had frustrated the people's plans to rebuild the house of the Lord. This situation persisted during the entire reign of Cyrus and down to the reign of Darius (Ezra 4:5). In the ancient world the building of temples was the prerogative and responsibility of kings, and Israel shared this point of view. The time for rebuilding the temple, therefore, had not yet come, especially because the Persian king had not yet ordered the work to be done (so Koole).

The lack of funds was probably another setback for the people. Because of the extensive and persistent drought, the labor of their hands had produced nothing (vv. 10, 11), and they themselves were without food and

46. Koole refers to Brockelmann, *Syntax*, § 29b.

drink (vv. 6, 9). How could they rightly justify the expenditure involved in rebuilding the house of the Lord? According to Zech. 8:10 even the times were dangerous: "No one could go about his business safely because of his enemy."

The people could even have ventured a theological argument, with reference to Ezek. 37:24–28; 40–43, suggesting that they had to wait for the coming of the Messiah, whose task it would be to restore the temple and its worship (so Van Hoonacker). It has even been suggested that a miraculous provision of a new temple was expected, because Ezekiel was "shown" the temple he described, without mentioning the necessity of its reconstruction. "Rebuilding was a betrayal of the eschatological hope."[47] Older exegetes (Jerome, Rashi, Kimchi) have pointed out that the prophesied seventy years (Jer. 25:11–14) may have been a consideration for not commencing work on the temple, because the end of that period, reckoned from the time of the destruction of the Solomonic temple (587 B.C.), had not yet come in 520 B.C.

These and similar considerations,[48] however, did not seem to have impressed the Lord. They were not in accordance with the blessings and the obligations of his covenant relationship. A people who acted and argued in this manner could not be designated as "my people." They had disregarded the attitude of their ancestor Abraham who believed the Lord (Gen. 15:6), and they had forgotten God's word through Isaiah: "If you do not stand firm in your faith, you will not stand at all" (7:9); "The one who trusts will never be dismayed" (28:16); "In repentance and rest is your salvation, in quietness and trust is your strength" (30:15). They had confused their priorities as people of God, and subsequently had drawn the wrong conclusions with regard to their obligations. The element of revelation in God's reference to them as "these people" is to confront them with the real issues at stake.

This indication of God's people as *hāʿām hazzeh,* "these people,"[49] is peculiar to the preexilic prophecies of doom. Isaiah was admonished "not to follow the way of this people" (8:11), and Jeremiah was told to refrain from praying for "this people" (7:16). Haggai continued in this line of

47. Cf. R. G. Hamerton-Kelly, "The Temple and the Origins of Jewish Apocalyptic," *VT* 20 (1970) 12; and Baldwin.

48. In Ezek. 11:3 the nature of the advice about house-building is not clear; cf. A. W. Blackwood, Jr., *Ezekiel: Prophecy of Hope* (Grand Rapids: Baker, 1965), p. 84. Cf. also Jer. 29:5.

49. Mitchell (p. 45) rightly draws attention to these "ominous" words, for here, as in Isa. 8:6 and often elsewhere, the phrase "these people" betrays impatience and disapproval. In the NT we have a similar use of *hē genéa haútē;* cf. Matt. 23:36; Mark 8:38; Luke 11:30, 50–51; 17:25. See also Beuken, op. cit., p. 29n.3; and Elliger, ATD, p. 86.

prophecy (cf. also 2:14). Koole draws attention to a remarkable shift in emphasis in the postexilic use of the term. In Zech. 8:6 the variant "remnant of this people" is used to stress their lack of faith, obviously in a salvation context (cf. 8:11–13). Koole deems it implicitly possible in Haggai's reference also: the people dare not believe in salvation or ensuing blessings. Here the expression is used in Haggai's address to the leaders of the people. This use, implicitly, must have reminded them of their own responsibilities, which, according to vv. 12–15a, were not without consequence.

3, 4 Verses 3 and 4 form a structural unit and concern the messenger formula and its content.[50] Both these verses represent an extensive parallelism of v. 2. Substantially "these people" (v. 2) is contrasted with "this house" (v. 4), and the same applies to the contrast between "a time to build" (v. 2) and "a time to dwell" (v. 4). The repetition of the messenger formula in v. 3 has already been explained above (on v. 2). The main difference between vv. 1– 2 and vv. 3ff. concerns the persons addressed by God's messenger. After he had conveyed to the leaders the people's argument about the inconvenient time, Haggai addressed the people themselves. We may assume that both messages were delivered in separate venues, the one in the privacy of Zerubbabel's dwelling, and the other in the center of the festival activities, perhaps in the forecourt on the temple site. It is clear that the two messages presuppose a time lapse, but the exact amount of time between them cannot be established with certainty. We tend to agree with the point of view that both messages were delivered on the same day. Zerubbabel and Joshua received their message on the first day of the sixth month, and this day, being a festive occasion, was appropriate for the prophet to address the people. The repetition of the messenger formula probably served a rhetorical purpose, to emphasize the fact that God did not leave himself without witness in the actual situation of his people, or else to prevent the people from regarding their own argument (v. 2) as the word of God (so Von Orelli). According to Baldwin the emphatic introduction of the messenger formula is understandable when we assume that the spokesmen of the people had been heckling the prophet.

4 The prophet challenges the people's priorities.[51] They have attributed their lack of concern for the rebuilding of the temple to their own adverse economical circumstances, but the word of the Lord is going to

50. Cf. Beuken, op. cit., p. 30.

51. Beuken, op. cit., p. 30, distinguishes two series of verses in the pericope 1:4–11: one which deals with the people's negligence to rebuild the temple (vv. 4, 7, 8, 9b), and the other which concerns the adverse economical circumstances (vv. 5, 6, 9a, 10–11). Cf. his exposition of the "genetic" development of vv. 3–11 on pp. 187–89.

expose their excuses. The pronoun *you* is repeated to give strong emphasis to the suffix of the same person: Is it a time for you, (for) you to dwell in your well-built houses?"[52] They have argued that the time for rebuilding the temple has not yet come (v. 2). But now, what about themselves? Their "time" seems not to be inconvenient.

With this question the word of God is probing into the spiritual background of their formal indifference and lack of fervor in the service of the Lord. The argument of the inopportune time is obviously unfounded, because the people apparently have had time for something else—not for God and his temple but for themselves *(lāḵem).* The diagnosis of God's word reveals that God's people, who had recently been delivered from the Babylonian captivity, did not comply with the very essence of the covenant relationship to seek first his kingdom and his righteousness, with the subsequent promise that "all these things"—houses, material (and spiritual) blessings—would be given to them as well (Matt. 6:33).

The ensuing antithesis suggests the people's attitude and answers their economically defined argument. *Their houses* are well built: paneled, roofed-in, decorated, while *this house,* the temple, remains a ruin.

A major problem concerns the meaning of *s^e^p̱ûnîm*. The word is a Qal passive participle from the root *sāp̱an*, which means "to cover," "to roof in," "to panel." Thus the expression *b^e^ḇāttêḵem s^e^p̱ûnîm* can be rendered: "your houses (that are) covered/roofed/paneled." The first and last possibilities suggest the adorning of the houses with wood paneling. In this sense the word is used in 1 K. 7:7 (Solomon's throne hall was "covered" [NIV], "finished" [RSV], had "cedar panels" [TEV]) and Jer. 22:14.

Concerning Jehoahaz, one of the evil kings of Judah, Jer. 22:14 states that he built himself a palace with spacious rooms and large windows, "paneling it with cedar" (RSV). In 1 K. 6:15 it is said that Solomon decorated the interior walls of the temple, "paneling them from the floor of the temple to the ceiling" (NIV). The word translated "paneling," however, is not *sāpan* but *sāpâ*. The custom of decorating the inner walls by applying panels of cedar to cover them cannot be denied, although it seems that it was restricted to large and expensive buildings, for example, the temple and the palaces of kings. In Haggai the point of reference could have been either the decoration or the finishing of the houses. On the one hand the people could have decorated their houses with excessive wood supplies, while that specific commodity was totally absent as far as the temple was concerned (cf. v. 8). On the other hand the point of comparison could have been the completion of the houses, by providing the necessary roofs, while the temple

52. See GKC, § 135g; König, *Syntax,* § 19.

still remained a ruin. The ancient versions (Aquila, LXX, Vulg.) seem to support the notion of the roofing-in of the houses. Perhaps both points of reference must be considered in trying to explain the prophet's argument. He is contrasting their total lack of concern in regard to the house of the Lord with their zeal for their own houses. They had both the time and the means to decorate (to cover/panel) or to complete (to roof-in) their houses, while the required building material for the temple still had to be gathered, and the temple itself remained a ruin![53]

We agree with some scholars that we must not overestimate the general conditions of the dwellings at that time.[54] The people were experiencing adverse economical circumstances; Jerusalem seemed to have had only a small number of inhabitants (Zech. 1:16), even seventy-five years later (Neh. 7:4). The point of the argument, however, is that the people have exerted themselves literally to "run" on behalf of their own houses (v. 9), while nothing was done to rebuild the temple.

The Hebrew word *ḥārēḇ*, from a root meaning "to be void of water and vegetation," "to be dried up," and also "to be desolate," "to lie in ruins," is used by Haggai in the sense of the desolation of the temple (cf. v. 9; Jer. 22:5; 33:10–12; Ezek. 36:35, 38; Neh. 2:3, 17). This description seems contrary to the narrative in Ezra 3:6–13, according to which the work on the temple had already begun about fifteen years before. The people gave money to pay the expenses, and even sent to the cities of Tyre and Sidon to obtain cedar trees from the Lebanon. They succeeded in laying the foundation of the temple, but then their work was frustrated by their enemies (Ezra 4). Accordingly, F. I. Andersen suggests that *ḥārēḇ* must rather be translated "deserted," with the remark that "it is not unknown for a prophet to indulge in hyperbole."[55] But a deserted foundation still leaves the temple itself a ruin.

5, 6 Verses 5 and 6 are connected with vv. 2, 3, and 4 both by logic *(wᵉʿattâ)*[56] and by their content. They denote the relationship between the

53. Wiseman's comment is appropriate: "Should people live in *panelled houses* while wood is in short supply for the House of God? The technical term *(sāpan)* is used of decorative panels (1 K. 7:7) and of roofing beams (1 K. 6:9) and might have been chosen as a play on the identically spelt Aramaic/Babylonian verb *sāpānu,* meaning 'flattened (crushed)', a sidelong glance at the contrasting state of the Lord's House" (p. 783). For alternative views, cf. Rudolph; Ackroyd, *Exile,* p. 155n.9; Koole; et al., all of whom translate "paneled"; Mitchell; Baldwin; Winton Thomas; Steck, *ZAW* 3 (1971) 362, all of whom translate "roofed-in."

54. N. H. and J. Ridderbos, Koole, et al.

55. F. I. Andersen, "Who Built the Second Temple?" *Australian Biblical Review* 6 (1958) 1ff.

56. Cf. H. Brongers, "Bemerkungen zum Gebrauch des adverbialen *wʿattāh* im AT," *VT* 15 (1965) 289–99.

desolation of the temple and the adverse economical circumstances of the people.

And now. This expression presupposes a conclusion drawn from the preceding statement, and introduces a new statement. *this is what the Lord Almighty says.* The messenger formula emphasizes the revelatory aspect of the following message. *Consider your ways* (lit. "set your heart upon your ways"). This charge to "heed" or to "consider" is one of Haggai's characteristic expressions (vv. 5, 7; 2:15, 18). In Isa. 41:20-24 *śîm lēḇ,* "set (your) heart," or just "set," is synonymous with the Hebrew verbs for "understand" *(hiśkîl),* "see" *(rā'â),* and "know" *(yāḏaʿ).*[57] In the context these verbs concern the apprehension of the real meaning of the historical and eschatological "events." The same applies to the expression "to set your hearts upon." The people must consider, must give careful thought to, their circumstances and experiences, in order that they may deduce from them the correct conclusions. They must consider their situation and fate from the point of view of what God had wanted from and had intended for them. "You must set your hearts upon your ways *[ʿal-darḵêḵem],"* in the double sense of "what you have been doing, and what it is leading to."[58] They have acted in the normal way, they have sown their grain, have indulged themselves in eating and drinking, they have clothed themselves, and some of them even have hired themselves out to earn their wages, but the net result was a bitter disappointment. "Your ways," therefore, reflects both what they have done and what they have achieved. According to Haggai the onus rests with them to consider the real issue in connection with their experiences. They must come to grips with the problem of cause and effect in their specific circumstances. He does not explain to them the cause of their misery, although it is suggested in his reference to the deplorable condition of God's temple.

What has befallen the people of God?[59]

First, *you have sowed (or planted) much (grain), and brought in little.* According to Brockelmann the perfect of *zᵉraʿtem,* "you have sowed," is an affirming perfect, which could be translated in the present, the idea

57. Cf. also 1 Sam. 9:20; 21:13; 25:25; 2 Sam. 13:13; 19:20; Isa. 57:1; Jer. 12:11; etc.; and with the verb *šîṯ:* Exod. 7:23; Ps. 48:14; Prov. 24:32; 27:23.

58. Cf. Driver, and Jerome: *quae feceritis et quae passi sitis;* also A. Gros, *Le thème de la Route dans le Bible* (1954); and Koole. According to G. A. Smith "your ways" cannot mean here, as elsewhere, "your conduct," but obviously from what follows, "the ways you have been led, the way things have gone for you—the barren seasons and little income" (p. 238n.9).

59. The literary form of the following statements is called by D. Hillers (*Treaty Curses and the Old Testament Prophets* [Rome: Pontifical Biblical Institute, 1964], pp. 28–29) "futility-curses," and by Beuken (op. cit., pp. 189–93) *Wirkungslosigkeitsfluche.* Both scholars refer to extrabiblical instances of these "curses"; cf. Hillers, pp. 28, 61; Beuken, p. 190n.2.

being that it happened occasionally. Every time they have sown their grain, they have experienced the same result. This is borne out by 2:15–19, which suggests that the failure of crops was experienced in consecutive years. They have sown abundantly. The Hiphil infinitive absolute *harbēh*[60] has the meaning of an adverb: "much," "a great amount." The conditions for sowing seemed to have been favorable, or else they have minded the word "whoever watches the wind (clouds) will not plant" (Eccl. 11:4, NIV). The harvest, however, was disappointing. They have brought in *little* (Heb. *m*^{e}*ʿaṭ*), which is exactly the opposite of abundance!

Grain or corn was harvested at the end of May or the beginning of June. When we consider that Haggai had addressed the people on the twenty-ninth of August, we may assume that the people's disappointment was still fresh in their minds. The crop failure was but part of their disillusionment. Even the present provisions of their basic everyday needs such as food, drink, clothing, and wages did not have the required effect.

In the description of the people's plight, the prophet uses a series of infinitives absolute as the continuation of the preceding finite verb "sow," in order to bring out the verbal idea in a clear and more expressive manner.[61] In a few instances the infinitive construct with the preposition *l*^{e} and the conjunction is used to establish a certain and emphatic relationship with the preceding verb.[62] This "excited style" and emphasis can be effectively rendered as follows: "Your intention was to eat and to drink, and indeed you have been busy doing it, *but* with a disappointing result: you do not have enough food to satisfy yourselves, and do not have enough drink to get drunk on [NEB], or to become satisfied [Von Orelli]. You don't avail yourselves of ." The Hebrew word *šēḵar* need not imply becoming drunk, but may indicate abundance; cf. Aram. *r*^{e}*wāyā*. This is supported by the parallel word *l*^{e}*šōḇʿâ*, "to become satiated."

The description also includes clothing and wages. You intend to put on clothes, and are indeed doing it, *but* nobody is getting warm (lit. "there is no warmth for any one of you"). The pronoun with the preposition *l*^{e} is an individualizing singular: "every one of you."[63] Various reasons are suggested for this particular experience: because of the drought the sheep could not provide the necessary wool for the fabrication of clothes (Cyrillus); because they could not earn enough, they did not have the required money to

60. For the feminine form, cf. H. Bauer and P. Leander, *Historische Grammatik der hebräischen Sprache des Alten Testamentes* (Halle: Niemeyer, 1922; repr. Hildesheim: Olms, 1965), § 43d.

61. Cf. GKC, § 113z; Gemser, § 270d.

62. See GKC, § 114p.

63. Cf. Rudolph; P. Joüon, *Grammaire de l'hébreu biblique* (Rome: Pontifical Biblical Institute, 1923, repr. 1965), § 152d.

buy the necessary clothes (Hitzig); the lack of nutrition caused them to feel cold despite their clothes (Driver, et al.). Whatever the reason(s), their clothes did not have the desired effect.

When people are obliged to hire themselves out for wages, they do not enjoy the benefit of it, because it is as if they had put the wages into a pouch with holes (RSV). The nominal sentence is being used with rhetorical effect (Koole). There is no reason to doubt the authenticity of the second *miśtakkēr*. Two manuscripts have the imperfect (cf. *BHS*), and some of the ancient versions (LXX, Vulg.) have a finite verb, but we agree with Koole that this could have been due to the problems of translating in a different language. The verb *śāḵar* means "to hire someone for wages," and it applies in various contexts: one may hire a priest (Judg. 18:4), an army (2 Sam. 10:6), a goldsmith (Isa. 46:6). In Hag. 1:6 the verb is in the Hithpael and has a reflexive meaning: "to hire oneself out." The assumption is that at least some of the people were obliged to do it. The semantic field of this word is defined by the noun *śāḵîr,* meaning "a day-laborer," "a hired laborer," "a wage-earner" (Exod. 12:45). The situation was in itself humiliating (cf. Mal. 3:5; Lev. 19:13; 25:6), but the people's experience was that the wages they earned in such a manner were of no avail: their money simply disappeared as if the purse they put it in was full of holes. The prophet's figure of speech is indeed striking. The hired laborers earned their wages, but those wages were totally insufficient to cope with their material needs, probably due to the rising costs, the depreciation of the wages, and the general economical malaise.

It is important to note that this reference to a "purse" containing wages is the first in the OT. In earlier times big chunks of silver were simply gathered in a piece of cloth. In Gen. 42:35 and Prov. 7:20 the Hebrew word *ṣᵉrôr* is rendered too technically by "pouch" (NIV); it simply means "to wrap up," to make a "bundle" of the pieces of silver (cf. RSV). From the sixth century B.C. onward it became the practice to carry a pouch in the form of a leather bag, which could be tied up at the top. Thus the Hebrew word *ṣᵉrôr,* "a thing that is being wrapped up," could be used to denote such a purse. In these "pouches" minted coins were kept. These coins became extant in the Persian period (cf. Ezra 2:69). But it is uncertain whether the minted coins were known to Haggai, because according to Zech. 11:12 the shekels of silver were still being weighed out (cf. Baldwin). It was also customary to put rough and pointed pieces of silver in "pouches" when business transactions were being settled. The sharp edges of these pieces of silver occasionally were responsible for holes in the "pouches."[64]

64. Cf. R. Loewe, "The earliest biblical allusion to coined money," *PEQ* 87 (1955) 141–50, with literature.

The theological perspective on the word of God to the people is that their adverse economical circumstances were not the result of mere natural phenomena but were due to God's judgment. We have a similar picture of God's judgment as the main cause of the people's general malaise in Mic. 6:9-16. Some of the features in this picture of disaster are similar to that in Haggai: "You shall eat, but not be satisfied" (Mic. 6:14), "you shall sow, but not reap" (v. 15), "you will tread grapes, but not drink wine" (v. 15b). The theological context of Haggai's message is the covenant relationship, with its blessings and sanctions in the form of curses or judgments. An aspect of God's blessing was that his people should eat and become satisfied (Deut. 6:11), but the same applies to his curse: "You shall eat, and not be satisfied" (Lev. 26:26). In Deut. 28:38, 39 this specific curse was pronounced: "You shall carry (sow) much seed into the field, and shall gather little in; for the locust shall consume it. You shall plant vineyards and dress them, but you shall neither drink of the wine nor gather the grapes; for the worm shall eat them." In vv. 47 and 48 we read: "Because you did not serve the Lord your God with joyfulness . . . therefore you shall serve your enemies whom the Lord will send against you in hunger and thirst, in nakedness, and in want of all things."

The real point in the prophet's appeal to the people to consider their ways (v. 5) is to remind them of the vertical dimension in their relationship to God, and to urge them to relate their present malaise to the covenantal sanction in the form of God's judgment. This turn in God's "argument" with his people is aptly introduced by the *wᵉʿattâ,* "and now," at the beginning of v. 5.[65]

7 Most scholars have a contextual problem with v. 7b: *Consider your ways,* because it is "a mere clerical repetition from verse 5" (G. A. Smith), and because it apparently does not link with v. 8. The proposed solution to this problem is either to delete v. 7b as a later addition (*BHK, BHS,* Wellhausen, et al.), or to rearrange its position in the context. The following options have been suggested: v. 7b must be transposed after v. 8 (Ehrlich, Nötscher, Horst, Chary, et al.), the whole of v. 7 is placed after v. 8 (Halevy, Van Hoonacker, Deden, Gelin, Eissfeldt, et al.), or vv. 7 and 8 "would read well after verse 11" (JPSV, note; cf. *BHK*).

These and similar proposals to rearrange the text are not supported by any textual evidence, neither by the ancient versions nor by the Murabbaʿat fragments. We are, therefore, bound to make sense out of the Hebrew text as it stands.

The context of v. 7 could be established in two ways. Either it could be considered the closing link of a circular composition, starting with v. 5,

65. Cf. n.56 above, and J. Ridderbos, Koole, et al.

or we could reconsider the exact meaning of v. 7b in the specific context with v. 8.

According to our structural analysis of vv. 5-7, we may regard this section as a literary unit, commencing and closing with the same statement. The repetition of the injunction to the people to "consider your ways" has the effect of stressing the divine appeal for their repentance and conversion. If only they could become aware of their sinful negligence of God's temple, and repent themselves, the way would be paved for them to act according to the message formulated in v. 8.

The second possible solution to the contextual problem, suggested by Mitchell, Koole, et al., is that the expression in v. 7b need not have the same purport as the one in v. 5b. In v. 5b the point of reference is the past (and present) experiences of the people, but in v. 7b the relationship between cause and effect, conduct and fate, suggests that if they mend their ways now, they may experience the blessings of the Lord in the future. In this sense v. 7b may be regarded as an introduction to v. 8: If the people react favorably to the prophet's summons to rebuild the temple (v. 8), they will definitely and actually observe God's pleasure and experience his subsequent blessings. This explanation also allows for the repetition of the messenger formula, *This is what the Lord Almighty says,* in v. 7a. In v. 5a the implied suggestion was the pronouncement of judgment, in v. 7a it is the promise of God's blessings.

8 Structurally this verse seems to be without any direct link to the preceding or following verses. It occupies a somewhat independent position. As such it receives special emphasis and conveys the central theme of Haggai's message.[66] In direct and positive terms the people were charged with the duty to rebuild the temple. This claim to obey the command of the Lord unconditionally, in spite of the adverse circumstances and the inopportune time, presupposes an act of faith, a venture in the firm belief and trust that God will comply to their material needs if only they would first seek his kingdom (Matt. 6:33).

Go up into the hills, get timber, and rebuild the house. The purport of

66. According to Koole the central theme of the pericope is expressed in v. 4: They dwelled in paneled houses, while the Lord's house remained a ruin. Elliger's point of departure in explaining the central message of the pericope is the fear of the Lord (v. 12). He considers this the key to understanding the pericope. The main purport of the whole discourse is to restore, i.e., to rouse up, the true fear of the Lord. The decisive verse, however, is v. 8, with its vital reference to the pleasure of the Lord. According to Elliger vv. 7 and 8 form "dem Herzstuck in der Mitte der Komposition" (ATD, p. 87). This emphasis on the significance of v. 8 in its context is endorsed by Beuken, op. cit., p. 185.

this charge is clear. It consists of three separate commands, like the shots of an automatic weapon, focusing the people's attention on the climax of the series: "and rebuild the house."

They must ascend *the hills* (Heb. *hāhār,* lit. "mountain"). The intention was not to send them to a specific mountain, but in general to the Judean mountains or hills surrounding Jerusalem, which at that time were still covered with forest. Nehemiah besought Artaxerxes to supply him with a letter of introduction to Asaph, "keeper of the king's forest," so that he might give him timber "to make beams for the gates of the fortress of the temple, and for the wall of the city, and for the house which I shall occupy" (Neh. 2:8). From Neh. 8:15–16 we learn that olive, myrtle, and palm were available, because the people were sent "out to the hills" to bring back branches from these trees to make booths.

It is remarkable that the categorical command confines itself to the obtaining of *timber* only. Various explanations have been offered for this. According to some the specific command really has a comprehensive intent: the order to bring back timber includes all the materials needed for rebuilding the temple. This point of view, taken by Keil, is, however, not supported by the clear meaning of the text. The people have to go up into the hills to get *ʿēṣ,* "wood," "timber," which is a specific commodity.

A second explanation is that of Ehrlich. Based on an account in Josephus (*Ant.* 11.4 [75–119]), Ehrlich claims that the Jews at first erected a wooden temple. But this deduction from Josephus's narrative is incorrect. Josephus mentions money given to "the masons and to the carpenters," and everything that was necessary for the maintenance of the workmen (11.4.1 [78]). No mention is made of a wooden structure representing the completed temple.

Jerome alluded to a tradition among the Jews according to which the walls of the Solomonic temple remained intact after the catastrophe of 587 B.C., thus requiring wood only for the reconstruction of the temple. This point of view, however, is contrary to the specific reference to the temple being a ruin (v. 4), and that the rebuilding was effected by laying "one stone on another" (2:15).

Koole again suggests that the acquired timber was necessary in the primary stages of the temple's reconstruction, in order to make scaffolds and to remove stones and other forms of debris before the real rebuilding could begin. The wood could also have been used to reinforce the walls, in accordance with Cyrus's "memorandum" in Ezra 6:3-5, where it is specified to build the walls alternatively with three courses of large stones and one of timbers (v. 4).

The most probable solution is that of Von Orelli, et al. In the ruins of the temple and in its immediate vicinity were ample stones for building purposes. Because all the timber of the temple was burned in 587 B.C., it was necessary only to obtain large quantities of timber from the forests on the nearby hills surrounding Jerusalem.[67]

A minor issue in connection with the required timber is the question of its quality. We know that olive, myrtle, and palm wood were available (Neh. 8:15), but it is doubtful whether they would have been suitable for supporting the roof. According to Neh. 2:8, however, it seemed possible. It was also possible that the cedar logs which were brought from Lebanon at the command of Cyrus (Ezra 3:7) were still available and were sufficient heavy timber, long enough to stretch from wall to wall in order to support the roof of the temple. According to Drusius, Haggai was referring to these cedar logs, with the command to bring them up to the temple mountain. This point of view, however, is contrary to the specific injunction *to go up into* the hills and bring the timber, and not the other way round.

Mitchell again deems Ezra 3:7 to be a duplicate of Hag. 1:8a. The mountain to which Haggai referred was not the Judean mountain range, but the Lebanon, and this command to get the timber concerned the first group of returned exiles. This explanation, though ingenious, is without a solid basis in the text. The Lebanon is nowhere referred to simply as "the mountain."

In the time of Solomon "all Israel" were forced to hew stone and to carry loads (1 K. 5:13-18). The Lord's command through Haggai was also indicative, but suggested voluntary service.

The consequence and relevance of the rebuilding of the temple is spelled out: *Then I will again take pleasure in it and will reveal my glory.* This is the significant perspective on the function and purpose of the temple. It concerns God's pleasure and honor.

The Hebrew word *rāṣâ* has a wide range of meaning and is rendered by various English words: pleasure, favor, acceptance, delight, love, devotion. It is used as a synonym of a number of Hebrew words, such as *ḥāpēṣ,* "delight" (Ps. 51:18 [Eng. 16]); *nāḇaṭ,* "to look at," or in a cultic context "to accept graciously" (cf. Amos 5:22); *nāśā' pānîm,* "to accept one" (lit. "to lift up his face," Mal. 1:8); *ḥeseḏ,* "lovingkindness"; *ḥānan,* "to be gracious to someone"; *rāḥam,* "to have compassion on"; *y^ešû'â,* "salvation" (Ps. 149:4); *'āhēḇ,* "love" (Prov. 3:12); etc. It is also used as an antonym to remembering iniquity and punishing sins (Jer. 14:10; Hos. 8:13), to consuming by the sword, by famine, and by pestilence (Jer. 14:12), and to rejection (Ps. 77:8 [Eng. 7]).

67. In Ezek. 6:1–14 the prophecy against the "mountains of Israel" is in reality directed against the territory of Israel. Cf. also Ezek. 19:9; 20:40; 33:28; etc.

In addition to its various meanings it is especially a cultic term.[68] The word is used when a priest declares a sacrifice to be acceptable to God, a sacrifice with which God is pleased. Even when the objects of God's pleasure are people and not sacrifices, they mostly concern people who are bringing their offerings to the Lord. In Deut. 33:11 Moses beseeches the Lord to be pleased with the work of Levi's (or the priesthood's) hands, presupposing their sacrificial ministry. According to Hos. 8:13 the Lord will not be pleased with Ephraim, although they offered sacrifices to the Lord. In Ezek. 20:40 the Lord promised to accept Israel, requiring of them their offerings. In Mal. 1:8 God's pleasure (actually displeasure) concerns priests and people because of their offerings.

In this semantic scope of reference the rebuilt temple will achieve the status of an acceptable offering in which the Lord again will take pleasure, with all the overtones of his covenantal love *(ḥeseḏ),* mercy *(ḥānan),* and compassion *(rāḥam).*

The Lord will take pleasure *in it* (Heb. *bô*), that is, not so much in the process of the rebuilding of the temple but in the finished product.

reveal my glory. The Hebrew verb *'ekkāḇd(ā)* is a Niphal, which may have a passive or reflexive meaning.[69] Many scholars prefer the passive sense: The Lord will be honored by the rebuilding of the temple (so André, Budde, Halevy, Gelin, et al.) The TEV renders: "and will be worshiped as I should be." Koole may be right that the passive meaning suggests a mere repetition of the injunction of v. 8a: the people must rebuild the temple and in that way honor the Lord, rather than promulgating their own interests. But God has already promised his pleasure when they have completed the temple. Accordingly, some scholars add a subjective element to the passive

68. Beuken, op. cit., p. 185n.3, emphasizes the technical cultic meaning of the word in this context. Cf. also G. von Rad, *Old Testament Theology,* tr. D. M. G. Stalker (New York: Harper & Row, 1962), I:261–62; Beuken, op. cit., p. 187. The specific religious or cultic meaning of *rāṣâ* is also found in texts like Amos 5:22: "Even though you bring me burnt offerings . . . I will not *accept [rāṣâ]* them"; Mic. 6:7: "will the Lord *be pleased* with thousands of rams . . . ?"; Ps. 51:18 (Eng. 16): "you do not *delight [ḥāpēṣ]* in sacrifice . . . you do not *take pleasure [rāṣâ]* in burnt offerings"; etc.

69. Text-critically we have either a *ketib* or a *qere* possibility: according to the text as it was written *(ketib),* the verb is an imperfect indicative: "and I will honor myself," or "and I will be honored," but according to the way it should be read *(qere),* it is a cohortative: "that I may honor myself," or "that I may be honored." Rudolph maintains that the meaning of the cohortative resembles that of the imperfect. A third alternative is that the original had a paragogic *-āh,* which was dropped by the Jews, because this *-āh* represented the fifth one, and according to them five things were missed in the second temple: the ark, the holy fire, the shekinah, the spirit of prophecy, and the urim and thummim (cf. Von Orelli).

sense: the Lord will consider himself honored when they have rebuilt the temple (so Hitzig, Mitchell, Elliger, et al.). But even then the honoring of the Lord will be an afterthought. In the words "I will take pleasure in it," "I will look on it with favor" (JPSV), we have the active deed of God's acceptance and the declaration of his pleasure concerning the temple and the people who build it. The same active sense is implied in the next statement: God will reveal his glory (so Koole, et al.).

In a number of texts God's honor or glory is manifested in his judgments (cf. Isa. 40:66; Exod. 14:4, 17-18; Lev. 10:3; Ezek. 28:22; 39:13). In Haggai the Lord's *kāḇôḏ* is not his destructive presence, but rather his presence with all his covenant love and compassion. See the commentary on Mal. 1:6 for a discussion of the semantic range of *kāḇôḏ,* "honor," "glory."[70]

God's promise that he will take pleasure in the rebuilt temple and will grant them the honor of his salutary presence is emphasized by the concluding *says the Lord.* Koole rightly stresses the significance of this formula in the context of the people's apathy and despondency.

9–11 The structural analysis of these verses is as follows.

Verse 9a is an extended parallel of v. 6, continuing the picture of the people's malaise. Verse 9b-e draws the conclusion and provides the reason for the adverse circumstances of the people. The reason for these conditions was already implied in vv. 2 and 4, but here it is explicitly stated. As such it has a revelatory character. The point of view of the temple desolation is emphasized, while the people busied themselves with their own homes. Verse 9d and e constitutes a chiasm and is an antithetic parallelism:

My house which *['ᵃšer hû']* remains a ruin
while you are running each for his own house.

The "excited style," because of the infinitive absolute in v. 6, is continued in v. 9a. In v. 9 we have an accumulation of o-sounds.

Verses 10 and 11 are again an extended parallel to vv. 6 and 9a. Verses 10 and 11 comprise the relationship between a general (v. 10) and specific (v. 11) statement, while the elements of v. 11 reflect a shifting from the general to the particular application of God's judgment. In v. 10 we have a chiastic construction:

Have withheld . . . the heavens
the earth . . . has withheld.

In v. 11 the use of the Hebrew word *ḥōreḇ,* "drought," has an implied inference to the *ḥārēḇ,* "ruin," of the temple.

70. See also W. Zimmerli, *Ezekiel,* Hermeneia, tr. R. E. Clements (Philadelphia: Fortress, 1979), 1:53–54.

It must be conceded that vv. 9-11 are, substantially and linguistically, a continuation of vv. 5 and 6. The fact remains, however, that the present arrangement of the Hebrew text is supported by all the ancient versions, including the fragments from Murabba'at, and that the order of the verses can be explained in an apprehensible manner. There is no need to question their context or authenticity.[71]

It is important to note that vv. 9-11 are not a mere repetition of vv. 5 and 6, but are an extended parallel, with their own perspectives and emphases. The new element in v. 9, for instance, is the explicit reference to the act of God, which is then fully explained in vv. 10 and 11. We may agree with Koole's observation concerning the relationship between vv. 5-6, 7-8, and 9-11. In vv. 5-6 the contemporaneous economic plight of the people is described; in vv. 7-8 the promise of a restored situation is implied, when the people would obey the command to rebuild the temple, and in vv. 9-11 it is explicitly stated that the people's present-day circumstances were due to their negligence concerning the rebuilding of the temple.

9 *You have been expecting much.* For the use of an infinitive absolute in a hurried or otherwise excited style, cf. v. 6.[72] The expression *pānâ 'el-harbēh,* "turn yourselves to much," is a parallel to *zᵉraʿtem harbēh,* "you have sowed much," of v. 6, but with a difference in meaning. The Hebrew verb *pānâ,* "turn toward a direction," with the preposition *'el,* means "look for," "expect." The implication is "with eagerness," "with expectation." They have already sown abundantly (v. 6), and it seems that the grown grain is in accordance with their expectations. They have turned with eagerness to the fields, which superficially had the promise of an abundant harvest.

but look, it turned out to be little. The superficial evaluation of the crops was not borne out by what they in fact yielded. The harvest itself turned out to be little. In Hebrew the expression is unusual: *wᵉhinnēh limʿaṭ,* "and look! it amounts to *[lᵉ]* little." So also the Vulgate: *et ecce, factum est minus.* The LXX, Syriac (Pesh.), and Targum, however, seem to have read *wᵉhāyâ,* "and it was," instead of *wᵉhinnēh,* "and look." Many scholars propose to alter the text accordingly (cf. Chary, G. A. Smith, et al.). But we agree with other scholars that the present expression itself makes good sense, and that there is no need to alter the text. In Jer. 8:15 (cf. 14:19) we have an analogous expression: "we hoped . . . for a time of healing, but

71. Beuken, op. cit., pp. 200–202, considers vv. 10 and 11 a retrospection on the announcement of judgment, with v. 11 an additional note on the intervention of God. This and similar views on the secondary nature of these verses do not allow for the structural and substantial context esp. of vv. 9–11.

72. See also GKC, § 113z, aa; Brockelmann, *Syntax,* § 46b.

there was *[wehinnēh]* only terror" (lit. "and look! terror"). The only problem in our text is the added preposition *le*, which, however, may be regarded as an emphatic *lamed.*[73] An emphasis is being placed upon the disappointment of the people: "they have turned themselves with expectation to reap an abundant harvest, and look, it amounted to just a little."

The main reason for the people's disillusionment is explained in the following statement: *And when you brought it [i.e., the harvest] home, I blew on it!* There are two problems in connection with this statement. The first concerns the chronological order of the events, and the second the purport of the Hebrew verb *nāpaḥ* in this context. The obvious sequence of the events according to the text is that the harvest was first brought home, and after it was stored up the Lord came and blew on it. The harvest itself then was relatively abundant, but afterward something happened to reduce its value and bulk. On this basis, some solutions to the problem were ventured. Jerome's explanation is that the *exsufflavi* caused the grain to lose its nutritional value. According to Cyrillus the portion of the harvest allotted to the farmers was reduced to a minimum, apparently because they were obliged to borrow grain for food, and now they had to return that portion with accumulative interest. Others interpreted the disappointment with the harvest in terms of the damage done to the supplies, either because some of it was stolen or because it was eaten away by vermin.[74] These and similar explanations are indeed feasible. The harvest itself was brought in, but it was of no avail to the farmers and to all who had relied upon it for sustenance.

The problem of what has happened to the harvest is, however, closely linked with the meaning of the Hebrew verb *nāpaḥ*. Its general meaning is "to blow," and with the preposition *be*, "to blow on" something. In Ezek. 22:21 the Lord "blew on" Israel with his fiery wrath. The blowing here has the sense of fanning up a fire in order to melt the dross away from the silver. In Ezek. 37:9 the Spirit breathes into those who were slain, so that they may live. In this text the blowing has a figurative meaning. The same applies to Hag. 1:9. The Lord will blow on the (supplies of the) harvest.

The explanations offered are varied. According to Wellhausen and others the blowing here is a form of magic, with reference to Job 4:9: "By the breath *[nišmat]* of God they are destroyed, and by the blast *[rûaḥ]* of his anger they are consumed." Although *nāpaḥ* is not used, the idea is the same. The supplies will dwindle away in a mysterious manner. It is, however,

73. Cf. F. Nötscher, *VT* 3 (1953) 380; Beuken, op. cit., p. 185; Steck, op. cit., p. 369n.42. According to Rudolph, p. 29, this assumption is unnecessary.

74. See Rashi; G. Dalman, *Arbeit und Sitte in Palästina* (repr. Hildesheim: Olms, 1964), III:206.

unthinkable that Haggai would have resorted to magic in describing what God will do to the people's harvest.

Another explanation of the whole phrase is that of F. Peter. According to him "what you brought home" really means "what you have offered at the temple," with reference to Mal. 1:13, where *hēḇē'*, "to bring," has the meaning of "bringing to sacrifice." In addition, the word *habbāyiṯ,* "the house," is used occasionally to denote the temple. Although the temple was not fully built, enough of it was left to regard it as a temple. When God "blows" on the sacrifices, he detests them, he disregards them. This is what the people have done to the altar, according to Mal. 1:13: they sniffed at it, they had contempt for it.

This explanation was already known to and rejected by Jerome. The *habbāyiṯ* of v. 9 could not have been the temple, because at that time it still was a ruin. The rest of Peter's assumption is contrary to the context, both of v. 6 and of vv. 10-11. The point of reference in all the statements in these verses is the distinction between an expected abundance and an experienced insufficiency. The idea of offering is foreign to the immediate context.[75]

The solution of the problem must be looked for in vv. 10-11. The Lord had called for a drought, and this was the reason why the crops failed. Koole correctly tries to relate God's "blast" on the people's harvest with his calling forth of a "drought." Because the "breath" *(rûaḥ)* of the Lord blows on them, the grass withers and the flowers fall (Isa. 40:7); "scarcely are they planted, scarcely sown, scarcely has their stem taken root in the earth, when he blows upon them, and they wither" (Isa. 40:24). The parallel between Hag. 1:9 and the texts from Isa. 40 is strengthened because the verbs are also synonymous. The only difference is that the withering of the grass, flowers, and wheat is easily explained, but the drought or dry wind (Isa. 40:24) could not have had the same effect on the supplies of grain in the storage rooms!

Koole's ultimate solution is that the perfect *nāp̱aḥtî* in v. 9 must be understood as a pluperfect, chronologically preceding the first verb: "I have already blown on that which you have brought home" (cf. Exod. 10:13). What they have brought home is not only quantitatively insufficient because of God's blowing by means of the drought, but also qualitively inferior. Like chaff before the wind, the net result of their labors dwindled away. This was not the consequence of any kind of magic or fate, but of a deliberate act of God. He did it. It was an aspect of his judgment, the enforcement of his covenantal sanction.

75. Beuken, op. cit., pp. 187–88; Koole, p. 41; and Rudolph, pp. 29–30, rightly reject the identification of *habbayiṯ* here with the temple (contra F. Peter, "Haggai 1:9," *TZ* 2 [1951] 150–51; Deden; Ackroyd, *Exile,* p. 158; and Steck, op. cit., p. 370n.46).

In terms of a question-answer schema, the Lord poses the question: *why* (Heb. *yaʿan meh*)?[76] and answers: *because* (Heb. *yaʿan*). The obvious reason for the people's plight must not be misunderstood. It is "because of." The nominal construction expresses a condition and emphasizes the subject: *because of my house, it* [Heb. *hûʾ*] *being a ruin, while you are running each for, on behalf of, his own house.*[77] The antithetic parallelisms are obvious: "my house" over against "their houses," the ruin of the temple contrary to their fervor on behalf of their own houses. They literally *ran* in their eagerness to be busy with their own dwellings.

An interesting problem concerns the identity of the people who are busy working on their own houses. They obviously could not have been the people who returned shortly after the end of the Exile (ca. 539/38 B.C.; cf. Ezra 3), because it may be taken for granted that they would have finished their own building projects by 520 B.C., the time of Haggai. But then what does this expression "to run each on behalf of his own house" really mean?

It is possible that the addressees could have included exiles who had returned at the very beginning. The text does not distinguish between the different groups of returned exiles (contra Mitchell, et al.). But then the people's endeavors with regard to their houses must be explained accordingly. The people who had returned earlier during the reign of Cyrus have obviously already built their houses, but they were ever since busying themselves with the decoration and expansion of their homes. The essence of the argument is that they, whoever they might have been, continually (participle) busied themselves with their own dwellings, while they disgracefully neglected the house of the Lord. Their priorities were precisely the opposite to the "law" of God's kingdom, as expressed in Matt. 6:33.

10, 11 God's judgment is explained negatively in v. 10 and positively in v. 11. Because the people have lost sight of their priorities and obligations, *That is why the skies because of you have withheld their moisture and the earth has withheld its yield.* The Hebrew text, supported by the Targum and the fragments from Murabbaʿat, has *ʿal-kēn ʿalêḵem,* "therefore, because of you." The general consensus of scholarly opinion is to delete *ʿalêḵem,* because it is "unparsable, not found in the LXX and probably a clerical error by dittography from the preceding *ʿal-kēn.*"[78]

Scholars who have maintained the Hebrew text interpret the preposition *ʿal* to mean either *above you* (Vulg., André, Budde, Sellin, Van Hoon-

76. Cf. LXX *diá toúto táde,* deleting the interrogative clause.

77. For this construction see Gemser, § 280; Joüon, *Grammaire,* § 158a; Brockelmann, *Syntax,* § 152a.

78. So G. A. Smith; cf. *BHS,* Chary, et al.

acker, Nötscher, Horst), *against you* (Hitzig), or *on account of you* (Targ., Dhorme, Rudolph, NIV). The second alternative, "against you," suggests a verb of movement and is therefore unlikely. It is even impossible if the *ʿalêḵem* is applied to vv. 10b and 11 (so Rudolph). Against the first alternative, "above you," it is argued that it presupposes *taḥtêḵem,* "under you" (cf. Ibn Ezra and Kimchi who stress the meaning of the suffix in this context: above *your* country). The argument against the third alternative, "on account of you," viz., that *ʿalêḵem* would then be a mere repetition of *ʿal-kēn,* seems unconvincing (contra Koole). The emphasis is on the suffix: therefore, because of *you.* This is a very important element of the argument. God's action concerns what the people have done. His judgment is because of their sins (cf. Rudolph). The same meaning of *ʿal* is found in Jer. 1:16: "I will pronounce my judgments on my people *because of* [Heb. *ʿal*] their wickedness" (NIV).

the skies have withheld their moisture. A syntactical and textual problem concerns the Hebrew phrase *kāleʾû šāmayim miṭṭāl.* The verb *kālāʾ* is generally used transitively (with *min,* "from") in the sense of "withholding something from someone" (cf. Gen. 23:6). In the Hebrew text the meaning would literally be that the heavens are withholding something/somebody from the dew, which does not make sense. Thus two alterations to the text have been suggested: either to delete the preposition *min* as a probable dittography (André, Wellhausen, Driver, G. A. Smith, et al.), or to transpose the *m* and to read *ṭallām,* "their dew" (*BHK, BHS,* Marti, Budde, Sellin, Elliger, et al.). Another likely proposal is to emend the text in accordance with the Targum, and to read *māṭār,* "rain" (cf. Deden, Gelin, Horst, Chary, *BHS,* etc.).

We agree with Van Hoonacker, Koole, et al., however, in maintaining the Hebrew text. In accordance with Gen. 8:2 and Ezek. 31:15 we may assume an implicit object to the verb *kālāʾ*, viz., *gešem,* "rain," and explain the preposition *min* in a privative sense, "to be without dew" (cf. Von Orelli). Or else we may use the preposition *min* in the sense of the Arabic *mîn ʾel-beyān,* or as an explicative *min,* simply translated by *namely:* "The heavens have withheld, namely, dew" (cf. Gen. 7:22).[79]

In this case there is also no need to exchange "moisture" (lit. "dew") with "rain" (contra Targ.). The idea that dew, indispensable for a country like Palestine, was given by the heavens (Zech. 8:12) reflects the language of observation and daily experience, and is supported by the Ugaritic expression *ṭl šmm,* "the dew of the heavens."[80] Isaac's blessing of his son Jacob

79. See GKC, § 119wn.2.

80. Rudolph rejects the idea of an analogy with Ugaritic (against M. Dahood, *Bib* 45 [1964] 412). Beuken, on the other hand, endorses Dahood's suggestion

concerns "the dew of heaven" (Gen. 27:28), and the same blessing is echoed in Deut. 33:28: "So Israel will live in safety alone; Jacob's spring is secure in a land of grain and new wine, where the heavens drop dew" (NIV). Instead of this blessing, the postexilic community experienced just the opposite: "the heavens withheld their dew," their indispensable moisture, according to the Lord's pronounced judgment in Lev. 26:19; Deut. 28:23; and 1 K. 17:1. In maintaining the word *ṭāl* in this context, we agree with the Notes on the TEV that in much of the world dew has little importance for agriculture, and that it is advisable for modern translators to render the word *ṭāl* with "moisture."

and the earth has withheld its yield. When the heavens or skies (JPSV) withheld their moisture (dew), the earth or land inevitably withheld its produce. The Hebrew word *yᵉḇûl,* "produce," "yield," is derived from the root *yāḇal,* "to bring," and is used to indicate that which the land or soil yields, namely, its produce or crops. The full expression is an aspect of the promised blessing. In Lev. 26:4 the Lord promised his obedient people (cf. v. 3): "I will send you rain in its season, and the ground will yield its crops." This is echoed by the psalmists in Ps. 67:7 (Eng. 6) and 85:13 (Eng. 12) (cf. also Ezek. 34:27; Zech. 8:12). The direct opposite to this formula of blessing is the pronouncement of judgment as a punishment for disobedience: "your strength shall be spent in vain, for your land shall not yield its increase" (Lev. 26:20; cf. also Deut. 11:17).

In Haggai's time the people's experience was related to God's word, and they had occasion to distinguish the aspect of judgment. If only they had given careful thought to their ways (vv. 5, 7), they would have been able to detect the relationship between the crop failure and God's judgment. They could not have pled ignorance for failing to recognize God's hand in their agricultural and economic malaise (cf. Baldwin). They were expected to know and consider the "Law" (Lev. 26:20; cf. v. 4) and the "Prophets" (Amos 4:6-10; Hos. 4:10; Mic. 6:15) in such experiences.[81]

11 *I have summoned a drought.* The lack of moisture and the failure of crops (v. 10) were due to the fact that God had called for a drought. This is

---

to read *miṭṭôl,* the Qal infinitive of the *denominative ṭll* (cf. 1 Aqht 41), which is also implied in Deut. 33:13 (cf. M. Dahood, *Ugaritic Lexicography* [Vatican City: Biblioteca Apostolica Vaticana, 1964], p. 90).

81. G. A. Smith's observation is interesting but unacceptable: "For ourselves Haggai's appeal to the barren seasons and poverty of the people as proof of God's anger with their selfishness must raise questions" (pp. 239–40). This interpretation ignores the character and significance of God's covenantal relationship with his people, with its sanctions and blessings.

the positive aspect in the prophet's explanation for the people's adverse circumstances. The central point of reference in this pronouncement is *God.* He commanded the heavens to withdraw their moisture, and that happened because he called for a drought. There is no need to emend the Hebrew verb to read "I covered" (*wa'ekrām;* cf. North), because the idea that God has called (Heb. *qārā'*) a specific form of judgment, such as famine or something else on the land (cf. 2 K. 8:1; Ps. 105:16), is well attested in the OT.[82] The same applies to the proposals to read either *ḥērem,* "ban," "what is banned" (so Halevy, with reference to Mal. 3:24 [Eng. 4:6]) or *ḥereḇ,* "sword" (so LXX, Pesh.; cf. Jer. 25:29), instead of *ḥōreḇ,* "drought" (cf. one Targ. ms. which reads *yuḇûšâ,* "dryness," "drought," and Rudolph). Koole rightly pointed out that these alterations would be in contradiction to the context of v. 10, but also would miss the point in this oracle of judgment, namely, the play on words between the *ruin* (*ḥārēḇ,* vv. 4, 9) of the temple and the *drought (ḥōreḇ)* that God has called forth. When the people are giving careful thought to what happened to them, they must consider this relationship between "ruin" and "drought." The one is the cause and explanation of the other.[83]

The effect of the drought is felt *upon the fields and upon the mountains* and on the main agricultural products: *grain, new wine, and oil,* being (including) *all that the ground produces.* In this description the areas affected by the drought move from the general to the specific. First, the extent of the drought is described. It is called on the *fields* and on the *mountains.* The Hebrew word *'ereṣ* means "ground" (Gen. 18:2; 38:9; etc.), "piece of land" (Gen. 23:15), "territory" (Gen. 47:13; plur. Isa. 37:18), and "totality of land," "earth." The semantics of this word are here defined by the situation and context. It concerns the experiences of the postexilic community in the minor province of Jerusalem-Judah. The extent of the *'ereṣ* therefore is effectively confined to their territory. It could either refer to the territory as a whole, with the mountains as a part of it (NEB, JPSV), or to a separate portion of the land, that which is being cultivated, the fields (NIV), distinguishing it from the mountains. We prefer the second alternative. The distinction between the "fields" and the "mountains" is to emphasize two

82. The objects of God's calling forth in the prophetic literature are mainly the enemies, the sword, or fire (Isa. 13:2; Jer. 1:15; 25:29; 34:17; Ezek. 38:21; Amos 7:4). When drought is the object, it mainly concerns Babylon or Egypt (Isa. 19:6; 37:25; Jer. 50:38; 51:36; Ezek. 30:12). In Deut. 28:22 and Hos. 13:15, however, the judgment concerns Israel. Cf. Beuken, op. cit., p. 201.

83. Chary also stresses the double antithesis: "*ma* Maison est en ruine *tous* s'affairent à *leur* maison (v. 10); ma Maison est une ruine *ḥārēḇ,* voilà, pourquoi vous accable la sècheresse *ḥōreḇ.*"

areas which were seriously affected by the drought: the cultivated area, corresponding with *hā'ᵃḏāmâ* in the following phrase and "the fruits of labor," and the noncultivated area, the *mountains,* which usually get the most rain.[84] In this way both the seriousness and the severity of the drought are stressed.

The effect of the drought is specified with reference to the three most important agricultural products of Palestine: *grain, new wine, and oil.* The idea of course is that the drought will affect the "grainfields, vineyards, and olive orchards" (so TEV), with the result that they would not yield the crops that are derived from them. These three products are mentioned together in a great number of texts.[85] When Israel faithfully obeys God's commands, he will send "rain for your land . . . that you may gather in your grain and your wine and your oil" (Deut. 11:14). The shares due to the priests were the firstfruits of their grain, new wine, and oil (Deut. 18:4). In Hosea's time Israel had acknowledged that God was the One who gave them the grain, the new wine, and the oil (2:24 [Eng. 22]).

The Hebrew word *dāḡān* is used to indicate "corn" or "grain," and is regarded an archaic term for *leḥem,* "bread," "food." *Tîrôš* is also regarded an archaic word for wine in ritual and poetic texts. It is derived from the root *yāraš* II, "to tread," "to press (grapes)" (cf. Mic. 6:15), and is translated "new wine," the juice of newly pressed grapes.

The third product is *yiṣhār,* from the root *ṣāhar,* "to press out oil." The first meaning of *yiṣhār* is "to glare," and then "oil," "the juice of olives." According to L. Koehler this word is archaic for the general term *šemen,* "(olive) oil."[86] The contention is that these words lost their specific meaning and eventually became a general indication for food, wine, and oil. The fact remains, however, that this trilogy is referred to in the following books of the OT: Numbers (18:12, in an inverted order), Deuteronomy (7:13; 11:14; 12:17; 14:23; 18:4; 28:51), Jeremiah (31:12), Hosea (2:10, 24 [Eng. 8, 22]), Joel (1:10; 2:19), Haggai (1:11), Nehemiah (5:11; 10:40; 13:5, 12), and 2 Chronicles (31:5; 32:28). The meaning of newly pressed grape juice and olive juice is reflected in Joel 2:24: "The threshing floors will be filled with grain; the vats will overflow with new wine and oil" (cf. also Mic. 6:15).

By way of summary it is said that the drought will be called on *all that the ground produces.* This translation assumes the insertion of *kol,* "everything," with a number of Hebrew manuscripts and some ancient

84. Cf. Dalman, *Arbeit und Sitte in Palästina,* I:309ff.
85. Beuken, op. cit., p. 202, considers this index a cliche.
86. L. Koehler, *JSS* 1 (1956) 9–10.

versions (cf. *BHS*). Nothing will be excluded from this severe drought. Everything that grows, and especially everything that yields food for man and beast, will be affected by it. This of course will have a devastating effect on man and animals alike, and on the achievements of their toil.

The effect of the drought on *man and beast* is that they would be without food and water: they would suffer famine *(rāʿāḇ),* a typical aspect of God's pronounced judgment on a disobedient people (2 K. 8:1; Ps. 105:16). The use of the article in both (singular!) words is to determine the class, as it was universally known. The employment of the names as collectives, to denote the sum total of individuals belonging to the specific class (thus *hā'āḏām,* "the man," and *habbᵉhēmâ,* "the beast") includes everyone belonging to the well-defined class.[87] The drought, therefore, will affect all people and every animal in the territory. The Hebrew word *bᵉhēmâ,* commonly used as a collective, means animals in general, as opposed not only to human beings (Exod. 9:9) but also to birds, fish, and reptiles (1 K. 5:13 [Eng. 4:33]); it can also refer to wild animals, and more often domestic animals, cattle, including sheep. We prefer the translation *beast* (JPSV) or *animals* (NEB) to *cattle* (RSV, NIV), because the drought would be felt by animals in general. The idea of totality is adequately expressed by the juxtaposition of the opposites *man and beast.*[88]

The inclusion of animals in such contexts along with human beings is characteristic of the OT. The love and righteousness of the Lord are manifested in the preservation of both "man *['āḏām]* and beast *[bᵉhēmâ]*" (Ps. 36:7 [Eng. 6]). The anger and wrath of the Lord will be poured out on "man and beast" (Jer. 7:20), and he will strike down those who live in this city— "both man and beast" (Jer. 21:6). In Joel 1:18 the animals are included in the general lamentation because of the locusts and drought.

In the OT animals and human beings are related; the animals are part of mankind's environment and the objects of human responsibility.[89] Thus when the people of God consider their ways (vv. 5, 7), they will have to give careful thought to the extent and seriousness of their guilt, which caused the suffering not only of themselves, but also of nature as such, with the deliberate inclusion of the animals.

Ultimately the drought will affect *all the fruits of labor.* The words

87. See GKC, § 126l-n.

88. Cf. also Gen. 6:7; Exod. 9:25; Lev. 27:28; Num. 3:13; Jer. 31:27; 36:29; Ezek. 14:13; Jon. 4:11; Zeph. 1:3; Zech. 2:8 (Eng. 4); Ps. 135:8; etc.

89. Cf. Marie L. Henry, *Das Tier im religiösen Bewusstsein des alttestamentlichen Menschen* (Tübingen: Mohr, 1958).

y^e^gîa^c^ kappayim (lit. "toil of the hands") are usually connected with a suffix (cf. Gen. 31:42; Ps. 128:2; Job 10:3). The LXX and Peshitta read "their hands," but the context (v. 10) rather favors a suffix of the second person plural: "your hands." There is, however, no need to alter the text, because the suffix may be implied in the translation. The Hebrew word *y^e^gîa^c^* means "labor," "work," or the product of labor, "gain." It is derived from a root meaning "to grow tired," "to weary," "to exert oneself," "to take pains for." The element of tiresomeness is included in the meaning of the word. *Y^e^gîa^c^* is *labor fatigans* (Zorell), "toil" (cf. Isa. 49:4; Mal. 1:13).

Even the people's most strenuous efforts to obtain food will be of no avail. Nothing will grow (NEB) on account of the severe drought. Because the Hebrew word *kap* could mean either the "palm" of the hand or the "sole" of the foot, some scholars tend to include the labor of man and beast, with reference to Zech. 8:10: "Before that time there were no wages for man and beast" (NIV). This possibility, however, is excluded by the dual form of the word, which indicates the two hands of a person, not the four feet of an animal.

This then was the divine diagnosis of the people's plight: There was a significant connection between the *ḥārēḇ* and the *ḥōreḇ,* between the temple's "ruin" and the experienced "drought." The people considered the adverse circumstances to be a decisive argument against the rebuilding of the temple. The Lord, however, revealed to them that the drought was his punishment for their lack of spiritual fervor and commitment in rebuilding the temple. The postexilic community's priorities were awry: they had not first sought the kingdom of God; rather, they were busy concerning themselves with their own "kingdoms," their selfish interests and conveniences.

A sermon on this pericope may have as its theme: prophetic light on temple ruin and drought. How are we to evaluate human experiences, the character and plight of our times? We may approach this problem from two different angles: (1) From the point of view of our human considerations, with its obvious conclusion: because of the adverse circumstances, this is an inopportune time to avail ourselves in the service of the kingdom of God. (2) From the point of view of divine revelation and priorities: the drought, or whatever malaise there might be, is God's punishment for our waywardness, apathy, and negligence in committing ourselves to serve the Lord and to promulgate his kingdom. Israel and the Church tended, throughout their history, to depend on the first criterion rather than on the second one. The prophet Haggai reminds us to evaluate our lives and circumstances in the light of the Word of God, and to seek first his kingdom and his righteousness (Matt. 6:33).

B. THE RESPONSE OF LEADERS AND PEOPLE (1:12–15a)

12 *Zerubbabel son of Shealtiel*[1] *and the high priest Joshua son of Jehozadak and the whole remnant of the people then gave heed*[2] *to the command*[3] *of the Lord their God, and to the message of the prophet Haggai, with which the Lord their God had sent him. And the people feared before the Lord.*
13 *Haggai, the Lord's messenger,*[4] *fulfilling the Lord's mission,*[5] *spoke to the people, "I am with you, declares the Lord."*
14 *Then the Lord roused the spirit of Zerubbabel son of Shealtiel, the governor of Judah, and the spirit of the high priest Joshua, son of Jehozadak, and the spirit of the whole remnant of the people. They came and set to work on the house of the Lord Almighty, their God.*
15 *(This was) on the twenty-fourth day of the sixth month in the second year of King Darius.*

God's word did not return to him empty (Isa. 55:11). The leaders and people responded favorably to the prophet's exhortation (1:1–11) to rebuild the temple.

According to our structural analysis vv. 12-15 constitute a structural unit in conjunction with the preceding section.[6] It describes in a rhythmic prose style[7] the positive response of the community to the word of the Lord as it was conveyed to them by Haggai. Leaders and people reacted according to the two primary biblical responses to the self-disclosure of God, viz., to *hear* and to *fear* (D. R. Jones). These responses, significant as they were, may, however, entail negative attitudes. Therefore, it was of the utmost importance that the Lord himself should encourage the people with the promise that he would be with them (v. 13), and to activate them in rebuilding the house of the Lord (v. 14). Structurally, therefore, v. 12 constitutes

1. Lit. "Shaltiel." The shortened form also occurs in 1:14; 2:2. The form Shealtiel is found in 1:1; 2:23; and five times in Chronicles.

2. Lit. "listened to," "obeyed."

3. Lit. "the voice."

4. Targ. reads "the prophet"; cf. 1:1, 3, 12; 2:1, 10.

5. Lit. "according to the commission of the Lord."

6. Bear makes no break between this and the preceding sections, but there is manuscript authority for beginning a new section here, as Mitchell correctly notes, with reference to Ginsburg.

7. So D. J. Wiseman, contra Elliger, et al. According to Van der Woude the style reveals dependence upon Deuteronomistic idiomatic expressions and diction, although with its own vocabulary. Deuteronomistic expressions are: "to obey the voice of the Lord"; "the Lord, their God"; "the remnant of the people." The author's own: "the messenger of the Lord"; "according to the commission of the Lord."

the conjunction between the word of God in 1:1–11 and his promise in v. 13. Verse 14 may be regarded a connecting link with the contents of ch. 2 (so Koole). The suggestion that this passage was the work of a redactor (so Van der Woude) is in itself hypothetical and irrelevant for its understanding.[8]

12 The impact of Haggai's sermon was such that leaders and people unanimously decided to resume work on the temple. They *gave heed,* that is, obeyed, the word of the Lord conveyed to them by Haggai. In Hebrew the predicate preceding two or more subjects frequently agrees in gender and number with the first and nearest subject.[9] *Šāmaʿ*, "to hear," constructed with *b^eqôl,* "in the voice," has the meaning "to heed a request" (Gen. 30:6), or "to hear" in the sense of "to obey" (Gen. 22:18). The leaders and people therefore listened with attention, interest, and submission (Mitchell); they responded favorably to the prophetic message and acknowledged the validity and purport of it. Koole may have a point in distinguishing between the way leaders and people obeyed the word of God: the leaders responded to the reminder of their responsibility in connection with the temple, and the people acknowledged the validity of the rebuke concerning their wrong priorities. In essence, however, both leaders and people responded to the central theme of Haggai's message as it was expressed in v. 8: "Go up into the hills, get timber, and rebuild the house."

The expression "to hear the voice of the Lord" usually refers to the obedience to the revealed commands and decrees of the Lord.[10] During the

8. According to Van der Woude Haggai could not have been the author, esp. because mention is made of "the remnant of the people" (1:12, 14), while Haggai himself refers to "the people of the land" (2:4) or to "these people" (1:2; 2:14). Doubts, albeit of a different nature, are also expressed by Rudolph and Beuken. According to Rudolph 1:1–15 is addressed to the leaders only, and therefore the words concerning "the remnant of the people" must be deleted. Beuken regards 1:12–14 as a historical notice (op. cit., pp. 31–49, 184–208).

Beuken's theory about the Chronistic milieu of the editor is, according to him, endorsed by the author's focus on the leaders. He refers to Freedman's characterization of the Chronicler: for him "monarchy and prophecy go hand in hand. . . . Throughout the kings are confronted, warned and advised by a line of prophets . . . down to Haggai and Zechariah who filled this role in the time of Zerubbabel" ("The Chronicler's Purpose," *CBQ* 23 [1961] 440). This theory suffers from a semantic overloading, however. The confrontation of leaders by the prophets is not confined to the work of the Chronicler but is part and parcel of the function of a prophet as messenger of the Lord.

9. See GKC, § 146f.

10. Cf. A. K. Fenz, *Auf Jahwes Stimme hören: Ein biblische Begriffsuntersuchung* (Wien: Herder, 1964). This expression occurs 75 in the OT, 71 times in a form similar to that in our text. It belongs to the terminology of the covenant (Fenz,

period prior to the Exile Israel "would not listen and were as stiff-necked as their fathers, who did not trust in the Lord their God" (2 K. 17:14, NIV; cf. vv. 7–23). Now the leaders and people again trusted in the Lord and listened to his word. According to Van der Woude this response is not the same as the renewal of the covenant, but is similar to Jer. 42:21, the acceptance of the prophet's message. In Jer. 42:21 the prophet admonishes the people because they still "have not obeyed the voice of the Lord your God in anything that he sent me to tell you." The same interpretation applies to our text: the people responded to the specific message of the prophet to rebuild the temple (v. 8). This interpretation is correct, but of course it need not exclude the covenantal relationship as the implied background of both the prophet's message and the people's response.[11]

Haggai's summons was obeyed by *Zerubbabel son of Shealtiel and the high priest Joshua son of Jehozadak and the whole remnant of the people*. There is no need to add with the LXX and Vulgate the title "governor of Judah," with reference to 1:1, 14; 2:2, 21. It is also omitted in 2:4, 23. According to Rudolph, 1:1–15 is addressed to the leaders only, and therefore the phrase "and the whole remnant of the people" must be deleted as secondary. This point of view, however, is not supported by any textual evidence and is at variance with the whole context of this pericope.

the whole remnant of the people is a fixed expression in the prophetic literature to denote those who have survived the catastrophe caused by God's judgment. The term does not, of itself, describe either those who returned from exile or those who remained in the land, but all who survived to be the true Israel, the people of God in the restricted area of Jerusalem and Judah (Jones). The TEV renders this phrase "all the people who had returned from the exile." They are referred to as "these people" (1:2), "the people" (1:12, 13), "all the remnant of the people" (1:14; 2:2), "all the people of the land" (2:4). We may assume that the covenantal aspect of the "remnant" theme, which was characteristic of the prophecies of Isaiah, Jeremiah, and Amos, is also implied in Haggai's prophecy. In this connection the listening of the people acquires a deeper meaning: those who obeyed the word of the Lord were the "remnant" as the representatives of God's own people, the people of the covenant.[12]

---

p. 49), and denotes that all the stipulations of the covenant had been met. Cf. Beuken, op. cit., p. 33.

11. This is also endorsed by Beuken, op. cit., p. 33. To listen to the voice of the Lord is a covenant command *(Bundesangebot)*, with reference to Exod. 19:3–8, the *locus princeps* in this connection, and to N. Lohfink, *Scholastik* 36 (1961) 298ff.

12. So Koole; cf. Werner E. Müller (ed. by H. D. Preuss), *Die Vorstellung vom Rest im Alten Testament* (Neukirchen: Neukirchener, 1939, repr. 1973). See also

The command (Heb. *qôl,* lit. "voice") of the Lord is not at variance with *the message* (Heb. *d^e^ḇārîm,* lit. "words") of the prophet. In essence both amount to the same: they both concern the revelation of God's will in connection with the rebuilding of the temple. Calvin's comment is still worthwhile: "the word of God is not distinguished from the words of the prophet, as though the prophet had added anything of his own. Haggai . . . ascribed these words to himself, not that he devised anything himself . . . but that he only distinguished between God . . . and his minister," with reference to Exod. 14:31; Judg. 7:20; and Acts 15:28. Brandenburg also pointedly remarked that the leaders and the people would not have made a distinction between the voice of the Lord and the words of the prophet, in the sense that they would have been inclined to listen to the former and not to the latter. Thus the copula connecting the two phrases must be interpreted in an explanatory sense: "to wit," "namely":[13] "the voice of the Lord, namely, the words of the prophet." The distinction between the prepositions *b^e^,* "in," and *ʿal,* "over," in this context must not be overemphasized. The Hebrew verb *šāmaʿ*, "hear," is usually construed with an accusative, but also with various prepositions, including *b^e^, ʾel, l^e^,* and *ʿal* (cf., e.g., Isa. 42:24; Jer. 35:18; Neh. 9:16). Therefore, there is no need either to delete *ʿal* (Duhm), or to substitute *ʾel* (Wellhausen, et al.), "because *ʿal* would have been a frequent mistake of the copyists in the later books, and one easily made after writing it eight times in verse 11" (Mitchell). The ancient versions differ in rendering the second preposition: the LXX and Vulgate have the same construction as for *b^e^,* and the Peshitta and Targum both have *l^e^*.

The divine character of the prophet's message is also assumed in the following phrase: *kaʾ^a^šer š^e^lāḥô YHWH,* which is usually rendered "because the Lord has sent him." On the basis of some manuscripts of the LXX which read *prós autoús,* the Vulgate's *ad ipsos,* and a manuscript of the Targum that reads *lwthwn,* most scholars add *ʾ^a^lêhem,* "to them," or else substitute "to them" for *ʾ^ĕ^lōhêhem,* "their God." The alternative readings could then be rendered as follows: "because the Lord their God has sent him to them," or "because the Lord has sent him to them."[14] Van der Woude may be correct in rejecting the proposed emendations, because in both cases the assumption is that reference is made to the sending of the prophet instead of his

G. Hasel, *The Remnant: The History and Theology of the Remnant Idea from Genesis to Isaiah,* 2nd ed., Andrews University Monographs 5 (Berrien Springs, Mich.: Andrews University, 1975).

13. See GKC, § 154n.1(b).

14. See M. Bogaert, "Les suffixes verbaux non accusatifs dans le sémitique nord-occidental et particulièrement en hébreu," *Bib* 45 (1964) 220–47.

message. His solution to the problem of *ka'ašer* in this context is that it must be regarded not as a conjunction but as the introductory word of an independent relative clause.[15] The phrase, then, can best be rendered: "according *[kᵉ]* to that which the Lord their God has sent him." According to this explanation the "words of the prophet" were in full agreement with the message which God had given Haggai, and, therefore, with the voice of the Lord itself. A striking parallel is Exod. 4:28: "Then Moses told Aaron everything the Lord had sent him to say" (cf. also Isa. 55:11; 1 K. 20:9; Prov. 26:6).

And the people feared[16] *before the Lord.* This is the second aspect of their response. This "fear" is not a reverential attitude toward the Lord, which manifests itself in obedience to and trust in the God of the covenant (so Mitchell, Sellin, Elliger, Amsler, et al.), but it is an expression of their holy awe, their terror because of the wrath of the Lord (so Keil, Ridderbos, Smit, Koole, Baldwin, Van der Woude, et al.). The expression "to fear before" (Heb. *yārē' mipnê*), in the sense of "awe, terror," is also found in Exod. 9:30: "fear the Lord," Deut. 5:5: "afraid of the fire" (cf. 1 K. 3:28; Jer. 42:11). The word *pānîm,* "face," as part of the prepositional expression "before" *(mipnê),* sometimes means "anger," "wrath" (e.g., Ps. 9:4 [Eng. 3]: "they stumbled and perished before you," i.e., because of your wrath; and in Jer. 4:26: "all its cities were laid in ruins before the Lord, before his fierce anger"). To obey the word of the Lord is to acknowledge one's own sinfulness and condemnation. Leaders and people alike became aware of the fact that the drought was due to God's judgment, because they sinfully withheld the honor that was due to him. Such a sense of guilt can easily manifest itself in a feeling of dread and anguish, because of God's continuous wrath and judgments (so Van der Woude).

13 In the midst of the fear-stricken people, the comforting word was conveyed to them by Haggai, the Lord's messenger, fulfilling the Lord's mission (JPSV): "I am with you."

The genuineness of this verse has been seriously questioned, first by Böhme[17] and subsequently by the majority of scholars. The reasons for the prevailing opinion are: (a) it disturbs, without reinforcing, the narrative, especially between vv. 12 and 14; (b) the terminology used for the prophet

15. See GKC, § 138e, f.

16. Cf. J. Becker, *Gottesfurcht im Alten Testament* (Rome: Pontifical Biblical Institute, 1965), pp. 205ff. He distinguishes between a cultic and an ethical concept of fear. Beuken, op. cit., p. 36, differs from Becker, and rightly emphasizes the covenantal element in this concept.

17. W. Böhme, "Zu Maleachi und Haggai," *ZAW* 7 (1887) 215–16.

and his message is a substantial reiteration of v. 12; (c) Haggai is here called not "the prophet," as in every previous case in which his name has been mentioned (vv. 1, 3, 12), but "the messenger of the Lord." According to Keil the main reason for the interpolation of v. 13 was to emphasize Haggai's position as extraordinary messenger and representative of the Lord, just as the priest is seen in Mal. 2:7 as the permanent messenger of the Lord.

This criticism of the authenticity of v. 13, however, can not be maintained. Verse 13 contains an indispensable element in the response of the leaders and people to the word of the Lord. Trust and consolation must be substituted for their fear before they could be stirred up (v. 14) to begin work on the temple. It is quite natural that the same word of encouragement should be repeated in 2:4, where leaders and people are being admonished to be strong and work. The argument that the terminology used for the prophet and his message coincides with that of v. 12 rests on the assumption that v. 12b refers to the mission of Haggai instead of to his message. The designation of the prophet as "messenger of the Lord" also indicates a prophet in 2 Chr. 36:15, 17 and in Isa. 44:26. It is not a rare title. In fact, it is quite common, especially in the earlier portions of the OT, where it denotes "the messenger of the Lord" as the manifestation of the personal presence of the Lord. Mitchell rightly admits that the "compiler [sic!] of the prophecies of Haggai might, without exciting comment, have called the prophet *the messenger of Yahweh*."[18]

With the same emphasis with which v. 12 has equated the words of the prophet with the message which God has given him, it is declared in v. 13 that the word of encouragement which the prophet addressed to the people is in full agreement with the mission *(b^e^mal'^a^k̲û̲t̲)* of the Lord, which was conveyed to them by "the messenger of the Lord." The expression *b^e^mal'^a^k̲ût̲ YHWH* means "according to the mission of the Lord," rather than "by virtue of the mission of the Lord" (Rudolph). Just as in v. 12 the emphasis is placed on the agreement between the message of the prophet and the "voice," "word," "mission" of the Lord. For the use of the preposition *b^e^* in the sense of "according to," see Gen. 1:27: "God created man according to *[b^e^]* his own image."[19]

The phrase *I am with you* is the customary assurance of God's

18. Cf. A. S. Van der Woude, "De Mal'ak Jahweh: Een Godsbode," *NTT* 18 (1963–64) 1–13. According to Koole, who enumerates three different meanings attached to the expression "messenger of the Lord," the peculiarity is not that Haggai is called a "messenger of the Lord," but that this identification is used rather than the more common designation "the prophet."

19. Cf. W. H. Gispen, *Genesis,* COT (Kampen: Kok, 1974), 1:73, 75; and Exod. 25:40; 30:32; Isa. 10:24, 26; Ezra 10:3.

merciful, guiding presence in a variety of situations: in an oracle of promise (Amos 5:14), in theophanies (Gen. 28:15; Judg. 6:12), in the calling of prophets (Exod. 3:12; Jer. 1:8, 19). This was the experience of persons like Moses (Exod. 3:12; 33:14), Gideon (Judg. 6:16), and Jeremiah (1:8); this was also an aspect of Christ's promise to his disciples (Matt. 28:20). In some contexts the promise of God's support and blessing is joined with the injunction "fear not" (Gen. 26:24; Isa. 41:10; 43:5; Jer. 1:8). Although this reassurance is not added to the promise of the text, we may assume its presence here, with reference to v. 12.

The promise of God's personal presence, support, and blessing is the very foundation of the community's consolation, which will enable them to overcome their anxieties and to start anew the work on the temple. Calvin's remark is most appropriate: "Though then they had all attended to God's command, it was yet necessary that they should be strengthened by a new promise: for men can be encouraged, and their indifference can be corrected by no other means, to such a degree, as when God offers and promises his help." In this sense v. 13 constitutes a connecting link between the people's sense of guilt and fright (v. 12) and their eagerness and dedication (v. 14) to commence the work.

The point of view that the expression "I am with you" originally was connected with the wanderings of nomads, and that the promise really entails God's protective, accompanying, combating, and guiding presence on their way, has a sociological basis which does not comply with the covenantal relationship between God and his people.[20] Van der Woude rightly maintains that our expression is better derived from a cultic (sic!)-prophetic oracle of promise than to assume a priestly (and sociological!) origin.[21]

14 The willingness to dedicate oneself to the service of the Lord is also a gift from the Lord (cf. Phil. 2:13). Leaders and people were stirred up

20. Cf. H. D. Preuss, ". . . ich will mit dir sein!" *ZAW* 80 (1968) 139-73; idem, in *TDOT*, I:449–63; D. Vetter, *THAT*, II:325–28.

21. Cf. W. C. van Unnik, "*Dominus Vobiscum:* The Background of a Liturgical Formula," in *New Testament Essays: Studies in Memory of T. W. Manson*, ed. A. J. B. Higgins (Manchester: University of Manchester Press, 1959), pp. 270–305. He draws attention to the fact that the formula with the second person plural is rare (Hag. 1:13; 2:4; Jer. 42:11; cf. Zech. 8:12); the second person singular, however, with the preposition *min*, occurs many times.

Beuken's conclusion is that Hag. 1:13b belongs to the *Gattung* of the priestly salvation oracle (op. cit., p. 41); it functions within the context of the renewal of the covenant (p. 45). Cf. J. Begrich, "Das priesterliche Heilsorakel," *ZAW* 52 (1934) 81–92 (repr. in *Gesammelte Schriften zum Alten Testament*, Theologische Bücherei 21 [München: Kaiser, 1964], pp. 217–31).

out of their inertia and apathy to the dynamic of a spiritual revival.[22] The secret of this dedication was not so much the indispensable message of the prophet but the Lord himself.

Then the Lord roused the spirit.[23] The spirit *(rûaḥ)* of man is associated with his mind (Ps. 32:21), disposition (1 K. 21:5), temper, and courage (Josh. 2:11). It has a dynamic aspect. It is susceptible to inspiration and can be moved to do something (cf. Gen. 45:27: because Jacob was told about Joseph, his spirit revived *[ḥāyâ]*).[24]

roused. The Hiphil of *yāʿar* means "wake up" (Zech. 4:1), "disturb" (Deut. 32:11), "stir up," "set in motion" (Isa. 41:2). The expression occasionally is used of non-Israelites, for instance, in Jer. 51:1: "I will stir up the spirit of a destroyer"; v. 11: "The Lord has stirred up the spirit of the kings of the Medes"; 1 Chr. 5:26: "So the God of Israel stirred up the spirit of Pul king of Assyria"; 2 Chr. 21:16: "The Lord stirred up against Jehoram the anger of the Philistines"; Ezra 1:1: "The Lord stirred up *[ʿûr]* the spirit *[rûaḥ]* of Cyrus" (cf. also Isa. 41:2; Jer. 50:9). All these instances concerned political heads of state. The same applies to the civil and religious leaders of the postexilic community: *Zerubbabel,* who is here again called *governor* to emphasize the importance to the Jews of having the enthusiastic support of the civil head of the community in their enterprise (Mitchell); for the same reason *Joshua* is given the title *the high priest* in this connection. God's initiative directed itself primarily to those persons whom he had chosen to perform his purposes, who were chiefly responsible for the work at hand. In their leaders the authoritative structure of the people of God was affirmed and honored.

The responsibility also rests on *the whole remnant of the people.* Koole rightly deduced that the community itself was allotted adulthood, with reference to Joel 3:1, 2 (Eng. 2:28, 29). The people were involved in the responsible task of rebuilding the temple and serving the Lord. They could not hide themselves behind the argument that they did not belong to the leader corps, and that they, therefore, were not responsible for rebuilding the

22. Cf. H. Bardtke, "Der Erweckungsgedanke," in *Von Ugarit nach Qumran,* BZAW 77, Fest. O. Eissfeldt, ed. J. Hempel, et al. (Berlin: Töpelmann, 1958), pp. 9–24.

23. According to Beuken, op. cit., p. 31, this is a pure Chronistic expression (cf. 1 Chr. 5:26; 2 Chr. 21:16; 36:22; Ezra 1:1, 5), and belongs to the editorial framework.

24. Cf. J. H. Scheepers, *Die Gees van God en die gees van die mens in die Ou Testament* (Kampen: Kok, 1960), p. 61; D. Lys, *Ruach, le souffle dans l'Ancien Testament* (Paris: Presses Universitaires de France, 1962), pp. 230ff.

temple. Among the surrounding nations this was specifically the liability of the king.

It is worthwhile to note that the stirring up of the spirit of the people to rebuild the temple has had its own history. It already began when the first exiles returned to their country. In Ezra 1:5 it is stated that the community and the religious leaders along with "everyone whose spirit God had stirred *[ʿûr]*," prepared to go up and build the house of the Lord in Jerusalem. It is, therefore, a comforting thought that God's initiative to "move" the hearts and spirits of his people to become active in his service does not vanish or diminish in the course of time. He does not abandon his work!

Calvin finds in this passage support for his doctrine of the human will. God, he says, did not merely confirm a free volition, but produced the willing mind among the people. Baldwin rightly endorses this point of view: "Behind the willing response of both leaders and people was the silent working of the Lord, creating a willing attitude by his Spirit," with reference to Zech. 4:6: "Not by might nor by power, but by my spirit, says the Lord Almighty."

The result of the stirring up of the leaders' and people's spirits was that they began work on the house of the Lord. Literally it reads: "and they came and did the mission/work in/on the house of the Lord." The two Hebrew verbs *bôʾ*, "come," and *ʿāśâ*, "make," may have a separate (so Van der Woude) or a joint meaning (so Marti, Koole, Rudolph) in this context. In both instances the emphasis is placed on the inceptive, denoting the beginning of an action. *They came and began to work* (so NIV; cf. NEB), "they came and set to work" (NAB, JB), "they set to work" (JPSV).

The emphasis is on the people's changed attitude. They were motivated by the Lord to begin work on the temple. The idiom employed, literally "*in* the house of the Lord," does not imply that the temple was already partly built, or even that the foundation had been laid. The preposition *b*ᵉ, "in," can also be translated with "on," for instance, "on Horeb" (1 K. 8:9), "on the seventh day" (Gen. 2:2), and it is frequently used in constructions in which but a part of the object is affected.[25] The idea, expressed in this manner, is that the work in connection with the temple has started, without suggesting that they were actually engaged in the process of rebuilding the temple. Baldwin, therefore, incorrectly implies from the use of the preposition *b*ᵉ that the shell of the building remained. This point of view, already advocated by Jerome, is in direct contradiction to the description of the temple as a ruin (1:4, 9). Zech. 6:15 is a striking parallel to Hag. 1:12–14.

25. BDB, p. 88, s.v. "*b*ᵉ," I.2.b.

"Those who are far away will come and will build *[bānâ]* the temple [lit. *in* the temple] of the Lord." Here the function of the preposition b^e is merely to stress the object, as a substitute for the accusative.[26] It is also not necessary to blame "the redactor" for this "optimistic view" on the reality of the rebuilding of the temple, as is done by Van der Woude. To *begin* a work does not imply that the work already has progressed to a certain stage. This was certainly not the case. According to Haggai himself (2:4) it remained necessary to encourage the people to complete the task.

The term *ʿāśâ m*^{e}*lā'ḵâ,* "do the work," may denote activities of renovation, such as are described in 2 K. 22:5–6: "Have them entrust it to the men appointed to supervise the work *[ʿōśê hamm*^{e}*lā'ḵâ]* on [so ketib] the temple. And have these men pay the workers who repair *(l*^{e}*ʿōśê hamm*^{e}*lā'ḵâ)* the temple of the Lord" (NIV). The word *m*^{e}*lā'ḵâ,* therefore, can refer to various stages of the work, even of the preparatory work, consisting of the removal of debris from the site and acquiring the necessary materials. We may assume, therefore, that the "work" mentioned in our text was also of a preparatory nature.

15 According to this verse the work began *on the twenty-fourth day of the sixth month,* that is, in mid-September 520 B.C. It is important to note that twenty-three days had elapsed since Haggai first addressed leaders and people (1:1, 3). It may be assumed that the leaders and people responded favorably and immediately to the prophet's exhortation when he first addressed them. At that time their spirits were stirred up to rebuild the temple. It is evident, therefore, that the revival mentioned in v. 14 did not occur in a short space of time or on a specific day. A number of reasons have been offered for this lapse of time between the message of the prophet and the actual beginning of work on the temple. The initial revival of the spirits of leaders and people could have resulted in preliminary activities, such as organizing the work force, indulging in consultations, and carefully planning the undertaking. We may allow for quite a period of time for the preparatory work. In addition to this consideration, Baldwin rightly reminded us that the sixth month was a month of harvesting, when urgent tasks in the orchards and fields would have to be completed. Twenty-three days would allow that work to be finished, after which the work at the temple site could begin in earnest.

These and similar circumstances could have caused this lapse of time. When the work officially began, it was necessary to mark it with the mentioning of the specific date. This would also explain the positioning of

26. W. L. Holladay, *A Concise Hebrew and Aramaic Lexicon of the Old Testament* (Grand Rapids: Eerdmans, 1971), p. 32, s.v. "b^e," no. 19.

the date not at the beginning of a statement, as was customary (1:1, 15b–2:1, 10; cf. Zech. 1:1; 7:1), but at the end.

There is, therefore, no need to regard v. 15a as an interpolation, or as originally the introduction to a separate paragraph, of which the end is extinct (Klostermann, Sellin, Rothstein), or which follows in 2:15–19 (*BHS* and a number of scholars). Van der Woude rightly suggests as an additional consideration for the present position of the date that it forms an inclusio with 1:1: between the first (1:1) and twenty-fourth (1:15a) day of the same month something actually happened!

Traditionally v. 15 was regarded as a unit and combined with the following passage to form the first verse of ch. 2 (so in the LXX, Vetus Latina, Vulg., Pesh., and a number of later editions). The consensus of modern opinion, however, is that the double dating suggests a division between v. 15a and 15b–2:1, and that the usual order of year-month-day, when reference is made to the kingship of Darius, endorses this division. An alternative point of view, however, is that the phrase *in the second year of King Darius* (v. 15b) really does double duty: it concerns both dates. These clauses could be rendered as follows: "(It happened) on the twenty-fourth day of the sixth month in the second year of King Darius. (In the second year of King Darius), on the twenty-first day of the seventh month" (cf. Notes to the TEV translation, NIV, Groot NB).

According to many scholars the number of the month ("the sixth") is suspect. The definite article with the preposition *b^e* in *baššiššî* is deemed impossible after *lāḥōḏeš,* "the month." The construction of a number with definite article and the preposition *b^e*, however, is not altogether exceptional. In Ezek. 1:1, for instance, the dating is *bah^{a}miššâ lāḥōḏeš,* "on the fifth of the month." The position of the number with regard to its noun varies considerably,[27] but this does not affect the form in which it is constructed. Furthermore, it makes sense to explain "on the sixth" as being in the absolute state,[28] emphasizing the fact that it really happened in the *sixth* month and not in the "seventh" (2:1), or on the twenty-fourth day of the "ninth" month (2:10). It therefore really need not be deemed a gloss.[29]

The theme of this passage can be defined as the people's favorable

27. See GKC, § 134.

28. See GKC, § 134c.

29. Budde calls the indication of the *sixth* month a "slight" interpretation (*ZAW* 26 [1906] 13). He is followed by Nowack, Mitchell, Horst, et al. Beuken endorses this explanation (op. cit., p. 48). He also agrees with the majority of scholars that v. 15a is secondary. He favors the point of view of Sellin and Rothstein (followed by the majority, e.g., H. W. Wolff, Brandenburg, *BHK*, *BHS*, etc.) that v. 15a is continued in 2:15–19 (op. cit., p. 13nn.2 and 3, and p. 49).

response to God's initiatives. The full emphasis is on God's initiatives. He spoke to the people through his messenger, the prophet Haggai. He promises them his gracious and abiding presence, counteracting their sense of fear and guilt. He activates them to engage themselves to work on his temple, thereby endorsing the word of the apostle: "For it is God who works in you to will and to act according to his good purpose" (Phil. 2:13, NIV). The task that leaders and people are on the point of performing concerns not their interests but the house of the Lord, the seat of his living presence in the midst of his people—in terms of the NT, the Church (cf. 1 Cor. 3:16; 2 Cor. 6:16; Eph. 2:19–22; 1 Pet. 2:5; etc.). The leaders and people reacted according to the typical biblical responses to the self-disclosure of God: they obeyed the word of the Lord, they humbled themselves under the mighty hand of God, and they acted according to his good purpose!

In the NT God's initiative is predominantly revealed in the vicarious work of his Son, our Lord Jesus Christ. "For God so loved the world that he gave his only Son, that whoever believes in him should not perish but have eternal life" (John 3:16). The response required of the NT Church remains the same as that which was evidenced in the book of Haggai.

II. THE PROMISED GLORY OF THE NEW TEMPLE (1:15b–2:9)

1:15b *In the second year of King Darius*
2:1 *on the twenty-first day of the seventh month, the word of the Lord came through*[1] *the prophet Haggai:*
2 *Speak to Zerubbabel son of Shealtiel the governor of Judah, and to the high priest Joshua son of Jehozadak, and to the remnant*[2] *of the people (and ask them):*
3 *Who is there left*[3] *among you who saw this house in its former splendor? How*[4] *does it look to you now? Does it not seem to you like*[5] *nothing?*
4 *But now, be strong, O Zerubbabel, says the Lord, be strong, O high priest Joshua son of Jehozadak, and be strong, all you people of the land, says the Lord, and act!*[6] *For I am with you, says the Lord Almighty,*
5 *according to the promise*[7] *I made with you when you came out of Egypt: my Spirit will always remain among you.*[8] *Do not fear!*[9]
6 *For thus says the Lord Almighty: In just a little while*[10] *longer*[11] *I will shake the heavens and the earth, the sea and the dry land.*

1. Heb. *bᵉyaḏ*. The fragments from Murabba'at have *'el,* which seems to fit the context. See the commentary below. Beuken maintains *bᵉyaḏ,* contra Budde, Mitchell, Sellin, Deden, Deissler, Rudolph, et al. (op. cit., p. 51).

2. LXX, Pesh., and Vetus Latina read "and to *all* the remnant"; cf. 1:14. See the commentary below.

3. Lit. "(is) the one who is left." It is a distributive singular; cf. GKC, §§ 126t, 145l, m; König, *Syntax,* § 300; and Gen. 14:13; Ezek. 24:26, 27; 33:21, 22. The LXX omits, probably due to homoioteleuton.

4. Lit. "According to which."

5. Heb. *kᵉ* can also be used with the thing which is compared, and not only with that with which it is compared; cf. Gen. 44:18b; Judg. 8:18b; Isa. 24:2.

6. For the absolute use of *'āśâ,* cf. Gen. 30:30; Ruth 2:19 (1 Chr. 28:20).

7. These words are omitted by LXX and Pesh.; see the commentary below.

8. Targ. explains: "my prophets teach."

9. LXX renders positively: "have courage."

10. Vulg. *adhuc unum modicum est;* cf. KB, p. 27. LXX and Pesh. render *'aḥaṯ* as an adverb: "once"; cf. Exod. 30:10; Lev. 16:34; 2 K. 6:10.

11. Lit. "a little (time) is it." LXX, Pesh., and Heb. 12:26 omit.

7 *I will shake all the nations. And the precious things*[12] *of all the nations shall come, and I will fill this house with glory, says the Lord Almighty.*
8 *Silver is mine and gold is mine, says the Lord Almighty.*
9 *The glory of this latter house shall be greater than that of the former one, says the Lord Almighty. And in this place I will grant peace,*[13] *says the Lord Almighty.*

It was about seven weeks since Haggai's message to leaders and people to rebuild the temple (1:1–11), and nearly four weeks after work actually began (1:12–15a), that Haggai was given a new word from the Lord in order to encourage them to take heart and resume work. In the meantime something happened to discourage the people and to frustrate their efforts to rebuild the temple. Various reasons have been suggested for the people's discouragement. According to Mitchell (cf. Keil, Van der Woude, etc.) "this prophecy was designed to meet an emergency arising from the despondency that overtook the builders as soon as they realised the magnitude of their task and the slenderness of their resources."

Now that four weeks of work had been done since the rebuilding of the temple actually started (1:15a), people coming up to the Feast of Tabernacles passed unfavorable comments on the project. It would be four years before the restoration was complete, but already they were expressing the view that the new temple could never be the equal of the old (D. R. Jones).

Baldwin rightly suggests two main and additional obstacles to the work. First, the preparatory work took longer than was expected. Much time was consumed in clearing the site of rubble, re-dressing stone that was fit for use, organizing teams of workmen for their particular tasks. Such preparations on a sixty-year-old ruin, without any mechanical aids, would tax the endurance of even the most enthusiastic worker. Second, progress would have been delayed during the seventh month by the major festivals on which no work would be allowed. In addition to sabbath rest days, the first day of the month was the Feast of Trumpets, and the tenth the Day of Atonement (Lev. 23:3–32). Then on the fifteenth day the Feast of Tabernacles began (Lev. 23:33–36, 39–43; Deut. 16:13–15), which lasted for seven days. It would be understandable if the enthusiasm was frustrated by a lack of progress due to the compulsory holidays. Whatever the reasons might have been for the delay, it was again necessary to admonish leaders and people to

12. The plural form of the verb requires a collective meaning of *ḥemdâ*. So rightly LXX *tá eklektá*. Pesh. and Targ. have the singular, but then the causal form of the verb: "they brought the precious things."

13. Pesh. "my salvation."

take heart and resume work on the temple, and to assure them that the Lord himself would provide the required material and adornment.

This section of Haggai's prophecies consists of seven sentences with a number of subclauses (see the Introduction).

The unity of this pericope has unwarrantably been questioned. According to Elliger, Horst, Junker, Deissler, et al., it consists of two independent prophecies, which, however, were delivered on the same day. The main reason for this distinction is the various references to the Lord: as *YHWH* (2:3–5), and as *YHWH ṣ^{e}ḇā’ôṯ* (2:6–9). But both references occur throughout the book in an unorganized manner: *YHWH* with *’āmar* (1:8) and with *n^{e}’um* (1:13; 2:4a, c, 14b, 17c, 23c), and *YHWH ṣ^{e}ḇā’ôṯ* with *’āmar* (1:5a, 7, 9; 2:6, 11) and with *n^{e}’um* (1:9b; 2:4d, 8, 9b, 23a, c). According to the present Hebrew text both names occur in v. 4. The use of the divine name is too casual to provide a sound basis for distinguishing between separate sections of Haggai's prophecy. Moreover, v. 9, with its reference to "this house" and "the former glory," forms an inclusio with v. 3, warranting the structural unity of this section. This unity is endorsed by the fact that vv. 6–9 are structurally connected with the preceding verses by means of the causal conjunction *kî,* "for," "because."[14]

1:15b The date *in the second year of King Darius* need not be deemed "a scribal error" (Mitchell, et al.), but could have served double duty: as a part of the preceding date (in 1:15a), which has the sequence day-month-year (as in 2:10; cf. Num. 1:1; Ezra 6:15; Zech. 1:7), and as a part of the following date, with its sequence year-month-day (as in 1:1 and twenty other instances in the OT).

More significant is the reference to the month and day: *in the seventh (month), on the twenty-first (day) of the month.* The seventh month is Tishri, also called Ethanim (1 K. 8:2), and corresponds with our September-October. The twenty-first day of this month coincides approximately with 17 October.

According to the current calendar this was an important day in the Feast of Tabernacles. This feast began on the fifteenth day of the month and lasted for seven days. The twenty-first day, therefore, was the seventh day of the feast (cf. Lev. 23:33–43; Num. 29:12–39; Deut. 16:13–15; Ezek.

14. So, correctly, Van der Woude. Beuken, op. cit., pp. 52–64, endorses the interdependence of the various elements of this section, but distinguishes a threefold structure:

4–5: the accession to office
6–9a: salvation oracle
9b: the redrafting of the salvation oracle.

45:25). Because no specific reference is made in this passage to this feast, scholars are inclined to consider the feast irrelevant for this prophecy (cf. Keil, et al.). The fact remains, however, that the allusion to "this house" (v. 3; cf. 1:4) suggests Haggai's presence on the temple site, which was the cultic center of the day's festivals. On the Feast of Tabernacles, which was instituted as a "statute for ever throughout your generations" (Lev. 23:41), the whole population moved out of their homes to live in booths, made of "branches of palm trees, and boughs of leafy trees, and willows" (Lev. 23:40), for seven days in happy memory of God's sustenance and protection during the Exodus wanderings. It was also an occasion of rejoicing in the harvest, the warranty of God's faithfulness to his promises (cf. Baldwin). An additional motivation was the remembrance that on the seventh month, so many years ago, Solomon had dedicated the glorious temple with its sacred objects (1 K. 8:2). On no other month, therefore, was the attention of the people more directed to the glory of "the former house," and during no other feast were they reminded more of the future than on this Feast of Tabernacles, heralding as it did the new (civil) year (cf. Van der Woude).

At this occasion, however, the rejoicing was subdued: the crops had failed (1:11), and the present ruin of the temple contrasted sharply with the remembrance of God's merciful support and guidance in the history of his people. At this feast, under these circumstances, the word of the Lord again came to and through Haggai to encourage leaders and people to resume work on the temple.

The question is whether the word of God had come "to" or "through" Haggai.[15] The problem with the prepositional phrase *b^e^yaḏ* (lit. "in the hand of," "through") in this connection is that it is part of a direct speech, followed by *lē'mōr: 'ĕmār-nā'*, "saying: Speak to." The versions testify in favor of *b^e^yaḏ*, "through." The Murabba'at fragments, however, read *'el,* "to." Koole discusses this problem at length and concludes that *b^e^yaḏ* must be rendered in the sense of *'el,* "to." Thus the word of the Lord came to the prophet Haggai in the sense that it reached him. According to Koole the emphasis is therefore on the reception of the revelation rather than on the communication of it.

A close comparison of 2:1, 2 with the analogous 1:1, however, suggests that the solution must be found in another direction. 2:1, 2 are a concise expression of the explicit statement (cf. 1:1) that the word of the Lord came *through (b^e^yaḏ)* the prophet Haggai *to ('el)* Zerubbabel . . . saying *(lē'mōr)*. That word which Haggai was called upon to communicate now consists in the following: "Speak to leaders and people and ask them." The people

15. Cf. n.1 above.

addressed by the word of God through Haggai are implied in 2:1, because they are explicitly mentioned in 2:2 (cf. also Van der Woude). Thus the general meaning of *bᵉyaḏ*, "through," can be maintained, but the idea of receiving the message must also be assumed (cf. Isa. 20:2).[16] This is fully in accordance with the very nature of prophecy and the function of a prophet: to *communicate* the revealed word of God, which he has *received*. These two elements of a prophet's function cannot be divorced from one another.

In his commission Haggai was instructed to address himself to the previously mentioned civil and religious heads of the community, both with their full official titles. This time it also includes *the remnant of the people* (cf. 1:12, 14 with 1:1). The LXX, Vetus Latina, and Peshitta insert "all" *(kōl)* before "remnant" in order to equate this reading with 1:12 and 14. The Vulgate and Targum are in accordance with the Hebrew text. The addition of "all" is not necessary. It is easier to assume its presence than its omission (contra most scholars, e.g., Nowack, Marti, Mitchell, *BHS, BHK*).

3 The prophet begins his message on the temple site by posing a question to those among the people who might have been old enough to have witnessed the relative splendor of the Solomonic temple at the time of its demolishment by Nebuchadnezzar II in 587 B.C. *Mî ḇāḵem* is a predicative construction, literally, "who is among you?"

left. The Niphal participle with the definite article, *hanniš'ār*, means "such a one who was left over." The definite article expresses attributival definiteness: it is not meant to denote a whole class, but only that part of it which applies to the given case.[17] Thus here it refers to those individuals (singular with distributive force) who have survived the catastrophe and who were part of the "remnant" of God's people (cf. Isa. 4:3; Ezra 1:4).[18]

The question is whether there was anyone left in 520 B.C. who had witnessed the temple of Solomon before its final destruction in 587 B.C. In the time mentioned in Ezra 3, there were surely "many of the priests and Levites and heads of fathers' houses, old men who had seen the first house" (v. 12). That was in 536 B.C., a mere fifty years after the destruction of the temple. According to some scholars it seems impossible for people at the time of Haggai and under the circumstances of the Exile to have attained the age of at least seventy years. According to them Haggai's question, therefore, must have a rhetorical intent: it does not concern people who have

16. Rudolph concedes that Isa. 20:3 is the only analogous instance where *bᵉyaḏ* is used in a similar context, but according to him there is a difference: in the Isaiah text it is used to express a symbolic act. The problem with this explanation, however, is that it is not so much a question of interpretation but of syntax!

17. See GKC, § 126t; cf. Koole, Rudolph, et al.

18. See n.3 above.

actually seen the Solomonic temple, but rather those who had memories of it, based on literature (Ps. 137) or oral tradition.[19] This assumption, however, is unlikely, first, because it is contrary to the explicit terms of the question; second, because "memories" were the joint heritage of the whole community, not merely of a few individuals "among you"; and third, because the comparison concerns the *seeing (rā'â)* of both the former and the present state of the temple.

It is important to evaluate the *former* state of the temple. It surely had lost much of its previous splendor during successive raids and the plundering of its contents.[20] In the fifth year of King Rehoboam, Shishak king of Egypt attacked Jerusalem and carried off the treasures of the temple of the Lord (1 K. 14:25, 26). When Hazael king of Aram attacked Jerusalem, Joash king of Judah took all the sacred objects dedicated by his fathers and sent them as ransom to Hazael (2 K. 12:17, 18). The same "plundering" of the temple objects, this time in deference to the king of Assyria, was done by King Ahaz (2 K. 16:17, 18) and later by Hezekiah, who redeemed Jerusalem in return for "all the silver that was found in the house of the Lord . . . the gold from the doors of the temple of the Lord, and from the doorposts" (2 K. 18:13–16). In the eighth year of his reign (597 B.C.) Nebuchadnezzar king of Babylon "removed all the treasures from the temple of the Lord . . . and took away all the gold articles that Solomon had made for the temple of the Lord" (2 K. 24:12–13, NIV).

The reference in our text, therefore, could not have been to the original glory of the Solomonic temple, but must be to that which it still contained after Nebuchadnezzar carried Jehoiakim into exile (in 597 B.C.; cf. Jer. 27:16–22). Before its final destruction in 587 B.C. the temple itself and its imposing complex of buildings were still intact, and the elderly people who had seen it could still have remembered its magnificence.

Haggai implores the elderly people to compare the *former splendor* of *this house* with its present condition. The antithesis is between "former" *(hāri'šôn)* and "now" *('attâ)*. It is important to note that the comparison does not concern two separate temples. In both cases the reference is to "this house." Thus it concerns the one temple in its twofold condition: before its destruction and at the present time. The point, however, is that the temple at that time was not yet rebuilt. The work had hardly begun and seemed to have

19. So, e.g., Mitchell, Koole, Van der Woude. After overcoming their grief (Ps. 137:2–11), the remembrance of the temple was kept alive in the exilic worship by singing Pss. 26:8; 27:4; 42; 63:3; and 84 (so Rudolph).

20. Solomon's temple in itself was relatively small. Rudolph compares it with a medium-size town church. According to him distance lends enchantment to the view.

already been frustrated. The so-called second temple, which the people were admonished to rebuild, would only be completed four years later, on the third day of the month Adar, in the sixth year of the reign of King Darius (Ezra 6:15), in the spring of 515 B.C.

How does it look to you now? There was hardly any comparison between the former and the present state of the temple. The interrogative particle *mâ* is used in the sense of "how" (cf. Gen. 44:16; 1 Sam. 10:27; etc.). The object "it" refers back to "this house." *Does it not seem to you like nothing* (lit. "is the likeness of it not like nothing in your eyes?")? The interrogative particle with the negative suggests a positive answer. It implies knowledge and understanding of the subject. The comparative particle *k*[e] can be construed with the thing or person that is compared (cf. Gen. 44:18b: "for you are like Pharaoh himself," lit.: "for like you, the like is Pharaoh"; Judg. 8:18b; Isa. 42:2; etc.).[21] Both comparisons refer to the same object: the present state of the temple.

The disappointment did not concern so much the vastness of the present construction. According to the decree of Cyrus the rebuilt temple would have been ninety feet high and ninety feet wide (Ezra 6:3), which would have exceeded that of Solomon. The disappointment was rather on account of the lack of suitable material and the absence of sacred objects, such as the ark of the covenant. The new temple, they realized, would never be like the old. They had no resources to pay skilled craftsmen from abroad, as Solomon had done, and they could not begin to think of covering the interior with gold (1 K. 6:21, 22). In spite of the work already done, there was nothing to show for it. The new temple, even in terms of the proposed reconstruction, did not comply with the promises of the earlier prophets for the grand renovation in the messianic age. The problem is that the unfavorable comparison between the present and the past undermined all incentive to persevere (so Baldwin, correctly). Thus the people needed to be encouraged again.

4 Haggai's message in these circumstances has two aspects: (1) leaders and people are encouraged to be strong, to take heart, and to work (v. 4), and (2) God himself will solve the problem of the "filling" of the temple (vv. 5–9).

But now. The diagnosis of the situation was disheartening. The logical consequence would have been to sympathize with leaders and people, to condone their lack of incentive and dedication. But Haggai does the

21. For the form and meaning of *kāmōhû,* "the likeness of it," see GKC, § 103k. Both comparisons here refer to the same object: the present state of the temple.

contrary. With his *w^eʿattâ* (lit. "and now") the prophet not only introduces a new thought but prepares the way for his surprisingly new approach toward the people's dilemma.

be strong. The people are not consoled but are encouraged to be or become strong, to have courage. The Hebrew verb *ḥāzaq* denotes a frame of mind which enables one to pursue or initiate something with fervor and diligence (cf. Josh. 1:6, 7, 9; Judg. 7:11). In this case it is to *act* (Heb. *ʿśâ,* "do [something]"; the implied object is *m^elā'ḵâ,* "work"; cf. 1:14). Leaders and people must not be discouraged, but must join hands and forces in diligently promoting the significant task of rebuilding the temple of the Lord. The responsibility of each leader, and of the people individually and jointly, is emphasized by the repetition of the command *be strong* (singular), with the exhortation to all of them together to *act* (plural!).

The expression *all you people of the land* refers to the postexilic community (as in Zech. 7:5), and is synonymous to "all the remnant of the people" (Hag. 1:12, 14; 2:2). In the books of Ezra (4:4) and Nehemiah (10:29) the reference is to the semi-heathen population in the vicinity. Elsewhere the expression is defined similarly (e.g., 2 K. 11:14, 18–20; 15:5; Ezek. 45:22; 46:3, 9).[22] The omission of "son of Shealtiel" is as noticeable as the occurrence of "the high priest" in direct address, yet there is no evidence to warrant the insertion of the former or the omission of the latter (so Mitchell, correctly).

For I am with you,[23] says the Lord Almighty. The encouragement to leaders and people alike is endorsed by and is rooted in the Lord's promise that he will be with them. Compare the commentary on 1:13, and also Ezra 10:4 and 1 Chr. 28:20.

5 In its present form v. 5a asserts that God's Word and Spirit will

22. The preexilic connotation of this expression is the free, landowning, endowed citizens with fully military and political rights. So E. Würthwein, in *Biblisch-Historisches Handwörterbuch,* 3 vols., ed. B. Reicke and L. Rost (Göttingen: Vandenhoeck & Ruprecht, 1962–66), I:81; idem, *Der amm ha'arez im Alten Testament,* BWANT 4/17 (Stuttgart: Kohlhammer, 1936), pp. 51ff. Beuken, op. cit., p. 220nn.1 and 3, is of the opinion that the countryfolk could not have participated in the rebuilding of the temple, and that the expression must have the same meaning as in Ezra-Nehemiah: the syncretistic population (contra R. J. Coggins, "The Interpretation of Ezra 4:4," *JTS* 16 [1965] 124–27). See also A. R. Hulst, in *THAT,* II:299–302.

23. According to Beuken, op. cit., pp. 53–60, vv. 4 and 5 do not belong to the message of the prophet (vv. 6–9a) but are from the Chronistic editor. His reason is that an "assistance formula" ("I am with you") fits in with the Chronistic "accession to office" but not in the structure of a prophecy (p. 57). Here the preconceived mold determines the interpretation.

be in the midst of his people as they were during all the events of the deliverance from the Egyptian bondage. Because of that, the people need not be afraid.

according to the promise I made with you when you came out of Egypt (lit. "the word which I have cut with you when you came out of Egypt"). The consensus of scholarly opinion is that this phrase must be considered a gloss, because (1) it is wanting in the LXX, Vetus Latina, and Peshitta; (2) no attempt to construe this phrase with the surrounding context has proven satisfactory; and (3) it breaks the connection between two clauses in vv. 4 and 5 that were evidently meant to be parallel, viz., "I am with you" (v. 4) and "my Spirit will always remain among you." Baldwin suggests that a scribe's marginal reference to Exod. 29:45, 46 may have become incorporated into the text. The glossator would have deemed the promise that God would be with them (v. 4) as the quintessence of salvation, which he then expressed in terms of "the word" (*'eṯ haddāḇār,* v. 5a). This would have been in accordance with the later doctrine of "Word" and "Spirit." According to Koole the OT here anticipates the meaning of the NT's *lógos* and *pneúma*.

There are two main structural problems concerning v. 5a. (1) The unusual position of *'eṯ* at the beginning of this phrase. None of the three different explanations offered for this position is appropriate. *'eṯ*'s ordinary function is to denote the direct object of the verb, but in this case the presupposed preceding verb is wanting. Thus some scholars add or imply a verb like *zāḵar,* "mention," "remember" (Ewald, Ridderbos). The phrase then would read, "remember the word [or promise] which I made [lit. cut] with you." The implied verb is arbitrary, however. Another possible approach is to explain *'eṯ* as emphasizing the nominative, literally, "the word-which-I-have-cut-with-you and my Spirit remains with you." The participle *'ōmeḏeṯ,* "abide," "remain," is then used as predicate for both "word" and "Spirit."[24] It must be granted that although this explanation may be possible, it still is exceptional and syntactically awkward. A third approach explains *'eṯ* as denoting the preposition "with," in conjunction with "my Spirit" (cf. Isa. 59:21; Marti, Sellin, et al.), but this solution is also not satisfactory.

(2) The use of the Hebrew verb *kāraṯ,* "cut off," with *haddāḇār,* "the word," is exceptional. The verb is usually construed with *bᵉrîṯ,* "covenant," and in this connection denotes the cutting up of a sacrificial animal, or the cutting up of an animal in the space between the parties, as a ceremony to

24. See Joüon, *Grammaire,* § 125j; Brockelmann, *Syntax,* § 31b; J. Hoftijzer, "Remarks concerning the use of the particle *'t* in Classical Hebrew," *OTS* 14 (1965) 1–99; cf. Ezek. 17:14.

establish an agreement or conclude a covenant. Applying the principle of *lectio difficilor,* Rudolph has a point that it is methodologically unwarranted to substitute "the covenant" for "the word,"[25] because no one would have done that if "the covenant" belonged to the original text. Another possibility, however, is that the prophet wanted to stress the terms in which the covenant was expressed, which consisted in "the word" (of promise). Most modern versions rightly render *haddāḇār* as "promise,"[26] in the sphere of God's covenant with his people, which would explain the use of the verb *kāraṯ* in this connection (cf. RSV: "according to the promise that I made you"; JPSV: "so I promised you"; NIV: "This is what I covenanted with you"; etc.).

The phrase then is connected with the previous promise "to be with them" (v. 4), and is a further elaboration of it. The promise that God would be with his people was already made way back in the history of Israel, especially in connection with the classical event of the Exodus, and it is still in vogue in the present situation of his people. According to the New Afrikaans Version the promise is linked with the assertion that the Lord's Spirit will remain (participle) with the people for ever.

Whatever the interpretation given to this phrase might be, it is clear that it was meant to interpret the prophet's allusion to the presence and power of God at the Exodus (D. R. Jones), and to apply this as a continual promise for the present situation. This historical accrediting and endorsing of God's promises for the present and future is in full accordance with the historical and prophetical traditions in the history of revelation (cf. the preamble to the Decalogue, Exod. 20:2; Deut. 1:6–8; 4:1–14; 5:1–6; 29:1–26; Amos 2:9–11; Mic. 6:4–5; etc.).

my Spirit will always remain among you. The Hebrew participle *ʿōmeḏeṯ,* "abides," denotes continuous action and includes both past and present within its meaning. The use of the word in connection with "my Spirit" is unusual. According to some scholars the allusion seems to be to the "pillar of cloud" (Heb. *ʿammûḏ*), which accompanied the people of God on their journey (cf. Exod. 33:9). In this case "my Spirit" has a specific meaning. He does not function primarily as the renewing factor in the lives of God's people, because then we would have expected "within you" *(beqirbeḵem)* and not "among you" *(beṯôḵeḵem)* (cf. Ezek. 36:26, 27; Isa. 59:21). The reference here rather corresponds with the function of the Spirit as it was

25. As it is done by Budde, Horst, Gelin, Chary, et al.

26. Van der Woude equates "the word" with the covenantal *tôrâ,* which was given at Sinai, with reference to Deut. 4:2; 13:1 (Eng. 12:32); 30:14; Ps. 119:105; Prov. 6:23; Heb. 2:2. This "gloss" originates from someone who lived in the time when the Pentateuch was canonized (p. 47).

expressed in Isa. 63:7–14, especially vv. 11–14: "Where is he who put in the midst of them his holy Spirit, who caused his glorious arm to go at the right hand of Moses. . . . Like cattle that go down into the valley, the Spirit of the Lord gave them rest. . . . So thou didst lead thy people, to make for thyself a glorious name" (cf. Isa. 44:3; 32:1–15; Zech. 4:6). Koole, therefore, may be correct in identifying God with his Spirit, and equating both parallel clauses, "I am with you" and "my Spirit remains among you." Both instances concern the promise of God's guiding, sustaining, and abiding presence among leaders and people. They can and may rely on the Lord. He remains in full command of every situation and circumstance. Therefore the prophet says, *Do not fear!* (cf. Exod. 14:13). The people who bow in awe before the Lord (1:12) must not be afraid to serve the Lord.

6–8 These verses announce what the Lord intends doing on behalf of the rebuilding of the temple: he will harness his sovereign sway over nature and nations in order to provide the wealth that would be necessary to fill this house with glory. In what the Lord is about to accomplish, leaders and people will observe the reason *(kî)* for God's assurance and encouragement that he will be with them, and that they, therefore, need not be afraid (vv. 4, 5). The considerations of their lack of wealth and material are irrelevant. The Lord is their King and Shepherd, they shall want nothing in the service of the Lord. He is Lord Almighty, and this is what he says.

6 *In just a little while longer I will shake the heavens and the earth, the sea and the dry land.* The first phrase, *ʿôḏ ʾaḥaṯ meʿaṭ hîʾ* (lit. "once again, a little while is it"), is disputed. In the LXX, Peshitta, and Heb. 12:26 the last two words are omitted. They are, therefore, deemed to be a gloss. According to Wellhausen, who is followed by many scholars, the whole phrase was the result of a combination of two separate idioms: "yet once," and "yet a short while and I. . . ." Various suggestions have been made to solve this problem. Because *ʾaḥaṯ* is feminine and therefore cannot be construed with the masculine word *meʿaṭ* (cf. Lev. 25:52), some scholars delete it. According to Van der Woude the best explanation is to regard *meʿaṭ hîʾ* as an explanatory remark on *ʾaḥaṯ*, the assumption being that *ʾaḥaṯ* has the uncommon meaning of "a short while," "unexpectedly," "suddenly" (cf. Prov. 28:18). This would have prompted a glossator to explain the meaning by adding: that is, *meʿaṭ*, "a little (while)." Van der Woude suggests reading "again one moment and," with the deletion of the explanatory remark (cf. also Von Orelli, Elliger, Gelin, Horst). According to him the rendering of *ʾaḥaṯ* in the sense of "once" (Exod. 30:10; Ps. 89:36), as opposed to "frequently," "often," with *ʿôḏ*, "yet," "again," implies a contradiction in terms: "yet once, again once." The idea of an explanatory addition to the original expression seems feasible, but this need not have been the work of a glossator. The phrase, therefore, can be explained as it stands and rendered "again, for once, (it is) in a short while" (so also Rudolph, Koole, *BHS*).

Whatever the solution to this problem might be, the message is clear: God is going to act in a powerful and sudden manner. He is going to *shake* (violently) nature and nations (vv. 6, 7a). The Hiphil participle *marʿîš* in v. 6 has the function of a *futurum instans* after a specification of time.[27] The idea is that it is going to happen in the immediate future.

The Lord will shake *the heavens and the earth*. In Hebrew totality is often expressed by means of the combination of opposite terms, like good and evil, or here, "heaven and earth." The idea is that the whole universe will be shaken. It is not necessary to delete "the sea and the dry land," as "evidently a gloss" (so Mitchell, et al.). Mitchell's reasons for this assumption—that it not only unduly lengthens one of the members of a parallelism but also introduces details inconsistent with the context, details which belong to the field of the later apocalypses (cf. Joel 3:3, 4 [Eng. 2:30, 31]; Isa. 24:1ff.)—are not conclusive. The first objection is arbitrary, because the style of Haggai is nowhere strictly poetical in the Western sense of the word, and the second reason presupposes an incorrect explanation of the imagery used here.

Scholars differ with regard to the underlying motifs for the imagery of the shaking of nature and nations. According to some the imagery was suggested by the storms that sometimes sweep over Palestine (cf. Isa. 2:12–22; Jer. 5:4, 5; Nah. 1:3–6). The later prophets employed it with other similar material in their pictures of the inauguration of the messianic age (cf. Ezek. 33:19–33; Isa. 13:13; 24:18–23; Joel 4:15–21 [Eng. 3:15–21]).

Others assume a literal series (participle) of shakings in the form of earthquakes, with reference to Amos 1:1; 8:8; 9:15; Isa. 2:13–21; 13:13; 29:6; Joel 4:16 (Eng. 3:16); Ezek. 38:20; etc. According to Baldwin, Haggai foresees the whole universe in such a series of convulsions that every nation will gladly part with its treasures. The problem with this explanation, however, is that it attaches two different meanings to the same Hebrew verb *rāʿaš* in vv. 6 and 7: a literal and a figurative meaning. The imagery must be explained in such a way that it will have a bearing on the theme of this section, viz., that the Lord himself will provide the means for "filling" the temple with splendor.

Therefore, it seems preferable to agree with the explanation according to which the Hiphil of the verb *rāʿaš*, "cause to quake," "shake (violently)," belongs to the terminology of the epiphany during the holy war,

27. See Joüon, *Grammaire*, § 121; GKC, § 116p.

when God will intervene on behalf of his people (cf. Judg. 5:4 par. Ps. 68:9 [Eng. 8]; 2 Sam. 22:8 par. Ps. 18:8 [Eng. 7]; Isa. 13:13; 24:18; etc.). The divine intervention also causes the nations (v. 7) to "shake" (cf. Exod. 15:16; Isa. 24:18; Ezek. 38:20; Hab. 3:6). The motifs are derived from the universal and the military-political context of the Day of the Lord: not only the earth, but heaven and earth, the whole universe will be affected by the divine shaking (so Koole, Van der Woude).

7 The real purpose of the cosmic commotion was to engage the nations as instruments on behalf of the rebuilding of the temple: *I will shake all the nations*. The contribution of the nations to the worship of the Lord is a pervasive motif in both OT and NT. The primary theological concept is God's sovereign reign over the nations (Ps. 47:9 [Eng. 8]; cf. Ps. 2:8; 7:9 [Eng. 8]; 22:29 [Eng. 28]; 82:8; 99:1; Jer. 10:7; 2 Chr. 20:6; etc.), and the promise that all nations will share in the salvation and blessing of Abraham (Gen. 12:3; 18:18; 22:18; 26:4; Gal. 3:8) and Israel (Exod. 19:5, 6; Ruth 1:16; 1 K. 8:43 par. 2 Chr. 6:33; etc.). The contributions of the nations are expressly stated in Isa. 60:5: "Then you shall see and be radiant . . . because the abundance of the sea shall be turned to you, the wealth of the nations shall come to you"; Isa. 61:6: "You shall eat the wealth of the nations, and in their riches you shall glory" (cf. 66:20); Zech. 14:14: "And the wealth of all the nations round about shall be collected, gold, silver, and garments in great abundance"; and Rev. 21:26: "They shall bring into it the glory and the honor of the nations."

In our text *the precious things of all the nations shall come*. In this presentation we must retain the concept of the holy war. These things will become available to the project of the rebuilding and furnishing of the temple, not as voluntary offerings (Mitchell), but as "spoils" dedicated to the Victor in the holy war (cf. Josh. 6:19; Mic. 4:13). The "things" thus devoted to the Lord and his sanctuary are described as *ḥemdaṯ*, singular construct of *ḥemdâ*, "something desirable," "precious." Here it does not denote jewels (Hitzig) or the beloved ones (Dan. 11:37), but those things which the nations desire and deem precious (cf. 1 Sam. 9:20; Isa. 2:16; Hos. 13:15; Nah. 2:10 [Eng. 9]; Dan. 11:8; 2 Chr. 32:27; 36:10). The proposed alteration of the singular into a plural *ḥămûḏôṯ* (cf. LXX *tá eklektá*, *BHS*, etc.) is unnecessary because the plural of the verb (*bā'û*, "they will come") occasionally is construed with a singular word with a collective meaning.[28] The singular form is supported by the Vulgate, Peshitta, and Targum.

The older commentators of the early and medieval church, following

28. So, correctly, Van der Woude, Koole, et al., against Wellhausen, Nowack, Marti, Duhm, Mitchell, Sellin, Nötscher, Elliger, Winton Thomas, Deissler, Horst, Chary, Amsler. See GKC, § 145b-e.

the singular of the Vulgate, "and then will come the desire of all the nations," interpreted this verse as referring to the Messiah, citing the incidents recorded in Luke 2:22–26 as fulfillment of Haggai's prophecy. Luther was especially adamant in emphasizing the christological exegesis of this verse: the prophecy of Haggai, according to him, is fulfilled in Christ; a mere eschatological interpretation is *contra fidem,* it deprives Christ of the honor that is due to him and denies the fact of the Christ event in a similar manner as it was done by the Jews. Calvin allows that this explanation is possible, but he rightly rejects it in favor of his first explanation, viz., that nations shall come and bring with them everything that is precious.

The AV still maintains the christological interpretation by rendering, in accord with the Vulgate, "and the desire of all nations shall come." It is significant to note that Luther's translation: "Da sol denn kommen aller Heiden Trost" ("then will come the consolation of all [the] heathen"), is reflected in some modern hymnals, for instance in the *Evangelisches Kirchengesangbuch* 5:4 (cf. 10:1): "Wo bleibst du, Trost der ganzen Welt" ("where are you, [the] consolation of the whole world"), and in the Dutch *Liedboek voor de Kerken,* 128:4: "Waar blijft Gij toch o' wereld's troost, die wij verbeiden onverpoost" ("where are you, O Consolation of the world, for whom we are waiting unceasingly")?

This interpretation is now generally abandoned, for it is clear from v. 8, as Calvin already pointed out, that the "glory," "wealth" of the last clause of v. 7 is that of silver and gold, and thus it is not a delightful or desired person but precious things that are destined to come to the new sanctuary (so Mitchell, et al., correctly).

With these "precious things" the Lord will *fill this house with glory.* "This house" is the new temple-to-be. The Piel form of the verb *mālā'* emphasizes the fact that something is *filled* with something, in this case, this house with glory. The idea of abundance is stressed. Beauty will be added upon beauty until the temple is filled with splendor. Leaders and people need not be discouraged because of the time of financial stringency and lack of resources. God is never short of funds (Baldwin)!

This house will be filled with *kāḇôḏ*. This is not God's glory, but the abundance and preciousness of the desired things which will become available to the temple. Leaders and people may take heart. God is taking the initiative, and he warrants it.

says the Lord Almighty. There is no textual evidence to "excite suspicion" (Mitchell) concerning this form of expression, just because it is rare in Haggai and Zechariah. *'āmar* and *nᵉ'um* are interchangeable, and they occur with *YHWH ṣᵉḇā'ôṯ* not less than three and five times respectively in this section of Haggai.

8 The reason for the previous assertion that God will provide the wealth of the nations to enhance the splendor of the temple is given in this verse: *Silver is mine and gold is mine* (lit. "to me are the silver and the gold"). God is not dependent on the insufficient and insignificant material and resources of the people to accomplish his purpose with the new temple. All the material wealth is his. The reference to silver and gold has a double meaning: it concerns the totality of all precious things, and it emphasizes the intrinsic value of this material wealth. Everything is at his disposal: every beast of the forest, the cattle on a thousand hills (Ps. 50:10). In v. 8, however, the allusion is not so much to the absolute ownership of God because he is the Creator and Sustainer of all things (cf. Exod. 19:5; Ps. 24:1), but to him as Victor in the holy war on his day. The totality of spoils from all the nations are at his disposal (cf. Ps. 60:8–10 [Eng. 6–8]; Josh. 6:19; Mic. 4:13; Koole, Van der Woude). And this will become available for the rebuilding and decoration of the temple.

The tendency to interpret v. 8 spiritually is contrary to the explicit terms of Haggai's message. The first and direct meaning is as stated above. Leaders and people need not be disheartened on observing the meager and insignificant resources they had at hand. God himself will provide abundantly and gloriously. This is endorsed in v. 9.

This interpretation, of course, does not exclude a twofold perspective: on the Day of the Lord as the theological context, and on the history of its fulfillment. To both these aspects we will have to turn in our summary of the message of this pericope.

9 This verse depicts the result of God's actions on behalf of the temple: the temple's subsequent and future glory and splendor will be greater than that of the former, and God will grant peace in this place.

The comparison between the "latter" *(hā'aḥ^{a}rôn)* and the "former" *(hāri'šôn)* concerns the "glory" or "splendor" *(kāḇôḏ)*, and not "this house."[29] The rendering of the Vulgate, therefore, is inappropriate: *gloria domus istius novissimae* (so also Luther, AV, Marck, Calvin, etc.). The expression "this house" here, as in v. 3, refers to the continuous existence of the temple, in spite of the vicissitudes of its dramatic history and now also of its ruined and unfinished condition (so Mitchell, et al.). By its former *glory*, therefore, is meant the splendor it possessed before it was demolished and burned down by Nebuchadnezzar in 587 B.C. When the Lord has accomplished that which he intended doing (vv. 6, 7), the later glory of the temple will surpass the former glory.

The fulfillment of this promise has a literal and an eschatological

29. Cf. 2:3; Joüon, *Grammaire,* §§ 143h, 139a.2.

application. Contrary to Calvin's assertion that Herod's temple was counterfeit, an attempt of Satan to deceive by impostures and crafts that he might draw away the minds of the godly from the beauty of the spiritual temple, the temple built by Herod was indeed heralded as magnificent (Mark 13:1). The eschatological application, however, transcends the empirical significance of "this house," and must be evaluated first in terms of the contribution of God himself, and second in terms of the context of the Day of the Lord, and therefore as a reality of faith. In essence the OT temple finds its ultimate fulfillment in the "Lord of the temple," who is greater than the temple (Matt. 12:6), namely, Jesus Christ (cf. John 2:13–22). The final fulfillment coincides with the consummation, when the temple would be superseded by the Lord Almighty and the Lamb as the city's temple (Rev. 21:22–27).

In accord with the imagery of the holy war, and the spoils which belong to the Victor (cf. Mic. 4:13), the promise *in this place I will grant peace* must be explained. The *bammāqôm hazzeh* is the place of which the Lord has said "My name shall be there" (1 K. 8:29); actually the reference is to both the temple and Jerusalem, the city of peace (cf. 2 K. 22:16–20; Jer. 7:3, 6; 28:3–6; also Ps. 46:5 [Eng. 4]; 48:1–13 [Eng. 2–14]).[30] The demonstrative pronoun *hazzeh,* "this," joins "this house" (v. 9a; cf. v. 7) and "this place" (v. 9b). The primary point of reference, therefore, is the temple. But in the message of the preexilic prophets the announcement of peace includes Jerusalem. It is therefore not either/or, but both Mount Zion and the Holy City (Jer. 7:3, 6; 14:13; etc.).

These places will experience *peace (šālôm).*[31] In trying to define the meaning and scope of this peace, it is important to distinguish between the messages of the "false" and the "true" prophets in this respect. In Jer. 14:13 the prophet accuses "the prophets" who kept telling the people, "you shall not see the sword, nor shall you have famine, but I will give you assured peace in this place" (cf. Mic. 3:5, 11). The "peace" which they proclaimed in the name of the Lord was a product of their own theology, which assumed a static, automatic relationship between God and his people, and the inviolability of the people of God and of their institutions, especially of Jerusalem and the temple. This point of view is an essential aspect of the "doctrine" of the false prophets and therefore must not be equated with the preexilic salvation-prophets, as is done by Van der Woude. The idea of peace as part

30. So, correctly, Koole, Van der Woude. To exclude the temple on the grounds that it was not completed (so André, Nowack, J. Ridderbos, Winton Thomas) is to misunderstand the purport of this prophecy, alluding as it does to the future.

31. It cannot be established with certainty whether *šālôm* was meant to allude to Jerusalem (Ackroyd) or to Solomon (Beuken).

of the promise of salvation is inherent in the messages of both the false and the true prophets. They differ with regard to the conditions of peace and the application thereof. In the case of the false prophets no specific religious or ethical conditions were required, apart from the external fact of belonging to the chosen people. On that assumption the promise and application of peace are unconditional.

According to the true prophets, including Haggai, the peace as part of the eschatological promises presupposes the renewal of the covenantal relationship between God and his people and consists of all the blessings of the messianic age. The prerequisite for the people to share in this peace is faith. "If you do not stand firm in your faith, you will not stand at all" (Isa. 7:9, NIV). When their conduct is sinful, defying the Lord's glorious presence, Jerusalem will stagger and Judah will fall (Isa. 3:8). The promised peace is not unconditional. This also applies in our text. The condition for peace remains wholehearted submission to the command of the Lord to rebuild the temple and a sincere dedication to accomplish this task.

The promise of "peace" in "this place" also has an eschatological perspective, in full accord especially with the message of Isaiah. In Haggai, however, the messianic motif is not explicit but is implied in the concept of the pilgrimage of the nations toward Jerusalem (cf. Isa. 2:1–4), with the wealth of their "precious things" (cf. Isa. 60:2; 66:12). Koole rightly identifies two new elements in Haggai's preaching: the pilgrimage of the nations is joined with the eschatological motif of the holy war, and the gifts of the nations are intended not for Israel but for the temple. According to Koole the significance of the pilgrimage of the nations for the splendor of the temple presupposes two circumstances: because the nations have plundered the temple they were obliged to make amends according to the *ius talionis,* and Israel became acquainted in the Exile with the economical function of the heathen temples, namely, as a safe place for the accumulation and keeping of the nations' wealth.

In line with this traditio-historical fact, Haggai foresees Jerusalem as the capital of the world, with the new temple being the economic center, in the sense of a world bank, where the wealth of the nations could be deposited. This eschatological and universal scene constitutes the point of reference for the meaning of the promised peace. It includes not only well-being in general but also prosperity, success, safety, inviolability, the stabilization of all relationships, internally and internationally, peace within and with the neighboring countries—in short, every imaginable gift in eschatological perspective. The antonym of "peace" is *rāʿ*, "of bad quality," "inferior," "disagreeable," "unwholesome," "disaster," as opposed to "prosperity" (Isa. 45:7), "harmful" as opposed to hopeful and having a future (Jer. 29:11);

a synonym of "peace" is *ṭôḇ,* "good," in every variety of meaning (cf. 1 K. 22:8, 12).[32]

The idea is that the wealth and splendor of the new temple will be immense and astonishing. The *kāḇôḏ* of this temple would not be that it lasted ten years longer than that of Solomon (so Rashi, Kimchi), but that it would be provided with real gold and silver, the result of the pilgrimage of the nations. For the contemporaries of Haggai and even for the subsequent generations this amazing promise was contrary to reality. Nehemiah and Malachi accused the people for their negligence in providing the necessary contributions for the temple worship. Later Judaism understood this prophecy in the sense of a royal subsidy for the temple (2 Macc. 3:1–2). In Heb. 12:26–29 the promise is applied to a kingdom that cannot be shaken, assuming the motifs both of the holy war and of the pilgrimage of the nations.

The LXX adds to the Hebrew text "even peace of soul unto preservation [2 Chr. 14:12] to every one that lays foundations to erect this temple." This addition, however, could not have been a part of the original text. Jerome gave the reasons for rejecting it when he characterized the phrase in the LXX as "superfluous and hardly consistent," and noted that the words were not regarded as genuine. The addition of the LXX seems to derive from Ezra 9:9 as a gloss on *šālôm,* in order to apply the "peace" specifically to those who have assisted in the rebuilding of the temple (so Rudolph, et al.).

The theme of 1:15b–2:9 can best be expressed in terms of reality and promise in connection with the house of the Lord.

The reality gave rise to both rejoicing and sadness. They began work on the house of the Lord Almighty (1:14), which caused them to rejoice, but at the same time they were sad because of their sinful negligence, and especially because of the unfavorable comparison with the former reality and splendor of the Solomonic temple. This sadness was expressed in three books of the Bible: Ezra 3:12, 13, where no one could distinguish between the shouts for joy and the weeping; Zech. 4:10, where the question is asked: "Who despises the day of small things?" (NIV); and Hag. 2:3.

Under the NT dispensation the same reaction to the reality concerning the Church is appropriate. There is reason to rejoice because it concerns the church of Jesus Christ, but at the same time the people of God have reason to humiliate themselves because of their own apathy and lack of dedication in promoting the life and function of the spiritual "house of the Lord." When the reality of the Church in its present state is compared, not

32. Cf. H. H. Schmid, *Šālôm, "Frieden" im Alten Orient und im Alten Testament,* Stuttgarter Bibelstudien 51 (Stuttgart: Katholisches Bibelwerk, 1971), p. 84.

with that of Solomon or of Zerubbabel or of Herod, but with the life in paradise, and even with the early church as it is described in Acts 4:32–35, then we surely have reason for sadness.

The purpose of the prophecy of Haggai, however, was not to discourage the people of God but to encourage them. They must take heart, or in terms of Zech. 4:10, they must not despise the day of small things. God has allotted his promise to this house.

The promise really was astounding: "The glory of this latter house shall be greater than that of the former one" (2:9). The secret and warranty of this promise lies in what God himself will do to encourage and activate them and to fill the house with glory: he will be with them (1:13; 2:4), he will shake universe and nations, and he will cause the precious things of the nations to be at the disposal of the builders. The result of God's intervention on behalf of the temple is the perspective on its future glory and "peace." In answering the vexing problem whether this promise has been fulfilled, we must allow for a fulfillment in stages.

(a) The temple was completed after four years, also due to "the precious things" decreed by Cyrus, endorsed by Darius (Ezra 6), and presented by Artaxerxes (Ezra 7:15); this temple, expanded and adorned by Herod, was indeed of greater splendor than the contemporaries of Haggai could have imagined (Mark 13:1). An additional aspect of the glory of this temple was that it was attended by more proselytes than was the case with the temple of Solomon (N. H. Ridderbos), and especially that it was visited by the Lord himself.

(b) The terms of the promise will be fully realized when Christ comes again. Then we will receive a kingdom that cannot be shaken (Heb. 12:26–28). Then the glory and honor of the nations will be brought into it (Rev. 21:24, 26). It is true that the temple as a sanctuary in itself will disappear (Rev. 21:22), but the essence of this promise will be fulfilled in the New Jerusalem, where "the dwelling of God is with men" (Rev. 21:3; cf. in more detail J. Ridderbos).

(c) Although the terms of the prophecy do not allow their application to the first coming of Christ and to the Church, this application may be implied. In Christ the very essence and purpose of the OT temple is fulfilled, "for in him all the fulness of God was pleased to dwell, and through him to reconcile to himself all things" (Col. 1:19, 20). In and through Christ the Church and believers became the temple of God (1 Cor. 3:16; 6:19; 2 Cor. 6:16; Eph. 2:21, 22).

The promise of the future glory of the temple has in itself became a reality in Christ, but at the same time retained its character as a promise with its perspective on the full realization at the second coming of Christ.

III. BLESSINGS FOR A DEFILED PEOPLE (2:10–19)

10 *On the twenty-fourth day of the ninth (month), in the second year of Darius, the word of the Lord came to the prophet Haggai:*
11 *"Thus says the Lord Almighty:*[1] *Ask*[2] *the priests for a ruling of law:*
12 *If a person carries consecrated meat in the fold of his garment, and touches with his fold bread, stew, wine, oil, or any kind of food, will it become consecrated?" In reply, the priests said, "No."*
13 *Haggai then said, "If someone defiled through contact with a corpse*[3] *touches anyone of these, will it be defiled?" And the priests replied, "It becomes defiled."*
14 *Thereupon Haggai responded: "This is how this people and this nation is in my sight, says the Lord. Whatever they do, and whatever they offer there,*[4] *it is defiled.*[5]
15 *Now consider this carefully from this day on, from the time when one stone is laid on another in the Lord's temple,*
16 *how they (the days) will become.*[6] *(Before) if one came to a heap*[7] *of*

1. There is no reason to delete the messenger formula because it was addressed to the prophet only (against Budde, Rudolph). God's command involved the people as such.

2. The LXX has a plural form, which is contrary to v. 13a.

3. This meaning of *nep̱eš* is endorsed by Lev. 22:1, 4; etc. Cf. M. Seligson, *The Meaning of "nefes met" in the Old Testament* (Helsinki: Societas Orientalis Fennica, 1951); cf. also LXX, Vulg.

4. Rudolph and Joüon (*Bib* 10 [1929] 418–19) prefer: "and where they brought (offerings)." But the point is more the defiled offering than the defiled place where they were brought.

5. The LXX rephrases the last words of this verse: "and whosoever shall approach them shall be defiled"; it also has an extensive addition: "because of their early burdens: they shall be pained because of their toils; and you have hated him that reproved in the gates." The last part of this addition, perhaps taken from Amos 5:10, is without support from the other witnesses to the text; cf. P. R. Ackroyd, *JJS* 7 (1956) 163–67.

6. Lit. "since they were," "away from their being" (Rudolph), i.e., "before they were there." See the commentary below.

7. I.e., of grain.

twenty (measures),[8] *there were but ten; and if one came to a wine vat*
to skim off fifty (measures), the press[9] *would yield only twenty.*
17 *(Before) I struck you—all the works of your hands—with blight and*
mildew and hail, yet you did not (turn) to me,[10] *says the Lord.*
18 *Take note, from this day onward, from the twenty-fourth day of the*
ninth month, the day[11] *that the foundation of the Lord's temple was*
laid, consider carefully:
19 *Is there yet any seed left in the barn? Do the vine and the fig tree, the*
pomegranate and the olive tree still[12] *yield nothing? From this day*
on I will bless (you)."

Exegetical and translational problems often come in clusters.[13] This comment is especially applicable to this section of Haggai's prophecies. The problems are text-critical, literary-historical, and exegetical. Numerous glosses are assumed, and the majority of commentators deny the unity of this section, with subsequent differences in the interpretation of its contents.

In its present form, this section presents the word of the Lord to Haggai, commissioning him to obtain answers from the priests on a twofold question pertaining to ritual purity and impurity. The answers are applied to the people: because of their impurity they have defiled whatever they have done and whatever they have offered. In 2:15–19 Haggai promises that the future would be better than the past, with the assurance as the theme of this section: "From this day on I will bless you."

A structural analysis of this section amounts to the following: sentence 1 (v. 10) stands apart and provides the date and messenger formula, with a marked difference in wording, compared with 1:1 and 1:15b.

Sentence 2 (vv. 11–13) consists of a number of subclauses or embedded sentences which constitute a unity. It introduces the word of the Lord with the request to the priests for an official ruling *(tôrâ)* on a matter of ritual,

8. Lit. "to a heap of twenty." The "measures" here and in v. 16b are implied, because the issue in this "argument" is not so much the assumed measure but the relative numbers. The LXX supplied a measurement: *sáton,* the equivalent of Heb. *s*ᵉ'*â*. The Vulg. has *viginti modiorum,* "twenty bushels."

9. Heb. *pûrâ* is deleted by Pesh. and translated as a kind of measurement by LXX, Vulg., and Targ. Rudolph's remark is appropriate: one does not explain words with a clear meaning with unknown words (against those who regard *pûrâ* as a gloss).

10. Lit. "there was not with you to me." Cf. Amos 4:9 and the commentary below.

11. Lit. "namely, since the day." For *l*ᵉ, "namely," see KB, p. 465, no. 20.

12. Lit. "and until." The translation is according to the LXX and Vulg., "still," *w*ᵉ*ʿôḏ,* instead of *w*ᵉ*ʿaḏ*.

13. See David J. Clark, "Problems in Haggai 2:15–19," *BT* 34 (1983) 432–39.

concerning the distinction between ritually pure and impure (Lev. 10:8–11; also Exod. 29:31, 37; Lev. 6:18, 27, 28).

Sentence 3 (v. 14) provides the application of the preceding official ruling on the people in the sight of the Lord: as a defiled nation they have defiled whatever they have done and all their sacrifices.

Sentences 4–7 (vv. 15–17) form a literary unit. The people are reminded of what they have experienced in the past because of their uncleanness. That was before one stone was laid on another in the Lord's temple. The connection with the preceding verses is evident. The official ruling by the priests must be applied to the defilement of "this people," and because of that *(w^{e}ʿattâ)* they must consider their past experiences as a token of God's displeasure with them.

Sentences 8–10 (vv. 18–19) are closely connected to the preceding verses but open a perspective on the people's subsequent experiences "from this day on." The central theme of this section as a whole is found in sentence 10: "From this day on I will bless you."

The literary unity of 2:10–14 and 2:15–19 was denied especially by J. W. Rothstein.[14] His point of departure is that the events described in Ezra 3:8–4:3 did not occur in 536 B.C. but in 520 B.C., and that "this people" in 2:14 does not refer to the remnant of Israel but to the Samaritans. As a matter of fact, the intent of 2:14 is to thwart the Samaritans from participating in the rebuilding of the temple, and that is why the twenty-fourth day of the ninth month in the second year of Darius is considered "the day of the birth of pure Judaism." The suggestion that 2:15–19 should follow 1:15a also originated with Rothstein, with the additional comment that this prophecy was delivered on the twenty-fourth of the *sixth* month![15]

This hypothesis of Rothstein found wide acceptance, especially among European scholars, with minor or major variations in the rearranging and interpretation of details. For example, Sellin and Deden, followed by NEB, transpose 1:13 between 1:15a and 2:15–19, with the resultant order of 1:14, 15, 13; 2:15–19, 10–14, 1–9, 20–23. Elliger concurs with this order of verses but modifies Rothstein's thesis concerning the Samaritans. They

14. Rothstein, *Juden und Samaritaner: Die grundlegende Scheidung von Judentum und Heidentum*, BWANT 3 (Leipzig: Hinrichs, 1908). The authenticity of this section was already questioned in 1895 by T. André, op. cit., pp. 24–39.

15. According to Horst (HAT, p. 197), followed by Deissler and Eissfeldt, the editor combined all sections which were dated on the twenty-fourth day into a separate paragraph, 2:10–23. See also I. H. Eybers, "The Rebuilding of the Temple according to Haggai and Zechariah," in *Studies in Old Testament Prophecy, OTWSA*, ed. W. C. van Wyk (Potchefstroom: Pro Rege, 1975), pp. 15–26. He transposes the whole of 2:15–23 to the end of ch. 1. According to him the book of Haggai originally ended with 2:14 (p. 19).

were not the descendants of the ten tribes who remained in their country after the fall of Samaria, but those of the foreign nations who were resettled in the towns of Samaria to replace the exiled Israelites (2 K. 17:24–41). The main reason for Haggai's prophecy here did not concern the rebuilding of the temple, but the question whether the Samaritans may participate in the offering ritual in Jerusalem.

Rudolph agrees with Rothstein's main thesis and distinguishes between "people" (*ʿam)* and "nation" *(gôy)*. The first refers to the indigenous descendants of Northern Israel and the second to the foreign elements, according to 2 K. 17:24–41 and Ezra 4:2. Rudolph, however, regards 2:10–19 as a literary unit. Others, like Chary and Amsler, agree with Rothstein's literary analysis but reject his anti-Samaritan interpretation of 2:10–14. According to them "this people" and "this nation" in v. 14 refer to the temple community.[16]

The main objections against the generally accepted theses and literary analysis of Rothstein, et al., are the following:

It is completely unsupported by any textual evidence. Even the fragments from Murabbaʿat strongly support the Hebrew text.

It is inconceivable that a redactor would have separated passages which originally belonged together in such an arbitrary way. In addition, the presupposed connection between 2:15–19 and 1:15a is not feasible at all. 2:15a starts with *weʿattâ,* "and now," introducing a turning point in a narrative or argument, with reference to something that has been said in the preceding passage. In the alleged original composition of 1:15a plus 2:15–19, the "and now" would refer to a date, contrary to its use elsewhere in Haggai (cf. 1:4, 5; 2:4). The proposed solution, according to this hypothesis, is either to assume an omission in the text of 1:15a, or to delete "and now."

It has rightly been pointed out that a form-critical analysis is in favor of the literary unity of 2:10–19. This section is structurally similar to 1:4–11 and 2:3–9: the account of the present situation is followed by an appeal, introduced by *weʿattâ,* and a divine promise. On this basis Van der Woude distinguishes between 2:10–14 (present situation), 2:15–17 (appeal), and 2:18–19 (promise).

The assumption that the events described in Ezra 3:8–4:3 really took place in 520 B.C., and not in 536 B.C., and that the Samaritan schism lies behind Haggai's oracle in 2:10–14, is disputable. To substantiate this hypothesis, the text must be emended, and a forced explanation must be given to the words "this people" and "this nation." The date in v. 18 is also either omitted as a gloss or brought into line by changing "ninth" to "sixth." The

16. According to Ackroyd (*Peake's Commentary,* pp. 563–64), the reference originally was to the returned exiles, but in the final editing of Haggai's prophecies it was meant as a word of judgment against the Samaritans.

effect is to leave vv. 10–14 isolated and to make possible the identification of "this people" (v. 14) with the Samaritans. Baldwin rightly questions this view. She asks, if it was Haggai's intention to allude to the Samaritans, why was he not more explicit? Why did he not mention the Samaritans by name? Moreover, the expression "this people" was used by Jeremiah to reproach the inhabitants of Judah (Jer. 6:19, 21; 14:10, 11), and by Haggai himself (1:2) to rebuke his compatriots. There is no evidence that he uses the expression in a different sense in this verse.

The historicity of the events described in Ezra 3:8–4:3 as having occurred in 536 B.C. need not be denied. See the Introduction for a discussion of this problem.

Van der Woude's attempt to establish the unity of the passage as a whole by suggesting that this prophecy was addressed to the priests only is not convincing. A consequence of this interpretation is that he has to consider v. 17 as a gloss, which, however, is not supported by textual evidence. According to him the theme of the passage can be described as a discussion between Haggai and the priests concerning the relationship between the current sacrificial practices and the anticipated divine blessing, seen against the background of the guarded attitude of the priests with regard to the prophet's exhortation to rebuild the temple. The argument is that the priests could have referred to the fact that the blessing was indeed not experienced, in spite of the offerings on the erected altar since the reign of Cyrus (Ezra 3). Would the rebuilding of the temple be any different in this connection? To this point of view Haggai addressed himself by asserting that the ineffectiveness of the sacrificial ritual was caused by the people's impurity, and that evidence of the divine blessing would manifest itself as soon as the rebuilding of the temple had started with zeal and dedication.

This suggested explanation according to which Haggai addressed himself to the priests only cannot be maintained. Both the experienced curses (vv. 16, 17) and the anticipated divine blessing (vv. 18, 19) are obviously directed to the people as such. The priests' part in this prophecy is only to provide an official ruling on a matter pertaining to ritual purity and impurity. The answer, then, is applied to the impurity of the people as the main reason for their adverse circumstances.

2:10–14 Haggai establishes the principle, on the basis of the priestly instruction, that ritual purity cannot be passed on by physical contact, whereas ritual defilement can. He applies this principle to the situation of his day: because the people's attitude toward the temple, and therefore toward the Lord himself, was wrong, their offerings had been unacceptable, and the Lord had not blessed them with good harvests.[17]

17. See Clark, op. cit., p. 432.

10 *On the twenty-fourth day of the ninth (month), in the second year of Darius.* The style of this introductory verse is, contrary to 1:1 and 1:15b–2:1a, that of official decrees (so Van der Woude). The title "king" is omitted (cf. 1:1; 1:15b), except in the Vulgate. The precise date, the equivalent of 18 December 520, is nowhere mentioned in the calendar of Israel's feasts as a special remembrance day. André's assumption, that because of the sacrifices implied in v. 14 this day originally was considered to be a feast day, is arbitrary, because no scriptural evidence can be offered to establish his point of view. The significance of this day is rather that it is precisely three months since work on the temple began (1:15), and two months since Haggai's previous sermon (2:1). According to v. 18 the foundation of the Lord's temple was laid on this day. This festive occasion, therefore, might have provided the incentive for Haggai to pronounce this prophecy.

the word of the Lord came to the prophet Haggai. Koole's argument that the preposition *'el*, "to," instead of *b^eyaḏ*, "through," emphasizes the reception of the revelation rather than the communication of it has but a relative significance.[18] Both aspects of the prophetical office are simultaneously applicable. The word received is destined to be communicated, according to the very definition of prophecy.

It is important to note that Zechariah had begun his ministry in Jerusalem a few weeks previously (Zech. 1:1). Zechariah's appeal to the people was to return to the Lord in order that he may return to them (1:3). The situation reflected in the prophecy of Haggai is that of an unrepentant people who have not taken the prophets' exhortations to heart. On this, the twenty-fourth day of the ninth month, Haggai still suggested their impurity before the Lord.

11 Haggai, evidently preaching on the temple site, must consult the priests. The words *thus says the Lord Almighty* endorse the divine command. Whether this command was directed to the prophet only (so Koole, Van der Woude) or meant as part of the prophet's message is irrelevant with regard to the prophecy as such. Haggai acted as God's messenger, with God's authority invested in him.

The priests were the official mediators of the divine *tôrâ*.[19] Their lips

18. The text tradition seems not to be consistent in this respect. Nowack reads *b^eyaḏ*, in accordance with Pesh. and Targ., supported by the codex of Hillel and the Editio Bombergiana. In *BHK* (Procksch) *'el* is maintained, supported by LXX, Vetus Latina, Vulg., and the Syrohexaplaris. Beuken, op. cit., pp. 65–66, affirms the reading of *'el*, because the prophecy does not concern specific addressees.

19. Cf. J. Begrich, "Die priesterliche Tora," *ZAW* 66 (1936) 63–88 (repr. in *Gesammelte Studien zum Alten Testament*, Theologische Bücherei 21 [München:

were destined to preserve knowledge and from their mouths people should seek instruction (Mal. 2:7; cf. Zech. 7:3). They were the keepers and interpreters of the divine instruction, the body of precepts through which God's way of life for mankind was made known. Eventually "Torah" came to refer to what we know as the Pentateuch (Baldwin). The task of the priests was to apply the principles of God's precepts, especially pertaining to ritual and ceremonial purity and impurity, on request of the people in concrete circumstances. This kind of instruction, comparable to the "word" *(dāḇār)* of the prophets and the "counsel" *(ʿēṣâ)* of the wise men (Jer. 18:18), is called *tôrâ*, "instruction," *Weisung*.[20]

That Haggai had *to ask (šeʾal-nāʾ)* the priests implies the acknowledgment of their authority on matters concerning instruction in the law. They were chosen out of all the tribes of Israel to stand and minister in the Lord's name always (Deut. 18:5; cf. 17:12). Because of their lack of zeal and ignorance of the law of God, the prophets sometimes had to reprimand them (Hos. 4:6; Mal. 2:7–9). According to some commentators this criticism must also be assumed in Hag. 2:10–14. In addressing himself to the ordinary priests, it seemed that Haggai intentionally ignored the high priest Joshua. There is, however, no reason to assume any discriminatory distinction between the high priest and his subordinates. Haggai's request concerns a matter of instruction which was the task of the ordinary priests and does not imply any form of reproof. It is true, however, that the priests at that time were as guilty as the people in not rebuilding the temple, but the point in question is now different.

12–13 Haggai poses two related questions pertaining to ritual purity and impurity.[21] There is no evidence for the contention that Haggai was not asking for information but that he applied a methodological device familiar to every teacher (contra Baldwin). The questions asked and the persons to whom the prophet addressed himself are in full accordance with the actual practice in Israel.

Lexicographically and grammatically it is important to note the following points. *Hēn*, "behold," usually emphasizes the following word but is here used as a conditional conjunction, introducing a question with regard to

---

Kaiser, 1964], pp. 232–60). See also P. J. Budd, "Priestly Instruction in Pre-Exilic Israel," *VT* 23 (1973) 1–14.

20. Cf. Deut. 33:10; Lev. 10:11; Jer. 18:18; Ezek. 44:23; Mal. 2:7. See Budd, op. cit., pp. 1–14; Begrich, op. cit., pp. 63–68.

21. Cf. H. J. Hermisson, *Sprache und Ritus im altisraelitischen Kult* (Neukirchen-Vluyn: Neukirchener, 1965), pp. 84–99.

the law.[22] *Nāga*ʿ, "touch," can be used with a number of prepositions without much difference in meaning: *ʾel,* "to" (v. 12), *b^e^,* "in" (v. 13), or *ʿal,* "on" (Isa. 6:7). The definite article with "bread" *(leḥem),* "stew" *(nāzîḏ),* and "wine" *(yayin)* denotes the specific kind.[23] The first question is answered with the negative *lōʾ*, "no," and the second by the repetition of the predicate: "It becomes defiled."[24] *Kol,* "all," construed with an indefinite singular noun, can be rendered "any one" or "all sorts."[25]

The first question is whether sanctity is transferable. *If a person carries consecrated meat in the fold of his garment, and touches with his fold* [LXX the fold of his garment] *bread, stew, wine, oil, or any kind of food, will it become consecrated?* Haggai refers to a man, any person, who carries (lit.) "holy flesh" in the (lit.) "wing" of his garment. This way of carrying things (cf. Ezek. 5:3), in the fold of one's cloak (2 K. 4:39), may suggest a certain regard for the object carried (Pressel). More important is the meaning of *b^e^śar-qōḏeš,* "holy flesh." This expression is found in one other text, Jer. 11:15, where the question is posed: "Can consecrated meat avert your punishment?" (NIV). In Ezek. 40:43 reference is made to the four tables for the burnt offerings, which were for the "flesh of the offerings" *(b^e^śar haq-qorḇān).* In 1 Sam. 21:4 (Eng. 5) mention is made of the "holy bread," in contrast to the ordinary bread. We may assume that "holy flesh" is flesh or meat dedicated to the altar; it is sacrificial meat in general.

Technically we have a few hints at the kind of meat intended. The fact that it is carried excludes meat for the burnt offering, because that is consumed in its entirety. The meat could have been that of the "peace" (RSV) or "fellowship" (NIV) offerings (1 K. 8:64), or that of the sin offering (Lev. 6:18 [Eng. 25]). The person who carries it in the fold of his garment, however, could only have been a priest in the case of a sin offering (cf. Lev. 6:19 [Eng. 26]). If the reference is made to anyone, the meat of a fellowship offering is meant (cf. Lev. 7:11–21).

These and similar technical considerations, however, must not be stressed, because the point of reference is the effect of "holy meat" in the fold of a garment on food. The fact that the meat is carried suggests that it is taken home, because the sanctuary where the meat was supposed to have been eaten (Lev. 6:19 [Eng. 26]; 7:6; Ezek. 46:20) was still a ruin.

The "holy meat" will consecrate anything it touches, in this case the fold of the garment in which it is carried, but not, as would be the case with

22. Cf. Jer. 3:1, "If a man divorces his wife"; cf. also Joüon, *Grammaire,* § 167l.

23. See Brockelmann, *Syntax,* § 21cB.

24. See Brockelmann, *Syntax,* § 56a.

25. See Joüon, *Grammaire,* § 139h.

the sin offering (Lev. 6:20 [Eng. 27]), anything else that is touched by the fold of the garment. This suggested ruling has no scriptural evidence and must have been part of Israel's oral tradition. The specified foods have a bearing on the agricultural products mentioned in 1:11 (cf. 2:16, 19). The context of the inquiry is the disappointment with the harvests.

In reply, the priests said, "No." The priests' answer to Haggai's first question is an apodictic No! Some scholars are of the opinion that the priests were at fault in giving a negative answer, with reference to Ezek. 44:19, which states that the clothes of the priests must be left in the sacred rooms when they go out to the outer court where the people are, so that they do not consecrate the people by means of their garments! A proposed solution to this problem is the distinction that is made between direct and indirect contact: when the contact is direct the consecration is effected, otherwise not (Wellhausen, Bloomhardt, Horst, Rudolph, et al.). In this case the garment itself will become consecrated, but not the things which are being touched by the garments. This point of view, however, is contrary to Ezek. 44:19, and does not solve the problem of the second contact, mentioned in v. 13, which is also indirect (so Amsler, Van der Woude). Perhaps Koole's suggestion is appropriate that we have to consider the fact of a ruined temple, and the situation in connection with it, to be the reason for such an interpretation: the circumstances implied a freer usage of the sacrificial meat (cf. Deut. 22:9; Josh. 6:19).

13 The answer to Haggai's second question is that ritual defilement is passed on by contact, like a contagious disease (Lev. 11:28; 22:4–7). The defilement in this case is caused by contact with a *corpse*. The *ṭᵉmēʾ nepeš,* "defilement of a person," is an abbreviation for *ṭᵉmēʾ nepeš mēṯ,* "defilement of a person of a dead body" (Lev. 21:11; 22:4; Num. 5:2; 9:6, 7, 10). Contact with a dead body causes defilement in the highest degree, even more than having an infectious skin disease or a discharge of any kind (Lev. 22:4). Persons who have become ceremonially unclean on account of a dead body are excluded from celebrating the Passover (Num. 9:6) and are sent away from the camp (Num. 5:2). To be ritually defiled disqualifies one from having part in the organized worship in all its functions and activities. The answer of the priests in the affirmative that the food would become contaminated when an unclean person touches it is in full accordance with the stipulations of the Law: the person who touches something defiled by a corpse will himself be unclean (Lev. 21:11; 22:4; Num. 5:2; 6:6–7; 9:6), and anything that an unclean person touches becomes unclean (Num. 19:22).

14 Haggai provides the application of the priests' instruction. A defiled people defiles everything it touches, the agricultural products and the offerings. *This is how.* The comparison, expressed in terms of the particle *kēn,* "so," which identifies the two points being compared, leads to the conclusion that "it," the food, is unclean. *it is defiled.* The conclusion is stated in the words of a priestly verdict: *ṭāmē' hû'*, "unclean is it!"[26] Haggai introduces a perspective on this uncleanliness of the people by stating that it is *in my sight* (*lᵉpānay,* lit. "before me"). Even if the people do not acknowledge this fact, it is known by the Lord.

Three main explanations are given of the intent of Haggai's conclusion. The moral explanation assumes the wrong attitude of the people toward the Lord as cause of their defilement. They were more inclined to further their own interests than to seek the kingdom of the Lord in the rebuilding of the temple. This moral and religious defilement affected the work of their hands and their offerings in a similar manner (so Calvin, Van Hoonacker, Mitchell, Chary, Ackroyd, May, etc.).

The second explanation concerns the cult and suggests that the cause of the defilement was the newly erected altar, which was unable, since 536 B.C., to sanctify the people, because the ruined temple evoked God's anger upon the people, their harvests, and their offerings (Wellhausen, Marti, Koch).

The third explanation is based on the anti-Samaritan interpretation, which explains *this people* and *this nation* as a reference not to the Jewish community but to the inhabitants of the province of Samaria, either the descendants of the ten tribes or of the foreign peoples who were resettled in that province. These "Samaritans" were eager to assist the Jews in rebuilding the temple, and eventually in participating in the sacrifices. Haggai rejected their proposal, however, because they were themselves contaminated by their syncretism (cf. 2 K. 17:29–41; Ezra 4:2) and therefore would have inevitably desecrated the temple (Rothstein, Nowack, Sellin, Horst, Deissler, Beuken, Rudolph), or the sacrifices (Elliger, Chary).

Although widely accepted, the third explanation cannot be maintained for the reasons we have already mentioned.[27] Haggai's reference to "this people" and "this nation" is in accordance with 1:2 and 2:4, and with the derogatory references to the defiled people in Jeremiah (cf. 6:19, 21; 7:28;

26. Beuken, op. cit., pp. 74–75, has a point in stressing the fact that the connection between *imago* and *res* does not lie in the comparison as such, but in the denunciation in terms of the declaration formulas: "impure is it," and "so" *(kēn).*

27. Deissler distinguishes two groups of people, consistent with the two questions pertaining to purity and impurity in vv. 12–13, dividing the people into a pure and an impure section (p. 495). Beuken, op. cit., identifies the *'ām* and the *gôy* by way of a hendiadys: the second word emphasizes a specific aspect of the first, with a *waw augmentativum* (cf. E. König, *Stilistik, Rhetorik, Poetik in buzug auf die biblische Literatur* [Leipzig: T. Weicker, 1900], pp. 160–61).

14:10, 11).[28] Elsewhere in the OT the terms *ʿam* and *gôy* are used synonymously for God's people.[29]

The very nature of the people's defilement is not mentioned but could be deduced from ch. 1: the people neglected the rebuilding of the temple, and thereby broke communication between themselves and the Lord (cf. Hag. 1:8; 2:9; Ezek. 36:22–38). Disobedience is the main reason for God's displeasure in their sacrifices. Salvation and blessings can only be expected when the Lord receives and retains the place of honor in the midst of the people. In this respect Haggai is in full accord with the criticism of the preexilic prophets concerning a sacrificial system and practice which does not comply with the covenant relationship with the Lord.[30]

15–19 Attention is now focused on the future, with a reminder (vv. 16–17), in parentheses and with reference to the preceding verses, of the people's past experiences. Verses 15 and 18–19 form an inclusio, emphasizing the theme that is expressed in v. 19b.[31]

28. Cf. K. Koch, "Haggai's unreines Volk," *ZAW* 79 (1967) 52–67; H. G. May, "'This People' and 'This Nation' in Haggai," *VT* 18 (1968) 190–97; T. N. Townsend, "Additional Comments on Haggai II 10–19," *VT* 18 (1968) 559–60. Beuken's argument, op. cit., p. 68n.2, that the reference to "this people/this nation" in the third person is in accordance with the prophetic *Gattung* against foreign nations, is valid in general but not conclusive in this context. He concedes that the same reference to "this nation" in 1:2 concerns Israel, but he assumes a difference in situation in the respective texts.

29. See Exod. 33:13; Isa. 1:4; 10:6; Zeph. 2:9; Ps. 33:13. See also A. R. Hulst, in *THAT,* II:290–325; Ackroyd, *Exile,* p. 167n.71. S. Talmon, "Synonymous Readings in the Textual Traditions of the OT," *Scripta Hierosolymitana* 8 (1961) 343, assumes two alternative readings: "so it is with this people," and "so it is with this nation." Cf. L. Rost, "Die Bezeichnungen für Land und Volk im AT," in *Festschrift O. Procksch,* ed. A. Alt, et al. (Leipzig: Deichert, Hinrichs, 1934), pp. 137–47.

30. Beuken, op. cit., pp. 71–74, says that Haggai denounced three things in his application of the priestly *tôrâ:* this people/nation, all the works of their hands, and what they have offered there. His conclusion, however, is that the half-heathen population was not allowed to participate in the rebuilding of the temple. The Chronistic editor later revealed the intent: the worship of the Samaritans is unacceptable. The essential aspect of the denunciation concerns the rebuilding of the temple. The work of their hands, therefore, concerns the building project as such. What they offered there is a later addition to the text. This ingenious conclusion of Beuken cannot be maintained, however. See the introduction to this pericope above.

According to Blenkinsopp, op. cit., p. 232, "the point, which concerned the entire community addressed rather than a section of it or a different group such as the Samaritans (Hag. 2:14; cf. 1:2), seems to be that whatever cult had been carried out since the destruction of the Temple had not rendered them acceptable to God but that, on the contrary, their polluted state had rendered their cult unacceptable." The reference is most likely to "syncretistic practices."

31. Rothstein's assertion that 2:15–19 was a salvation oracle at the beginning

"All the major problems [in the book of Haggai] come in the short section 2:15–19" (D. J. Clark). We will deal with the problems as we encounter them in the separate verses.

15 Haggai commences this section with *weʿattâ* (lit. "and now"). We have rejected the assumption that this word must be deemed a gloss which was introduced at a latter stage to link the two sections in the current arrangement (so Elliger, Horst, et al.). *Weʿattâ* is an integral part of Haggai's argument. It can be explained in a temporal sense, "now," "at the present moment" (cf. Num. 24:17; Mitchell), or as a conclusion drawn from the preceding statement and at the same time introducing a new thought. Both alternatives are appropriate here, with the emphasis perhaps on the second, in conjunction with its use in 1:5 and 2:4. The prophet draws his conclusion from the preceding instruction and application, implying that they must reflect on what they have experienced because of their impurity, and at the same time introducing the new thought on what the future will have in store for them.

consider this carefully (lit. "put your heart [on it])." This is an abbreviated form of the expression "put your heart on your ways" (cf. 1:5, 7), with the meaning "consider the relationship between your conduct and your experiences." The conduct was referred to in the preceding verses, and the experiences were implied in the conclusion that this people, with all they have achieved and offered, were impure (v. 14). In this context, however, the people's consideration is required for their new experiences, from now on and afterward.

A major problem in this context is the expression *from this day on (min-hayyôm hazzeh wāmāʿelâ).* The word *māʿelâ* can have a local sense, "above," "higher" (Deut. 28:43) or in connection with the age of a person, "older" (2 K. 3:21); in a temporal sense it usually refers to the future, "afterward" (1 Sam. 16:13; 30:25).[32]

According to Clark there are four main approaches to this problem.

1. It clearly points to the future. Most modern versions retain this meaning: "from this day onward" (RSV), "from this day and upward" (AV, RV), "from this day on" (NIV, with a note, "or 'to the days past'"). The

---

of the rebuilding of the temple has subsequently been endorsed by the majority of scholars. See Beuken, op. cit., pp. 208–16. On the other hand, K. Koch maintains that 2:15–19 originally formed a unit, in which the prophet declared the people as such, including the returned exiles, to be defiled, because they neglected the rebuilding of the temple.

32. There is not a single text where *māʿelâ* means "backward." So, correctly, also Beuken, op. cit., p. 209n.5. BDB, p. 751, allows for the possibility that the expression "from this day and upwards" could also imply "and back," but this hypothesis is not supported by GB, KB, Zorell, et al.

difficulty with this interpretation is that it hardly fits the description of the disillusionment with the food supplies in vv. 16 and 17.

2. The LXX and older Jewish and Christian scholars understood the phrase to mean "from this day backward," "and now look back over recent times down to this day."[33] This meaning would, indeed, fit the immediate context, which referred to past experiences. But this interpretation involves giving the phrase a meaning not found elsewhere, not even in 1 Sam. 30:25, and it is contrary to the meaning of the same expression in v. 18. LXX manuscripts have two different words: LXX B has *hyperánō,* "above," "before," and LXX A has *epánō,* "before," referring to both the past and the future, which is obviously an attempt to accommodate the problem phrase of v. 15 in its context.[34]

3. The difficulties with the above views have led other scholars to consider this phrase as a gloss, inserted from v. 18 by a copyist's error.

4. The fourth solution takes the phrase as referring to the future but assumes that the words "from this day onward" go only with the verb "consider." As it is rendered by JB: "Reflect carefully from today onward."

In order to decide which solution best fits the context, it is necessary to consider the main thrust of Haggai's message in this section, namely, to encourage the people with the blessing of the Lord, which they would experience "from now on and afterward" (v. 18). The problem phrase in v. 15a seems to anticipate the promise expressed in vv. 18 and 19, thereby forming an inclusio or a circular composition. The prophet starts his new thought *(wᵉʿattâ)* and ends his message with a perspective on the future, when God will again bless them. Van der Woude rightly compares the structure of 2:15–19 with that of 1:5–8. Just as 1:5b anticipates the command and promise of 1:7–8, 2:15a anticipates 2:18–19. The reference in 1:6 to the past adverse circumstances finds its parallel in 2:16 and 17: in both sections the promise of future blessings is contrasted with the past experiences of material malaise. Thus the best solution to this problem seems to be the last one: the people are encouraged to consider the new things to come, "from this day and onward." In vv. 16 and 17 they are reminded, parenthetically and by comparison, of their past experiences.

33. So JPSV, NEB, NAV, NBG, J. Ridderbos, Nötscher, Baldwin, Kittel (*Geschichte des Volkes Israel* [Stuttgart: 1929]). Van Hoonacker allows for this explanation, esp. in connection with v. 18, where he translates *māᵉʿlâ* "plus haut dans le passe" (cf. *Zorobabel et le second temple* [1891]; idem, *Nouvelles études sur la restauration juive apres l'exil de Babylone* [Gand: H. Engelcke, 1896]; idem, *Les douze petits prophètes* [Paris: J. Gabalda, 1906], p. 569).

34. This point of view is refuted by J. C. Matthes, "Miscellen," *ZAW* 22 (1903) 120–27.

The following phrase poses one of this section's major problems. It concerns the key word *miṭṭerem.* In this form, construed with the particle *min,* it occurs only here. The word *ṭerem,* with the meaning "beginning," is used in negative sentences as an adverb, "not yet," and in the sphere of past time to express actions and events which continued throughout a longer or shorter period, with the imperfect.[35] As a conjunction and preposition *ṭerem* is mainly used in the sense of "before." In our text *miṭṭerem* is used with the infinitive *śûm,* "to put, set, place."

To define the meaning of *miṭṭerem* in our text, it is necessary to establish its function in the context of Haggai's prophecy. The main issue is whether it refers to the past or to the future. It is obvious that this clause provides a narrower definition of time and is parallel to v. 15a. But what kind of parallelism is implied? If the parallelism is synonymous then both clauses may refer to either the past or the future. Referring to the past experiences of the people, *miṭṭerem* will have the meaning "before," or in its negative sense "not yet." Rudolph explains the particle *min* in its negative meaning of *ṭerem,* "not yet," "from-the-not-yet-being" (of the rebuilt temple). According to this explanation both clauses in v. 15 refer to what the people had experienced in the past: "And now look back over recent times down to this day: before one stone was laid on another in the Lord's temple" (NEB; cf. JPSV, NAV, etc.).

A second possibility is to have both clauses refer to the future. In this case *miṭṭerem* can only mean "immediately after," with *ṭerem* taken as a substantive in the sense of "beginning." Haggai's compatriots must turn their attention to the things that are going to happen "from this day and onward, from the beginning of the rebuilding of the temple" (so Van der Woude).

The parallelism between the clauses of v. 15 could also be antithetical, in which case the first clause would be taken to refer to the future and the second one, introduced by *miṭṭerem* in the sense of "before," to the past: "Now give careful thought to this from this day on—consider how things were before one stone was laid on another in the Lord's temple" (NIV).[36]

The ultimate solution of this problem must be found in the parallel structure of v. 18. With the exception of *Die Gute Nachricht* Bible, most modern versions render the different clauses of v. 18 in such a way that all of

35. For the adverbial use of *ṭerem* in a negative sentence, see GKC, § 152r; for its use with the imperfect to express continued action in the past, see GKC, § 107c.

36. According to Beuken, op. cit., v. 15b belongs to the parenthesis of the following verses, in which the attention is focused on the past. Cf. also Matthes, op. cit., p. 124.

them refer to the future: "Consider from this day onward, from the twenty-fourth day of the ninth month. Since the day that the foundation of the Lord's temple was laid, consider" (RSV; cf. NEB, NIV, JPSV, GN, NAV, etc.).

If our interpretation of v. 15 is correct, viz., that it anticipates what is clearly expressed in vv. 18 and 19, this verse must be explained accordingly. Verse 15b, therefore, reiterates v. 15a, providing a double dating. The people must consider what they will experience (a) from this day onward (v. 15a), that is, (b) from the beginning of the rebuilding of the temple (v. 15b). The difficulty with this explanation is that it does not seem to fit the description in vv. 16 and 17 of the people's past adverse circumstances. The solution to this problem is to consider vv. 16 and 17 as parenthetical (cf. Van der Woude, Koole, et al.).

from the time when one stone is laid on another in the Lord's temple. It is significant that the sanctuary is here referred to as *temple* (*hêḵāl;* cf. v. 18), and not "house" *(bayiṯ),* as elsewhere. In Zech. 8:9 both terms are used in a synonymous sense, but Ezra 3:9, 10 suggest a distinction between the main building, the *hêḵāl,* and the complex of buildings, the *bayiṯ* of the Lord (cf. Marti, Sellin, Koole). If this distinction is also implied here, it must be considered a distinction without a significant difference. The work on the main building had hardly started, and we may assume that the work on the outbuildings was at that time not even taken into consideration.[37]

The expression *one stone is laid on another* need not imply that the foundation was already laid (cf. v. 18). The function of this expression is to serve as a *terminus a quo,* referring to the time when the work on the temple actually and officially began. The purpose of this statement is not so much to furnish precise information concerning the building activities, but to mark the turning point in the people's experiences.

16 A major problem here is the opening word *mihyôṯām,* which seems to be the preposition *min* prefixed to the Qal infinitive of *hāyâ,* "to be," with the suffix of the third person plural. The difficulty concerns the word's meaning, authenticity, and context. The literal meaning is "since they were," which seems not to make sense. Therefore most scholars and modern versions follow the LXX in both emending the word and in joining it with the preceding statement. The LXX reads "what (manner of men) were you?" The emendations suggested are either *mah- hᵉyîṯem,* "how was it with

37. See also Rudolph, p. 45. He allows for the possibility that the *hêḵal YHWH* may be applied to the main building in contrast with the complex of buildings, but grants at the same time that it could have a meaning synonymous with "house"; cf. Zech. 8:9; Ezra 3:9–10. The issue is irrelevant, however; the rebuilding would inevitably start with the main building.

you?" (Nowack, Marti, Duhm, Smit, Ridderbos, Elliger, Mitchell, etc.; cf. *BHS*), or *mî-hᵉyîṯem,* "who were you"? (Budde, Sellin, Rudolph, Amsler, Koole, etc.). The questions imply that the condition of the people was discouraging before they began work on the temple, with the assumption that v. 15b refers to the past. This point of view is reflected in a number of modern versions: "how did you fare?" (RSV), "what state were you in?" (JB), "what was your plight?" (NEB); in other words, what sort of poor condition were you in? In all these instances the assumed context is the preceding verse. Clark's recommendation to translators is to join vv. 15 and 16 and number them 15–16, as it is done in the German Common Language Version, *Die Gute Nachricht* (cf. also NAV, RSV, NEB, etc.).

Our interpretation of v. 15 favors Van der Woude's solution to the problem. He emends *mihyôṯām* to *mahyôṯām,* "how they will be or become." The suffix "they" with the infinitive of *hāyâ,* "to be" or "to become," refers to the previously mentioned *days* (so also Hitzig, André, Von Orelli, Mitchell). Now that the rebuilding of the temple has started, a new period of time has begun, and the people's attention is drawn to how these days will be. According to this interpretation the first word of v. 16 is joined with v. 15, and especially with the opening exhortation of v. 15: "And now give careful thought . . . how they (the days) will become." This interpretation is in accordance with the structure of vv. 18 and 19a.

Before mentioning what the people will experience from this day onward, Haggai first reminds them of their past circumstances. The whole structure of his prophecy is based on the explicitly stated or implied antithesis between past and future in the people's experiences, as the direct result of their sinful negligence to rebuild the temple on the one hand, and God's initiatives on behalf of his temple and people on the other hand. That is why the topic of the people's past experiences can function appropriately within the context of the perspective on the Lord's subsequent blessing.

The prophet lets two examples suffice to explain the previous economic malaise. It concerns both food and drink. *(Before) if one came to a heap of twenty (measures), there were but ten; and if one came to a wine vat to skim off fifty (measures), the press would yield only twenty.* The Hebrew does not state what the "heap" was composed of, but the context makes it clear that food is in mind, and therefore "corn" (NEB) or "grain" (JPSV, note) is implied. The quantities in both instances are not explicitly defined.[38] The LXX mentions two specific measurements, the *sáta* (Heb. *sᵉʾâ*) and *metrētás* (Heb. *baṯ*). The point in question, however, is not so much the amounts but the difference between the people's expectation and what they

38. See GKC, § 134n.

actually got: the heap of corn in fact yielded only half the quantity that was expected from its bulk, and the wine vat yielded but 40 percent of what was rightfully expected. We agree with Clark (and Rudolph): "because it is the proportion which is in focus rather than the exact amount, it really does not matter much whether a translator uses a metric unit, an Anglo-Saxon unit, or a traditional unit from the language and culture of his readers." Most modern translations use the vague term "measures" for both the "corn" and the "wine" (cf. RSV, JB, NAV, NIV, JPSV).

wine vat. Hebrew *yeqeḇ* is strictly a wine press, "usually with two rock cavities, one above the other, connected by a channel, the upper for pressing, the lower for collecting."[39] Sometimes the reference is more specifically to the lower cavity of the wine press, the "wine vat" (Isa. 5:2); in other instances it defines both cavities together, or just the upper cavity, the "wine press" (Isa. 16:10; 2 K. 6:27).

Haggai also uses another word, *pûrâ,* which means the trough of a wine press (cf. Isa. 63:3, the only other place where it is used), but it may also include the vat underneath in which the juice is collected. Most scholars deem this word a gloss, intending to define *yeqeḇ* as a wine press rather than an oil press.[40] The JPSV, however, retains the word as part of the sentence and translates: "and if one came to a wine vat to skim off fifty measures, *the press* would yield only twenty," which makes sense. If the pressed grape juice is already in the wine vat, there could hardly be a divergence between expectation and reality, because the content of the "lower cavity" could have been precisely judged. The point, however, is that the amount of grapes in the upper cavity, in the "wine press," were such that it boosted the expectation, but in reality it yielded less juice than could rightfully have been expected. In the same manner, the grain had been of poor quality, and when threshed, had yielded less than the farmer would have expected when he saw the crop growing (cf. Clark).

The reasons for this discouraging experience are given in the following verse.

17 *I struck you—all the works of your hands—with blight and mildew.* The opening words of this verse occur also in Amos 4:9, and may even be a quotation from it.[41] The emphasis here lies on what God has done. He *struck* them. This word (the Hiphil of *nāḵâ*) is typical of the curses of the

39. See Holladay, *Concise Lexicon,* p. 141.

40. See n. 9 above; cf. Joel 2:24; Mic. 6:15; cf. also G. Dalman, *Arbeit und Sitte in Palästina,* IV:357 n. 11.

41. According to Beuken, op. cit., pp. 210–11, this verse also seems to be an interpolation, not because it is a free quotation from Amos 4:9, but because it was added to the judgment oracle of v. 16.

covenant (cf. Lev. 26:24; Deut. 28:22, 27, 28, 35; Mic. 6:13). *all the works of your hands.* Except for the pronoun, this phrase is the same as that translated "all the works of their hands" in 2:14. The reference is clearly to agricultural labor, and therefore the phrase can be translated "everything you tried to grow" (TEV).

Haggai mentions three of the immediate causes of the recent crop failures, thus adding one to the list mentioned in Amos 4:9: *blight and mildew and hail.* These are the instruments of God's judgment on his people.

blight. Hebrew *šiddāpôn,* from the verb *šāḏap,* "scorch" (by wind; cf. Gen. 41:6, 23, 27), means "scorching."[42] This term actually refers to the scorching effects of the hot east wind that sometimes blows across Palestine from the desert, and causes the grain to shrivel up (so Clark). The rendering "blight" is correct, though not strictly accurate. It denotes any disease or injury of plants resulting in withering, cessation of growth, and death of parts, like leaves, without rotting. The term "blight" emphasizes the result rather than the cause of the process of withering. Thus Clark may have a point in contrasting the "blight" and "mildew" as having been caused by opposite extremes of humidity: the one is a hot, dry wind, and the other a damp wind, perhaps from the Mediterranean.

mildew. The second term, *yērāqôn,* refers to a disease of the grain caused by a fungus which prevents it from ripening properly.[43] According to Van der Woude both drought and excessive rains can cause the disease of mildew.[44] The terms "blight" and "mildew" occur together elsewhere (Deut. 28:22; 1 K. 8:37; 2 Chr. 6:28), and, according to Clark, suggest extremes of dryness on the one hand and dampness on the other. His advice to translators is to render the phrase "I sent hot, dry winds to wither your grain, and damp winds to make it rot." This interpretation and translation emphasize the seriousness of the situation. The winds from the desert and from the Mediterranean will all be "ill winds," blowing nobody any good! From whichever direction the wind comes, it causes havoc with the crops.

hail (Heb. *bārāḏ*). In addition to the two main causes for crop failure, this third adverse weather condition is mentioned. It may also be associated with a wind blowing from the north (cf. Prov. 25:23). If the hail is heavy and accompanied by a strong wind, it can damage crops and even

42. See Deut. 28:22; 1 K. 8:37; 2 K. 19:26 par. Isa. 37:27 (according to 1QIs[a]); Amos 4:9; 2 Chr. 6:28. Se also Dalman, op. cit., II:333–34.

43. According to Dalman, op. cit., II:332, *Syringpais (scythris) temperatella.*

44. Van der Woude refers to J. Feliks, "Brand, Brnadkorn," in *Biblisch-Historisches Handwörterbuch,* 3 vols., ed. B. Reicke and L. Rost (Göttingen: Vandenhoeck & Ruprecht, 1962), I:269.

injure people and animals (cf. Exod. 9:25–35; Josh. 10:11). There is no reason to join "hail" with "all the work of your hands," and to consider it an addition by a glossator (so Van der Woude). "Hail" as an instrument of God's judgment is well attested both in history and prophecy (cf. Exod. 9:13–35 and Isa. 28:2).

yet you did not turn to me. The last part of Haggai's message is literally "there was not with you to me." There is no reason to emend this unusual form of expression. Driver notes a number of instances of similar Hebrew expressions. Thus in 2 K. 6:11 the king of Aram literally asked: "who from us to the king of Israel," that is, who is on the side of Israel's king. Hos. 3:3 has the awkward expression "even I with you," and Ezek. 36:9 reads "for I will (care) for you." Van der Woude rightly retains our text unchanged, and equates *'ên 'eṯᵉḵem,* "there was not with you," in meaning with *'ên kem,* "you were not." In *'eṯᵉḵem* the *'eṯ* syntagmeme functions as the subject of a noun sentence.[45] Van der Woude suggests the translation "but you did not (turn yourselves) to me." The renderings of the LXX, Vulgate, and Targum are essentially the same as that of the Hebrew text. Clark rightly observes that from a translator's point of view it does not matter greatly whether the text is emended, since the meaning is much the same either way. The NIV probably translates the Hebrew text as it stands: "yet you did not turn to me," while other translations (like RSV, JB, NEB, JPSV, etc.) translate the text as emended to conform to Amos 4:9: "yet you did not return to me." The difference is slight, and the meaning of either possibility is clearly expressed in plain language by TEV: "but still you did not repent." This indeed is the obvious meaning. That the opening words in v. 17 are (almost) the same as Amos 4:9 does not imply that the closing words must also be identical. The text-critical rule applies in this case also that preference must be given to the reading which is more difficult from the point of view of language and subject matter.[46]

According to Van der Woude v. 17 must be considered a later interpolation, because (1) the idea of the people's unrepentance does not comply with the rest of Haggai's message, especially in the context of a promise of future blessing; and (2) it is inconceivable that the cause of the curse on the land would be mentioned after the consequences have been stated. These and similar considerations are unconvincing, however. One of Van der Woude's main reasons for regarding v. 17 as a gloss is his conviction that the

45. See J. Hoftijzer, *OTS* 14 (1968) 76; P. P. Saydon, *VT* 14 (1964) 193, 207; J. Macdonald, *VT* 14 (1964) 270.

46. See E. Würthwein, *The Text of the Old Testament,* 4th ed., tr. E. Rhodes (Grand Rapids: Eerdmans, 1979), p. 116.

the whole section (vv. 10–19) was addressed to the priests only. The mention of agricultural products, therefore, would be inappropriate when the message was directed to priests. Admittedly, the motif of repentance does not figure explicitly in Haggai, but this does not exclude the implied assumption of repentance in the exhortation to "consider their ways" (1:5, 7; 2:15, 18).

Verse 17 ends with the words *says the Lord.* This is an additional emphasis on the fact that the words of the prophet were actually the message of the Lord.

18 Having looked back, Haggai now turns to his main theme, already alluded to in v. 15, and looks ahead *from this day onward.* The opening words of this verse are the same in Hebrew as those of 2:15, except for the first word in v. 15, *weʿattâ,* "and now," which is not repeated here.

The words *from this day onward* refer to the same day as that mentioned in 2:10, *the twenty-fourth day of the ninth month,*[47] that is, 18 December 520 B.C. Haggai states that this day was *the day that the foundation of the Lord's temple was laid.* According to Baldwin this is a solemn declaration, dated with the precision of a legal document. Once again Haggai sees the rebuilding of the temple as the event of crucial importance.

The reference to the laying of the "foundation" of the temple appears to clash with Ezra 3:10–13, which records a foundation-laying ceremony ca. 537 B.C. A number of scholars think that the narrative in Ezra 3 is mistaken and that no such ceremony took place at that time. At least Haggai and Zechariah seem not to have had any knowledge of such an event. Since the book of Haggai is reckoned as a good historical source, while the work of the Chronicler (in Ezra) is later and shows evidence of special interests, it has been assumed that Haggai's silence proves that there was no foundation-laying ceremony in 537 B.C. But this assumption is not very convincing. Ezra 4:1–5 states that because of the opposition of Judah's enemies the rebuilding of the temple was frustrated. The temple, therefore, remained and became progressively more of a "ruin," due to weather conditions, including winter rains. The question is whether Haggai (and Zech. 8:9, 10) refers to a newly laid foundation or to the new commencement of the rebuilding of the temple.

There are a number of considerations with regard to the solution of this problem. The laying of the foundation, mentioned in v. 18, must not be interpreted in a strict sense, as one would expect. It does not concern the

47. Since Rothstein the generally accepted view is that the date of v. 18b was an attempt to harmonize the text with 2:10. The same applies to the next date: "from the day. . . ." It is considered to be an epexegesis; cf. Beuken, op. cit., p. 210; also Rudolph, who regards "the ninth" to be an error.

original or primary laying of the foundation. The foundation of Solomon's temple apparently still remained intact, and there is no reason to doubt the historicity of the narrative in Ezra 3. Therefore, we must allow for a broader interpretation of the laying of the foundation. Wiseman points out that "more than one foundation ritual was commonly employed for building temples." In the case of the Jerusalem temple "it is likely that the first marked the subterranean foundation-laying and the second the first building at ground level as in ancient Mesopotamian practices."[48] Sellin's solution to this problem is that the restorer of a ruined building first searches for the original foundation (stone) and then provides his own foundation stone to lay alongside the other one. Baldwin and others hold that the word translated "lay the foundation" in Ezra 3:10–12 and Hag. 2:18 could be more accurately rendered "begin the restoration."[49] She believes that such a rendering would remove the apparent contradiction. Work did begin on the temple site in 537 B.C., only to cease shortly afterward until, as a result of Haggai's rebuke, it was resumed in 520 B.C. Baldwin's interpretation, of course, rests on the assumption that Solomon's temple was not razed to the ground but that much of the stonework remained intact after the fire (2 K. 25:9). The main need was for wood (Hag. 1:8) to replace what had been burnt. There was no question of relaying foundations (cf. Baldwin's Additional Note on "The day that the foundation of the Lord's temple was laid" [2:18]).

We agree with Clark that none of the presented views is without difficulties, but fortunately the translator does not have to resolve them. The Hebrew text, he says, is easy enough to understand and translate, and the translator should not try to alter it. This applies also to the interpretation of this text. The actual point in question is the rebuilding of the temple, as the event of crucial importance for the people in their relationship to the Lord. The laying of the "foundation" simply marks the actual and official commencement of the work on the temple, and this constitutes the *terminus a quo* of God's initiative to bless his people and of the people's own new experiences.

19 The Lord's pleasure (cf. 1:8) in the rebuilding of the temple will become evident from this day onward in the material blessings which he will bestow on his people.

48. Wiseman, in *NBC,* p. 784.

49. According to Rudolph, p. 46, *yāsaḏ* need not mean "to lay a foundation," but could imply the continued work, in the sense of restoration or renovation. He refers to A. Fernandez, *Bib* 2 (1921) 214; F. I. Andersen, *Australian Biblical Review* 6 (1958) 13ff.; and A. Gelston, *VT* 16 (1966) 232–35. A striking example of this meaning is found in 2 Chr. 24:27, where the restoration work of 24:4 is called *yᵉsôḏ*.

This verse also has a number of problems, but before we consider them it is appropriate to emphasize two points. First, the closing words of v. 19, "from this day on I will bless (you)," form the central theme of and climax to the whole paragraph 2:15–19. The second is that the earlier part of the verse, which contains the difficulties, must be interpreted in accordance with the plain sense of the later part (so Clark, correctly).

A prerequisite to the understanding of this verse is some knowledge concerning the climate and agricultural patterns of Palestine. Clark's summary is appropriate: "The summers extend from May to September, and are hot and almost completely dry. During this time, the main crops are harvested: wheat in May and June, and grapes in August and September. In October and November the early rains were expected. These softened the ground and allowed it to be ploughed and planted with grain seed for the following year's crop. During the winter months of December, January, and February, the weather grew colder, with rain at intervals, or even with snow. The farmers hoped for more rain in March or April to help the growing grain crops to mature well. Since the total rainfall over the whole year was not very great, even small decreases could have a severe effect on the crops, and cause real hardship to the people."

The first two phrases of v. 19 can be variously translated and pose interpretative difficulties. There are three main alternative translations. The first renders both phrases in the form of (rhetorical) questions: "Is the seed yet in the barn? Do the vine . . . still yield nothing?" (RSV). The second alternative renders the first phrase as a question and the second as a statement: "Is there yet any seed left in the barn? Until now, the vine . . . have not borne fruit" (NIV, NAV). According to the third alternative both phrases are rendered as statements: "take note while the seed is still in the granary, and the vine . . . have not yet borne fruit" (JPSV; cf. Groot NB, GN, TEV).

Is there yet any seed left in the barn? The answer to this question (lit. "is there yet seed in the grain pit?") could be either negative or positive. If the answer is no, we must still ask what the seed is and why it is not in the barn before we can understand the point of the question. Clark considers three different answers.

1. The seed is that which was gathered in the relatively poor harvest of the summer of 520 B.C., and it is not in the barn because there was so little of it that it has already been eaten. This interpretation fits the thought of vv. 16 and 17, but does not seem fully convincing, since it does not lead on well to the promise of blessing in the second half of the verse. If even the seed grain had been eaten, how could there be any harvest the following year?

2. The seed is that which is yet to be gathered from the harvest expected in the following summer of 519. It is not in the barn because there

has not yet been time for it to grow since the work on the temple was restarted. According to Mitchell, Haggai's argument in this connection is as follows: "You have not yet had a harvest since you began to work seriously on the temple. Do not be discouraged, for now that you have begun, you can be confident that the Lord will give you better harvests." This interpretation fits with the promise of blessing in the second half of the verse, but it is still not convincing because it does not follow well after vv. 16 and 17, and it makes the prophet ask the people what appears to be a silly question. Obviously in December the harvest of the following summer could not have been gathered in!

3. The seed is the seed grain remaining from the harvest of 520, and it is not in the barn because it has already been sown in the ground. This view is held by Cashdan and Baldwin. In this case, Haggai's argument would be: "You know what bad harvests you have had in the past [vv. 16–17]. But now consider the present. Since you started to rebuild the temple, the Lord has given enough rain to soften the earth and allow you to plant the seed for the next year's harvest [cf. also Marti, Van Hoonacker, Nötscher]. Take this as a sign of encouragement, for the Lord will certainly bless you with better harvests in the future." This interpretation fits both with the preceding verses and with the promise of blessing at the end of v. 19, and seems most probable according to Clark.

Clark goes on to discuss the possibilities if one takes the answer to this question as positive: "yes, the seed is still in the barn" (cf. AV: "Take note while the seed is still in the granary"; also Groot NB and GN).[50] In this case the "seed" must be the seed grain, as in answer (3) above, and if it is still in the granary, then it has not yet been planted. While this interpretation is grammatically possible, it does not fit well with the date of the prophecy in mid-December, since the sowing of the seed for the next year's harvest was normally done before then. If it had not been done by then, there could be little hope of a good harvest the following year, unless the promise "from

50. According to Beuken, op. cit., pp. 212–13, Rothstein showed the way: v. 19aβ establishes that the trees have not yet borne fruit. Then the same would apply to v. 19a: it must concern the adverse circumstances. Here Joüon (*Grammaire*, § 161b) suggests the simplest solution: the particle *h*^{a} has a *nuance exclamative*, an exclamatory meaning, "certes," "indeed." In this sense v. 19 is a confirmation *(Zugeständnis)* to the hearers. It is true that the infertility of the land still exists, but this must not lead to unbelief. Indeed, the seed is still in the granary; also the trees have not yet borne fruit, but from this day on the Lord will bless them. Beuken is adamant that the perfect of *nāśā'* cannot refer to the future; it refers to the conditions which prevailed up until now. This means that the first clause of v. 19 must also be explained in this sense (op. cit., p. 58n.1, and p. 212).

this day on I will bless you" really only will come into effect during 518, which seems to stress the actual thrust of the promise a bit too far.

In connection with this first question, it remains to note that *BHS* suggests that *migrāʿ*, "diminution," be read instead of *zeraʿ*, "seed," or that *nigraʿ*, "be reduced, lessened," be inserted (cf. Exod. 5:11: "your work will not be lessened in the least"). This last emendation is followed by NEB: "will the seed still be diminished in the barn?" (cf. JB). Presumably this is intended to mean "will you go on having bad harvests in the future?" Clark considers this rendering inappropriate and does not recommend it to translators.

The rendering and interpretation of v. 19b are also in dispute. To begin with we must consider three textual points. First, the interrogative particle which occurs with the first question is not repeated here. This of course need not be an insurmountable problem because the influence of the interrogative particle could also apply here. It is also grammatically possible to treat this second (implied) question as a negative statement: "Until now, the vine . . . have not borne fruit" (NIV; cf. RV). This interpretation coincides with the first answer to the rhetorical question of v. 19a: "Is the seed yet in the barn?" The assumption is that the various fruit trees have also not yielded any fruit (cf. André, Budde, J. Ridderbos). This interpretation fits with vv. 16–17 but makes for a very abrupt change to the promise of blessing at the end of v. 19. According to Van der Woude this interpretation is impossible.

The second textual point is that most modern translations follow the LXX in reading "still" (RSV, JB, NEB, NAV, JPSV, TEV) as the first word of the second question. This does not involve changing the consonants of the Hebrew text but simply supplying a different vowel: *ʿaḏ,* "to, until, during," becoming *ʿôḏ,* "again, still."

The third textual point is that several modern translations also follow the LXX in reading *nāśāʾ*, the word translated "yield" in the RSV, as a present participle rather than as a perfect tense.[51] Again, no change in the Hebrew consonants is involved. The effect of this reading is to give it a future rather than a past reference (RSV, JB, NEB, Moffatt). Clark concludes that these small emendations help to keep the two questions parallel with each other, and he recommends that translators accept them. According to him it seems better to regard v. 19 as containing two questions rather than one question and one statement.

51. So Nowack, Marti, Van Hoonacker, Duhm, Junker, Deissler; or as plural participle, Budde, Sellin, Deden, Horst.

The second question is then to be understood as "Do the vine . . . still yield nothing?" If the implied answer is no, then Haggai is saying in effect "The vines and fruit trees are looking in better condition now than they have looked for years at this time of year, December. You should therefore take hope for better yields in the future." This agrees with answer (3) to the first question, and helps to form an adequate link between vv. 16–17 and the promise of blessing in the last part of v. 19.

But if the implied answer to the second question is yes, the fruit trees still yield nothing, it would also seem to imply either negative answers (1) or (2) or else a positive answer to the first question. If the negative answers (1) or (2) are implied, then the resulting interpretation as a whole is open to the same objections as those answers. It also seems unlikely that the two questions would imply opposite answers. If a positive answer is to be given to both questions (as in JPSV: "take note, while the seed is still in the granary, and the vine . . . have not yet borne fruit"), then Haggai's argument would run: "take note now, even before the seed of the harvest of 519 has been sown, and before the fruit trees have started their spring growth, that the Lord has already promised to give you harvests in the future." Clark rightly comments that this interpretation forms an adequate link between vv. 16–17 and the promise of the future blessing, but that it does not fit with the stage of the agricultural cycle that would be expected in December. Rudolph's attempt to solve the problem by attributing to *nāśā'*, "to bear," the meaning "to sprout," is also contrary to the agricultural cycle, because in Palestine the time for fruit trees to bud is March-April.

Clark's best recommendation to translators in view of the bewildering variety of possible interpretations and combinations of interpretations is (a) to interpret both phrases as questions; (b) to supply a negative answer (3) to the first question; (c) to supply a negative answer to the second question; or (d) to translate the questions as statements and thus make clear what the implied answers are. He then suggests a possible translation base, which would bring out the meaning of the verse: "The seed grain is no longer in the barn but has already been sown. The grapevines, fig trees, pomegranates, and olive trees will not continue to give poor crops. From now on I will certainly bless you with good harvests."

Van der Woude arrives at the same interpretation, but with two alterations to the text. First, following the LXX he joins the last two words of v. 18 with v. 19, as is done in several modern translations, and reads: "Consider carefully whether there is still seed grain in the barn." The rain has already fallen, and the seed was already sown. This opens a perspective on the prospect of the blessing of a good harvest. This will become evident also with the olive tree: until now it did not yield its fruit, but from now on it will yield abundantly. According to Van der Woude (cf. *BHS*) the problem with other explanations is that they incorrectly regarded the words "the vine and the fig and the pomegranate" as being part of the original, whereas these words were added to the text.

The words *lōʾ nāśāʾ*, "has not borne," are really an asyndetical relative sentence in connection with *ʿēṣ hazzayiṯ,* "the olive tree." Thus the phrase "the olive, which has not borne fruit" constitutes a *casus pendans,* to which the following clause refers, but without the suffix of the object: "I will bless."[52] Van der Woude's suggestion is to read: "Consider carefully whether the seed grain is still in the barn. The olive tree also, that has not yet yielded fruit, I will bless from this day on."

We agree that the last words of v. 18 must be joined with v. 19. The people must consider carefully the nature of the surprising change that is about to occur: "Is the seed grain still in the barn?" The answer is no. But the same situation existed during previous seasons. The seed had been sown, but it yielded no crops because of the prevailing drought. This seed, which was already in the soil, will be blessed. The same (*weʿôḏ,* "and also," instead of *weʿaḏ,* "and to") applies to the grapevines and other fruit trees: until now they have not borne fruit. But consider this: From now on the Lord will bless them. There are no textual or other reasons for regarding the words "the vine and the fig tree, the pomegranate" as a gloss. The blessing of the Lord presupposes all the mentioned agricultural entities as general objects. To "bless" in this context refers primarily to agricultural success and amounts to providing an abundant harvest.

In this "blessing" the people again will experience the pleasure and loving-kindness of the Lord (cf. 1:8). Now that the rebuilding of the temple has started, the Lord will again look with favor upon his people and will manifest it in providing the crops they so dearly needed.

Along with the material blessings, the Lord will also cause something else to happen. They need not wait to hear what that would be. On the same day, the twenty-fourth of the (ninth) month, another prophecy was announced, this time concerning a new dispensation in which Zerubbabel would become the Lord's chosen signet ring!

God's promised blessings presuppose repentance and obedience. This is the general thrust of this passage. With reference to the official ruling of the priests pertaining to ceremonial purity and impurity, the prophet establishes that the people are unclean, and that everything they touch becomes unclean. It is important to note that the people's moral and religious

52. For this exception to the general rule see König, *Syntax,* § 341e; cf. 1 K. 14:11.

attitude is screened against the light of the priestly *tôrâ*. God's decrees and ordinances are the norm in establishing the correct relationship between the Lord and his people.

In his application Haggai confirms the people's impurity, which defiled whatever they have done and whatever they have offered. It is evident that they have continued with their sacrificial obligations by offering on the rebuilt altar, since the time of the exiles' first return (cf. Ezra 3:1–6). But these offerings had become impure! They were brought by unclean people! In a figurative sense, they had become unclean, because they were in contact with a corpse, in this case a ruined temple! Their disobedience and sinful negligence in rebuilding the temple were the cause of their defilement and of God's judgment (2:16, 17). The very heart of the matter was that they "did not turn to me" (2:17). Their covenant relationship with the Lord was directly and eternally affected by their failure to rebuild God's temple. The word of Samuel was applicable in the time of Haggai, as it was applied by the preexilic prophets:

> *Has the Lord as great delight in burnt offerings and sacrifices,*
> *as in obeying the voice of the Lord?*
> *Behold, to obey is better than sacrifice,*
> *and to hearken than the fat of rams.* (1 Sam. 15:22)

From the very day on which leaders and people again dedicated themselves to begin work on the temple, on the twenty-fourth day of the ninth month, the dạy when the foundation of the Lord's temple was laid, the blessing of the Lord would come into effect. "From this day on I will bless you" (2:19). Van der Woude rightly speaks of a *Realprolepsis* of the coming salvation in the promised abundance of harvest, and of a *Verbalprolepsis* in the announcement "I am with you" (1:13; 2:4).

The emphasis on the material blessings need not be considered inappropriate. The promise of 2:19 presupposes the curse which had rested upon the land, and it is therefore quite obvious that the blessing would entail a counteracting of that in the first place. But then, the promised *šālôm* (2:9) entails more than the expected abundance of harvests. It is true that the emphasis is laid upon material blessings, but the material blessings were in themselves proof of the restored relationship with God and a symbol and anticipation of the eschatological renewal of all things.

The history of this prophecy's fulfillment poses a problem. The promised blessing evidently did not materialize. In the time of Malachi, a few decades later, the people again suffered adverse economical circumstances. According to some scholars it is obvious that Haggai's prophecy was at fault. This conclusion is superficial, however, based as it is upon the assumption that the fulfillment of a prophecy must correspond literally and exactly with the terms of the promise. This assumption does not comply with the telescopic and epitomizing character of a prophecy, especially in its eschatological context. The promise of material blessings blends with the perspective on the ultimate bliss, with its varied applications centrally in the first and finally in the second advent of Christ.

In Haggai's prophecy, just as in that of Malachi (cf. 3:7–12), we must allow for the relationship between obedience and blessing. We agree in this regard with Van der Woude. According to him there is a correlation between the acts of God and those of man. One must not conceive of the renewal of the world in history as an unrelated act of God (*een sprong-gebeuren van Gods wege,* with reference to H. Berkhof). It is possible to obstruct God's salvation (cf. Mark 6:5; Acts 3:19). We are required to seek first his kingdom and his righteousness, with the promise that all these things will be given to us as well (Matt. 6:33).

The continuity in the message of this prophecy is to acknowledge and to appreciate the correlation between repentance and obedience on the one hand, and the promise of the eschatological salvation on the other hand. This is adequately expressed in Acts 3:19: "Repent therefore, and turn again, that your sins may be blotted out, that times of refreshing may come from the presence of the Lord" (cf. Van der Woude).

IV. ZERUBBABEL, THE LORD'S CHOSEN SIGNET RING (2:20–23)

20 *The word of the Lord came to Haggai a second time on the twenty-*
fourth day of the month:
21 *Tell Zerubbabel the governor of Judah: I am going to shake the*
heavens and the earth.[1]
22 *And I will overthrow the thrones of kingdoms and shatter the might of*
the kingdoms of the nations.[2] *I will overthrow chariots and their*
drivers; horses and their riders shall fall,[3] *each by the sword of his*
fellow.
23 *On that day, declares the Lord Almighty, I will take you, my servant*
Zerubbabel son of Shealtiel, declares the Lord, and I will make you
like a signet ring, for I have chosen you, declares the Lord Almighty.

Haggai's last recorded word[4] is addressed to one of the community's leaders, Zerubbabel, on the same day on which he had pronounced the previous prophecy (2:10–19), the twenty-fourth day of the (ninth) month. In traditional eschatological language, in terms of what he said before concerning the shaking of the universe and of the nations (2:6–9), Haggai again combines the cosmological with the military-political upheaval on the Lord's Day as a prelude to the ushering in of a new dispensation, in which Zerubbabel will become God's chosen man of the hour.

1. LXX adds "the sea and the dry land," in accordance with v. 6.

2. LXX adds "and I will overturn your entire might and I will erase your boundaries and I will strengthen my chosen one."

3. Cf. 1 Sam. 26:10; Isa. 34:7: "a descending" (into Sheol) is inappropriate because of the reference to the horses (so Rudolph).

4. Special literature on this pericope includes J. W. Rothstein, *Juden und Samaritaner,* pp. 42–52; E. König, *Die messianischen Weissagungen des Alten Testaments* (Stuttgart: Belser, 1923/1925), pp. 261–65; S. Mowinckel, *He That Cometh,* tr. G. W. Anderson (Oxford: Blackwell, 1956), pp. 119ff.; G. Sauer, "Serubbabel in der Sicht Haggais und Sacharjas," in *Das ferne und nahe Wort,* Fest. L. Rost, ed. A. Kuschke, BZAW 105 (Berlin: Töpelmann, 1967), pp. 199–207; K. M. Beyse, op. cit., pp. 52–58; K. Seybold, "Die Königserwartung bei den Propheten Haggai und Sacharja," *Judaica* 28 (1972) 69–78.

2:20–23 Zerubbabel, The Lord's Chosen Signet Ring

A structural analysis of this passage is as follows.

Sentence 1 (v. 20) consists of the messenger formula and date. Contrary to 1:1; 2:1, 10, the order of the elements here is first the messenger formula and then the date. The word of the Lord is directed "to" *('el)* Haggai, as in 2:10, and not "through" *(bᵉyaḏ)* him (cf. 1:1, 3; 2:1).

Sentence 2 (vv. 21, 22) has a number of embedded clauses:

2.0 The message of the Lord directed to Zerubbabel:

2.1 He will shake the universe (cf. 2:6b–7a).

2.2 He will overthrow royal thrones.

2.3 He will shatter the power of foreign kingdoms.

2.4 He will overthrow chariots and their drivers.

2.5 He will cause horses and their riders to fall in deadly combat.

It is important to note the following.

1. Sub-sentence 2.1 corresponds with 2:6b: The Lord is on the point of shaking (participle in the sense of a *futurum instans*) the heavens and the earth.

2. Contrary to 2:7, clauses 2.2 and 2.3 do not concern the wealth of the nations but the thrones, power, and kingdoms of the nations. The focus is different. In 2:7 the nations will contribute their wealth on behalf of the rebuilt temple, here their seats of power are overthrown and replaced to provide the necessary room for God's own representative.

3. Sub-sentences 2.2 and 2.3 form an extended parallelism. The same applies to sub-sentences 2.4 and 2.5, while sub-sentences 2.4 and 2.5 on the one hand are parallel to 2.2 and 2.3 on the other hand:

I will overthrow *[hāpaḵtî]* royal thrones (2.2)
I will overthrow *[hāpaḵtî]* chariots and their drivers (2.4)
I will shatter *[hišmaḏtî]* the power of foreign kingdoms (2.3)
(I will cause) horses and their riders to fall in deadly combat (2.5)

Sentence 3 (v. 23) also has a couple of sub-sentences:

3.0 The Lord Almighty declares that he will accomplish the following on that day:

3.1 He will adopt/take his servant Zerubbabel.

3.2 He will appoint him to be a signet ring.

3.3 He has chosen him for that reason.

It is important to note the following.

1. Sentence 3 is intimately connected with sentence 2, in the sense of cause and effect. The focus of the whole passage, therefore, is sentence 3, which in turn forms an inclusion with sub-sentence 2.0: "Tell Zerubbabel. . . ."

2. The position of the words "declares *[n^{e}'um]* the Lord Almighty" in sub-sentence 3.0 is exceptional. In general (cf. 1:9, 13; 2:4 [2 times], 8, 9, 14, 17, 23b, c) it concludes a preceding statement. In this case the position rather serves to emphasize the Lord as the one who makes this announcement, and to contrast him with the thrones and kingdoms of the nations. The Lord is the paramount subject, both in what he says and in what he does. To emphasize this fact, the formula "says the Lord (Almighty)" is repeated three times in sentence 3 (v. 23).

3. One of the four chiastic constructions in the book of Haggai (cf. 1:4, 9, 10) is found in sub-sentences 3.2 and 3.3:

I will set you — as a signet ring

For you — I have chosen.

The position of the preposition *b^{e}* with the suffix of the personal pronoun "you" at the beginning of sub-sentence 3.3 serves to emphasize the object of God's election: Zerubbabel!

The text of this section seems well preserved, with only minor variations, especially in the LXX. In v. 21 (MT 20) the LXX adds "the prophet" after Haggai, as is done elsewhere (cf. 1:1, 3, etc.). In v. 22 (MT 21) the LXX has a number of additions: "the son of Salathiel" after Zerubbabel, and at the end of the verse: "and the sea and the dry (land)," as in 2:7 (MT 6). In v. 23 (MT 22) the LXX renders "the thrones of kings" *(basiléōn),* instead of "the thrones of kingdoms." The Vulgate corresponds with the Hebrew text. The Targum renders "I have received you with pleasure," instead of "I have chosen you."

The background against which this prophecy must be interpreted is not so much the political and international turmoil caused by the accession to the throne by Darius, but rather, as Van der Woude rightly pointed out, the traditio-historical themes of the Day of the Lord and the restoration of the Davidic kingship.[5] In December 520 Darius had already conquered his enemies and restored peace in his realm (cf. Zech. 1:11). Of course, this need not exclude the possibility that the recent upheaval among the warring nations could have contributed to the imagery of v. 22. However, this prophecy is the second one on the same day, and no reference is even implied to the international scene in the previous section (2:10–19).

On the other hand, the idea of God's final and ultimate intervention

5. Cf. Beyse, op. cit., p. 54: both 2:21–23 and 2:6–9 are the result of a theophany in the interest of the people.

on behalf of his people forms an integral part of the whole texture of prophecy and is therefore not a foreign element in the work of Haggai. As was the case in 2:6–9, this prophecy reflects Haggai's eschatological *Naherwartung*.[6] The prophetic "time" (Gk. *kairós*) is imminent. Israel's ultimate restoration is at hand. A branch from the root of Jesse, the dynasty of David (Isa. 11:1), will bear fruit. Zerubbabel is projected on the screen as a representative of the coming Messiah, perhaps as being the Messiah.

The fact that the subsequent history had not verified the validity of this expectation need not imply a prophetic error. The fulfillment of prophecy is a complex matter; many times it occurs in stages, the one after the other. As time passed, and Zerubbabel was not honored as had been expected, the messianic hopes were transferred via his descendants, until they were fulfilled centrally in the first and will be fulfilled finally in the second coming of Christ.

It is important to note that the religious leader of the community, Joshua, does not figure in Haggai's eschatological expectation, as is the case with his contemporary, Zechariah. According to Van der Woude this was because Haggai expressed a certain criticism of Joshua (2:4) and was also aware of the priest's negligence in rebuilding the temple. This assumption seems unconvincing, however. In 2:4 the prophet's encouragement involves both leaders and people, without any distinction, and the lack of dedication among the priests was something they shared with the people and with Zerubbabel!

Perhaps Joshua was excluded from this prophecy because he was already included in the prophecy concerning the restoration of the public worship and the proposed rebuilt temple. The other main aspect of the future restoration was that of the kingdom of Israel, under a descendant of David. Cult and kingdom are integral parts of the one perspective on the great future.

20 For the last time the word of the Lord came *to* (*'el;* cf. 2:10) Haggai. This prophecy was on the same day as that addressed to the people in the previous section, that is, *on the twenty-fourth day of the (ninth) month* (cf. 2:10), which was identified in 2:18 as the day on which the "foundation" of the Lord's temple was laid.[7] We may, therefore, assume that the two prophecies had a bearing upon one another, perhaps in a twofold manner. First, they were pronounced on the same festive occasion, the actual and

6. Cf. K. Frör, *Weg zur Schriftauslegung* (Düsseldorf: Patmos, 1968), pp. 149–52.

7. The structure of the date is the same in Ezek. 24:1: word-event-date. So Beuken, op. cit., pp. 24 and 78.

official commencement of work on the temple, and second, both reflect the contours of God's blessing on his day. Van der Woude seems right in rejecting the generally accepted transposition of 2:15–19 to the end of 1:12–15a, and of the anti-Samaritan interpretation of 2:10–14, because nothing in 2:20–23 suggests such a problem.[8] The content of 2:20–23 cannot adequately be explained from the contemporary history, but rather has its basis in the traditio-historical theme of the Day of the Lord. The relationship between 2:10–19, as a literary unit, and 2:20–23 must be interpreted within the scope of the coming time of ultimate salvation and blessing. Now that the temple is being rebuilt, the people of the Lord may rightfully expect material blessings, but this would be just the beginning of the great renovation, when the thrones and powers of the enemies of Israel would be overthrown to provide room for the reign of God's chosen representative.

21 The prophecy is explicitly addressed to *Zerubbabel the governor of Judah.*[9] The LXX is consistent in harmonizing the different verses by adding "son of Salathiel" (cf. 1:1, 12, 14; 2:2). This time Zerubbabel is not reminded of the people's lack of interest in rebuilding the temple (1:1–3), his spirit is not being stirred up by the Lord (1:14), he is not encouraged to take heart (2:4) nor to assist in rebuilding the temple. In this prophecy Zerubbabel is not the object of the Lord's exhortation but the central figure. He is not only the recipient of God's unbelievable message but is himself the very focal point of its intent.[10] This is why v. 21a and v. 23 are structurally and substantially a unit.

Zerubbabel, the governor *(peḥâ)* of Judah, that well-known political leader of God's postexilic community, is the recipient of an overwhelming message. The Lord is going to repeat all his wondrous acts in the history of his people, now in an eschatological context, on behalf of Zerubbabel! In this astounding process he will shake heavens and earth, overthrow royal

8. Rothstein's contention is that this prophecy was inspired by the negative reaction Zerubbabel had experienced because he, following the directives of Haggai in 2:10–14, had rejected the proposal of the Samaritans to participate in the rebuilding of the temple (cf. Ezra 4:1–3). Because Zerubbabel obeyed the message of the Lord, he was elevated to the position which his disobedient grandfather Jehoiachin had forfeited (Jer. 22:24), becoming the Lord's signet ring. Cf. also Beuken, op. cit., p. 78.

9. There is no textual evidence to suggest that this title is an anachronism, added at a later stage of the transition of the text, contra Beuken, op. cit., p. 79.

10. Beyse, op. cit., p. 53, is of the opinion that Haggai addressed this prophecy to Zerubbabel in his absence, just as the prophets generally spoke about kings when they were absent. This point of view is possible but not decisive. Prophets had occasionally addressed themselves to the kings in person (cf. Nathan and David)!

thrones, shatter the power of foreign kingdoms, overthrow chariots and their drivers, and cause horses and their riders to fall in deadly combat.

First of all, God is *going to shake the heavens and the earth.* This announcement corresponds literally with 2:6a. In keeping with its general tendency to harmonize, the LXX adds "and the sea and the dry (land)," as in 2:6b. The Hiphil participle *marʿîš,* "cause to tremble," "shake (violently)," is here, as in 2:6 and elsewhere (cf. Zech. 2:13; 3:8; Isa. 3:1; 7:14; Jer. 30:10; etc.), used in the sense of a *futurum instans.* The action or event which it introduces is presented as imminent.[11] Here also the terminology belongs to the epiphany[12] during the holy war, when the Lord intervenes on behalf of his people, or in this case, in favor of his chosen signet ring. The cosmological events are an integral part of the Lord's ultimate and final act on his day and emphasize the sureness and seriousness of his intervention on that day.

22 The second and third acts of the Lord are expressed by an extended parallelism.

I will overthrow the thrones of kingdoms
and shatter the might of the kingdoms of the nations.

In this way one idea is expressed in a twofold manner; the second merely elaborates on the first. The Lord is in the act of annihilating the power bases of world empires, in order to establish the universal and absolute rule of his own representative, Zerubbabel.

overthrow. The Hebrew verb *hāpaḵ,* "turn (over on the other side)," "overturn," is repeated in this verse. In connection with the destruction of Sodom and Gomorrah (cf. Gen. 19, esp. vv. 21 and 25) it has become a Leitmotif in prophecies of doom (Sellin), such as Deut. 29:22 (Eng. 23): "It will be like the destruction *[keмahpēḵat]* of Sodom and Gomorrah, Admah and Zeboiim, which the Lord overthrew *[hāpaḵ]* in fierce anger" (NIV; cf. Isa. 1:7–9; Jer. 20:16; Amos 4:11; Lam. 4:6).

the thrones of kingdoms. The Lord will overturn *kissēʾ mamlāḵôṯ,* literally "the throne of kingdoms" (so RSV, NBG). Following the LXX, some modern versions have "the thrones of kings" (NEB, NAV; cf. NIV,

11. See GKC, § 116p.

12. See Th. C. Vriezen, *Hooflijdnen der Theologie van het Oude Testment,* 4th ed., p. 206 (= Eng. 2nd ed., p. 190), for a distinction between epiphany and theophany: theophany denoting God's immediate appearance to a human being, epiphany referring to God's appearance in order to vindicate his people. Vriezen refers to F. Schutenhaus, "Das Kommen und Erscheinen Gottes im AT," *ZAW* 41 (1964) 1ff.; C. Westermann, *Das Loben Gottes in den Psalmen,* 5th ed. (Göttingen: Vandenhoeck & Ruprecht, 1954), pp. 65ff. (= *The Praise of God in the Psalms,* tr. K. Crim [Richmond: John Knox, 1965], pp. 93–101).

Groot NB, Gute NB). But *mamlāḵâ* denotes a "kingdom," "dominion" (cf. Gen. 10:10; plur. in Deut. 28:25), and in the sense of an adjective, "the royal city" (1 Sam. 27:5), "a temple of the kingdom" (Amos 7:13). It may also be used in the sense of "king" (1 Sam. 10:28). Here we have a compound idea, with a substantive *kissē*ʾ, "chair," "seat of honor," "throne," followed by a genitive, *mamlāḵôṯ*. The compound idea must be expressed in the plural, because the plural of the *nomen rectum* is used; hence it should be translated not "the *throne* of kingdoms" (RSV) but "the *thrones* of the kingdoms" (JPSV).[13] It concerns the symbols of political and military power of the world empires. They will be overthrown and destroyed.

This idea is emphasized in the second part of the parallelism: *and shatter the might of the kingdoms of the nations.* The Hiphil of the Hebrew verb *šāmaḏ,* "exterminate," "destroy," is elsewhere used to denote God's judgment against the nations, in order to make room for other nations (Deut. 2:20–23), but especially for his own people (Deut. 9:1–6; Amos 2:9; Zech. 12:9). In this case the Lord will exterminate the *might* (or "strength," Heb. *ḥōzeq*) of the kingdoms of the nations. This reference must not be confined to the military power of the world empires (cf. Amos 6:13), although this is also implied. As an extended parallelism of v. 22a, it rephrases, by way of explication (so König), the *thrones* or power bases of the kingdoms, and this includes every aspect of their political, economical, international, and military might. *Kingdoms* of v. 22a is here explicated as *the kingdoms of the nations* to emphasize their identity over against the people of the Lord. In Jehoshaphat's prayer (2 Chr. 20:6–12) he acknowledges God's rule over all "the kingdoms of the nations," and that "power" *(kōaḥ)* and "might" *(gᵉḇûrâ)* are in his hand. He also mentions that God has displaced these nations in order to give this land forever to his people. The new act of God in the near future will, therefore, be in full accord with his mighty acts in the past on behalf of his people.

Throughout history the kingdoms of the nations have executed their might by way of military feats in conquering other nations, including the people and kings of Israel. An aspect and symbol of that military force were *chariots and their drivers, horses and their riders.* These will be overturned *(hāp̄aḵ)* by the Lord, and horses and their riders *shall fall (yāraḏ),* while the men are fighting among themselves. The motifs and imagery of this prophecy are derived from God's intervention in the history of his people. He hurled Pharaoh's chariots and army into the sea (Exod. 14:25; 15:4, 21; Isa. 43:17), and routed Sisera and all his chariots and army (Judg. 4:15); in Gideon's war against the Midianites the Lord caused the men throughout the

13. See GKC, § 124p-r.

camp to turn on each other with their swords (Judg. 7:22). The motif is again clearly that of the holy war, especially in its eschatological context. In Zech. 12:4 it is announced that the Lord will strike every horse with panic and its rider with madness. He will blind all the horses of the nations. This will happen "on that day," when Jerusalem's enemies will be destroyed. The verb *yārad̲,* usually meaning "go down," has a varied application, but means here "will go down in the slaughter" (so Jer. 48:15; cf. Isa. 34:7). They will be slain.

each by the sword of his fellow. These words, here translated literally, are deemed to be a gloss *(BHS),* because of the parallelism with v. 22c and because "horses do not carry swords" (Duhm). This objection, however, is too much in accordance with Western logic. In the situation of war, the fighting is first of all among men, but in its destructive force it also involves the horses. It is true that the parallelism is adversely affected by this phrase, but at the same time it represents a well-established motif in the context of the holy war (cf. Judg. 7:22; 1 Sam. 14:20; Ezek. 38:21; Zech. 14:13).

It is important to note that the initiative of this fivefold act rests completely with the Lord. He will cause all these things to happen. There is no mention of a third party, not even of the military feats of his own people. He alone is responsible for providing the scene on which his representative can operate with dignity and effectiveness. "The fact that Judah is small and defenceless makes no difference when God says *I will overthrow.* He will act, and Judah will not need to fight" (Baldwin).

23 What the Lord will do to the universe and the power bases of the foreign kingdoms (vv. 21b–22) concerns Zerubbabel. This is the focus of this passage and one of the main themes of the prophecy of Haggai (so also Van der Woude).[14] To endorse this, the self-revelation of the Lord is expressed three times in v. 23.

The vocabulary continues to have special significance (Baldwin). The expression *On that day* refers to God's incisive intervention on behalf of his representative (vv. 21–22) and has an eschatological context.[15] When the Lord has overthrown the world empires, he will *take (lāqaḥ)* Zerubbabel. The Hebrew verb is used here, as elsewhere (Gen. 24:7; Exod. 6:6 [Eng. 7]; Deut. 4:20; Amos 7:15; etc.), in the sense of special election,[16] though not in a dogmatic sense but rather in the sense of adoption, of appointing him to be

14. See also Beuken, op. cit., pp. 69, 80; Beyse, op. cit., p. 57.

15. It must not be considered a (mere) "editorial connective formula"—so P. A. Munch, *The Expression "Bajjom Hahu,"* Avhandlinger utgitt av Det Norske Videnskaps-Akademi I (Oslo: 1936), pp. 15–57.

16. So, correctly, Beuken, op. cit., p. 80.

a special representative of the Lord among his people. It is not necessary to deny this meaning of the word "take," as is done by Van der Woude. According to him the element of election is already expressed in the designation of Zerubbabel as "my servant" and in the affirmation "I have chosen you." The semantic field of all the words and expressions used is virtually the same: Zerubbabel is singled out for a special relationship with God and for an important function. He is "taken" by the Lord, he is the "servant of the Lord," appointed to be his "signet ring," for God has "chosen" him.

Zerubbabel son of Shealtiel is emphatically called *my servant (ayaḇdî)*. When referring to a single person, this title is especially applied to David (cf. 1 K. 11:34; Ps. 78:70ff.; Ezek. 34:23; 37:24) and also to "the servant of the Lord" in Isa. 40–55. The figure of the "servant" presupposes the idea of the favorite confidant of the king, one who remains in the vicinity of the king, who knows the mind and wishes of the king, and who executes the confidential assignments of his master. Without mentioning David or the Davidic dynasty, the idea is evidently implied. Zerubbabel will be more than a governor of Judah, he will be heir to the throne of his forebear and predecessor David, because he will have an absolute and universal reign. For that reason God has annihilated the thrones and the power bases of the kingdoms of the nations. Verse 23 is an antithetic parallel to vv. 21 and 22. In vv. 21–22 the subject matter was the thrones and might of the kingdoms of the nations; here, in v. 23, the thrones are not mentioned but clearly implied: Zerubbabel will become the messianic king in their stead!

We agree with Deissler and others that v. 23 represents a deliberate ambiguity. It does not say that Zerubbabel will become a king, nor does it elaborate on the scope and character of his rule. It must be remembered, however, that Haggai could not have propagated the idea of a new king in the context of the Persian empire. But this does not mean that Haggai has depoliticized the messianic expectation (contra Koole). Zerubbabel's kingship is not mentioned *expressis verbis*, but it is clearly implied.[17]

17. See Beyse, op. cit., pp. 58–64: "The origin of the expectation of a king in Haggai." The terms for a king, viz., *meleḵ, nāḡîḏ, nāśî'*, and *śar*, do not occur. The reason why the term *meleḵ*, indicating the ideal king, is shunned, is that the kingship of the preexilic kings has been discredited. This "king" will be subordinated to God, being his signet ring and servant. His election refers to the promises made to David (cf. 1 Sam. 16:8–10; 2 Sam. 6:21; 1 K. 8:16; Ps. 78:70; 1 Chr. 28:4); concerning the content of the promise, see 2 Sam. 7. This implies that the election of Zerubbabel concerns not only his person but also his descendants. If this deduction is correct, Zerubbabel could not have been conceived of as the Messiah (so Mowinckel, *He That Cometh*, p. 119; and R. T. Siebeneck, "The Messianism of Aggaeus and Proto-Zacharias," *CBQ* 19 [1957] 326; see Beyse, op. cit., p. 59n.3: "Because Zerubbabel was promised posterity, he could not have been 'the Messiah' "). This deduction and conclusion are arbitrary, however. The text itself represents Zerub-

I will make you like a signet ring. God will "set up," "appoint" (Heb. *śûm,* lit. "set") Zerubbabel as a signet ring. He will not actually become a signet ring, but will be "like" *(kᵉ)* one. A signet ring was so precious that, to guard it against theft or misuse by an unauthorized person, it was usually worn on a chain around the neck, or as a ring on the right hand. In Cant. 8:6 the bride beseeches her lover to set her "as a seal [signet ring] upon your heart, as a seal upon your arm." A use parallel to the sense of Cant. 8:6 is found in an Egyptian lovesong:

> *Oh, if I only were your signet ring*
> *that were (put on your finger)*
> *(there it would guard me)*
> *like something which gives you a beautiful life.*[18]

The seal or signet ring (Heb. *ḥôṯām*) was a symbol of authority. All official documents were authorized with the king's seal (cf. Esth. 8:10). In 1 K. 21:8 Jezebel wrote letters in Ahab's name and sealed them with his seal, thus endowing them with the authority of the king himself. It is important to note that the Judean king Jehoiachin was designated to be the signet ring on the Lord's right hand (Jer. 22:24). In his case, however, he was rejected. Now in our text the situation is reversed. Zerubbabel will be appointed to be the Lord's signet ring. This vivid figure of the signet ring attested to the renewed election of the Davidic line, represented by Zerubbabel, the person in whom God had again invested the authority, promised to David and his dynasty. Thus, the historical governor of Judah is elevated to fulfill his God-appointed destiny within the context of the coming and imminent future dispensation.

This explanation is shared by most scholars.[19] Junker, however, favors a purely historical context. Because the Lord will break the might of the nations, Zerubbabel need not be afraid: he will protect him as a signet ring. Thus he may continue rebuilding the temple without fear of the intrigues and hostility of his enemies. We agree with Van der Woude that this interpretation is contrary to the eschatological context of v. 23 and to the terms used, which are typical for the election of King David.[20]

---

babel as God's chosen one, within an eschatological context. That he was not the Messiah can only be deduced from the history of this prophecy's fulfillment.

18. For a German translation, see G. Gerleman, *Ruth/Das Hohelied,* BKAT 18 (Neukirchen-Vluyn: Neukirchener, 1965), p. 217.

19. According to D. Winton Thomas, Zerubbabel was destined to become the vice-regent of God on earth. Cf. Beyse, op. cit., p. 57, "he will be the Lord's vizier."

20. According to Beuken, op. cit., p. 81, v. 23b is a Chronistic verification of Zerubbabel's election, in terms of an expression which is typically although not

The crisis of the end-time, which is the context of this prophecy, is God's work. "He makes wars cease to the end of the earth; he breaks the bow, and shatters the spear, he burns the chariots with fire!" He admonishes the nations to acknowledge him as the Exalted One in the earth (Ps. 46:10–11 [Eng. 9–10]). The people of the Lord are but spectators, and all they can do is to encourage themselves to "behold the works of the Lord" (Ps. 46:9a [Eng. 8a]).

This has a specific application to our prophecy. The thrones, as symbols of the power bases of the kingdoms of the nations, along with their armed forces, will be annihilated in God's final judgment. This will be solely the work of the Lord. We agree with Van der Woude that the "thrones" mentioned in vv. 21–22 must not be restricted to the Persian empire but must be seen in an eschatological context.

The same applies to the prophecy concerning Zerubbabel: it has a wider perspective than the person of the Judean governor as a contemporary of the prophet. In the context of the eschaton the figure of the messianic king, as plenipotentiary of the Lord, has his place.[21] According to Van der Woude, he is the representative of the theocracy (cf. Ps. 72:1). In Zerubbabel, Haggai detected the *rector designatus* of God. Thereby he has legitimized the promise of the prophecy in 2 Sam. 7 concerning "the house of David," in a time when the idea of a Davidic king seemed to have been disregarded.[22] The messianic dignity in the eschatological future belonged to "the house of David." That is why it was said that God had already chosen Zerubbabel.[23]

---

exclusively Chronistical, of the election of the son of David. See also Th. C. Vriezen, *Erwählung Israels* (Zürich: Zwingli, 1953), pp. 36–50.

21. Beyse, op. cit., pp. 59–64, detects three trénds in the exilic and postexilic literature concerning the future ruler: (1) Among the prophets of the Exile, only Ezekiel expected a future ruler (see S. Herrmann, *Die prophetischen Heilserwartungen im Alten Testament,* BWANT 85 [Stuttgart: Kohlhammer, 1965], p. 269; contra W. Zimmerli, *Ezekiel,* Hermeneia, 2 vols., tr. J. D. Martin [Philadelphia: Fortress, 1979–83], II:277–79). (2) The Persian king Cyrus is highly regarded (see O. Plöger, *Theokratie und Eschatologie,* WMANT [Neukirchen-Vluyn: Neukirchener, 1959], p. 45 = *Theocracy and Eschatology,* tr. S. Rudman [Richmond: John Knox, 1968], pp. 42–43). (3) The idea of the rehabilitation of Jehoiachin according to 2 K. 25. Note also Beyse's remark that the idea of the reinstitution of the kingship did not function in the events ca. 520 B.C.

22. See K. Baltzer, "Das Ende des Staates Juda und die Messiasfrage," in *Studien zur Theologie der alttestamentlichen Überlieferungen,* Fest. G. von Rad, ed. R. Rendtorff and K. Koch (Neukirchen-Vluyn: Neukirchener, 1961), pp. 33–43.

23. Cf. n.17 above.

Van der Woude agrees with the majority of scholars that Haggai was mistaken in the person of the anointed one. Zerubbabel vanished from the scene soon after Haggai's prophecy was announced. But then Van der Woude rightly points out that with this evaluation not everything has been said. The prophecy concerning Zerubbabel was inspired by the quest for the legitimate king of the future.[24] Even after the demise of Zerubbabel, this expectation remained the perspective on the chosen "Son of God," to whom will be given dominion over all the nations of the earth (Pss. 2, 110; Matt. 28:18; Phil. 2:9–11; Heb. 1).

Van der Woude is also correct that the interpretation of the prophecy concerning Zerubbabel does not justify a typological exegesis, according to which Zerubbabel is seen as a foreshadowing of Jesus of Nazareth. If the prophecy is to be interpreted christologically, then the emphasis is, according to him, more on the second than on the first advent of Christ.

We may concede this interpretation, but then we would like to add that this perspective is according to the very nature of prophecy. Its content is projected on the ultimate and the final stage of God's intervention in history, with all its universal and cosmological aspects. The history of the fulfillment, however, reveals a salvation-historical dimension, which can only be ascertained in the light of Christ's vicarious work on the cross. In Rom. 1:1–4 Paul defines the gospel of God as that "which he promised beforehand through his prophets in the holy scriptures, the gospel concerning his Son, who was descended from David according to the flesh and designated Son of God in power according to the Spirit of holiness by his resurrection from the dead, Jesus Christ our Lord" (cf. Matt. 1:6–16; John 7:42).

The question whether Haggai had identified Zerubbabel with the promised Messiah may be left open. In Zech. 3:8 and 6:9–15 there seems to be a differentiation. The fact remains, however, that the promises concerning Zerubbabel were an actualization of the promise that the Messiah would be a descendant from the house of David (cf. Matt. 1:6–16; Luke 3:27).

The splendor of the new temple and the glory of the throne of David will, amid the turmoil in nature and among the nations, be fulfilled in Christ, centrally at his first and finally at his second advent. In this prophecy Haggai

24. Blenkinsopp, op. cit., p. 236, endorses this point of view: "Like other examples of the disconfirmation of eschatological predictions, in the Bible as elsewhere, the outcome was not complete collapse of the hopes entertained but rather a reassertion of goals, a rescheduling of the expected millennium"; he refers to R. P. Carroll, *When Prophecy Failed: Cognitive Dissonance in the Prophetic Traditions of the Old Testament* (New York: Seabury, 1979), pp. 157–83.

and his contemporaries were again encouraged that God would complete the good work that he began. The rebuilding of the temple and the reestablishment of the Davidic dynasty must be interpreted and evaluated in the context of this work of God.

In sum, the theme of this passage is God's signet ring applied to (1) Zerubbabel, (2) Christ, and (3) the Church.

The Book of
MALACHI

INTRODUCTION

I. SIGNIFICANCE AND CONTENTS

The great importance of the book of Malachi is generally acknowledged. It belongs to the Minor Prophets, so-called not because they are of less importance than Isaiah, Jeremiah, and Ezekiel, but, as Augustine expressed it, "because their message is comparatively short."[1] In this collection of Minor Prophets Malachi has always been placed last, again not because it was considered the least important of the Twelve, but because according to tradition it concluded the series of prophetic books. It was considered the "transition link between the two dispensations," "the skirt and boundary of Christianity" (Tertullian). The Jews referred to Malachi as the *ḥōṯam hanneḇî'îm*, "the seal of the Prophets," and as *'aḥărôn šeḇāhem*, "the last among them."

In the Bible we have a number of "last words." We may refer to those of Jacob (Gen. 49), Moses (Deuteronomy), Joshua (Josh. 23, 24), David (2 Sam. 23), Paul (2 Tim. 4), and Jesus (John 13–16). These, of course, were the last words of individuals. With Malachi, however, it was different. His prophecies were likely not his personal "last words." Yet his book as such contains the last words of a whole generation, a generation of prophets through whom God had revealed himself to his people in a unique way. With Malachi these instruments of God's revelation concluded their task and were dismissed from office until the time of the fulfillment not only of the Law but also of the Prophets (Matt. 5:17), in the advent of the great Prophet, our Lord Jesus Christ.

A careful study of the book of Malachi does not disappoint our expectations. In his own way he proclaims the word of God to his people, with an eye on their past, present, and future. He reminds them of the enduring love of God, of his sovereign election and divine covenant down through the generations (1:2–5); he rebukes the sins of the people and priests with respect to the public worship (1:6–2:9), to mixed marriages and di-

1. Augustine, *De Civitate Dei,* 18:29.

vorces (2:10–16), to their heretical theological concepts (2:17–3:5), and to their negligence of the compulsory contributions to the temple worship (3:6–12); and he proclaims the advent of the Day of the Lord (3:13–21 [Eng. 4:3]). In addition he reminds them of the law of Moses and the coming of the prophet Elijah (3:22–24 [Eng. 4:4–6]).

One should not condescend to a subjective comparison of the significance of the different books of the Bible, but one can assert positively that the preaching of the book of Malachi delves into matters that are fundamental for all time and therefore conveys an important message even to us and our generation.

II. TITLE AND AUTHOR

Each book of the OT has its own peculiar problems with matters of introduction. The most obvious problem with Malachi is undoubtedly the question whether the name *Malachi* should be regarded as a proper name or as a title.

The main arguments against the assumption that *Malachi* is to be regarded as a proper name are the following:

The similarity in the titles of Zech. 9:1; 12:1; and Mal. 1:1 points to a secondary origin, and to the fact that these prophecies were originally handed down anonymously.

The name *Malachi* was supposedly taken from 3:1 and has been introduced in the superscription as a *Stichwort,* indicating the author of the book.

In its present form the word *Malachi* means "my messenger," and according to most scholars this surely would not have been a suitable name to give to any child.

It is also significant that the name appears nowhere else in the OT and that later history apparently knows nothing of a person by that name.

The translation of both the LXX and the Targum suggests the idea that *Malachi* was not regarded as a proper name. The Targum added to the words "by Malachi" the note: "whose name is called Ezra the scribe." The LXX translated the same phrase "by the hand of his angel [or messenger]."

This tradition has been further established by a number of church fathers who regarded the term *malachi* as a mere appellative or title adopted by the prophet.

As an anonymous writer the person of "Malachi" has been variously identified. According to some Jewish scholars and church fathers he indeed was an angel who appeared in human form. According to others he was a historical figure, alternatively identified with Ezra, Haggai, Mordecai, or a certain Joshua. Many modern scholars agree that the book of Malachi was originally anonymous. The words "by the hand of Malachi" were added by an editor in order to distinguish this prophecy from the so-called anonymous prophecies of Zech. 9–11 and 12–14 and to obtain the desired number of twelve Minor Prophets.

These and similar arguments against *Malachi* being a proper name are indeed legitimate but not conclusive. The argument based upon the anonymity of Zech. 9–11; 12–14; and Malachi is merely a hypothesis. According to Baldwin, et al., Zech. 9–14 are an integral part of the book and not anonymous. The argument of anonymity therefore falls to the ground. The same applies to the consideration that "malachi" was an editor's title borrowed from 3:1. If so, the editor was not very well informed, for the rest of the sentence in Mal. 1:1 suggests the third person, and the borrowed word meaning "*my* messenger" does not suit the context. The correct alteration "*his* messenger" was made by the translators of the LXX, but this fact merely serves to reinforce the originality of the MT, being in this context the more difficult reading!

We agree that "my messenger" is not a suitable name to give to a child, but it might be appropriate if we may assume the meaning "messenger of the Lord."[1] It is also true that the name *Malachi* is not found elsewhere in the OT or in later Jewish literature, but this applies also to Jonah and Habakkuk. The argument that the words "by the hand of Malachi" were added to distinguish this prophecy from the "anonymous" prophecies of Zech. 9–11 and 12–14 and to obtain the desired number of twelve Minor Prophets is unacceptable, because the number of the Minor Prophets would then have been fourteen instead of twelve!

There are indeed valid reasons to regard *Malachi* as the proper name of a prophet. The main considerations are:

The analogy of the titles of other prophetic books in which reference is made to the author.

The fact that when the expression *b^eyaḏ* is used to indicate the human instrument of God's revelation it is normally followed by a proper name.

The tradition of the word as a proper name is really very old, as is evident from the rendering of the Peshitta, Theodotion, Symmachus, and the Vulgate.

2 Esdras, dating from the second century A.D., lists the twelve Minor Prophets, naming as the last three books Aggaeus, Secharias, and Malachias, with the remark concerning Malachi: "qui et angelus Domini

1. See Laetsch, pp. 507–508, for analogous theophoric names.

vocatus est" ("who is also called the angel [messenger] of the Lord"). "Malachi" is thus regarded as a proper name.

The Greek form, "Malachias," appears also in the superscription of the book in the LXX. Hence the LXX's rendering, "his messenger," may be only a different form of the Hebrew word, *malkî yāhû,* in the sense of "messenger of the Lord." The *yod* is taken as a *yod compaginis,* as is the case in *ʿabdî* (1 Chr. 6:44), *ʿabdîʾel* (1 Chr. 5:15; cf. *ʿabdeʾel,* Jer. 36:26), and *buqqî* (Num. 34:22; Ezra 7:14) compared with *buqqîyāhû* (1 Chr. 25:4, 13).[2]

In the absence of compelling arguments to the contrary it is logical to accept that the prophet was called Malachi. This conclusion of Baldwin is endorsed by a number of scholars.[3] According to G. A. Smith "it is true that neither in form nor in meaning is there any insuperable obstacle to our understanding *mal'akhi* as the name of a person." Any one of the meanings "my angel," "my messenger," or "angelicus" could have been a natural name for a Jewish child and especially for a prophet, according to Smith.

In preferring the term *Malachi* as an indication of the prophet's name, we must admit that nothing more about his person and personal circumstances are known than his book reveals. The legends surrounding his person are totally unreliable. "Malachi" is represented to us in terms of the meaning of his name as "a messenger of the Lord," and in that we are reminded that the message is more important than the identity and circumstances of the messenger (cf. John 3:30).

According to the heading of this book the different messages were communicated by *(beyad)* Malachi. Without any doubt these dialogues were originally delivered in an oral form. The question whether Malachi must also be considered the author of the written copy of his speeches cannot be answered with any certainty.

III. DATE

Although we do not have any direct indication of Malachi's date, neither in Scripture nor in tradition, we may deduce from indirect evidence the approximate date of the prophecy. Scholars are agreed that the prophet could not have been living in the preexilic times, in the time of the Exile, or outside of Palestine. There is quite a consensus of opinion that he prophesied in the postexilic era. This is partly indicated by the reference in 1:8 to a *peḥâ,* a rather vague title for a dignitary representing a foreign government. Orig-

2. See GKC, § 90k-n.
3. Cf. P. A. Verhoef, *Maleachi,* COT (Kampen: Kok, 1972), pp. 9–16.

inally an Assyrian word, it was used to indicate a "governor" in the time of the Babylonian and Persian empires. Reference to this title is assumed to indicate the postexilic era, due to supporting evidence. The book of Malachi presupposes the existence of the temple, and this excludes the time of the Babylonian Exile. Before the Exile Judah was not administered by a *peḥâ,* which leaves us with the conclusion that the "governor" of Mal. 1:8 must have been a Persian dignitary.

Scholars are also agreed that Malachi must be dated after the time of Haggai and Zechariah. They had stirred up the returned exiles to rebuild the temple, which was completed in 515 B.C. (Ezra 5–6). As far as Malachi was concerned, this event already belonged to the past. The book assumes the existence of the temple (1:10; 3:1, 8), and presupposes a (long!) time of spiritual decline, because the temple worship had already deteriorated to such an extent that the priests and people had to be reproved by the prophet with regard to their malpractices (1:6–14; 2:1–9; 3:6–12).

Since the conditions and the specific sins which are described in the book of Malachi correspond to those in the books of Ezra and Nehemiah, the prophet must have been their contemporary. Scholars differ only on whether Malachi must be dated before, contemporary with, or after Ezra and Nehemiah. An additional complication enters the argument because of the assumed uncertainty about the date of Ezra's arrival in Jerusalem and his relationship to Nehemiah. According to many modern scholars Nehemiah preceded Ezra. But we are content with the traditional representation of the course of events as they appear in the books of Ezra and Nehemiah.[1] According to this point of view Ezra arrived in Palestine in 458 B.C. with a group of exiles; he was followed by Nehemiah in 445 B.C. Both of them worked together for a time in Jerusalem. After a sojourn of twelve years Nehemiah returned to Susa in 433 B.C., and again after an unknown period of time returned to Jerusalem for a second visit.

A "very generally accepted view" (Adamson) among modern scholars is that Malachi preceded Ezra-Nehemiah (or Nehemiah-Ezra).[2] The main considerations for this point of view are the following:

Malachi obviously does not seem to have known either the persons or the work of Ezra and Nehemiah.

Malachi does not refer to recent legislation such as Ezra and Nehemiah introduced (Ezra 10:3; Neh. 13:13, 23–27), especially in connection with Nehemiah's denunciation of mixed marriages (2:10–12), and of the

1. Cf. H. H. Grosheide, *Ezra-Nehemia,* COT (Kampen: Kok, 1963), I:35–49, for a thorough discussion of this problem.

2. For an anthology of views and dates, see my *Maleachi,* COT, pp. 19–20.

people's failure to provide the compulsory contributions for the maintenance of the temple staff (3:6–12).

Malachi seemingly did not have a knowledge of the "Priestly Code," but rather "moves within the orbit of Deuteronomistic conceptions."[3] Since the "Priestly Code" received its final redaction ca. 444 B.C. according to many scholars, Malachi must be dated before that time.

In the light of these and similar considerations Malachi is often dated in the period after the rebuilding of the temple in 515 B.C. and some time before Ezra came to Jerusalem in 458 B.C. Those who think that Ezra followed Nehemiah would date Malachi some time before 445 B.C. Any endeavor to be more specific about the date must be considered only an intelligent guess.

Most convincing, however, is the opinion of those scholars who maintain that the prophecy of Malachi "fits the situation in which Nehemiah worked as snugly as a bone fits its socket" (J. M. P. Smith). More precisely, the period between Nehemiah's two visits to Jerusalem (i.e., shortly after 433 B.C.) seems preferable for the following reasons:[4]

The considerations in favor of a date prior to that of Ezra-Nehemiah are not conclusive, especially because some of the arguments are based upon the Documentary Hypothesis.

It is true that Malachi did not refer to Ezra and Nehemiah. But the same applies to Samuel's attitude toward the ark of the covenant, to Isaiah's relationship toward the reform of Hezekiah, to Jeremiah's seeming indifference toward the reform of Josiah. According to Bright "Jeremiah's precise attitude toward the great reform must remain a mystery."[5] This *argumentum e silentio* can indeed be brought to bear upon the pre-Ezra date. If Malachi preceded Ezra it is significant that the author of Ezra's book referred to the prophets Haggai and Zechariah (5:1; 6:14) but did not mention Malachi's dialogues concerning some of the very aspects of Ezra's reform.

The absence in Malachi of reference to legislation introduced by Ezra concerning mixed marriages (Ezra 10:3) must be viewed in the context of Ezra's failure to procure permanent results. Nehemiah himself was obliged to introduce similar measures against mixed marriages at the time of his second visit (13:23–29), contrary to the acceptance by the people of the covenant obligations during his first visit (10:28–30). The introduction of "recent legislation" seemed not to have had any permanent effect on the behavior of the covenant people in those postexilic times.

3. So C. Kuhl, *The Prophets of Israel,* 2nd ed. (Edinburgh: Oliver & Boyd, 1963), p. 167. See also Blenkinsopp, *History of Prophecy in Israel,* p. 241.

4. For more detailed discussion see my *Maleachi,* COT, pp. 16–31.

5. J. Bright, *The Kingdom of God* (Nashville: Abingdon, 1953), p. 106.

The main argument that the prophecy of Malachi "agrees with the stylistic and intellectual influence of Deuteronomy, while there is no trace of influence of the Priestly Code" (Sellin-Fohrer) cannot be maintained. Malachi's prophecy concerning the compulsory contributions presupposes the legislation of "P" rather than that of "D" (so rightly G. A. Smith, A. Bentzen, et al.). Wellhausen, Horst, and others concede that Malachi referred to "P"-legislation, but they maintain that those elements of legislation consisted of handed-down material before the final redaction of the Priestly Code. This explanation seems feasible, but at the same time it contradicts the exclusive point of view that in Malachi "no trace of influence of the Priestly Code" is to be found.

Some of the positive indications of the time of Malachi's ministry are the following:

Prior to the arrival of Nehemiah the maintenance of the temple worship was sponsored by the Persian government (Ezra 6:6–12; 7:12–26). Malachi's appeal to the people to bring the tithes and the offerings to the house of the Lord (3:6–12) actually gained real significance after the renewal of the covenant in the days of Nehemiah, when the people had accepted their own responsibilities for the maintenance of the temple staff and worship (Neh. 10).

Because Nehemiah himself voluntarily relinquished what was due to him as governor (Neh. 5:1–8), it is obvious that Mal. 1:8 could not be referring to the governorship of Nehemiah. This indeed suggests a date when Nehemiah was absent from Jerusalem, most likely during his sojourn in Susa between his two visits to Jerusalem.

A comparison of the priests' and Levites' attitude toward the temple and its worship in the postexilic period up to the time of Nehemiah's first visit and that which is reflected in the book of Malachi leads to the conclusion that the evidence from Malachi corresponds with the situation described by Nehemiah on the occasion of his second visit (Neh. 13:28, 29). In the previous period the attitudes of priests and Levites were generally favorable (Ezra 3:8–13; 6:16; Neh. 3:1, 17; 8:7–9, 12, 14–19; 9:4–15, 38; 10:28, 29; 12:30). During Nehemiah's second visit he charged them with defiling "the priesthood and the covenant of the priesthood and the Levites" (Neh. 13:29).

The correspondence between the accusations of Malachi and those of Nehemiah (during his second visit) is evident and remarkable. Both of them charged the people with entering into mixed marriages (Mal. 2:10–12; Neh. 13:25–27). Both were concerned about the people's failure to bring the compulsory contributions for the maintenance of the temple staff (Mal. 3:6–12; Neh. 13:10–14, 31). The negligence of the priestly function was suggested by Nehemiah (13:9, 30) but spelled out by Malachi (1:6–2:9). The main difference between Malachi and Nehemiah concerns the desecration of the sabbath, which only Nehemiah mentions (13:15–22). On the whole, therefore, J. M. P. Smith's assertion (quoted above) that Malachi's book fits the situation well is correct.

Without being dogmatic about the precise date of Malachi, we favor the period between Nehemiah's two visits, that is, shortly after 433 B.C. Thus Malachi must be read against the background of the facts recorded in Neh. 10:1–13:5 on the one hand and in Neh. 13:6–31 on the other hand.

IV. HISTORICAL BACKGROUND

What were the circumstances of the postexilic period, especially that of the second half of the fifth century B.C.? This century may be defined as a "dark age." The data and evidence concerning the history of this period are lacking, and the material found in the books of Ezra, Nehemiah, and Malachi must suffice.

The political history of the Jews at this time was inseparably bound up with the Persian empire.[1] Under the same Darius I (522–486) who gave the Jews permission to rebuild the temple (2 Chr. 36:22, 23; Ezra 1:3; 6:3–12), the Persian empire obtained its vastest extent, stretching from the Indus Valley in the east to the Aegean Sea in the west, from the Jaxartes in the north to as far south as Libya. The magnitude and vastness of this empire certainly posed a great temptation to the people of God. Jews who were scattered far and wide in this empire made themselves at home, while the Jews in Palestine disclosed their openness to this world empire by a loss of their theocratic consciousness and by a failure to acknowledge and maintain the spiritual secret of their existence as the treasured possession of the Lord. The books of Ezra, Nehemiah, and Malachi testify to this fact. A nation that is prepared to serve God with sacrifices that they will not dare to offer to their heathen governor (1:8) is a nation that has lost its perspective on God as their Father and Lord (1:6). What remains of the spiritual identity of such a nation if it identifies itself through mixed marriages with the heathen world (2:10–12)? The people of such a nation act faithlessly to one another, profaning the covenant of God with their fathers.

The circumstances in which the approximately 50,000[2] returned exiles found themselves in the small province of Judah were critical in many respects. In a certain sense the coming of Ezra coincided with the disturbances caused by the war between the Persians and Egyptians. According to

1. Cf. J. Bright, *A History of Israel,* p. 356.
2. According to W. F. Albright, *Biblical Period,* p. 93.

some scholars this war was one of the causes of the ultimate failure of Ezra's initial reform (Reinke, Grosheide). Thus when Nehemiah appeared on the scene some years later, the colony was in a state of deep decline. The walls of Jerusalem were still further destroyed, presumably by the Egyptians and Persians, and everywhere conditions were bad. The exorbitant profits of the rich, together with the compulsory contributions to the Persians for the waging of their wars, caused many to sink into poverty, to mortgage their property, and to give their sons and daughters into slavery.

In these circumstances Nehemiah came into office and vigorously improved the general living conditions. The walls were rebuilt, the covetousness of the rich was reprimanded, the priests were admonished to observe their duties and to see that everything that had been acquired illegally was returned to its rightful owner. Nehemiah himself voluntarily relinquished the income that was due to him as a governor (Neh. 5:1–8). After all the preliminary work had been completed, the covenant was renewed; the nation agreed to keep the Law of Moses, to provide means for the support of the temple and its service. After a period of twelve years, in which time Nehemiah performed his comprehensive reform, he again returned to Persia (Neh. 12:44–47; 13:6).

On his second visit to Palestine Nehemiah found that many of the abuses which he had abolished during his first visit were again being practiced by the people (Neh. 13:6–31). The sabbath was desecrated (13:15–22). Contrary to the stipulations of Deut. 23:3–7, many Ammonites and Moabites were accommodated into the community life of the covenant people. The priest Eliashib fitted out a room for his relative, the Ammonite Tobiah (Neh. 2:10), in the courts of the house of God (13:7–9). Tyrian merchants established themselves in Jerusalem and to their hearts' content sold their wares to the children of Judah on the sabbath (13:16). Fraternization with the heathen fellow citizens developed into mixed marriages on a large scale (13:23–29). The children born from those marriages could not even speak the Judean language (13:24). This comment is interesting, because it gives us reason to believe that Nehemiah returned to Jerusalem for the second time only after a number of years, because the children from the mixed marriages could already talk when Nehemiah revisited Palestine.

In this general context Malachi was called to fulfill his prophetic ministry. With the exception of the desecration of the sabbath (Neh. 13:15–22), he rebuked all the abuses mentioned in Neh. 13:6–31. It is therefore recommended that the prophecy of Malachi be read against the background of Neh. 13, just as Neh. 13 is only fully understood in the light of Neh. 10. The sinful behavior and practices that are opposed in ch. 13 are in fact the very things that the people on the occasion of the renewal of the covenant

(Neh. 10) promised not to do: to marry foreign women, to desecrate the sabbath, and to neglect the temple offerings.

V. COMPOSITION AND STRUCTURE

In its present form the book of Malachi consists of three chapters in the Hebrew OT, as opposed to four chapters in the LXX, Vulgate, and modern versions. The fourth chapter of the translations corresponds with the last six verses of the Hebrew text: 3:19–24 = 4:1–6. The chapter division of the translations is arbitrary, because the first three verses of their ch. 4, at least, are an integral part of the preceding pericope.

Scholars generally agree that the book is composed of a number of prophecies, each with a similar structure. The most common division, which is followed in this commentary, distinguishes seven separate pericopes apart from the heading (1:1). They are 1:2–5; 1:6–14; 2:1–9; 2:10–16; 2:17–3:5; 3:6–12; 3:13–21 (Eng. 4:3); with 3:22–24 (Eng. 4:4–6) as an addendum.

The different dialogues of Malachi are alternately directed to the people (1:2–5; 2:10–16; 2:17–3:5; 3:13–21 [Eng. 4:3]) and against the priests (1:6–2:9), which caused some scholars to rearrange the various pericopes in the following manner: 1:2–5; 2:10–16; 1:6–2:9; 2:17–3:5; 3:13–21 (Eng. 4:3).[1] According to Gerhard Wallis the different pericopes concerning the priests (1:6–2:9; 3:1–4) and the people (1:2–5; 2:10–16; 2:17; 3:5; 3:6–12; 3:13–21 [Eng. 4:3]) were indeed separate units, which progressed in a parallel manner from exhortation (1:6–14 par. 1:2–5; 2:10–16), via threat (2:1–9 par. 3:5, 9), to *Heilswort* (3:1–4 par. 3:16–21 [Eng. 4:3]). These sets of pericopes initially were independent, but because of the similar concepts, they ultimately were composed in their present form.[2]

The attempts to rearrange Malachi's dialogues must be deemed arbitrary for the following reasons. (1) The different dialogues were originally expressed in an oral form, probably on separate occasions. (2) We really do not know the motives and the process which led to the present composition of the book. (3) At least some pericopes were directed against both priests and people (1:6–14; 2:17–3:5; 3:6–12). (4) The distinction between exhortations, threats, and words of salvation may only be regarded as relatively correct. We agree with Marti, et al., that the present composition is in itself significant. Just as every pericope commences with a specific theme, the

1. So, e.g., Kuhl, *Prophets of Israel,* p. 167.

2. G. Wallis, "Wesen und Struktur der Botschaft Maleachis," in *Das ferne und nahe Wort,* Fest. L. Rost, ed. F. Maass, BZAW 105 (Berlin: Töpelmann, 1967), pp. 229–37.

book as a whole is introduced by a comprehensive and pervasive theme (1:2–5), viz., that God loves his treasured possession, a theme that is again suggested in the concluding verses (3:23, 24 [Eng. 4:5, 6]), with a perspective on the renewal of the covenant between fathers and children. The only pericope that seems misplaced in its general context is 3:6–12, but we have no reason to rearrange it in order to connect it either with 1:6–2:9 (Elliger, et al.) or with 1:2–5 (Haller, Sellin, et al.). Within the comprehensive theme of God's love for his people, this pericope establishes that Israel's adversities were not due to the fact that the Lord had changed but because of the people's habit of turning away from God's decrees.

Our conclusion is that we lack evidence to ascertain without any doubt the diachronical process which eventually led from the oral dialogues to the present composition of the book. At the same time we deem every attempt to rearrange the different pericopes as hypothetical and arbitrary.

VI. UNITY AND AUTHENTICITY

Most scholars agree on the essential unity of this book. According to Robert C. Dentan it is evident from distinctive traits that the various dialogues are the product of "a single mind." The book reveals uniformity in language and vocabulary, it presupposes the same historical background, and it is notably characterized by a typical style of dialogue, reflected at the beginning of each main section (cf. 1:2, 6, 13; 2:14, 17; 3:7, 13).

The authenticity of the book as a whole is commonly acknowledged, with the exception of a couple of passages. According to Curt Kuhl "the almost general consensus of critical opinion is that the dicta on mixed marriages (2:11, 12) and above all the conclusion of the book (3:22–24 = 4:4–6) are later interpolations." Other verses sometimes queried as later additions to the text are, apart from the heading (1:1), 1:11–14; 2:2, 7; and 3:1b.

The main reasons for regarding the conclusion of the book (3:22–24 [Eng. 4:4–6]) as secondary are the lack of continuity with the preceding prophecy, the absence of Malachi's dialogue style, and especially the assumed dependence of these verses upon Deuteronomy. These and similar arguments are arbitrary, however. We agree with Baldwin: "if these verses were added as a later appendix, they are in keeping with the concise, hortatory style of the rest of the book, and could have come from Malachi's hand." As a matter of fact, in these verses the prophet appropriately focused his attention on the two most significant themes of his general message: the Law and the Prophets, the covenant and the coming Day of the Lord.

Baldwin rightly concluded: "Emphasis on the law of Moses (4:4) and on the figure of Elijah (4:5, 6) summed up all that God's servants had stood for throughout the centuries. When the law and the prophets were put together in one collection of sacred texts, these twin references looked forward to the consummation of the purpose for which both were given."[1] In the exegesis we will return to some of the arguments against the authenticity of these verses.

According to the "consensus of critical opinion" the dicta on mixed marriages (2:11, 12 or 2:11–13a) are later additions, mainly because Malachi's reference to "the daughter of a foreign god" (v. 11) is contrary to his otherwise "sympathetic" allusions to the heathen nations (1:11), and because this passage originally dealt only with divorces (2:14–16). Both these arguments are inconclusive. The assumed contradiction between particularism (2:11) and universalism (1:11) rests upon an exegesis of 1:11 according to which the heathen nations as such are represented as the bringers of "pure sacrifices" to the name of the Lord. We will deal with this point of view in the exegesis of 1:11. This verse neither teaches universalism in the pregnant sense of the word nor does it conflict with the rest of Malachi's message.

We agree with Baldwin and other interpreters that the evidence for regarding the other verses mentioned as later additions is so slight and so dependent on subjective factors that it is best to accept the text as it stands.[2]

VII. STYLE

We have already referred to Malachi's "disputation method," reflected at the beginning of each main section of his book. Scholars differ in trying to define this method. It has been variously typified as a form of dialogue (Aalders), as casuistic-dialectic (Holtzmann), as didactic-dialectic (G. L. Robinson, Freeman), as disputation (E. Pfeiffer),[1] as *Diskussionsworte oder Streitgespräche* (H. J. Boecker),[2] and as *Streitreden* (Wallis). The characteristic feature of Malachi's style is that each main section of the book is structured according to the scheme statement-question-motivation. In

1. Baldwin, pp. 214–15.

2. For a more detailed discussion on matters pertaining to the authenticity of Malachi's book, see my *Maleachi,* COT, pp. 37–42.

1. E. Pfeiffer, "Die Disputationswörte im Buche Maleachi," *EvT* 19 (1959) 546–68.

2. H. J. Boecker, "Bemerkungen zur formgeschichtlichen Terminologie des Buches Maleachi," *ZAW* 78 (1966) 78–80.

some cases the three elements of the dialogue are expressed in single sentences (e.g., 1:2; 2:17; 3:13).

The opening statement in 1:2 is: "I have loved you, says the Lord." The people's reaction follows immediately: "But you say, In what manner have you loved us?" This response provides the opportunity to explain the motivation for the initial statement: "Was not Esau Jacob's brother, says the Lord. . . ."

In other pericopes (1:6–2:9; 2:10–16; and 3:6–12) the structure of the dialogue is more complex. In 1:6–14, for instance, we have the following pattern. The prophet commences his accusation with a generally accepted statement that a father is honored by his son and a master by his servant. This is followed by the application in terms of another indisputable truth that God is the Father and the Lord of his people. At this stage the prophet introduces the accusation, still in general terms, that the priests are in the habit of despising the name of the Lord. To this the priests respond with the question: "In what manner have we despised your name?" The motivation in terms of a more specific statement is that they have offered defiled food on the Lord's altar. This accusation is flatly denied: "How have we defiled you?" The priests' response causes the prophet to specify his accusation a little more concretely: "By saying that the table of the Lord is contemptible." The purport of this accusation is then further explained in vv. 8–10.

It is noteworthy that the prophet's statements are generally indisputable and absolute (cf. 1:2, 6; 2:10, 17; 3:6, 13). They are expressed positively (1:2, 6, 7; 2:13, 17; 3:6, 7, 13) or in terms of a rhetorical question (1:6b; 2:10; 3:8) or even as an exhortation (3:7). They are also represented either as the word of God (1:2, 6, 7; 3:6, 7, 8, 13) or as the word of the prophet (2:10, 13, 17). The responses from the addressees are usually short and suggest total ignorance and an assumed innocence. The motivation, introduced with or without a specific formula, is expressed in terms of a word of salvation (1:2–5; 2:10–12; 3:16–18; 3:20, 21 [Eng. 4:2, 3]) or as an exhortation or threat (1:7–14; 2:10–16; 2:17–3:5; 3:9; 3:19, 20 [Eng. 4:1, 2]).

This style, which characterizes all of Malachi's dialogues, was not confined to this prophet. C. Westermann discusses the disputation with reference to Mic. 2:6–11, where the prophet quotes his opponents, and Isa. 28:23–29.[3] Dialogues between the Lord and his people are found in Jer. 2:23–25, 29, 30, 34–37; 3:1–5; 8:8, 9. According to E. Balla, Amos 3:2,

3. Westermann, *Basic Forms of Prophetic Speech,* tr. H. C. White (London: Lutterworth, Philadelphia: Westminster, 1967), includes a section on the disputation, p. 201.

12; 5:18–20; and 5:24, 25 can also be regarded as a form of disputation.[4] Other examples of this style are Isa. 40:27–31; 49:14–21; Jer. 13:11, 12; 15:1, 2; Ezek. 12:21–28; 18:2, 19, 25; and Zech. 1–6.

This style was also common in the later Jewish literature, especially in the Mishnah and Talmud. It was also found in the work of Greek authors and even in Paul's manner in proclaiming the gospel. Because of this resemblance between the style of Malachi and the later Jewish literature, some scholars, like Duhm and Sellin, dispute the originality of Malachi's diction, but unjustly so. Malachi's style could rather be compared with the vigorous dialogue of the public orator. "The short sentences and direct style characteristic of Malachi are marks of the spoken word, so that, even allowing for a certain amount of editorial arrangement, the impression remains that the very words of the prophet are here recorded" (Baldwin).

Whether the dialogues reflected the actual response of Malachi's opponents is uncertain. It seems unlikely that they would have reacted in the precise terms of the dialogue, especially when an answer to the Lord himself is involved (e.g., 1:2, "In what manner have you loved us?"; 3:7, "How are we to return [to you]?"). On the other hand we may assume a certain reality in the minds and acts of the addressees that would correspond with the words that were put into their mouths. According to Adamson the origin of Malachi's dialogues must be found in "the protesting and questioning cries of the hecklers, when he first delivered his message on the streets." Baldwin rightly suggests that "Malachi reads the attitudes of his people and intuitively puts their thoughts into words, so gaining their attention before driving home his word from the Lord."

Scholars tend to disagree in their assessment of the language and literary quality of the book. German scholars have attempted to translate Malachi as poetry in their belief that the original oracles were in poetic form. This is obviously the reason for the many proposed alterations *metri causa* in both *BHK* and *BHS*. The book of Malachi, however, is written in prose, with a few traces of a rhythmical pattern (e.g., 1:11 [4+3, 4+3, 3+3]; 3:1 [3+3, 3+3 (4), 4+4]; 3:6 [3+3], 3:7 [3+3, 4+3+3]). We do not share the negative evaluation of the literary quality of the book. According to De Wette it reflects the languid, lifeless spirit of an author who has tried but was unable to express his thoughts adequately. Although Edelkoort and others appreciate the clear and plain style of the book, they deny it any literary quality, especially because of an assumed absence of figurative language.

The opposite point of view is taken, for instance, by Bewer. Accord-

4. E. Balla, *Die Droh- und Scheltworte des Amos* (Leipzig: A. Edelman, 1926).

ing to him "there is a freshness in the lively debates of the little book that makes it interesting reading. It is written in prose which sometimes has the rhythmic swing of poetry."[5] We share this appreciation. It is true that Malachi does not employ any particular literary structure in order to convey his meaning.[6] The subjects with which he deals follow one another apparently haphazardly (Baldwin), but this is only one side of the story. In the discussion below on the structural analysis it will become clear that the author has indeed employed literary devices in order to convey his meaning, not only within the various pericopes but also in the book as a whole. Elements of the covenantal structure are reflected in the composition of the book. The introductory pericope (1:2–5) resembles the historical prologue of the Decalogue. The liabilities of the covenant were not met by the people, however, and the prophet draws attention to this in his subsequent dialogues. In his presentation of the different subjects there is indeed "a logical progression from election and privilege (1:2–5) to the inevitability of judgment (3:13–4:3)" (Baldwin). Within the separate pericopes we have an astonishing concreteness and a dramatical heightening of the tension in the prophet's dialogue.

This is especially apparent in 2:10–12. The prophet commences by posing an undeniable statement in the form of a rhetorical question: "Do we not have one Father and Creator?" Without answering his own question, he confronts the people and himself with a grave accusation: "Why then are we faithless to one another?" The seriousness of this accusation is then spelled out in general terms: "Judah has broken faith; a detestable thing has been committed . . . Judah has desecrated the sanctuary of the Lord." At this stage of high tension the denouement of the accusation is effected: "By marrying the daughter of a foreign god." The elements of the inner structure of this paragraph are an integral whole and amount to the following. Because the covenant people are attached to one another through faith in the one and only God, the introduction of a "foreign" element in the form of mixed marriages is a fundamental violation of this intimate bond, and therefore the transgressor himself must be detached from this bond and eliminated from "the tents of Jacob." The literary composition of this paragraph is such that its merit cannot be denied.

The book of Malachi is not without figurative speech. For example,

5. J. Bewer, *The Literature of the Old Testament*, rev. ed. (New York: Columbia University, 1933), p. 258.

6. See esp. E. Wendland, "Linear and Concentric Patterns in Malachi," *BT* 36 (1985) 108–21, for a thorough investigation into the literary-structural analysis of the book. See also S. D. Snyman, "Antiteses in die boek Maleagi," Ph.D. diss., University of Pretoria, 1985.

the relationship between God and his people is compared with that between a son and his father and a servant and his master (1:6). The priests are admonished literally to soften the Lord's (severe) face by patting his cheeks (1:9). The Lord will spread on the faces of the people "the offal" of their sacrifices (2:3). Reliable instruction in the law was in the mouth of the priests (2:6); "the lips of a priest preserve knowledge" (2:7). The purifying judgment is likened to "a refiner's fire or a launderer's soap" (3:2), and the day of the Lord is represented as a burning furnace and a shining sun (3:19–20 [Eng. 4:1–2]). All these and similar examples of figurative speech are taken from life and are effectively utilized in the prophet's dialogues.

A literary device which occurs a number of times is chiasm.[7] Here we shall cite only one example; in the commentary proper we will deal more fully with this device. In 1:2–3 the statement "Yet I have loved Jacob, but Esau I have hated" is chiastically structured to emphasize the point in question.[8]

The prophet is also fond of parallelism. For instance: "A son honors (his) father and a servant his master" (1:6). The significance of this parallelism is that each member provides the missing element in the other member. The first member lacks the personal pronoun "his," and the second the verb "honor," which can also have the sense of "fear."

Finally, it is important to note that the language of Malachi is on the whole pure Hebrew. Reinke detects only two foreign words, viz., *rāšaš* (1:4; cf. Jer. 5:17) and the title *peḥâ* (1:8), but *rāšaš* need not be regarded as an Aramaism.

VIII. TEXT

With a few minor exceptions the Hebrew text (MT) makes good sense and appears to be well preserved. In our commentary we have favored the following minor emendations: *g*ᵉ*ḇûl,* "the territory of," instead of *lig*ᵉ*bûl,* "with regard to the territory of" (1:5); *niḇgôḏ,* Qal imperfect first person plural, instead of *niḇgaḏ,* Niphal perfect third person singular (2:10); *śōnē*ʾ, Qal active participle, instead of *śānē*ʾ, Qal perfect third person singular (2:16).

7. Cf. A. R. Ceresko, "The Function of Chiasmus in Hebrew Poetry," *CBQ* 40 (1978) 6; S. D. Snyman, "Chiasmes in Mal. 1:2–5," *Skrif en Kerk* (Jan. 1984) 17-22; and now esp. Snyman's doctoral thesis, op. cit., for the identification and discussion of all the chiasms in Malachi.

8. Cf. S. D. Snyman, "Haat Jahwe vir Esau? ('n Verkenning van Mal. 1:3a)," *NGTT* 25 (1984) 358–62.

Two verses (2:15, 16) show signs of an attempt to restore their meaning, without any great success. In particular v. 15 is grammatically and syntactically incomplete (see the commentary below). The Jewish scribes have suggested an alteration in the text, reading *'ôṯî* instead of *'ôṯô* in either 1:12 *(BHK)* or 1:13 *(BHS)*.

The MT is generally supported by the ancient versions. The variant readings, which indeed exist, can be explained in an adequate way. Most of these variants are due to the normal process of translating from one language into another. Even the fairly high number of additions and omissions do not necessarily imply a different Hebrew *Vorlage;* they may be interpreted as characteristic of the versions concerned. With regard to a number of meaningful variants, we have given preference to the more difficult reading of the MT. The Qumran manuscripts do not cast any direct light on the MT.[1]

The LXX is an important witness to the text. In the apparatus of *BHK,* and to a lesser degree also in *BHS,* the variant readings are nearly all taken from the LXX (א, A, Φ). In the first paragraph of *BHK*'s apparatus 6 variants are Greek additions to the MT, and 12 can be considered real alternative readings. In *BHK*'s second paragraph another 21 instances of variant readings taken from the LXX are quoted to support the editor's (O. Procksch) proposed alterations. *BHS* refers 29 times to the LXX in order to support the editor's (K. Elliger) suggestions for the alteration of the MT. Although both editors of the Hebrew editions have incorporated quite a bit of material from the LXX into their apparatuses, it must be pointed out that even these references represent only a selected portion of the available data. Attention is drawn in the commentary to additional material. The LXX generally keeps close to the MT, but at times it is characterized by "verbose expansion" (J. M. P. Smith). A few typical examples of arbitrary additions are to be found in 1:1, 7; 2:2, 4; 3:2, 5, 8, 19 (Eng. 4:1).

The LXX's division in pericopes is slightly different from that of the MT. Mal. 2:17a is connected with the preceding verse (16), and the same applies to 3:6 and 3:16, both of which are connected with the preceding pericope. In accordance with a later Jewish tradition the LXX has a different arrangement of the last three verses (3:22–24 [Eng. 4:4–6]). The LXX's alteration, viz., 23, 24, 22 (Eng. 5, 6, 4), most likely reflects an attempt to end the book on a less threatening note. It need not represent a different Hebrew *Vorlage*. The translation of the LXX is especially characterized by

1. The Qumran mss. have a quotation from Mal. 1:10 (CD 6:11–14), and a fragment with references to and commentary on Mal. 1:13–14 (5QapMal 10; cf. *DJD*, III:180). Cf. A. S. Van der Woude, *Haggai, Maleachi*, POT (Nijkerk: Callenbach, 1982), p. 81n.3.

the tendency to interpret and to paraphrase difficult words and phrases. Reference to the following examples will suffice here (we will deal with them more fully in the commentary): 1:3, 7, 9, 10; 2:2, 3, 4, 10, 11, 12, 13, 16; 3:5, 6–7, 8, 9, 10, 11, 15, 16, 17, 19, 23, 24 (Eng. 4:1, 5, 6).

The translation of the Peshitta generally presupposes the MT. The influence of the LXX is evident in the following verses: 1:3, 4, 10, 13, 14; 2:2, 3, 4, 11, 13; 3:16. In a few instances the Peshitta's translation conforms to that of Targum Jonathan: 1:2, 13; 2:3, 12. A number of its variant readings are due to the common problems concerning translations. This obviously is the case in passages like 1:1, 2, 3, 4, 5, 6, 8, 9, 10, 11; 2:4, 12, 13, 16; 3:5, 6, 7, 9. There are also a number of syntactical differences, for instance, in 3:1 (imperfect instead of perfect), 3:2 (passive participle instead of infinitive construct), 3:3 (infinitve construct instead of participle), etc. The Peshitta has a number of additions (1:4; 2:11; 3:6, 11, 19 [Eng. 4:1]) and omissions (1:4, 9, 12, 14; 2:2, 16; 3:11). A different arrangement of sentences is found in 1:2 and 3:9. The textual evidence of the Peshitta is neglected in *BHK;* with the exception of 2:15 Procksch did not refer to the Peshitta in his apparatus. *BHS* is much better in this regard; in his apparatus Elliger refers to the Peshitta eight times (1:3, 12, 13 [twice]; 2:3, 17; 3:8, 16).

The Targum Jonathan also presupposes the MT. Its rendering has a significant element of paraphrase in terms of later Jewish convictions. Typical examples are the following: 1:9 ("And now, pray to the Lord God, and he will answer our prayers"), 1:11 ("among the heathen, and in every season in which you toil and in which I answered your prayers, my name is great and will be sanctified by you and your prayers will be like a pure offering to my name"). Compare also 2:12, 15; 3:1, 5, 6, 7, 12, 23, and 24 (Eng. 4:5, 6). Targum Jonathan is also neglected in Procksch's apparatus, with only one reference (1:13), while Elliger refers to it four times (1:12; 2:15, 17; and 3:8).

The Vulgate has also been slighted in the two Hebrew editions. *BHK* does not refer to it at all, while *BHS* refers to it only six times (1:8; 2:3, 9, 15, 17; 3:8). With a few exceptions the Vulgate is a dependable witness to the MT. In a number of cases it supports the reading of the MT over against that of the other ancient versions (1:7, 12, 13, 14; 2:2, 4, 7, 11; 3:16). In a few instances the Vulgate deviates from the MT (1:3, *in dracones deserti* instead of "the desert jackals"; 1:10, *gratuito,* "without cost," instead of *frustra,* "in vain"; 2:3, *ego projiciam vobis brachium,* "I will cast away the arm for you").

In conclusion we may say that the MT is preferable to the ancient versions and has unduly been emended by the editors of both *BHK* and *BHS*.

IX. CANONICITY

The canonicity of Malachi has never been disputed. It was known as part of the Twelve by Jesus ben Sira (49:10; cf. 48:10 with Mal. 3:24 [Eng. 4:6]). The NT does not directly mention either the prophet or his book. But we have a number of quotations and reminiscences from its content. The most important examples are Rom. 9:13 (Mal. 1:2, 3); Matt. 11:10; Mark 1:2; Luke 1:76; 7:27 (Mal. 3:1); Matt. 11:14; 17:10–12; Mark 9:11, 12; Luke 1:17 (Mal. 3:23, 24 [Eng. 4:5, 6]). Other resemblances of ideas are Mal. 1:11 (John 4:21, 23); 2:10 (Acts 17:26; 1 Cor. 8:6); 2:15 (Matt. 19:4,5); 2:17 (2 Pet. 3:4); 3:2 (Matt. 3:11, 12); 3:6 (Jas. 1:17); 3:7 (Acts 7:51); 3:12 (Luke 1:48); 3:16 (Rev. 20:12); 3:19 (Eng. 4:1) (2 Thess. 1:8; Matt. 3:10; Luke 3:9); 3:20 (Eng. 4:2) (Luke 1:78; John 1:4,9; 12:46; 2 Pet. 1:19; Rev. 2:28).

X. STRUCTURAL ANALYSIS

In this commentary we have applied a modest structural analysis to the book of Malachi. It concerns mainly the division of the book into pericopes, the analysis of sentences (prose), stichoi (poetry), and discourses, and a consideration of various literary devices.[1]

Apart from the heading (1:1) and the epilogue (3:22–24 [Eng. 4:4–6]), we have divided Malachi into seven pericopes: 1:2–5; 1:6–14; 2:1–9; 2:10–16; 2:17–3:5; 3:6–12; 3:13–21 (Eng. 4:3).

In 1:2–5 the central theme is expressed in v. 2a (sentence 1) and again suggested in v. 5 (sentences 10 and 11). The composition of this discourse is therefore circular; it begins and concludes with the same theme. In accordance with Malachi's disputation method, the general structure of the pericope could be divided into God's statement (v. 2a), the people's response (v. 2b), and God's motivation (v. 2c–4), with the suggestion that the people will have to acknowledge God's love for them (v. 5). The pericope is characterized by its employment of chiasms and especially antithetical structures. Sentences 1 and 2 (v. 2a and b) are chiastically structured:

"*I have loved* you, *says the Lord*
But *you say,* In what manner *have you loved* us?

The same applies to sentences 4 and 5 (v. 2d, 3a):

I have loved Jacob
but *Esau I have hated.*

1. For a more detailed structural analysis of the book of Malachi, see E. Wendland, "Linear and Concentric Patterns in Malachi," *BT* 36 (1985) 108–21.

Sentences 6 and 9 (v. 3b and 4c) constitute a synonymous parallelism:

I have turned his mountains into a wasteland. . . .
They will be called: the wicked country. . . .

Sentences 7 and 8 (v. 4a, b) are also structured as an antithetical parallelism: the Lord's resolution (sentence 8) will cancel Edom's intention (sentence 7). Each sentence has its own antithetical elements: "crushed" versus "rebuild" (7, v. 4a), "build" versus "demolish," and "they" versus "I" (8, v. 4b). According to its content sentences 6–9 (vv. 3b–4c) provide an extension of sentence 5 (v. 3a), an application of the statement that God has hated Esau.

Sentences 10 and 11 (v. 5) again constitute an antithesis to the people's retort in sentence 2 (v. 2b). They will see with their own eyes! This pericope must be considered as a preamble to the following discourses. The people are confronted with the "gospel" of God's love before they are reprimanded because of their sins.

In 1:6–14 the main theme is expressed in v. 11 (sentences 17–19). God has pleasure in *pure* offerings! The composition of this discourse is therefore according to the model that has the theme in the middle. The pericope is thus divided into two main sections. Section A has the following structure:

1. The accusation, sentences 1–8 (vv. 6–8b). In accordance with Malachi's style, the accusation is expressed in terms of a statement (sentences 1–2, v. 6c) and the motivation for that statement (sentences 4–8, vv. 7–8b). The motivation again consists of a statement (sentence 4, v. 7a), a response (sentence 5, v. 7b), and the final motivation (sentences 6–8, vv. 7c–8b).

2. God's evaluation, sentences 9–16 (vv. 8c–10c). God's displeasure is likened to that of the governor (sentences 9–13, vv. 8c–9c). God's displeasure is confirmed (sentences 14–16, v. 10).

3. The great antithesis, sentences 17–19 (v. 11). The very antithesis of God's accusation with regard to the defective offerings of the priests and people in Jerusalem (sentences 1–16, vv. 6–10) is his affirmation that pure offerings are being brought to the honor of his name from elsewhere (sentences 17–19, v. 11). This is the real purport of the discourse. God's pleasure is in the bringing of *pure* offerings.

Section B (sentences 20–28, vv. 12–14) is on the whole a repetition, with minor variations, of section A:

1. Sentences 20–24 (vv. 12–13d) repeat the content of sentences 1–8 (vv. 6–8b).

2. Sentences 25–26 (vv. 13e–14a) are a repetition of sentences 9–16 (vv. 8c–10).

3. Sentences 27–28 (v. 14b, c) in a certain sense repeat the content of sentences 17–19 (v. 11).

This pericope is pervaded with parallelisms and key words. In sentences 1–3 (v. 6) we have several parallelisms, with the key words *'āḇ, alāḏôn, kāḇaḏ, bāzâ šēm*. In sentences 4 and 5 (v. 7a, b) *gā'al* is the connecting word. In sentences 6–8 (vv. 7c–8b) the key word *nāḡaš* is taken from sentence 4 (v. 7a) and made concrete in sentences 7 and 8 (v. 8a, b). Sentences 9 and 10 (v. 8c, d) are parallel to sentences 11 and 13 (v. 9a, c). Sentence 9 is parallel to sentence 11:

> *offer them to your governor!*
> *Try then to appease God!*

Sentence 10 is parallel to sentence 13:

> *Would he . . . show you favor, says the Lord Almighty*
> *Would he show his favor . . . says the Lord Almighty.*

Sentence 12 (v. 9b) disrupts the parallelism of sentences 9–13, and with good reason. In the surrounding sentences the discourse is expressed in general terms, but with sentence 12—"You have done this"—the accusation is applied in a concrete manner. With sentences 14–16 (v. 10) a clear answer is given to the series of questions introduced by the interrogative particle *ha* in sentences 9–13 (vv. 8c–9c). The doors leading up to the altar may be shut, because the Lord has no pleasure in the offerings presented to him.

The very important statement of sentences 17–19 (v. 11) emphasizes the positive side of God's pleasure. Sentences 17 and 19 are parallel, both expressing the greatness of God's name among the nations. These sentences flank sentence 18, which must be considered the key conception of the whole pericope and the most significant antithesis of the preceding sentences 1–16. It concerns the *minḥâ ṭehôrâ*, the "pure offering."

Sentences 20–28 may be considered a repetition of the preceding accusation, in order to emphasize its seriousness, with one new element which explicates the involvement of the laity. The structural analysis of this pericope suggests its unity and contradicts the deprecatory assessment of the sacrifices as such.

The literary structure of 2:1–9 comprises four subsections.

1. A general statement concerning the duty and privilege of the priests to honor the name of the Lord (sentence 1, v. 1).

2. God's judgment because of the priests' failure to comply to "his command" (sentences 2–7, vv. 2–3). The judgment is first spelled out in

climactic style (sentences 2–4, v. 2), then expanded in more detail (sentences 5–7, v. 3).

3. The covenant with Levi (sentences 8–23, vv. 4–8). The composition of this main section is circular. The theme of both the beginning and concluding sentences (8 and 23) is "the covenant with Levi." But between the knowledge of the covenant (sentence 8) and its annulment (sentence 23), the antithesis between the classical (or ideal) and the contemporary priesthood is stressed. Following the introductory remarks concerning the upholding of the covenant with Levi (sentence 8, v. 4), the dual content of the covenant is expounded.

On the one hand it consists of life and peace, which are provided/given by God (sentences 9 and 10, v. 5a, b), and on the other hand its content is reverence, to which the classical priesthood complied (sentences 11 and 12, v. 5c, d). This last statement is especially emphasized in sentence 13 (v. 5e): "And (the classical priesthood) stood in awe of my name." This emphasis on the priests' obligation is most significant in the light of the accusation directed against the contemporary priesthood. The content of the priestly office is then indicated in sentences 14 and 15 (v. 6a and b). His instruction in the law is adequate and reliable. It involves two categories of persons: the lives and conduct of the priests themselves, and the lives and conduct of the "many" (sentences 16–22, vv. 6c–8b). Sentences 21 and 22 (v. 8a, b) are antithetical to sentences 16 and 17 (v. 6c, d). In between these antithetical sections the content of the priestly office is again emphasized (sentences 18–20, v. 7). Sentences 18 and 19 are chiastically structured:

> *the lips* of a priest preserve *knowledge*
> *instruction in the law* they seek from his *mouth*.

The office of the priest is summarized in sentence 20 (v. 7c):

> *He is a messenger of the Lord Almighty.*

The essence of section C can be condensed in terms of the two sentences which stand apart and are thereby emphasized: 13 and 20 (vv. 5f and 7c). According to these sentences a priest is a person who reveres the Lord and stands in awe of his name (sentence 13), and "a messenger of the Lord," implying both the moral integrity of his own person and his influence on "many," by way of a reliable instruction in the law.

4. This subsection consists of a concluding judgment on the contemporary priesthood, because they have annulled the covenant with Levi and have misused their elevated office (sentence 24, v. 9). The structural analysis of this pericope provides points of relief to the basic theme concerning the

remarkable contents of God's covenant with Levi, and the priesthood's obligations toward themselves and their community.

The pericope 2:10–16 is concerned with two mutually related vices: mixed marriages (sentences 1–8, vv. 10–12), and divorce (sentences 9–22, vv. 13–16). We have already referred to the complex character of Malachi's discourse in this section. We may analyze it as follows:

a. The deepest motivation for the accusation against the covenant people is their intimate relationship toward God. This is expressed by way of a question in sentences 1 and 2 (v. 10a and b), which are nearly a perfect parallelism:

Have we not . . . one Father
has not one God . . . us?

b. The accusation is pronounced, first, in general terms (sentences 3–6, vv. 10c–11c), and then with a specific application (sentence 7, v. 11d): "By marrying the daughter of a foreign god." It is important to consider the key words in this passage: *bāgaḏ* and *ḥillēl*. In sentence 3 (v. 10c) they are used in a vague sense, with a nearer definition of the subject in sentences 4 (the country of Judah) and 6 (the people of Judah). Both these terms, "to act faithlessly" and "to profane," are then applied to the phenomenon of mixed marriages (sentence 7, v. 11d).

c. The judgment is pronounced upon those people who have contracted mixed marriages and at the same time have with impertinence indulged in offering to the Lord (sentence 8, v. 12).

Note especially the inner structure of this passage. It concerns the intimate bond between the people and their God, and of the people among themselves. This covenant relationship is endangered when a "foreign" element is introduced by way of a religiously mixed marriage. Such marriages reflect faithlessness and profane the covenant. The whole spectrum of the covenant relationship is hereby affected. Because of the seriousness of this transgression, the culprits must be removed from the covenant community.

The next subsection may be analyzed as follows:

a. The accusation of being unfaithful toward the legal wife is introduced by the well-known pattern of statement-question-answer (sentences 9–13, vv. 13–14).

b. The deepest motivation for marriage fidelity and for the prohibition of divorce is both the intimate bond between the marriage couple as an institution of God himself and the deep concern for the kingdom of God (sentences 14–16, v. 15a–c).

c. The people are admonished to "guard their spirits" and not to be faithless to the wife of their youth, because God's severe displeasure ("hate") is directed against the culprits who have divorced their legal wives and have simultaneously indulged in religious activities, covering their clothes with the spattered blood of the sacrificial animals (sentences 17–22, vv. 15d–16).

This subsection has a number of parallelisms, which are helpful in conveying the meaning of its message. The admonishment to "take heed to yourselves" is stressed in the parallel sentences 17 and 21 (vv. 15d and 16c). The people are twice reprimanded not to be unfaithful (sentences 18 and 22, vv. 15e and 16d). The most significant parallelism is between sentences 19 and 20 (v. 16a and b). God hates both the sending away (of the legal wives) and the covering (of the clothes with violence). With reference to the first subsection (sentence 8, v. 12), we have here the same combination of transgression and a seeming act of piety.

The pericope 2:17–3:5 has a significant structure. It concerns God's answer to the people's "theological" considerations with regard to God's attitudes and acts on behalf of his people. The scope of reference is eschatological. In sentences 1–3 (2:17) the prophet applies his disputation method, statement-question-answer, and reveals the twofold reproach of the people against the Lord. According to them (a) God approves of evil, and therefore they asked, (b) where is the God of justice? The answer to this twofold reproach is given in sentences 4–18 (3:1–5).

First we have an answer in vague and general terms: (a) a messenger of the Lord will prepare his way (sentences 4–5, 3:1a, b), (b) the Lord will arrive suddenly (sentences 6–7, v. 1c, d), and (c) his arrival will be unpleasant (sentences 8–9, v. 2a, b).

In sentences 10–16 (vv. 2c–4) the prophet answers the first reproach of the people, viz., that God approves of evil. The negation of this reproach is strongly implied: God is going to purify his people. He will do it "like a refiner's fire, and like a launderer's soap!" Sentences 17–18 (v. 5) provide the answer to the second reproach, viz., "where is the God of justice?" The answer is that he is not dead or far away. On the contrary, he will draw near to them for judgment. He will be in a hurry to testify against them, with the implication that he will also judge them. It is important to note that the *mišpāṭ* of the people's reproach (2:17) figures prominently in the second answer (sentence 17, v. 5a).

This pericope also has its quota of literary devices. Sentences 1 and 2 are chiastically structured:

> *You weary* the Lord *with your words,*
> Yet *you say* wherein *have we wearied* (him)?

The same chiastic pattern is found in sentences 6 and 7 (v. 1c, d):

> *Suddenly he will come . . . the Lord you are seeking,*
> *The angel . . . in whom you delight. Behold, he comes.*

Sentences 8 and 9 (3:2a, b) are parallel. The key word in sentences 6–9 is *bô'*, "he comes," with its synonym, the Niphal of *rā'â,* "to appear." Sentences 10 and 11 (3:2c, d) are again parallel. In sentences 12 and 14 (3:3a and c) the figures of speech are parallel. In sentence 13 (3:3b) the implication is evident, because God's purifying activity concerns Levi. The key concept in sentences 10–14 is "to purify." Sentences 15 and 16 (3:3d, 4a) are parallel, denoting the consequence of the preceding process of purifying. In sentence 17 (3:5a) the key concept is *mišpāṭ,* "judgment," and in sentence 18 (3:5b) the roll of court is enumerated. The structural analysis emphasizes the inherent unity of this pericope and highlights the central theme of God's answer to the people's "theological concerns."

In the pericope 3:6–12 the central motif is the broken relationship between God and his people. In sentences 1–4 (3:6–7b) the situation is defined: (a) God has not changed. The evidence is the very existence of the people (sentences 1 and 2, v. 6); (b) the people, however, have continually disregarded God's decrees (sentences 3 and 4, v. 7a and b). This theme of God versus people permeates the entire pericope.

Sentence 5 (v. 7c) provides the key to the relationship between God and people. It is remarkably structured. The parallelism of the twofold *turn to (šûḇ 'el)* is chiastically arranged: you-I-I-you. The very essence of the relationship comprises a turning of one to another.

Sentences 5–12 (vv. 7c–9) are structured according to Malachi's disputation method: (a) statement (sentence 5: "Return to me, and I will return to you"), (b) question (sentence 6: "Why do we have to return?"), and (c) answer (sentences 7–12)—this answer being structured according to the same three-part pattern: (i) statement (sentences 7–8, v. 8a, b), (ii) question (sentence 9, v. 8c), and (iii) answer (sentences 10–12, vv. 8d–9).

The key words in this section are *šûḇ* (sentences 5, 6, v. 7c, d) and *qāḇaʿ* (sentences 7–9, v. 8a–c).

In sentences 13–16 (vv. 10–12) the renewal of the relationship between God and people in terms of sentence 5 (v. 7c) is expounded in a concrete manner. The people must *return* to the Lord by bringing the whole tithe into the storehouse (sentence 13, v. 10a), and God will again *turn* to his people by restoring to them material blessings (sentences 14–16, vv. 10b–12). According to this analysis the material obligations and promises are highlighted in the context of the relationship between God and his people.

The pericope 3:13–21 (Eng. 4:3) may be divided into three subsections. The first cluster of sentences is 1–3 (vv. 13–15), of which 1 and 2 are chiastically structured:

you—our conversation—against you

The well-known disputation method of statement-question-answer results in the distinction between the futility of religion and the prosperity of the wicked. The whole pericope is dominated by the antithesis between the righteous and the wicked. The second cluster of sentences is 4–9 (vv. 16–17), which comprises two parallel sections: (a) sentences 4–6 (v. 16a–c), and (b) sentences 7–9 (vv. 16d–17b). In this section the relationship between God and the righteous is expounded:

Those who feared the Lord spoke to one another (sentence 4).
God takes heed of them (sentences 5–6).
Those who feared the Lord kept his name in mind (sentence 7).
God will spare them as his treasured possession (sentences 8–9).

The third cluster of sentences is 10–17 (vv. 18–21 [Eng. 4:3]), which again can be subdivided into four sections: (a) sentence 10 (v. 18) with an internal parallelism emphasizes the real antithesis between the righteous and the wicked. This antithesis will reveal itself in the following manner: (b) the wicked will be destroyed on the day of the Lord (sentences 11–13); (c) for those who feared the Lord the righteousness will be like a shining sun (sentences 14–16); (d) the righteous will overcome the wicked on the day which God will create (sentence 17).

This pericope abounds with parallel phrases. This is especially evident in sentences 4–9 (vv. 16–17). Sentences 4 and 7 (v. 16a and 16d) are parallel, concerning the acts and attitudes of the righteous, and the same applies to sentences 4–6 over against sentences 8–9 (v. 16b, c and v. 17a, b), describing God's reaction. Sentence 10 (v. 18) has an internal parallelism, and sentences 11 and 13 (v. 19a and c) are both dominated by "the day that comes." It is worthwhile to note that the "coming day" of sentences 11 and 13 is more clearly defined in sentence 17 (v. 21 [Eng. 4:3]) as "the day which I will make." This reference to the "day of the Lord" provides the referential scope for the antithesis between the righteous and the wicked. On that day the distinction between those two categories of people within Israel will become apparent, and at the same time God will reveal himself as the one who takes heed and who will judge.

The more or less independent addition to Malachi's prophecy, 2:22–24 (Eng. 4:4–6), has two foci: the one (sentence 1, v. 22 [Eng. 4:4]) concerns the law of Moses, and the other one (sentences 2–4, vv. 23–24 [Eng. 4:5–6]) the prophet Elijah.

Sentence 1 (v. 22) has no specific literary structure, but it is nevertheless interesting in the way the *tôraṯ Mōšeh,* "the law of Moses," is defined. It consists of *ḥuqqîm ûmišpāṭîm,* "decrees and ordinances," it was "commanded" by the Lord to Moses at Horeb, and it was destined for "all Israel." A key word is the imperative plural of *zāḵar,* "to remember." Israel was admonished to remember the law of Moses.

Sentences 2–4 (vv. 23–24 [Eng. 4:5–6]) represent the second focus, concerning the prophet Elijah. Structurally the emphasis is on sentence 3 (v. 24a [Eng. 4:6a]). It consists of two parallel phrases, each dominated by *lēḇ . . . ʿal,* "hearts . . . to," and with *ʾāḇ* and *bēn* chiastically structured. On both sides of sentence 3, emphasizing the urgent need for a change of heart, are the parallel sentences 2 and 4 (vv. 23 and 24b [4:5, 6b]). Both these sentences are dominated by the idea of God's coming:

> *Look . . . the great and terrible day of the Lord comes. . . .*
> *Or else I will come and strike the land with the ban.*

The referential scope of Elijah's appearance and function is the eschatological occasion of God's coming on his great and terrible day.

XI. MESSAGE

In trying to assess the message of Malachi it is necessary to define the context and referential scope of his prophecy. Several possibilities have been suggested.[1] According to Nagelsbach, Volck, et al., the contents can be expressed with a reference to the past, present, and future. Their referential scope, therefore, is chronologically defined. Horst, Vriezen, and Botterweck content themselves with three basic elements in Malachi's prophecy, viz., the eschatological, cultic-legalistic, and particularistic aspects. T. J. Marshall confines himself to a number of theological ideas, such as the love of God, the theocratic covenant, the ideal priesthood, the universalistic perspective, the theodicy, and Malachi's conception of "the grand renovation." According to O. Procksch Malachi's message must be assessed in the light of the significance of the temple and cult for the postexilic community. Without denying the importance of these and similar approaches to the

1. The different approaches to the message of Malachi are spelled out in more detail in my *Maleachi,* COT, pp. 49–69. See A. van Selms, "The Inner Cohesion of the Book of Malachi," in *Studies in Old Testament Prophecy, OTWSA,* 1970/71 (Potchefstroom: Pro Rege, 1975), pp. 27–40.

central themes and motifs of Malachi's message, we share Baldwin's view that the concept of covenant is to be regarded as fundamental to Malachi's teaching.[2]

A few preliminary remarks are necessary. It is important to translate the covenantal content of Malachi's message in terms of the historical and religious background of his time. According to our date for his prophecy, Malachi delivered his speeches to the same audience to which Ezra and Nehemiah directed themselves in their renewal of the covenant, and to which Nehemiah would again address himself on the occasion of his second visit. Therefore we may assume that the themes of Malachi's message would be related to the specific and concrete situation of that period.

A second consideration is that the concept of covenant in Malachi's message does not resemble the classical structure of the late second-millennium covenants, or even the varying scheme of the covenants from the first millennium.[3] In Malachi the covenant is implied as the systematic principle of all the prophet's dialogues, the fundamental presupposition of his message. Apart from that we may discern relevant covenantal features throughout Malachi's book.

A third preliminary remark is that this approach to Malachi's message radically contradicts the tendency to disparage Malachi and belittle his message on the assumption that the creative period of prophecy had passed and that Malachi was more like a scribe or a casuist than a prophet, interested merely in the details of the ritual and in applying the letter of the law. This approach is totally at variance with the content and purport of Malachi's message.

The main features of the covenant, reflected in Malachi's prophecy, can be summarized as follows. The preamble or title, identifying the author of the covenant and expounding the majesty of the great king, does not precede Malachi's prophecy but is evident throughout. The Lord, who initiated the covenant, is really the central figure and spokesman. He is the dynamic and unifying center, not only of the OT as such (Hasel), but also of the book of Malachi. Out of a total of fifty-five verses, forty-seven record in the first person the address of the Lord of Israel (the exceptions being 1:1; 2:11–15, 17; 3:16). Baldwin rightly remarks: "This use of the first person

2. See Baldwin. Cf. also S. L. MacKenzie and H. N. Wallace, "Covenant Themes in Malachi," *CBQ* 45 (1983) 549–63. We may also refer to the unpublished M.Th. thesis of L. C. H. Fourie, "Die betekenis van die verbond as sleutel vir Maleagi," University of Stellenbosch, 1982.

3. Cf. K. A. Kitchen, *Ancient Orient and Old Testament* (London: Tyndale, Chicago: Inter-Varsity, 1966), pp. 94–96.

presents a vivid encounter between God and the people, unsurpassed in the prophetic books."[4]

God is the all-important subject of Malachi's dialogues. This is evident from the way he is introduced. Twenty-one times he is called Yahweh, the God of the covenant (1:1, 2, 4, 5, 7, 13; 2:11, 12, 13, 14, 17; 3:3, 4, 6, 13, 16, 23 [Eng. 4:5]; in some verses more than once: 1:2; 2:17; 3:16). Twenty-four times he is referred to as *YHWH ṣᵉḇā'ôṯ,* "the Lord Almighty," who has sovereign sway over all in heaven and on earth as his army (1:4, 6, 8, 9, 10, 11, 12, 14; 2:2, 4, 7, 8, 12, 16; 3:1, 5, 7, 10, 11, 12, 14, 17, 19, 21 [Eng. 4:3]). He is the supreme Lord, as expressed in the name *'ᵃḏônîm* (1:6), *hā'āḏôn* (3:1), and *'ᵃḏōnāy* (1:12, 14). In a few instances he is called *'ᵉlōhîm* (2:15; 3:8, 14, 15, 18). The meaningful combination that expresses his covenant relationship toward Israel is *YHWH 'ᵉlōhê yiśrā'ēl* (2:16) and *'ᵉlōhê hammišpāṭ* (2:17). With the name *'el* his divinity is contrasted with mankind, thus emphasizing God as the Incomparable One. By virtue of the covenant relationship the Lord refers to himself as a Father, which implies that Israel is his son (2:10; cf. 1:6). He is also referred to as *'ēḏ mᵉmāhēr,* "the quick witness" (3:5), and especially as *meleḵ gāḏôl,* "the great king" (1:14). In the ancient Near East this title is an indication of the author and initiator of the covenant relationship. In Malachi this great King also has revealed himself in his name (1:6, 11, 14; 2:2, 5; 3:16, 20) and presence (3:16).

The preamble is usually followed by a historical prologue or retrospect, mentioning previous relations between the two parties involved. Malachi does not provide an extensive historical prologue, but the introductory pericope, 1:2–5, may be regarded as such, especially the significant statement which constitutes the pervasive theme of the pericope: "I have loved you" (v. 2). Apart from this reference to the great King's attitude toward and concern for his covenant people, the whole prophecy testifies to the dynamic of God's holy and glorious presence. God's living intercourse with his people is expressed in terms of human acts and affections: he loves (1:2; 2:11), hates (1:3; 2:13, 16), is angry (1:4), is wearied (2:17), has pleasure and displeasure (1:10, 13; 3:4); he threatens (2:3; 3:11), blesses (3:10–12), and curses (2:2, 9, 12; 3:9). We agree with Oskar Holtzmann that Malachi, just as Job and Jonah, is full of "a striving for God."

Another element of the ancient covenants is the stipulations, which were both basic and detailed. In the book of Malachi the obligations are not expressly formulated but rather assumed. It is stated, however, that Israel habitually and continually has turned away from God's decrees (3:7), and in

4. Baldwin, p. 216.

the epilogue Israel was admonished to remember the law of Moses, consisting of decrees and ordinances (3:22 [Eng. 4:4]). The terms of the "instruction in the law" (2:6, 7) and the assumed written "law of Moses" (3:22 [Eng. 4:4]) must be implied. We may assume that the various stipulations in Malachi corresponded with "the book of the law of Moses" which Ezra expounded to the assembly of Israel (Neh. 8–10). Scholars differ with regard to the identity and scope of this "book." The general point of view is that it must be identified with Deuteronomy, with the exclusion of the "Priestly Code." We do not share this exclusive identification of Malachi's stipulations with Deuteronomy, but rather consider the Pentateuch as such as the legal background for Malachi's accusations. In the "roll of court," enumerating Israel's transgressions (3:5), and in the prophet's injunction concerning the compulsory contributions (3:6–12), the "material" of the "Priestly Code" is implied.

The main point in assessing the stipulations expounded or assumed in Malachi is that their referential scope is the covenantal relationship between God and his people. The deprecation of Malachi as one merely interested in the details of ritual (1:6–14) and "being possessed with an especial zeal for the seemly worship of God" (Lattey, with reference to 3:6–12) neglects the significance of the covenant relationship and implies the obscuring of the moral and religious issues which that entails.

The stipulations assumed in the book of Malachi concern the bringing of pure offerings (1:6–14), the priestly office of instruction in the law (2:1–9), the violation and desecration of the intimate bond between God and his people; and among the covenant people themselves, by means of religiously defined intermarriages and divorce (2:10–16), the law of retribution in vindicating the justice of God in permitting evil to exist (2:17–3:5), the maintenance of the temple staff and worship (3:6–12), and the distinction between the righteous and the wicked in eschatological perspective (3:13–21 [Eng. 4:3]). It is apparent that Malachi's "stipulations" embrace both the Law and the Prophets. It is therefore appropriate that his epilogue would remind the people of both "the law of Moses" and the covenant-restoring activities of Elijah, the representative of the Prophets.

In Malachi we also have the element of the invoking of witnesses. These, however, were not the gods, as in the ancient Near Eastern vassal treaties, but Yahweh himself (3:5). He will be "a quick witness against" (*'ēḏ m^{e}mahēr b^e*) a number of transgressors in Israel. In connection with God, the word "witness" implies both prosecutor and judge, as in Mic. 1:2 (cf. Mal. 2:14). In a certain sense the reference to "the angel of the covenant" may be interpreted as a witness to the maintenance and well-being of the covenant.

The prophecy of Malachi has its share of sanctions, in the sense of blessings and curses. The main passages in which the blessings are implied or expressed are 1:2–5; 2:2; 3:10–12; and the curses are in 1:4, 10, 13, 14; 2:2, 3, 9, 12, 13, 15, 16; 3:9, 11, 12. In all these passages the confirmation or annulment of the covenant relationship between God and his people is assumed.

The blessings and curses of the covenant are fundamental aspects of Malachi's representation of "the day of the Lord" (2:17–3:5; 3:13–21 [Eng. 4:3]). For a detailed discussion of this concept and the manner in which it is applied in the book of Malachi, see the summary at the end of the commentary on 3:13–21 (Eng. 4:3).

The message of Malachi obtains its theological purport and referential scope and perspective when it is assessed in the light of God's covenant with his people. The God of whom Malachi is speaking is the great King, the sovereign God of the covenant. The vassal partner in this covenant relationship is a couple of thousand returned exiles along with an unknown number who have stayed behind, subjected to a foreign government (1:8), experiencing plagues and pests (3:11, 12), a people whose spirituality (1:6–2:9; 3:6–12) and the moral aspects of their family life (2:10–16) are in deep decline, wrestling with the problem of vindicating the justice of God in the face of their adverse circumstances (2:17–3:5; 3:13–21 [Eng. 4:3]), but nevertheless, Israel (1:1, 5; 2:11), "the sanctuary of the Lord," which he loves, his treasured possession (2:11).

Malachi's preaching concerning this people must not be regarded as a purely particularistic or chauvinistic exercise on his part. The whole purport of his message concerns the well-being of the covenant relationship and was directed toward Israel's obligation to comply with its stipulations. In the history of revelation, and also in the prophecy of Malachi, temple and worship must not be considered purely ritualistic and without moral and religious significance. Indeed, they were instrumental to the renewal and the confirmation of the covenant relationship. The fundamental concept in this regard is *yir'a̱t YHWH*, "the fear of the Lord" (1:6, 11, 14; 2:2, 5; 3:16, 20 [Eng. 4:2]). The perspective on the coming "day of the Lord," providing the eschatological solution for all the questions and problems regarding retribution and theodicy, really obtains its theological content and purport in the context of the covenant: the judgment is the consequence of Israel's profaning the covenant of the fathers, and the blessings are the benefits of "life and peace," which are elements of God's covenant of grace.

The message of Malachi is confined to Israel as the covenant people. But this focus does not exclude a perspective on the universal purport and application of the concept of covenant. The God of the covenant is simultaneously the great King in both judgment and blessing even beyond the boundaries of Israel: Edom is the object of his eternal wrath (1:4), his name is to be feared among the nations (1:14), and far and wide over the Zion of all the earth there will be those who will present pure offerings to the honor of his name (1:11).

We agree with Baldwin that Malachi's remarkable ethical thrust has lost none of its cutting edge. His teaching, both negative and positive, strikes at the heart of nominal, easy-going Christianity just as it did at that of Judaism.

Malachi's message comprises a number of ultimates in the history of OT revelation. The way the love of God for his people is introduced and acclaimed (1:2–5) is comparable only with Deuteronomy (4:32–34; 7:6–8; 10:14, 15; 23:5) and Hosea (3:1; 11:8, 9; 14:5). The universalistic perspective on all peoples being incorporated into the kingdom of God is a general trend of prophecy (cf. Isa. 2:2–4; 11:10; 42:1–7; 45:14, 22, 23; 49:6; 51:4, 5; 66:18–23; Jer. 3:17; Amos 9:13; Zech. 8:20–23; 14:16), but the idea of the sanctification of the whole earth to become one grand Zion is found only in Mal. 1:11 (perhaps also in Isa. 19:19 and Zeph. 2:11). The conception of the importance and dignity of the priesthood presented in Mal. 2:5c–7, especially with regard to their teaching function, is unsurpassed elsewhere in the OT.

The same applies to Malachi's "ethics" on the marriage life of the covenant people (2:10–16). Scholars are generally agreed that nowhere else in the OT do we find such an elevated view of marriage as in this passage of Malachi. Nowhere else is divorce condemned in such explicit terms, and nowhere else is the purpose of marriage expounded in such a manner. It serves to procreate citizens not only for the kingdom of Israel but above all for the kingdom of God! Some aspects of Malachi's eschatology are also unique in the history of revelation, especially the notion that the Day of the Lord will be preceded by a "forerunner" (3:1, 23 [Eng. 4:5]).

In the relevant summaries to the different pericopes we have tried to relate the message of Malachi to the Church of the new dispensation.

TEXT AND COMMENTARY

I. HEADING (1:1)

1 *An oracle: The word of the Lord to Israel through Malachi.*

The problems of authenticity, of the relationship of this heading to Zech. 9:1 and 12:1, and especially of the purport of the name Malachi were considered in the Introduction. The textual variants in the LXX, Targum, and Peshitta are of no consequence. In the LXX *b^e^yaḏ mal'āḵî* is rendered "In the hand of the angel (messenger)," with the additional phrase, "Place it upon your hearts," taken from either Hag. 2:15 and 18 or Mal. 2:2. The Targum paraphrases the term *mal'āḵî* by adding "Whose name is called Ezra, the scribe." According to the Peshitta the heading refers to the "words" of the Lord.

In its present form the heading emphasizes the content, address, and instrument of the prophecy. The content of Malachi's prophecy is defined by the words *maśśā'* and *d^e^ḇar YHWH*. The Hebrew word *maśśā'*, especially in the context of prophecy, has been the subject of detailed studies. The word itself is a *maqṭal* form of the root *nāśā'*,[1] which means "to lift up," "to bear a burden," hence the meaning of the word is primarily "lifting," "the carrying of a burden," and then by a natural extension of meaning, "that which is lifted up," a "load" or "burden." In this sense it has a wide application in the OT. It is rendered "load" (Exod. 23:5); "carrying," along with that which is being carried (Num. 4:15–49); "burden" (Ps. 38:5 [Eng. 4]), and also "burden" in the sense of "responsibility" (Num. 11:11, 17) and even of "nuisance" (2 Sam. 15:33); "partiality" (2 Chr. 19:7); etc.

The main problem is to define the exact meaning of the word in a prophetic context. The division of scholarly opinion concerns, on the one hand, whether the word inevitably denotes a prophecy of judgment or, on the other hand, whether it could also mean "that which is lifted up," in this case "the voice," with the derived meaning of "utterance," "proclamation," "pronouncement," "oracle." We need not enter into this interesting discus-

1. Cf. P. A. H. de Boer, "An Inquiry into the Meaning of the Term *massa*," *OTS* 5 (1948) 197.

sion.[2] Both points of view can be substantiated by evidence taken from Scripture, the rendering of the ancient versions, and the history of translation and exegesis. It is sufficient to say that the tendency in lexicons and concordances to distinguish two words, one meaning "load" and the other "oracle," is unnecessary, because both meanings can be attributed to the semantic domain of the word *maśśā'*. We may concede to the opinion that in prophecy the word *maśśā'* generally acquires an ominous sense linked up with the catastrophic nature of many prophecies. In this sense the word usually denotes a pronouncement of utmost importance, a prophecy of judgment. In the context of such prophecies the word can be rendered by "burden imposed on." On the other hand, we have to consider that *maśśā'* is virtually a technical synonym of *d^{e}ḇar YHWH* (2 K. 9:25, 26), and that the idiomatic expression of "the lifting up of the voice," in regard to the utterances of the Lord, must also be conceived of in a solemn manner. Our conclusion would be that both approaches to the meaning of *maśśā'* will have to consider the seriousness of the message that is conveyed by this word in a prophetical context. Therefore we may agree with J. G. Baldwin that though the word "oracle" persists for want of a more accurate term, there is more to this heading than that word would suggest. "It lays stress on the prophet's sense of constraint in giving the message that follows." This "sense of constraint" is of course clearly suggested by the rendering of *maśśā'* as a "burden" which is imposed on the prophet, who like the loadbearer has no alternative but to accept and to discharge his duty. On the other hand, we may also agree with Baldwin that the idea of compulsion, urgency, dread, must be added to the rather neutral term "oracle." It signifies a pronouncement of utmost importance.

The syntactical relationship between *maśśā'* and *d^{e}ḇar YHWH* in the heading is differently assessed. In accordance with the conjunctive accent of the Masoretes *(mēr^{e}ḵā')* and the rendering of some of the ancient versions (LXX, Vulg.), most scholars during the previous centuries and even some of the modern interpreters give preference to the genitive relationship and translate: "The oracle of the word of the Lord" (so RSV). An alternative to this is the appositional relationship, expressed in the following translation: "An oracle: The word of the Lord" (so NIV). The third alternative is to maintain the separateness of both elements and translate: "An oracle. The

2. In addition to the article by De Boer (see n.1 above), relevant studies in this regard include H. S. Gehman, "The 'Burden' of the Prophets," *JQR* 21 (1940–41) 107–21; R. B. Y. Scott, "The Meaning of 'massa' as an Oracle Title," *JBL* 67 (1948) v–vi; J. A. Naude, "'Massa' in the Old Testament with Special Reference to the Prophets," in *Biblical Essays, OTWSA* (Potchefstroom: Pro Rege, 1966), pp. 91–100. For a detailed discussion see my *Maleachi,* COT, pp. 71–78.

word of the Lord" (so NEB). All these alternatives are grammatically appropriate. The conjunctive accent presupposes both the genitive (Gen. 17:13; Isa. 23:5) and the appositional (Ezek. 22:18; 1 Chr. 15:19) relationships. The third alternative is strongly advocated on the basis of Zech. 9:1 and 12:1.

There is, however, no need for an exclusive choice between the alternatives. The main consideration is that both elements of the heading amount to the same, that the content of the prophecy is thus described as a divine special revelation, as the living word of the revealing God, as the "burden," the "word," the message of the Lord. Our translation of the heading presupposes the second alternative as being more in accordance with the close relationship between *maśśā'* and *d^e^bar YHWH*.

Everywhere in the OT the expression "the word of the Lord" denotes the divine revelation. It is significant that the expression is mostly construed with the divine name Yahweh. There are only a few exceptions where reference is made to "the word of God" *(d^e^ḇar 'ĕlōhîm)* (Judg. 3:20; 1 Sam. 9:27; 2 Sam. 16:23; 1 K. 12:22; 1 Chr. 17:3). The point in question is, however, that the alternative expressions are substantially the same (cf. 1 K. 12:22 with 1 Chr. 17:3), that all bear witness to the fact that the Lord has revealed himself, and that the divine name Yahweh is especially connected with the *revelatio specialis.*[3] By this name he has revealed himself to Israel (Exod. 3:14–16; 6:1, 2) and has spoken through the prophets.

In considering the nature of "the word of the Lord," it is important to note that, with a few exceptions (Gen. 15:1, 4; Judg. 3:20; 1 K. 6:11; 2 K. 15:12), this "word" was mediated by the prophets, both the so-called prophets of the deed (Moses, Samuel, Nathan, Shemaiah [1 K. 12:22], Jehu son of Hanani [1 K. 16:1, 7], Elijah, etc.), and the "literary" prophets, with the exception of Obadiah, Nahum, and Habakkuk, who did not use the expression "the word of the Lord."

The etymology of *dāḇār* suggests the idea of background, of content. According to Procksch nothing is in itself *dāḇār,* but everything has a *dāḇār,* that is, has a background and meaning.[4] He distinguishes two elements in this concept: a noetic and a dynamic element. The *dāḇār* contains a *nous,* an element of thought, and it is filled with *power.* This would apply especially to the word of the Lord. It does not only convey understanding, but it is also dynamic. It goes out from the mouth of the Lord, and it does not return to him empty; it accomplishes that which he desires and achieves the

3. According to Th. C. Vriezen, *An Outline of Old Testament Theology,* rev. ed. (Wageningen: Veenman; Oxford: Blackwell, 1970), p. 345, "Yahweh represents the *revelatio specialis,* El the *revelatio generalis.*"

4. Procksch, in *TDNT,* IV:92. Procksch's approach has been criticized by J. Barr.

purpose for which he sent it (Isa. 55:11; cf. Isa. 9:7; Jer. 23:29; Heb. 4:12). Procksch rightly asserts that the word of the Lord has been the decisive power in the history of Israel since the days of Samuel. Every time the true prophets spoke *biḏᵉḇar YHWH,* "by the word of the Lord" (1 K. 13), things would happen *kiḏᵉḇar YHWH,* "according to the word of the Lord" (1 K. 12:24; 15:29; 16:12, 34). God revealed himself through his word, conveying the content of his will and establishing the fact of his divine presence.

Realizing the danger of the semantic overloading of meaning, and that the meaning of a word is specifically determined by its context, we have reason to consider the legitimacy of both the noetic and dynamic elements of the word of the Lord. As part of the heading of a prophetical book, such as Malachi, the expression indicates the content of the prophecy as being the veritable word of the Lord.

The prophecy of Malachi was directed *'el-yiśrā'ēl,* "to Israel." This is its address or destination. We maintain the reading *'el* and assume the accompanying verb *hāyâ:* "the word of the Lord which came to. . . ." In Hag. 1:1 we have an analogous expression with the verb *hāyâ* and the preposition *'el:* "The word of the Lord came through the prophet Haggai to . . ." (cf. Jer. 1:2; Ezek. 1:3; Hos. 1:1; Joel 1:1; Mic. 1:1; Zeph. 1:1; Zech. 1:1). The reading *'el* is substantiated by the Vulgate *ad.* The LXX has *epi,* which corresponds with the *'al* of Zech. 12:1, and both the Peshitta and Targum. The reading *'al* presupposes a meaning for *maśśā'* in the sense of "a burden imposed on." This need not be the case in our text.

The name *Israel* is used in the OT to denote Jacob, the second son of Isaac (Gen. 32), the twelve tribes of Israel, the ten tribes, and ultimately, the remnant of the nation after the Exile (Jer. 2, 31; Ezek. 3, 4, 5, 6, 12, 14, 21; and esp. the books of Ezra and Nehemiah).[5] It also occurs in 1 Maccabees (3:35; 4:11; and 30:31) and in the NT (Acts 3:12; 4:8; 13:17; etc.). It is also found on coins, denoting a *šeqel yiśrā'ēl.*

In the book of Malachi, *Israel* (1:1, 5; 2:11, 16; 3:22 [Eng. 4:1]) is also called Judah (2:11; 3:4), Jacob (2:12; cf. 1:2), and descendants of Jacob (3:6). This name is not used to distinguish between the people and the priests (cf. 1 Chr. 9:2; Ezra 9:1; 10:5), but is an indication of "the whole remnant of the people" (Hag. 1:12, 14). This comprehensive term is used to denote the covenant nation, the exiles mainly from the tribes of Judah, Benjamin, and Levi, together with the descendants of those who remained behind (cf. 2 K.

5. See A. R. Hulst, *Wat betekent de naam Israel in het Oude Testament?* (Miniaturen: Wageningen, 1962). See also L. M. Muntingh, "'Israel' in Old Testament and Jewish Apocalyptic Literature," *The Exilic Period. Aspects of Apocalypticism,* ed. W. C. van Wyk (*OTSWA* 25 [1982] and 26 [1983]; Pretoria: University of Pretoria, 1984), pp. 109–29.

25:12; Ezek. 33:24; Lamentations).[6] It is important to stress the unique significance of the term *Israel* in this historical context. It is a mere remnant of God's people, but as such it represents the entire nation. Irrespective of their numbers, failures, and sins, they still were the representatives of the people of God, the bearers of his promises, the mediators of his revelation (cf. Rom. 9:4, 5).

The mentioning of the name Israel also suggests the people's responsibility in terms of the expression "noblesse oblige." The indicative of their eminent position corresponds with the imperative of their calling to be the holy covenant nation. The prophecy of Malachi stresses both points of view.

The third element of the heading concerns itself with the instrument of the prophecy. The content of the prophecy is directed to the covenant people of God in the context of their historical setting through the instrumentality *(bᵉyaḏ)* of *mal'āḵî*. *Bᵉyaḏ* is a compound preposition, and is used here in the construct state to denote the human instrument of that which the Lord has spoken *(dibbēr),* has sent *(šālaḥ),* has ordained *(ṣiwwâ),* has given *(nāṯan),* has proclaimed *(qārā'),* or against which he has warned *('ûḏ).* In most cases the Lord is the subject, the content of his act is the revelation, and his instruments are the prophets. Analogical expressions are "by/from the mouth of" (*mippî,* Ezra 1:1), "in your mouth" (*bᵉp̄îḵā,* 1 K. 17:24). The compound preposition *bᵉyaḏ* corresponds with the *bᵉ-instrumentalis* (cf. 1 Sam. 28:15).[7] As part of a heading to prophetic utterances, it is also found in Isa. 20:2; Jer. 50:1; Hag. 1:1; 2:1, 10.

The meaning of *bᵉyaḏ* is literally "in or through the hand of," that is, "through" or "by means of." The prophet is represented as the "hand" that accepts and communicates the word of the Lord, that acts as its mediator.

The human (i.e., the prophetical) instrument mediating the word of the Lord is indicated as *mal'āḵî,* literally, "my messenger," or in its proposed more extensive form *mal'āḵîyāhû,* "messenger of Yahweh." We have already dealt with the problem of whether this name is to be regarded as an appellative, title, or proper name. We still have reason to believe that Malachi was the name of a historical person, even though nothing else is known concerning his personality, family, occupation, and circumstances.

This significant heading to the prophecy of Malachi is also applicable to the people of God under the new dispensation. It reminds us of the content of the word of God, not only as "Good News for Modern Man," but also as his "burden," his "prophecy" of judgment, his word, which conveys truth but is at the same time a dynamic power which changes lives through

6. So, correctly, H. H. Grosheide, *De terugkeer uit de Ballingschap,* Exegetica 2/4 (The Hague: Uitgeverij van Keulen, 1957), p. 38.

7. See GKC, § 119o-q.

the Spirit of God. This word of the Lord must be proclaimed to an exceptionally important group of people, the Church of the new dispensation, representing the whole of mankind. This group of people are of such importance in the whole economy of God's dealings with mankind that they are destined to be both the aspect and the instrument of God's kingdom.

The heading of Malachi's prophecy reminds us that the instrument is neither the creator nor the sustainer of either the gospel or the Church but is just the hand which receives and mediates, "the messenger" of the Lord who is charged with the calling to deliver the message, even though it might be an unbearable "burden" for both the instrument and the addressees. This presupposes total dedication, a self-sacrificing humility, but at the same time a boldness of faith, to proclaim such a message to such a people in the name of such a God. According to the book of Malachi this message contains good news, but also the sharp edge of God's divine judgment.

II. GOD'S LOVE FOR ISRAEL (1:2–5)

2 *I have loved*[1] *you, says the Lord.*
But you say,[2] *In what manner have you loved us?*
Was not[3] *Esau Jacob's brother?*[4] *says the Lord.*[5]
Yet I have loved Jacob,
3 *but Esau I have hated.*[6]

1. The Hebrew perfect may also be rendered in the present tense: "I love you" (cf. GKC, § 106g; S. R. Driver, *A Treatise on the Use of Tenses in Hebrew,* 3rd ed. [Oxford: Clarendon, 1874], § 11). A. S. Van der Woude prefers this translation, because the people's response presupposes a concrete and present situation. The one possibility does not exclude the other, however. The prophet's argument is based upon God's continuous love, during the whole of Israel's history, including the present time.

2. The first two sentences are chiastically structured. Cf. S. D. Snyman, "Chiasmes in Mal. 1:2–5," *Skrif en Kerk* (Jan. 1984) 17–22; idem, "Haat Jahwe vir Esau? ('n Verkenning van Mal. 1:3a)," *NGTT* 25 (1984) 358–62.

3. The interrogative particle connected with the negative, *h^a^lō'*, presupposes an answer in the affirmative: "Was not (Esau) a brother?" Answer: "Yes, of course." Cf. A. van Selms, "The Inner Cohesion of the Book of Malachi," in *Studies in Old Testament Prophecy, OTWSA,* ed. W. C. van Wyk (Potchefstroom: Pro Rege, 1975), pp. 27–40.

4. In Hebrew the preposition *l^e^* before "Jacob" denotes the genitive construction after the indefinite word *'āḥ:* "*a* brother *of* Jacob." Cf. GKC, § 129.

5. The proposition to delete *n^e^'um YHWH* metri causa *(BHK)* is unnecessary. This expression occurs only once in this passage, but it conforms to Malachi's general appeal to divine authority (so, rightly, J. M. P. Smith).

6. Sentences 4 and 5 (vv. 2d, 3a) are chiastically structured:

I have loved . . . Jacob
Esau . . . I have hated.

Sentences 3–5 (vv. 2c–3) are mutually connected through the names of Esau and Jacob, the sequence of which also has a chiastic pattern.

I have turned[7] *his mountains*[8] *into a wasteland*
and his inheritance (into a habitation)
for the desert jackals.[9]
4 *If*[10] *Edom would say: We have been crushed,*
but we will rebuild[11] *the ruins,*
then says the Lord Almighty: They may build,
but I will demolish.[12]
They will be called[13] *the Wicked Country,*
A People Always under the Wrath of the Lord!
5 *Your own eyes will see it,*
and you will say:
Great[14] *is the Lord over*[15] *the territory of Israel!*

The first pericope of Malachi's prophecy resembles the preamble of the Decalogue and presupposes God's covenant relationship with his people. It

7. The Hebrew verb governs two accusatives: "I have put his mountains to a wasteland." The imperfect with *waw*-consecutive refers to facts of history; cf. GKC, § 111.

8. The LXX has "his borders," but this is obviously a slip of the pen, the translator having chosen a word with a similar sound but with the wrong meaning (*tá hória autoú* instead of *tá oreiá autoú*).

9. See the commentary below on this translation.

10. The *kî* has conditional force: "supposing that," "if." See GKC, § 159bb; see also Vulg., Pesh., and Targ.

11. Lit. "we shall return and we shall build." For our translation, see the commentary below and GKC, § 120d.

12. Sentences 7 and 8 (v. 4a and b) are structured as an antithetical parallelism, with antithetical elements within each sentence: the *intention* of Edom against the *resolution* of the Lord. Cf. crushed/rebuild (sentence 7); they/I, build/demolish (sentence 8). Sentences 6–9 (vv. 3b–4) form a separate unit, which is dominated by words of judgment against Edom. Sentences 6 and 9 (vv. 3b and 4e) are structured as a synonymous parallelism, and the whole of this unit is an expansion of sentence 5: "but Esau I have hated."

13. Lit. "And they will call them." The third person plural is sometimes used to express an indefinite subject, which can be rendered by a passive: "They will be called." See GKC, § 144f, g. There is, therefore, no need to alter the text.

14. Heb. *yigdal,* Qal 3rd singular imperfect (not jussive), in the active sense of "to be great," "to manifest oneself as great." Sentences 10 and 11 (v. 5) are substantially the antithesis of sentence 2, "But you say, in what manner have you loved us?"

15. Heb. *mēʿal* means "over," "above," "upon"; see LXX *hyperánō* and Vulg. *super*. Many modern versions (NBG, RSV, NEB, NIV) and scholars (Reinke, pp. 246–47; Pressel, p. 378; G. A. Smith; Marti; Lattey; Smit; Brockington; Brandenburg; Edgar; etc.) prefer the rendering "beyond." See the commentary below.

The suggestion to read *g*ᵉ*ḇûl,* instead of *lig*ᵉ*ḇûl,* is based on an alleged dittography of *l*ᵉ (see *BHS*).

may be considered a general introduction to the prophecy,[16] in which attention is being drawn to the fact that the Lord has loved his people. This initial statement is of great significance. The tenor of the rest of the prophecy is one of judgment. The Lord is going to admonish and judge his people because of their sins in various spheres of their lives. But before addressing them with the stipulations and obligations of the law, he confronts them with the gospel: "I have loved you."

According to its structure we could summarize the content of this pericope as follows:

Sentences 1–2 (v. 1): God's declared love is called in question.

Sentences 3–9 (vv. 2–4): God's love for Israel is demonstrated by his judgment of Edom.

Sentences 10–11 (v. 5): God's love is being acknowledged by Israel.

It is important for the analysis of the discourse of this pericope to emphasize its basic theme. Contrary to a superficial impression, that theme is not the judgment of Edom but God's covenant love for Israel. This is the initial statement, the pervasive presupposition, and the culmination of the entire discourse.

2–3a The Lord himself is addressing the people. He declares to them his unaltered and continuous love. *I have loved you.* The Hebrew perfect frequently denotes an action resulting in a state which may be of longer or shorter duration, according to the context (cf. Gen. 4:6, 9; 32:10). Where the consequence of such action or the action itself continues into the present, we may render it in the present tense: "I love you."[17] This rule also applies to the perfect in our text. God's love began far back in the history of his people and remained in force through their entire history until the present day. We prefer the rendering "I have loved you," however, because the argument is based upon God's continuous love during the whole of Israel's history, including the present time. Malachi himself provides an eloquent commentary on God's abiding love in 3:6: the reason for Israel's continued existence is that the Lord has not changed.

The etymology of *'āhēḇ* is uncertain. Some scholars relate the word to a root *ḥāḇaḇ,* meaning "to be on fire," but then in the sense of "to love" (cf. Deut. 33:3). This meaning is also found in other semitic languages and

16. So, e.g., Keil; J. M. P. Smith; N. Ridderbos, in *De Bijbel . . . van verklarende aantekeningen voorzien,* vol. 2 (Kampen: Kok, 1954). Von Bulmerincq unjustly disconnected this passage from the following, dating it in ca. 485 B.C. (pp. 132–36).

17. See GKC, § 106g; Driver, *Tenses,* § 11.

in Mishnaic Hebrew.[18] It is doubtful, however, whether the two roots *'hb* and *ḥbb* can be related to one another in such a manner.[19]

'āhēḇ is the ordinary Hebrew word for "love." According to Quell its primary basis is the sexual relationship, with reference to Gen. 24:67; 1 Sam. 18:20; Hos. 3:1.[20] Snaith, on the other hand, presupposes the relationship of a dignitary toward one in need, and refers to Gen. 29:18; 37:3; Deut. 4:37; and 1 Sam. 18:1, 16.[21]

The modern approach, however, is not to rely too much on the etymology of words. Quell rightly concedes that *'āhēḇ* is used to express other relationships as well, for instance, the love of parents for their children (Gen. 22:2; 25:28), the mutual love between friends (1 Sam. 18:1, 3; 20:7), and even to denote the relationship between a slave and his master (Exod. 21:5). We are more interested in the word's meaning according to its usage. In this connection it is interesting to note that both the Peshitta and the Targum have substituted *rāḥam,* "to have compassion," "to bestow love on someone in need," for *'āhēḇ*. In the literature of the Christian era *'āhēḇ* seems to have vanished.[22]

The "love *['āhēḇ]* of God" occurs 32 times in the OT. The objects of his love are righteous deeds (Ps. 11:7; 33:5; 37:28; etc.), those who pursue righteousness (Prov. 15:9), and are in themselves righteous (Ps. 146:8). The Lord loves those he disciplines (Prov. 3:12; Heb. 12:6), and the alien (Deut. 10:18). Abraham is called "the loved one," the friend of God (Isa. 48:14). He loves Mount Zion (Ps. 78:68; 87:2) and his "sanctuary," here presumably Israel (Mal. 2:11). In most passages his love is directed toward Israel (Deut. 7:6–8; 7:13; 23:5; Ps. 47:5 [Eng. 4]; Isa. 43:4; Jer. 31:3; Hos. 11:1; 14:5; Mal. 1:2; 2:11) and their predecessors, the patriarchs (Deut. 4:37; 10:15).

The love of God for Israel is sovereign and unconditional. In a sense it is synonymous with election *(bāḥar)* and redemption *(yāša').*[23] This love-

18. Cf. N. Snaith, *The Distinctive Ideas of the Old Testament* (London: Epworth, 1944; repr. New York: Schocken, 1975), p. 131.

19. Cf. Quell, in *TDNT,* I:22; W. L. Moran, "The Ancient Near Eastern Background of the Love of God in Deuteronomy," *CBQ* 25 (1963) 77–87.

20. Quell, in *TDNT,* I:22. Cf. also J. Ziegler, *Die Liebe Gottes bei den Propheten,* Alttestamentliche Abhandlungen 11/3 (Münster: Aschendorffse Verlagsbuchhandlung, 1930); D. W. Thomas, "The Root *'hb* in Hebrew," *ZAW* 57 (1939) 57–64; G. Wallis, in *TDOT,* I:101–18; E. Jenni, in *THAT,* I:60–73.

21. Snaith, op. cit., p. 132.

22. See W. Jennings, *Lexicon to the Syriac New Testament* (Oxford: Clarendon, 1926).

23. According to C. Westermann, *Elements of Old Testament Theology,* tr. D. W. Stott (Atlanta: John Knox, 1982), p. 41, "election" is a static concept, which originated by way of "subsequent reflection *[nachträglicher Reflexion]* . . . looking back from a distance." The *locus classicus* Deut. 7:6–8 shows plainly, he says, the

election relationship between God and Israel is classically expressed in Deut. 7:6–8: "the Lord your God has chosen *[bāḥar]* you to be a people for his own possession, out of all the peoples that are on the face of the earth. It was not because you were more in number than any other people that the Lord set his love upon you and chose *[bāḥar]* you. . . . It was because the Lord loves *['āhēḇ]* you" (cf. Deut. 4:32–34; 10:14, 15; 23:5). The unconditional character of God's love for Israel is also stressed by Hosea, the prophet who was rightly called "the most magnificent preacher of God's love."[24] His love was that of a virtuous man toward an unworthy wife (Hos. 3:1; 11:8, 9; 14:5; cf. also Isa. 43:3, 4; 49:15; 54:5–8; Jer. 2:2–5, 31, 32; 31:3; Ezek. 16). In Jer. 31:3 God's love for Israel is defined as "an everlasting love" *('ahᵉḇaṯ 'ôlām)*. These components of the semantic domain of the word *'āhēḇ* are also present in the Lord's declaration of his love for Israel in our text. Historically it started with the calling of Abraham (Isa. 41:8; 2 Chr. 20:7), and with his love bestowed on the patriarchs (Deut. 4:37; 10:15). It was classically revealed in God's deliverance of Israel from the house of bondage (Deut. 4:34, 37; 7:8; 33:2, 3; Hos. 11:1), and, as the cause of the covenant relationship, it accompanied Israel's history.[25] In Lam. 3:22, 23 this truth is expressed in a striking manner: "Because of the Lord's great love *[ḥasḏê YHWH]* we are not consumed, for his compassions never fail" (NIV; cf. Mal. 3:6; Jas. 1:17).

In our text God's declared love for Israel is called in question. *But you say, In what manner have you loved us?* This style of dialogue is characteristic of Malachi's prophecy (cf. 1:6, 7; 2:14, 17; 3:7, 8, 13).[26] A sporadic use of this style is also found in Isa. 40:27–31; 49:14–21; Jer. 13:11, 12; 15:1, 2; Ezek. 18:2; and Zech. 1–6. It is a common trend in the later Jewish literature, especially in the Mishnah and Talmud. Because of this resemblance in style between Malachi and the Jewish rabbis, some scholars dispute the originality of Malachi's diction, but unjustly so.[27] Instead of

---

interpretative character of the concept of election. We cannot agree with Westermann, because of the hypothetical nature of his point of view. God's act of love and of choosing Israel presupposes a dynamic and living relationship.

24. So N. Peters, *Die Religion des AT* (München: J. Kosel and F. Pustet, 1920), p. 30; F. Buck, *Die Liebe Gottes beim Propheten Osea* (Rome: Pontifical Biblical Institute, 1953); J. Ziegler, *Liebe Gottes*.

25. Cf. Snaith, op. cit., p. 95.

26. Cf. E. Pfeiffer, "Die Disputationsworte im Buche Maleachi," *EvT* 19 (1959) 546–68; H. J. Boecker, "Bemerkungen zur formgeschichtlichen Terminologie des Buches Maleachi," *ZAW* 78 (1966) 78–80.

27. Cf. B. Duhm, *Die Theologie der Propheten als Grundlage für die innere Entwicklungsgeschichte der israelitischen Religion* (Bonn: Verlag von Adolph Marcus, 1875), p. 319; P. Volck, in *Realencyklopädie für protestantische*

being drab and stereotyped, Malachi's style could rather be compared with the lively dialogue of the popular orator.[28] The same method was applied in the works of Greek authors and by Paul in his proclamation of the gospel.[29]

The question whether the people really reacted in such a manner must be left open.[30] If not in actual words, this reaction may be assumed in the mind and acts of the people. Adamson may be right that the origin of Malachi's dialogues must be found in "the protesting and questioning cries of the hecklers, when he first delivered his message on the streets."[31]

In what manner have you loved us? The point of reference in this question is not so much the metaphysical truth of God's love for Israel, but rather the actual experience of that love in the people's concrete existence and adversities. In what has God manifested his love for them?[32] They bluntly denied the fact and significance of God's love. In a way this is an astonishing question. It presupposes the denunciation of both election and covenant, the annulment of their own wonderful history and of the fact that his compassions never fail, that they are new every morning (Lam. 3:22, 23).

Although one cannot condone the utterly irreligious and irresponsible character of this question, one may appreciate their attitude in the context of their experiences. Their expectations of a glorious renewal of their national life after the return from exile had been disappointed. The promised kingdom of the Messiah had still not dawned. Israel as a nation was not delivered and glorified. They still remained under Persian rule (1:8) and were suffering from pests and plagues (2:17; 3:11, 12). The words of Isa. 59:9–11 seem to reflect their own situation: "So justice is far from us, and righteousness does not reach us. We look for light, but all is darkness; for brightness, but we walk in deep shadows. Like the blind we grope along the

---

Theologie und Kirche, ed. J. J. Herzog, rev. A. Hauck (Leipzig: Hinrich, 1903), XII:110. According to Duhm the book of Malachi reflects the poverty *(Armuth)* of that time, as shown, e.g., by his style.

28. So R. Rendtorff, in *RGG,* IV:628–29.

29. For Greek authors see S. L. Edgar, p. 98; for Paul see E. P. Groenewald, "Die tweegesprek as verkondigingsmetode by Paulus," *NGTT* 4 (1962) 325–36.

30. Cf. A. H. Edelkoort, *De Christusverwachting in het Oude Testament* (Wageningen: H. Veenman, 1941), p. 473; Baldwin, p. 214, declares: "It is extremely unlikely that the words he puts into the mouth of his opponents were in fact voiced."

31. Adamson, "Malachi," in *NBC,* p. 764.

32. Cf. Gen. 15:8; Exod. 33:16; Quell, op. cit., p. 34n.71; H. Brandenburg: "How (do we recognize) that you love us?"

wall, feeling our way like men without eyes. . . . We look for justice, but find none; for deliverance, but it is far away" (NIV).

This questioning of God's love presupposes a situation in which it has become extremely difficult for the people to experience the reality of God's intervention on their behalf. It suggests a point in Israel's history a longer or shorter time after the exhilarating experiences of the return from exile and the rebuilding of the temple (Ezra 1, 3, 7, 8; Neh. 7; Hag. 2; Zech. 1–8). It was a time of low ebb, when it wearied priests and people to bring their sacrifices (1:13), when they deemed it irrelevant to do good or evil in the eyes of the Lord (2:17), and futile to serve him (3:14).

Because the Lord has not changed (3:6), he reacted to Israel's charge by giving concrete proof of his love. He is going to demonstrate his love by reminding his people of the distinction between Israel and Edom with regard to their respective fates and destinies. This proof could not be denied, because it was substantiated by the facts of history. It all started a long time ago. *Was not Esau Jacob's brother?*

The interrogative particle *hᵃ* connected with the negative *lō'* presupposes an answer in the affirmative: "Yes, of course!"[33] Esau was indeed Jacob's brother. In Hebrew the brotherhood is stressed more emphatically: "Was he not a brother, viz., Esau of Jacob?"[34] Note especially the sequence in this question. Esau is named first because he was the firstborn (Gen. 25:25, 26) and therefore entitled to the birthright, the person who could have claimed preferential treatment. The proposal to delete "says the Lord" (Heb. *nᵉ'um YHWH*) because of the meter (*BHK* and *BHS*) is unnecessary. This expression occurs only once, but it conforms to Malachi's general appeal to divine authority (so J. M. P. Smith, A. S. van der Woude, et al.).

Yet I have loved Jacob, but Esau I have hated. This statement is chiastically structured to emphasize the point in question.

I have loved . . . Jacob,
Esau . . . I have hated.[35]

The mystery and significance of God's love for Israel is especially evident from the fact that his preferential treatment was, contrary to the general custom and conception, not directed to Esau but to Jacob. This included both Jacob's and Esau's descendants.

How are we to assess the purport of the antithesis between God's

33. See n. 3 above.

34. See n. 4 above.

35. Cf. G. J. Botterweck, "Jakob habe ich lieb—Esau hasse ich," *BibLeb* 1 (1960) 36–38; S. D. Snyman, "Haat Jahwe vir Esau?", pp. 358–62.

"love" and "hate" in this context? We will have to reject statements like that of Edgar, according to whom Malachi's response is characterized "for its lack of depth." "How can God's love," he asks, "be demonstrated by comparing it to his hate for Esau? The reasoning is not altogether acceptable to us."[36] The same applies to the statement of Brockington according to whom "this attitude of Yahweh to Edom reflects . . . Israel's own attitude to Esau."[37] Would this also have been Paul's attitude when he referred to this statement in Rom. 9:13?

According to most scholars the contrasting concepts of "love" and "hate" must be interpreted in the sense of more or less. Laetsch represents this point of view. According to him "the Lord is speaking here not of absolute love embracing only one nation and of absolute hatred directed against another nation. The word hate is used in the sense of less love."[38]

It must be granted that the idea of a comparative contrast between love and hate is usually implied when it concerns the interrelationship between two persons, for instance, between two wives of the same husband. In Gen. 29:31 Leah is referred to as "the hated one" *(śᵉnûʾâ),* but in the previous verse we were told that Jacob "loved Rachel *more* than Leah" (cf. also 1 Sam. 1:2, 5; Luke 14:26). This comparative contrast between love and hate is unquestionably implied in Deut. 21:15–17. In connection with the birthright of the firstborn, a husband with two wives is admonished not to give preference to the son of his beloved wife if that son is not his firstborn. He must consider the right of the real firstborn, even though it is the son of the wife that he "hated." In this context the "hated" wife is the one that is less loved. In Hebrew the comparative relationship is sometimes expressed by merely joining the opposites, leaving it to the reader to assess the "dialectical" character of especially the negative statement.[39]

But the question is whether this idea of more or less reflects the real and significant meaning of the statement in our text. We do not believe so. The "love" that is spoken of in our text is sovereign and unconditional. It is *God's* "love" for Israel. It did not take into account the birthright prerogative of Esau (Gen. 25:25), the feelings or attitudes of the parents (Gen. 25:28), or even the moral imperfections of Jacob (Gen. 25:29–34) and his descendants throughout their history and in the time of Malachi. God's "love" was in no way conditioned by the moral qualities of its object, but emanated from his

36. Edgar, pp. 99–100.
37. Brockington, p. 656.
38. Laetsch, p. 512; also Elliger, ATD.
39. Cf. Kruse, "Die dialektische negation als semitisches Idiom," *VT* 4 (1954) 385–400.

sovereign will and mercy. This "love" is undefinable in terms of more or less.[40]

In a certain sense this is also true of God's "hate." This pericope describes its effect (1:3, 4) and its cause (1:4b). According to Michel this "hate" can be described in terms of "differentiation and disavowal, punishment and judgment."[41] The character of God's hate is evident when we consider the objects of his hate. He hates idolatry (Deut. 12:31; 16:22; Jer. 44:4; Hos. 9:15; Zech. 8:17), evildoers (Ps. 5:6 [Eng. 5]), the wicked and those who love violence (Ps. 11:5), robbery and iniquity (Isa. 61:8), and Israel's heathenized cult (Amos 5:21), as well as several vices mentioned in Prov. 6:16–19. The intensity of God's hate is emphasized when it is said that he "hates with all his soul" (Ps. 11:5, NEB), and especially when we consider the destructive effect of his hate: he will "destroy" those who tell lies (Ps. 5:7 [Eng. 6]), and on the wicked "he will rain fiery coals and burning sulfur" (Ps. 11:6, NIV).

In Hos. 9:15 the positive statement that God hated Israel because of all their wickedness is followed by the negative counterpart: "I will no longer love them." The gross effect will be that God will "drive them out of (his) house," out of the promised land and away from his divine presence.

In the light of scriptural evidence we are warned against reverting to human psychology in interpreting God's "love" and "hate." Both his love and hate are far more profound than the corresponding human sentiments. Both concern God's sovereign and radical decree. At the same time we must not interpret these divine "affections" in dogmatic terms. We disagree with Calvin, et al., that reference is made in our text to the predestination of Jacob to eternal life and the reprobation of Esau unto eternal damnation.[42] These ultimate destinies are not directly implied in our text and context. It concerns God's attitude toward his covenant people in terms of his elective love, and by way of illustration his attitude toward Edom and his descendants who were not included in the covenant relationship. The semantic scope of both terms, "love" and "hate," is primarily defined by the history of salvation.[43] In our nearer definition we must consider some appropriate distinctions.

40. Cf. G. C. Berkouwer, *De Verkiezing Gods* (Kampen: Kok, 1955), p. 77.

41. Michel, in *TDNT*, IV:691.

42. Cf. Schrenk, in *TDNT*, IV:179: "The reference here is not to salvation, but to position and to historical task." See also Botterweck, op. cit.: "Like Rom. 9:10–13, Mal. 1:3 does not refer to predestination." Cf. also Reinke; Laetsch; H. N. Ridderbos, *Romeinen* (Kampen: Kok, 1959), p. 228.

43. Cf. H. Velema, *Uitverkiezen en uitverkiesing in het NT* (Kampen: Kok, 1965).

God's "love" and "hate" concern first of all Jacob and Esau as individuals (Gen. 25:23). In sovereign liberty God drew Jacob to his side, inserting him into the holy lineage out of which the seed of the woman would be born (Gen. 3:15), and directing Esau to be on the side of the nations outside of his covenant relationship with Israel. In this sense "hate" does not imply that Esau was destined for eternal damnation. He merely became part of the nations at the fringe of the covenant people, and as such again entered into the scope of God's redemptive purposes (Gen. 12:1–3).

In the relative histories of the descendants of both Jacob and Esau, God's "love" and "hate" manifested themselves in a concrete manner. The territory and descendants of Edom emerged as a "wicked country" and as "a people with whom the Lord is angry for ever" (cf. Ezek. 25:12; 35:15; Obad. 10–16; Ps. 137:7; Lam. 4:21). In the process of the historical events God's contrasting attitudes of love and hate deepened in accordance with his everlasting compassion on the one hand and his righteous judgment on the other hand. In this sense God's "hate" has its correlation in Esau's "wickedness" (v. 4b). The effect of both "love" and "hate" will be that Jacob's descendants would be established in their country and those of Esau would be uprooted.[44]

The message of Malachi in this connection is in accordance with the testimony of Isa. 34–35 and 63:1–6, and of Ezek. 35–36. In Isa. 34–35 the prophecy of Israel's restoration as a nation is connected with the eschatological depiction of Edom's destruction. God's vengeance on Edom and his deliverance of Israel are interrelated on his "day," according to Isa. 63:1–6. The same vision on the relationship between Israel's restoration and Edom's destruction is found in Ezek. 35–36.

In the NT both "love" and "hate" are deepened to signify the participation or lack thereof in Christ's work of redemption.[45]

3b In the prophecy of Malachi the fact of this preferential love is stated without further explanation. The motivation is irrelevant. The statement amounts to saying that Israel would not be able to deny it. The history of the forefathers and of the nations that originated from them serves to confirm the fact. God has turned Edom's mountains, its indicated inheritance (Gen. 27:39),[46] into a wasteland, a habitation for the desert jackals.

44. Snyman, "Haat Jahwe vir Esau," p. 361, rightly draws attention to the chiastic and literary structure of the pericope, in which God's pronounced love and hate function. The focus is more on God's love for Jacob, not so much on his hate for Edom.

45. Cf. H. Velema, *Uitverkiezen en uitverkiesing in het NT* (Kampen: Kok, 1965), p. 111.

46. This does not imply that Edom's inheritance was initially a wasteland, although this may be suggested by the privative *min* in Gen. 27:39: "Your dwelling

Contrary to Israel, who also was destroyed on occasion, Edom's attempt to rebuild the ruins will be frustrated. The guilt of this nation and its fate are to be expressed in special names: the wicked country, a people always under the wrath of the Lord.

The Hebrew verb *'āśîm* governs two accusatives: *I have turned his mountains into a wasteland and his inheritance (into a habitation) for the desert jackals.* The imperfect with *waw* consecutive refers to facts of history. The LXX reads "his borders," but this is obviously a slip of the pen, choosing a word with a similar sound, *tá hória,* instead of *tá oreiá,* but with the wrong meaning. Since Cappellus most scholars emended the Heb. *l^e^tannôṯ,* "for the jackals," to *lin^e^wôṯ,* a shortened form of *lin^e^'ôṯ,* from the root *nāwâ* or *nā'â,* meaning "pastures" (of the wilderness). This rendering seems to be substantiated by the rendering of the LXX: *eis dómata,* "to habitations," a reading supported by the Peshitta and the Syro-Hexapla. It is also supported by scriptural evidence, where reference is made to "desert pastures" in a context of judgment (cf. Jer. 9:9 [Eng. 10]; 23:10; Joel 1:19, 20; 2:20; Ps. 65:13 [Eng. 12]). The main reason for this proposed emendation is that a feminine plural of the Hebrew word *tan,* "jackal," is unknown. But the ending *-ôṯ* originally was just another plural ending, without the definite distinction in gender.[47] The expression "jackals of the desert" is well attested to denote the effect of the divine judgment (cf. Isa. 35:7; Jer. 9:11 [Eng. 12]; 10:22; 49:33; 51:37; Ps. 44:20 [Eng. 19]; Job 30:29).

A significant point in our exegesis is to establish the scope of the historical reference to Edom's calamity. Three alternative historical events have been considered: (1) the possibility that Edom also was subdued by the Chaldeans shortly after 587 B.C.; (2) the calamities that ensued from the Persian-Egyptian wars; and (3) the invasion of Edom by the Nabateans.[48]

The argument of some scholars (e.g., Reinke, Keil, De Moor) that the comparison of Israel and Edom presupposes a simultaneous catastrophe and that it therefore must be connected with the Chaldean invasion of Judah in 587 B.C. is contrary to the facts of history. Instead of sharing Judah's calamity, Edom was elated because of Judah's downfall (cf. Ezek. 25:12; Obad. 10–16; Ps. 137:7; Lam. 4:21). According to Jer. 40:11 many Judeans fled to Edom and neighboring countries, and after a while returned to Judah. Therefore Edom's calamity could not have been simultaneous with that of

---

will be *away* from the earth's richness" (NIV). It became a wasteland and ruins because of God's judgment.

47. See Gemser, *Hebreeuse Spraakkuns,* § 95an.2.

48. So J. C. de Moor, *De Propheet Maleachi* (Amsterdam: Kirberger & Kesper, 1903), pp. 73–74.

Judah. According to Josephus (*Ant.* 10.9.7 [180–82]) Nebuchadnezzar invaded Ammon and Moab in the twenty-third year of his reign (582 B.C.), and the suggestion is that he could have conquered Edom as well. The facts remain, however, that Edom was not mentioned in Nebuchadnezzar's diary,[49] and that Edom eventually expanded its territory in a northerly direction during Judah's exile.[50]

The second alternative, proposed by Jahn, Hitzig, et al., is a mere hypothesis and cannot be substantiated by historical data. We have no evidence to prove that Edom was in any way involved in the Persian-Egyptian wars.[51]

Therefore we prefer the third alternative.[52] The Edomites gradually vacated their territory from the fifth century onward because of the occupation of their country by the Nabateans.[53] The details of this gradual overrunning of the Edomites by the Nabateans are unknown,[54] as is the attempt of Edom to restore the damage done and the nature of the divine interference (Lattey). We may assume, however, that the statement of v. 3 had a bearing upon calamities which befell Edom in the time of Malachi, and that this may be connected with the penetration of Edom's territory by the Nabateans.[55]

4 The notion that Edom would in the near future restore its national life, and that it would be able to rebuild the ruins of its cities and country, is going to be cancelled once and for all. Edom's assumed response is introduced by the particle *kî,* with conditional force: "If," "supposing that."[56]

We have been crushed. The Peshitta and Targum mistakenly derived the Hebrew word from a root *rôš,* "to be in want," "to be poor." The meaning

49. Cf. Josephus *Ant.* 10.9.7 (180–85); also M. Noth, *The History of Israel,* 2nd ed., tr. rev. P. Ackroyd (London: Black; New York: Harper & Row, 1960), pp. 293–94.

50. Cf. C. C. Torrey, "The Edomites in Southern Judah," *JBL* 27 (1898) 18.

51. Cf. B. Stade, *Geschichte des Volkes Israel* (Berlin: G. Grote, 1888), 2:112; G. A. Smith, p. 645.

52. First mentioned by Grätz, "Die Anfänge des Nabataer—Herrschaft," in *Monatschrift für Wissenschaft und Geschichte des Judenthums* (1875), pp. 60–66. Cf. also P. C. Hammond, *The Nabataeans—Their History, Culture and Archaeology,* Studies in Mediterranean Archaeology 37 (Gothenburg: P. Aström, 1973); J. I. Lawlor, *The Nabataeans in Historical Perspective* (Grand Rapids: Baker, 1974).

53. According to Torrey, op. cit., the Nabatean invasion of Edom's territory started in the 7th century B.C., and according to S. Cohen, in *IDB,* III:491, it may have been in the 6th century.

54. The first reference is found in the legends of Antigonus's campaigns in 312 B.C., as it was told by the Greek author Diodorus (Diodorus Siculus 19, pp. 94–100).

55. Cf. G. Smit, p. 142; Laetsch, p. 513; Deden, p. 306; Dentan, p. 1124.

56. See GKC, § 159bb.

of the Pual perfect from the root *rāšaš,* "to be crushed" or "destroyed," is supported by the rendering of the LXX and Vulgate. Edom realized their present condition. They have been crushed. Their cities and country have been laid waste.

Edom's intention is to *rebuild the ruins* (lit. "We shall return and we shall build"). In such a statement the principal idea is introduced by the second verb, while the first *(šûḇ)* contains the definition of the manner of action, thus: "We shall build again," "we shall rebuild."[57] It is important to note that v. 4a and b is structured as an antithetical parallelism. Edom's intention is radically cancelled by the Lord's resolution. They may try to overcome their national calamity, they may diligently endeavor to re-establish the political and socio-economic basis for the continuation of their existence. They may try to do all these things, but the Lord will not allow it to happen. He will *demolish.* He will tear down that which they wanted to rebuild, and in the process he is going to end Edom's history. The prophecy concerning Edom has described the full circle: the whole of this unit is the expansion of sentence 5 (v. 3a): "But Esau I have hated."

Israel must appreciate this fact. God's love for them has been and will be demonstrated in their own restoration. His "hate" for Edom will manifest itself in that country's total destruction. Israel must be reminded of God's ultimates in dealing with the righteous and the wicked, as they were expressed by Asaph: "When I tried to understand all this, it was oppressive to me till I entered the sanctuary of God; then I understood their final destiny" (Ps. 73:16–17, NIV)

Edom's fate and guilt are correlated. Both these aspects are expressed in proverbial names given "to them," that is, to both the country and the people. *They will be called the Wicked Country, A People Always under the Wrath of the Lord.* As a wicked country they will always experience the wrath and judgment of the Lord. For this same reason God has driven the nations of Palestine out before the Israelites (Deut. 9:4). As a people Edom's permanent ruins will always remind them of God's wrath. This will continue "for ever." The implication is that Edom, like Moab (Isa. 25:10), Babel (Isa. 13:1–14:23), and Egypt (Ezek. 30:3), is designated as God's permanent enemy. Also in later Jewish literature Edom became the symbol of the enemy of God (cf. 1QM 1:1, 2, 4 with 1QM 12:11).

This prophecy concerning the permanent ruin of Edom and the Edomites has been fulfilled in the subsequent history. The Nabateans drove them from their territory, and the Maccabees added to their distress. In 185 B.C. Judas Maccabeus crushed their resistance (1 Macc. 5:3, 65; 2 Macc.

57. See GKC, § 120d.

10:15–23, cf. Josephus *Ant.* 12.8.1 [327–29]), and fifty years later John Hyrcanus caused them to be circumcised. The end came in the time of Simon from Gerasa (cf. Josephus *BJ* 6.8.2 [378–86].[58]

5 Israel's duty and concern was to acknowledge the fact of God's love for his people, as he had demonstrated it in the histories and destinies of both Israel and Edom. *Your own eyes will see it.* You will unquestionably become aware of it. This will be the conclusive answer to your own arrogant question: "In what manner have you loved us?" This acknowledgment will cause you to rejoice in the confession that *Great is the Lord,* exalted "above," "over," "upon" the territory of Israel. The Hebrew verb *yigdal* is not a passive but an imperfect in the active sense of "to be great," "to manifest oneself as great." In Mic. 5:3 (Eng. 4) the idea of the Lord's greatness is applied to the universal reign of the Messiah, and in some of the psalms it is connected with the eschatological salvation (Ps. 35:27; 40:17 [Eng. 16]; 70:5 [Eng. 4]).

We deliberately prefer the translation of *mēʿal (l^e)* as *above,* because this is how it is rendered in all the passages where it is used, with the possible exception of 2 Chr. 24:20 and 26:19 (cf. Gen. 1:7; 1 Sam. 17:39; Ezek. 1:25; Jon. 4:6; Neh. 12:31, 37; 2 Chr. 13:4). The main reason for our preference is to be found in the analysis of the discourse: the pervading theme is God's love for his people. This theme is worked out negatively by demonstrating God's love in what happened and is going to happen to Edom, and is then emphasized by Israel's acknowledgment of the greatness of God's love for his covenant people and country. The greatness of the Lord is not so much seen in his judgment upon Edom, but rather in the manifestation of his love for Israel.[59] Our rendering of *mēʿal (l^e)* is supported by the LXX *hyperánō* and the Vulgate *super.* The alternative translation, "beyond," is supported by the Peshitta and Targum. The *territory of Israel* is preeminently contrasted with the *wicked country* of Edom: in one God's glory and love is manifested and acknowledged, in the other his anger is felt for ever.

58. Cf. Oskar Holtzmann, "Der Prophet Maleachi und der Ursprung des Pharisäerbundes," *Archiv für Religionswissenschaft* 19 (1931) 8; Laetsch, p. 209; N. Glueck, *The Other Side of the Jordan* (New Haven: American Schools of Oriental Research, 1940), p. 200.

59. According to E. Wendland, "Linear and Concentric Patterns in Malachi," *BT* 36 (1985) 120–21, the "epiphoric pressure exerted from 1:11 and 1:14 with regard to the repeated phrases, 'my name' and 'among the nations,' would lead one to see a corresponding pair in 1:5, viz. 'Yahweh' and '*beyond* the border of Israel' (rather than 'over the border of Israel')." This interpretation, of course, is possible, but the internal structure of the pericope in 1:2–5 favors our conclusion. This is endorsed by Snyman in his doctoral thesis, "Antiteses in die boek Maleagi," p. 81.

In sum, the Lord's love for his covenant people has been called in question by Israel, has been proven by God in the respective histories and destinies of Israel and Edom, and had to be acknowledged by Israel. God has demonstrated to us his unquestionable love in the "history" of his Son, our Lord and Savior, Jesus Christ (John 3:16), and our duty and privilege would be to acknowledge and proclaim this Good News.

III. GOD DEMANDS PURE OFFERINGS (1:6–14)

6 *A son honors (his)*[1] *father, and a servant his master.*[2]
If I am a Father, where[3] *is the honor due to me?*[4]
If I am a Master, where is the fear due to me?[5]
says the Lord Almighty to you, priests, who despise my name.[6]
But you ask, In what manner have we despised your name?
7 *You have offered defiled food on my altar,*
yet you ask, How have we defiled you?
By saying[7] *that the table of the Lord is contemptible.*[8]
8 *When*[9] *you bring a blind animal for sacrifice, there is nothing wrong,*

1. Although the pronominal suffix is not in the MT, it is clearly implied.

2. An intensive or majestic plural, according to Vriezen, *Outline of Old Testament Theology*, rev. ed., p. 344; cf. N. Walker, *VT* 7 (1957) 208; also Van der Woude. See also GKC, §§ 124e, 145h.

3. The interrogative particle *'ayyēh* (from *'ayay*) introduces direct questions. Cf. W. L. Holladay, *A Concise Hebrew and Aramaic Lexicon of the Old Testament* (Leiden: Brill; Grand Rapids: Eerdmans, 1971), p. 12. See GKC, § 150in.2, for a remark on the distinction between direct and indirect questions.

4. See GKC, § 135m.

5. The Pesh. reads "that you fear me." Cf. L. Kruse-Blinkenberg, "The Book of Malachi according to Codex Syro-Hexaplaris Ambrosianus," *ST* 21 (1967) 67. The Targ. reads *mar'eh*, "vision, image," incorrectly deriving the word from Heb. *rā'â*, "to see."

6. The Syro-Hexapla reads "Says the Almighty Lord, you priests who despise my name"; cf. Kruse-Blinkenberg, op. cit., p. 75.

7. See KB, s.v. *b*^{e}, no. 18 (p. 104), for the compound preposition *b*^{e} plus the infinitive.

8. For the variant readings of the LXX, see A. Rahlfs, ed., *Septuaginta II*, 5th ed. (Stuttgart: Württembergische Bibelanstalt, 1952). The LXX adds *kaí tá epitithémena brōmata exoudenōména*, "and the things thereon may be treated with contempt." Cf. v. 12—an example of the LXX's inclination to add (cf. J. Z. Schuurmans Stekhoven, *De Alexandrijnsche vertaling van het Dodekapropheton* [Leiden: Brill, 1887], p. 84).

9. Heb. *w*^{e}*ḵî* here introduces a conditional sentence; cf. GKC, § 159aa-bb.

or when you offer crippled or diseased animals, there is nothing wrong.
Do offer them to your governor!
Would he be pleased with you[10] *or*[11] *show you favor?*
says the Lord Almighty.
9 *Try then to appease God that he may be gracious to us.*[12]
You have done this.
Will he[13] *show his favor because of you? says the Lord Almighty.*[14]
10 *Oh, that one of you would shut the doors, that you would not kindle a fire upon my altar in vain.*
I have no pleasure in you, says the Lord Almighty,
and I will not be pleased with an offering from you.
11 *Verily, from the rising to the setting of the sun my name is great among the nations,*
in every place incense is offered to my name, a pure offering,
for my name is great among the nations, says the Lord Almighty.
12 *But you profane it by saying that the table of the Lord is defiled, and that its produce,*[15] *its food, is contemptible.*
13 *And you say, What*[16] *weariness!*[17]
And you[18] *sniff at it, says the Lord Almighty.*

10. The LXX reads "with it," reflecting an obvious tendency to harmonize. It should not be given preference, as is done by *BHK*/*BHS* and a number of scholars. See the same suffix in the parallel expression, *pāneyḵā*, "your face."

11. The conjunction *'ô*, "or" (GKC, § 104c), is used with the interrogative particle to introduce disjunctive questions (cf. GKC, § 150g). It is usually expressed by *'im . . . hᵃ* (cf. Brockelmann, *Syntax*, § 169c).

12. The LXX reads "and beseech him," probably to exempt the prophet *(us)* from having part in the guilt of the priests and people. Cf. F. Wutz, *Die Transkriptionen von der Septuaginta bis zu Hieronymus* (Stuttgart: Kohlhammer, 1933), p. 410.

13. LXX and Pesh. read the first person singular: "Shall *I* accept you?" The meaning remains the same.

14. There is no need to delete the last clause of this verse for the sake of meter. Cf. Rudolph, Van der Woude, et al.

15. The LXX and Vulg. both read "that which is placed upon" (LXX *tá epitithémena;* Vulg. *quod superponitur,* with the addition *cum igne, qui illud devorat*). Van der Woude suggests reading *nî' ḇô*, "the raw (meat) upon it," but this is unlikely.

16. Some of the ancient versions read the preposition *min*, "from," instead of *mâ*, "what."

17. On the form *mattᵉlā'â*, see GKC, §§ 20c, 37c, 147c; for other occurrences of *tᵉlā'â*, see Exod. 18:8; Num. 20:14; Neh. 9:32. Van der Woude translates *tᵉlā'â* with "gain": "Look, what gain do we get from it?" The meaning remains the same.

18. The Vulg. and Targ. concur with the MT. The LXX and Pesh. read the first person singular: "And *I* will blow against it." Thus they change the meaning:

You bring stolen, crippled, or diseased animals
and offer them as sacrifices.
Shall I accept it with pleasure from you? says the Lord.
14 *Cursed is the cheat*[19] *who, while having a male animal in his flock, which he has vowed, sacrifices a blemished animal to the Lord.*
For I am a great King, says the Lord Almighty,
and my name is feared[20] *among the nations.*

The indicative of God's unconditional love is not without the imperative to conform to the stipulations of God's *tôrâ*. After having reminded Israel of the indicative in vv. 2–5, Malachi now confronts them with the imperative. The first area of their behavior concerns the prescribed sacrifices in the restored temple.

In terms of the legal practice of that time and in accordance with Malachi's dialectical style, we may distinguish three elements: the accusation (v. 6), the motivation (vv. 7–8, 12–14), and the verdict (vv. 9–11). These elements can be translated into the following structural analysis: sentence-group A, comprising sentences 1–19 (vv. 6–11), and sentence-group B, a parallel group of sentences, 20–28 (vv. 12–14). In group A we have (1) the accusation (sentences 1–8, vv. 6–8b); (2) the motivation: (a) negatively (sentences 9–16, vv. 8c–10) and (b) positively (sentences 17–19, v. 11) stated. Group B is mainly a recapitulation of the three subdivisions of group A. The central theme of this prophecy is stated positively in sentences 17–19 (v. 11): God demands pure offerings. Israel has failed miserably in this regard. They have despised the name of the Lord by offering defiled sacrifices on his altar. This is the way in which they have responded to God's love for them.[21]

6 The accusation is expressed in a typical manner. It commences with a generally accepted statement that a father is honored by his son and a master by his servant.

---

instead of the priests showing contempt for the offerings, it is the Lord who shows contempt for the offerings. Cf. Kruse-Blinkenberg, *ST* 20 (1966) 98.

19. Heb. *nôḵēl* is a Qal active participle of *nāḵal*, meaning "to act cunningly," "to deceive"; it is not derived from the verb *yāḵal*, "to be able," "to have it in one's power," as it is rendered by the LXX *hós ḗn dynatós*. The Vulg.'s *dolosus* is in accordance with the Hebrew text.

20. Heb. *nôrā'* is a Niphal participle of *yārē'*, "to be revered," "to be dreaded," "inspiring fear." The Vulg.'s "horrible" corresponds with the MT, but the LXX's *epiphanés* is derived from Heb. *rā'â*, "to see."

21. Brandenburg, following G. A. Smith, distinguishes the attitude toward sacrifices in the time of Malachi from the attitude in the time of the earlier prophets.

The first part of this statement is fully in accordance with the Decalogue (Exod. 20:12; Deut. 5:16) and with the general custom (cf. Sir. 3:2–16), even among other Semitic peoples (cf. the Code of Hammurapi, §§ 186, 192, 193, 195). Nobody would justly deny it. The use of the imperfect (and not jussive!) denotes reiterated actions, implying what may be expected to occur time and again: a son usually and continually honors his father.[22]

(his) father. The pronoun "his" is spelled out in the Syriac, Arabic, and Ethiopic translations, but may be assumed in the Hebrew text as well. It is parallel to "his master" in the second clause, the suffix performing a "double duty."[23]

honors. The Hebrew word *kāḇaḏ* has one literal meaning and several figurative extensions.[24] Literally it means "heavy" *(gravem)*. The figurative extensions vary according to whether the item is culturally favored or disfavored.[25] It may be illustrated in the following manner:

Culturally favored	**Culturally neutral**	**Cuturally disfavored**
"riches"	"heavy"	"burdensome"
"respect"	"abundance"	"difficult"
"glory"	"grievous"	
"honor"		
"great"		

When a son honors his father he is acknowledging his "weight,"[26] his importance, his authority. This is tantamount to fearing, respecting

22. See GKC, § 107e, g. The Targ., Luther, Hitzig, Köhler, et al. have the jussive. Cf. Calvin, Reinke, Laetsch, et al., and the LXX, Pesh., and Vulg.

23. Van der Woude, p. 95.

24. The Piel form of *kāḇaḏ* occurs 38 times in the OT. It has various meanings: honor (Exod. 20:12), praise (Judg. 9:9), hardening (of hearts, 1 Sam. 6:6), console (2 Sam. 10:3), glorify (Isa. 25:3), serve (Isa. 43:23), make glorious (Isa. 60:13), etc. Synonyms are *yārē'*, "to fear" (Isa. 25:3), *hištaḥᵃwâ*, "to prostrate oneself" (Ps. 86:9), *hillēl*, "to praise" (Ps. 22:24 [Eng. 25]). Its antonyms include despise, treat with scorn; see *bāʿaḏ* (1 Sam. 2:29), *bôz* and *kālal* (1 Sam. 2:30), *nāzal* (Lam. 1:8), and *ḥārap̱* (Prov. 14:31).

25. According to E. A. Nida in a lecture on Bible translation. The figurative extensions could be elaborated in several more directions and on other levels. Many of these features can simply be explained linguistically.

26. In the ancient Near East the "weight" of a person was based on his material wealth. Cf. Gen. 31:1; 45:13; Num. 22:17, 37; 24:11; Ps. 49:17–18 (Eng. 16–17). In Isa. 5:13 "the men of rank" are considered the *kāḇôḏ* of the people. Cf. J. Pedersen, *Israel: Its Life and Culture,* 4 vols. repr. in 2 (London: Oxford University; Copenhagen: Branner og Korch, 1926), I–II:228.

(yārē') him (Lev. 19:3). Children who attack or curse their parents must be put to death (Exod. 21:15, 17). According to G. A. Smith, "in the old Semitic world, even to the human parent, honor was due before love."[27]

Similarly, a servant should honor his master. Some LXX manuscripts supply the verb *phobēthḗsetai,* "fears" (his master), which is basically correct, especially in connection with *môrā'î,* "my fear," in v. 6c. But *yeḵabbēḏ* from the previous phrase is implied here too, and simultaneously includes the idea of "fear" (cf. Isa. 25:3; 29:13; Ps. 22:24). The word *servant ('eḇeḏ)* may be taken in the sense of a "free" laborer or employee (Gen. 19:2; 26:24; Exod. 14:31) or a "slave" (Gen. 50:18; Exod. 12:44; Job 7:2; etc.). We may agree with Lattey that a servant in general, slave or free, is meant. "Slaves" in particular have no alternative but to "honor" their masters because they belong to them by right of purchase (Exod. 21:20, 21, 26, 27; Ps. 123:2; cf. the Code of Hammurapi, §§ 197–99, 205, 210, 282, etc.).

his master. The Hebrew word *'aḏōnāyw* is an intensive or majestic plural,[28] denoting a king (1 K. 22:17; Isa. 19:4) or God (Deut. 10:17; Ps. 136:3). The analogy of *'aḏônîm* and the parallel use of *'āḇ* require a singular meaning, "his master."

Another indisputable truth is that God is the Father and the Lord of his people.[29] Nobody could justly deny it. The father-son relationship between God and Israel was stated at the beginning of the Exodus deliverance, when Moses proclaimed the word of the Lord to Pharaoh: "Israel is my firstborn son. . . . Let my son go" (Exod. 4:22, 23; cf. Hos. 11:1). Afterward this relationship was mentioned explicitly (Deut. 32:6; Isa. 63:16; 64:8; Jer. 3:4, 19; Mal. 2:10; Ps. 89:27) or by way of comparing it with the human relationship between father and son (Deut. 1:31; 8:5; Ps. 103:13). L. M. Muntingh rightly observed that the father-son relationship between God and Israel must be considered a covenant relationship.[30] Elsewhere Israel was explicitly called the "son of God" (Exod. 4:22; Deut. 14:1; Isa. 45:11; Jer. 31:9; Hos. 11:1).

The idea of God being the Lord of Israel is nowhere expressly

27. G. A. Smith, p. 645.

28. See n.2 above.

29. The literature on the Fatherhood of God is extensive. Cf. M. G. Lagrange, "La paternité de Dieu dans l'Ancien Testament," *RB* 5 (1908) 481–99; Th. Paffrath, *Gott, Herr und Vater* (Paderborn: Bonifacius, 1930), pp. 567–70; L. Moraldi, "La Paternita de Dio nell' Antico Testaments," *Revista Biblica* 7 (1959) 44–56.

30. Muntingh, "Aanneming tot kinders in die teologie van Paulus," *NGTT* 9 (1967) 1–7.

mentioned in the OT but is obviously implied in the very nature of their relationship. Isaiah suggested God's lordship when he declared: "O Lord, our God, other lords besides thee have ruled over us, but thy name alone we acknowledge" (26:13; cf. Zeph. 3:9; Ps. 123:2). We may agree with E. Jacob that the fatherhood of God in the OT is an expression of his lordship.[31]

In parallel sentences and with direct questions God confronts the priests and people with the inevitable conclusion drawn from the fact of his fatherhood and lordship: "Where is the honor and fear due to me?" The possessive pronouns in both *keḇôḏî* and *môrā'î* are objective genitives, "my honor" and "my fear," in the sense of "that are due to me."

In connection with God the word *kāḇôḏ* has the figurative meaning of both "glory" and "honor." The "glory" of God is himself. This is implied in Ps. 57:6, 12 (Eng. 5, 11): "Be exalted, O God, above the heavens! Let thy glory be over all the earth!" "God" and "glory" are synonymous. According to Vriezen "*kabod* is the radiant power of His Being, as it were the external glorious manifestation of His mysterious holiness."[32] In this way God has revealed himself, both in the tabernacle (Exod. 40:34, 35; Num. 14:10; 16:42) and in the temple (1 K. 8:11; 2 Chr. 5:14; 7:1–3). God's glory was evident in the overpowering might of his acts through the phenomena of nature (Exod. 24:16, 17; Ps. 97:1–6). Human beings must be protected from the manifestation of his glory (Exod. 24:15, 16; 33:22; 40:34, 35), even though Moses wanted to see it (Exod. 33:18). In the great future the glory of God will manifest itself universally over all peoples and upon the whole earth (Num. 14:21; Isa. 6:3; 66:18, 19; Ezek. 39:21; 43:2; Hab. 2:14; Ps. 57:6, 12 [Eng. 5, 11]; 72:19; 108:6 [Eng. 5]).

The glory of God must be acknowledged by his people, and in this sense it is his "honor." To give glory to the Lord (Jer. 13:16) is to honor him. This is eloquently voiced by the psalmist: "Ascribe to the Lord, O mighty ones, ascribe to the Lord glory and strength. Ascribe to the Lord the glory due his name" (29:2–3 [Eng. 1–2], NIV).

The opposite evaluation of God is to regard him as insignificant, to deny him his "weight," to think: "The Lord will not do good, nor will he do ill" (Zeph. 1:12; cf. Isa. 5:18–20; 41:23; Jer. 10:5; Nah. 1:9; Mal. 2:17). This negative evaluation of God is implied in his question to the priests and people: *where is the honor due to me?* They have underestimated him, they have not paid him the respect that was due to him, they did not behave as a father might have rightly expected his sons to behave.

31. Jacob, *Theology of the Old Testament,* tr. A. W. Heathcote and P. J. Allcock (London: Hodder & Stoughton; New York: Harper and Brothers, 1958), pp. 61–62.

32. Vriezen, *An Outline of Old Testament Theology,* rev. ed., p. 299.

The same applies to the *fear* that was due to him. According to its general usage the emphasis of *môrā'*, "fear," is more on *timor*, "dread," "horror," "terror" (Gen. 9:2; Deut. 4:34; 11:25; 26:8; 34:12; Ps. 76:12–13 [11–12]; Isa. 8:12–13) than on *reverentia*, reverence, the loving fear of a child.[33] In our context, however, the "fear" that is due to God presupposes the covenant relationship between him and his people.[34] This suggests the idea of regard, respect, reverence, confidence, faith, trust. The parallelism of "Father" and "Lord" suggests that "fear" is synonymous with "honor."

The accusation is directed *lāḵem*, "to you." The identification of the addressees is one of the major problems of the exegesis of this paragraph. According to Ludwig Levy the assumption that the priests were the main sinners is to be regarded as the "great mistake" *(Hauptfehler)* in the exegesis of this portion.[35] The reference to "you priests" is meant ironically, the people as a whole pretending to be a priestly people! But we do not agree with this point of view. The persons concerned are both priests and people. The priests were the main transgressors, because they were acquainted with the stipulations of the *tôrâ* and were the mediators between God and his people in the service of the altar. The people were also guilty, however, because they provided the unworthy animals, and in doing so they were trying to deceive the Lord (v. 14). In v. 6, however, the priests were directly addressed.[36] They have returned along with other people, especially from the tribes of Judah and Benjamin, from the Babylonian Exile (Ezra 1:5; 7:7; Neh. 12:1–26), and were also referred to as "the sons of Levi" (3:3). The vexing problem of the relationship between priests and Levites will be discussed at the end of 2:1–9.

The accusation was that the "priests" have despised the name of the Lord. According to the participial form of the verb they were doing that continually.[37] They were in the habit of despising the Lord's name. It was

33. In all these passages *môrā'* is synonymous with "miraculous signs and wonders," "a mighty hand," "an outstretched arm," etc.; cf. Deut. 4:43; etc. In Gen. 9:2 "fear" is parallel to "dread." In Ps. 76:12 (Eng. 11) the Lord is represented as "the one to be feared," and according to v. 13 (Eng. 12) he is the judge of the rulers and kings of the earth.

34. Cf. F. C. Fensham, "Malediction and Benediction in Ancient Near Eastern Vassal-Treaties and the Old Testament," *ZAW* 74 (1962) 1–9; W. Eichrodt, *Theology of the Old Testament*, OTL, tr. J. A. Baker (London: SCM; Philadelphia: Westminster, 1967), II:268–77.

35. L. Levy, "Der Prophet Maleachi," in *Festschrift zum 75. jährigen Bestehen des jüdisch-theologischen Seminars der Fraenkelschen Stiftungen* (1929), II:273–84.

36. For the vocative with the definite article, "O priests," see GKC, § 126e, f.

37. See GKC, §§ 107d, 116.

precisely the opposite of "honoring" the Lord. The name of the Lord is the manifestation of his sacred being; it is himself not only in his revelation but also in the possibility of his being invoked.[38] The entire behavior and functioning of the priests were characterized by this attitude and conduct to "despise the name of the Lord." This is expressed in the appellative "despisers of my name."

In what manner have we despised your name? The priests, however, could not accept this accusation. They were not conscious of having done anything wrong. They respond, "In what manner and at what occasion have we done that?" We may agree with Baldwin that sinful attitudes are most often "secret faults," secret, that is, from the consciousness of the sinner, but they are not excused on that ground.[39] At the same time this unconsciousness tends to aggravate the sinfulness of the transgression, especially when it is the result of a blunting of the spiritual conscience.

Next the prophet is going to present his motivation.

7 Instead of honoring the name of the Lord, they have despised it by offering defiled, polluted food on his altar. In the MT the subject is not mentioned but assumed.[40] The participial form again stresses continuity. The priests were habitually and continually offering polluted food. The official task of the priests was to *offer* or "bring" (Hiphil of *nāgaš*) the sacrifices taken from and on behalf of the people to be put on *(ʿal)* the altar. This "approach" to the altar is a technical designation of the priests' office (Lev. 2:8), and is characteristically used by Malachi to denote the offering of sacrifices (1:8, 11; 2:12; 3:3; cf. Amos 5:25).

The problem with the *food* (i.e., the animal sacrifices, v. 8) was that it was *defiled*. The Hebrew word *meg̱ōʾāl* (from *gāʾal* II) does not mean "unworthy,"[41] but is used in the sense of "contaminated," "unfit," "to be rejected as unqualified." Hands (Isa. 59:3) or clothing (Isa. 63:3) may be "stained" or "defiled" (Lam. 4:14) with blood. Priests without family records were "excluded from the priesthood as "unclean" (Ezra 2:62; Neh.

38. Cf. Vriezen, op. cit., p. 208: "In the same way the . . . *name of God* can occur as something independent representing God, cf. Jer. 7, where the temple is the place that is called by God's name." Cf. H. Bietenhard, in *TDNT*, V:242–83.

39. Baldwin, p. 225.

40. See GKC, § 116s.

41. Cf. Wellhausen and Dummelow (p. 613), both of whom argue that the defective animals of v. 8 were not in themselves defiled. This is true, of course, but the point is that they did not comply with the stipulations of the law and were ritually unfit for sacrifices. Marti rightly observed that the verb does not occur in the sense of "be unworthy"; cf. Isa. 59:3; 63:3; Lam. 4:14; Zeph. 3:1; Dan. 1:8; Ezra 2:62; Neh. 7:64; 13:29. Van der Woude prefers the meaning "detestable" food. The point of reference, however, is that the sacrifices were ritually unfit.

7:64). Having been united in mixed marriages the priests had "defiled" the priestly office (Neh. 13:29). The term *defiled* thus has a strong cultic connotation. It means that the sacrifices are unqualified to be accepted as such. A sacrifice must be "pure," "clean" *(ṭᵉhôrâ)* and "perfect" *(tāmîm)* to be acceptable.[42] This pollution of the sacrifices also presupposes an attitude of mind which causes the priests to regard the table of the Lord as contemptible.

The reaction is stereotyped: *How have we defiled you?* The LXX, followed by the Vetus Latina, read "defiled it," meaning either the "food" or the "altar." Despite the fact that this reading is generally accepted,[43] we must give preference to the MT (supported by Syr. and Vulg.) as the more difficult reading. We agree with Lattey that "such vigorous phrasing would far more easily be changed than invented." The idea behind this "vigorous phrasing" is that the defiling of the sacrifices or of God's altar is in itself a defiling of the Lord.[44]

The answer to this question is *By saying that the table of the Lord is contemptible*. It is unlikely that these words were uttered. The intention clearly is that they have said it to themselves, that these words reflected their subconscious attitudes. We agree with Laetsch, "Even if they did not publicly use these exact words, their actions spoke louder than could any words that they regarded the Temple service not as an undeserved honor, but as a contemptible, miserable job."[45]

the table of the Lord. This expression is used only by Malachi in the OT, and only here and in v. 12. The Hebrew word *šulḥān* is used literally to denote an ordinary table (Judg. 1:7; etc.), or figuratively, for instance, when Israelites were accused of spreading a "table" for Fortune (Isa. 65:11; cf. Ps. 23:5; 69:23 [Eng. 22]; etc.). The table for "the bread of the presence" is implied to be a "table of the Lord" but is nowhere called by that name (Exod. 25:23–30; etc.). It is obvious that the prophet was not referring to this table, because he had blood sacrifices in mind. In Ezek. 40:39–43 tables were provided at the gates of the inner court for the purpose of slaughtering the

42. Cf. W. H. Gispen, "The Distinction between Clean and Unclean," *OTS* 5 (1948) 190–96; J. D. W. Kritzinger, *Qᵉhal Jahwe* (Kampen: Kok, 1957), p. 105. A sacrifice must be "perfect" (*tāmîm*, Exod. 12:5; 29:1; Lev. 1:3; 22:18–33; etc.), "without blemish" (*mûm*, Lev. 22:20, 21, 5; etc.), and "pure" (*ṭᵉhôrâ*, Mal. 1:11) to be acceptable.

43. Explicitly stated by F. Wutz, *Die Transkriptionen von der Septuaginta bis zu Hieronymus*, p. 286.

44. Cf. Reinke, p. 59; Pressel, p. 387; A. R. Johnson, *VTSup*, I (1953), p. 75. There is no need to delete this clause, as suggested by Wellhausen, Nowack, et al. Cf. G. A. Smith, p. 646.

45. Luther confirmed this point of view; cf. G. Krause, *Studien zu Luthers Auslegung der Kleinen Propheten* (Tübingen: Mohr, 1962), p. 377.

sacrifices, or for the utensils that were needed (v. 42). In Ezek. 41:22 the "table of incense" is called "the table that is before the Lord," whereas "table" in Ezek. 44:16 obviously referred to "the altar of burnt offering."[46] In our text "the table of the Lord" is synonymous with the altar on which defiled food has been offered and unfit animals have been sacrificed. The figurative meaning of "table" is derived from the meaning of sacrifices as being "food."[47]

This "table of the Lord" is deemed *contemptible*. There is no need to approach it with the necessary respect, to regard it as a sacred object in the service of a holy God. They have despised his name (v. 6) and therefore have no scruples in despising his altar.

8 The priests and people could not deny the prophet's accusation. Their sinful behavior was evident in the very sacrifices that they had offered on the altar. The evidence is irrefutable. *When you bring*. The Heb. *wᵉḵî* is used here in the sense of *wᵉʾim,* "and if, when," as in Hos. 13:15; Ps. 21:12; 37:24.[48] The prophet again uses his characteristic word *nāg̱aš,* "bring near," that is, "offer" (v. 7). What the addressees were doing was contrary to the stipulations of the *tôrâ*. A sacrificial animal has to be without defect *(tāmîm)* (Exod. 12:5; 29:1; Lev. 1:3; etc.) and without blemish *(mûm)* (Lev. 22:20, 21, 25; etc.). The *tôrâ* expressly forbade the offering of *blind, crippled,* or *diseased* animals. An *ʿiwwēr* was an animal blind in one or both eyes. The offering of such an animal was definitely prohibited (Lev. 22:22; Deut. 15:21). The same applied to a *pissēaḥ,* a lame or crippled animal (Deut. 15:21). It was allowed to be eaten, but could not be offered as a sacrifice. The participial form of the Hebrew word *ḥōleh,* "become weak or sick," is generally used to denote sick people, especially kings (Gen. 48:1; 1 Sam. 19:41; 1 K. 14:5; etc.). In Mal. 1:8, 13, and in a figurative sense also in Ezek. 34:4, 16, it refers to diseased animals. The law did not explicitly forbid the offering of such animals, but the prohibition is implied in the general stipulation that sacrificial animals must be without blemish or defect. These categories of animals are indeterminate, which means that every individual animal from these categories must be deemed unfit for sacrifice.

there is nothing wrong. The Hebrew expression *ʾên rāʿ*[49] is rendered

46. So, e.g., also Botterweck (*BibLeb* 1 [1960] 100–109) and Lattey.

47. Cf. R. de Vaux, *Ancient Israel,* pp. 413–14, on the religious significance of the altar.

48. See KB, s.v. *kî,* no. 19 (pp. 432–33).

49. In this form the expression is found only here. Both renderings, either as a rhetorical question or as a statement, are possible and meaningful, but we prefer the latter. Laetsch rightly contends that this brings out the wicked character of the addressees more forcefully. They ignored God's law deliberately. Cf. also Rudolph and Van der Woude.

by the LXX, Vulgate, Syriac, and Arabic translations in the sense of a rhetorical question: is it not bad? (cf. RSV, Berkeley); is that not wrong? (NIV). It is, however, more according to the general attitude of the priests and people to render the expression in terms of a positive statement, "there is nothing wrong" (cf. NEB) in offering such animals! Their infringement of the law was done deliberately. According to them there could be nothing wrong in accepting and offering defective animals. The main thing is to perform the sacrificial duties. The act of offering an animal is in itself beneficial. The ritual itself is working *ex opere operato*. They do not have to comply with the external stipulations of the law and with internal considerations of a reverent and spiritual attitude. Having despised the name of the Lord and his altar, it is merely a matter of consequence to offer defective animals!

The prophet's accusation and motivation concern both the priests and the people. The defective animals were presented by the people and accepted by the priests. Both these "acts" were contrary to the law (Lev. 22:13–33). The priests, however, were ultimately responsible for the sacrifices that were being brought upon the altar, and therefore their transgression was the more serious. As mediators between God and his people they ought to have remembered the Lord's admonition: "Among those who approach me I will show myself holy; in the sight of all the people I will be honored" (Lev. 10:3, NIV).

The prophet's decisive argument is that they would not dare to present such offerings by way of donations to their human governor. They can rest assured that the governor would not be pleased with them or show them favor. The conclusion is self-evident: if they could not present such offerings to their governor, much less should they to God!

Do offer them. The Hebrew word *qāraḇ* (Hiphil) means "to bring near." In the ritual of the cult it is a technical term for the act of the offering itself (cf. Hag. 2:14; 2 Chr. 35:12; etc.). In this context it is applied to the presentation to the governor either of the compulsory revenue (Judg. 3:17; Neh. 5:15) or a voluntary donation (Isa. 1:23; Ps. 72:10; Exod. 23:8; Deut. 16:19). The hypothetical character of the prophet's suggestion as well as the intention to please the governor favors the second alternative. "Presents were, as they are still, a common act of courtesy in the East" (Pusey).

to your governor. The Hebrew *peḥâ* (Akk. *paḥatu*) is a "rather vague title"[50] denoting a "governor," a *praefectus provinciae*,[51] a lower position than a "satrap." Presumably of Assyrian origin, this title generally desig-

50. So KB, p. 757.

51. So S. Mandelkern, *Veteris Testamenti Concordantiae* (repr. Jerusalem/Tel Aviv: Schocken, 1971), p. 947.

nates governors appointed by foreign rulers.[52] In Mal. 1:8 the governor may have been a representative of the Persian government (cf. Ezra 8:36; Neh. 2:7, 9; 3:7; Est. 3:12; 8:9; 9:3). We do not know whether he was a foreigner or an Israelite. Judean governors included Zerubbabel (Hag. 1:1, 14; 2:2, 21), Nehemiah (Neh. 5:14; 12:26), and a man called Bagoaz (Elephantine papyri). Scholars are in doubt whether the governor mentioned in our text could have been Nehemiah himself. Torrey deems it possible,[53] Laetsch is of the opinion that it "does not refer specifically to Nehemiah, but in general to any 'governor,'" while G. A. Smith maintains, and justly so, that it could not have been Nehemiah, because Nehemiah deliberately refused to accept the food allotted to the governor (Neh. 5:14, 15).

The identity of the "governor" is of little consequence in the context of the prophet's argument. He is reasoning from the minor to the major premise, from the human governor to the Lord and Father of his people.

Would he be pleased with you? The interrogative particle usually stands before the simple question, when the questioner is uncertain as to the answer to be expected. In other instances, like here, it is used in conjunction with questions to which a negative answer is to be expected.[54]

or (would he) show you favor? Literally, "would he lift up your face," that is, grant you a cordial reception (Gen. 32:20; etc.).[55] This expression is used here in *bonum partem,* but elsewhere in Malachi it has the sense of being partial (Mal. 2:9; cf. Lev. 19:15; etc.).

9 Parallel to the prophet's advice that they should bring the defective animals to their governor is his invitation to them to *Try then to appease God,* to try to placate him. The Heb. *ḥallû-nā' pᵉnê 'ēl* means literally "make weak," "soften," "soothe" the face of God, hence "appease" him.[56] The

52. Reference to this title is made in 1 K. 10:15; 20:24; 2 K. 18:24; Isa. 36:9; Jer. 51:23, 28, 57; Ezek. 23:6, 12, 26; Hag. 1:1, 14; 2:2, 21; Est. 3:12; 8:9; 9:3; Ezra 8:36; Neh. 2:7, 9; 3:7; 5:14, 15, 18; 12:26; 2 Chr. 9:14. See A. Alt, "Die Rolle Samarias bei der Entstehung des Judentums," in *Festschrift Otto Procksch,* pp. 5-28; F. C. Fensham, "*Peḥâ* in the Old Testament and the Ancient Near East," *Studies in the Chronicler, OTWSA* 19 (Potchefstroom: Pro Rege, 1976), pp. 44–52.

53. According to Torrey "there is nothing to preclude the possibility that the *pechah* mentioned in 1:8 was Nehemiah himself" (*JBL* 17 [1898] 14n.24). J. Bright formerly considered the governor to be either that of Samaria or even Nehemiah (*A History of Israel,* 2nd ed. [Philadelphia: Westminster, 1972], p. 378n.9), but he has now dropped the suggestion that the governor could have been Nehemiah (3rd ed., 1981, p. 377n.9). According to Van der Woude, the text and the date of Malachi's prophecy (ca. 480 B.C.!) preclude Nehemiah as a possibility.

54. See GKC, § 150d.

55. See KB, p. 635, s.v. *nś',* no. 5.

56. See D. R. Ap-Thomas, *VT* 6 (1956) 239–40; K. Seybold, "Reverenz

same expression is used in Zech. 7:2 and in Dan. 9:13. The imperative is strengthened by the particle *nāʾ*, but then in the sense of ridicule, as in Isa. 47:12.[57] The prophet's invitation is not to be taken seriously but is meant ironically. If they would not have a chance to secure the governor's favor with their detestable gifts, how would they ever be able to succeed in appeasing the stern face of God? The reference to *ʾēl*, "God," instead of "the Lord" dramatizes the contrast between him and the human governor.

that he may be gracious to us, "that he may show us mercy," suggests the merciful consequence of the prayerful approach to God, in order to beseech him, to appease him. The prophet's inclusion in this generally expected and experienced consequence does not imply that his advice must be taken seriously. This "natural" consequence of a humble beseeching of God is totally and radically excluded because of the priests' and people's attitudes and conduct.

The expression *You have done this,* literally "from your hand this has happened," is a circumstantial clause, meaning "while this is being done by your hand."[58] How could they expect God's favor even when they try to placate him with their prayers? This is explicitly stated by the prophet. *Will he show his favor because of you?* According to the RSV ("will he show favor to any of you?") the preposition *min* is used in a partitive sense, "any one of you." We prefer the causal sense: "because of you," "on your account." Because of the priests God will bestow no favor upon the people. In this way the immense responsibility of the priests to be the mediators between God and his people is again emphasized.

10 This verse expresses the thought that a closed temple, however terrible this may be, is preferable to the perpetuating of worthless worship. A worship that does not acknowledge and honor God is worse than no worship at all (Hellmuth Frey). It would be better to *shut the doors* rather than to continue bringing these unacceptable sacrifices. We agree with Brandenburg: "It is better to be speechless than to blaspheme. It is preferable to experience the agony of being far away from God than to deceive oneself by assuming that God will listen to the appeals of a hypocrite." The ancient versions have nearly all misinterpreted the opening sentence of v. 10.[59] The

---

und Gebet: Erwägungen zu der Wendung *ḥillā panîm," ZAW* 88 (1976) 2–16; idem, in *TDOT,* IV:407–409; Van der Woude, in *THAT,* II:456–57.

57. See GKC, § 110d.

58. See GKC, § 156d.

59. The LXX *dióti* reflects *kî gam* instead of *mî gam;* the LXX also reads the Hebrew verb as a Niphal, "shall be shut," and *tāʾîrû* as a singular: "because even among you the doors shall be shut, and (one) will not kindle (the fire of) my altar for

desiderative clause proper is here coordinated with an interrogative clause, literally, "Who are among you and would shut the doors," which is used to express a wish: "Oh, that there were one among you who would shut the doors."[60] The purport of this wish is strengthened by the emphasizing particle *gam,* "also," "even."[61]

The dual form of *d^e^lāṯayim* refers to the double doors which granted access either to the court of the priests, where the tables for sacrifice were situated (Baldwin), or to the inner court, where the altar of burnt offerings was located. Whichever doors were meant, the intention is that if those doors were shut, no offerings could be made. This is evident from the following sentence: *That you would not kindle a fire upon my altar in vain.*

kindle. The Hebrew verb *tā'îrû* is a Hiphil form derived from the root *'ôr,* "to become or be light," "to shine," "to light up," but in our context it has the meaning "to kindle a fire," "to alight," as in Isa. 27:11; 50:11; and Ps. 18:29 (Eng. 28).

in vain. The adverb *ḥinnām* means either *gratuito,* "freely," or *frustra,* "in vain." The LXX and Vulgate preferred the reading *gratuito,* and this was responsible for the incorrect interpretation that the priests were being paid for services rendered to the altar. The prophet's intention then would have been that there would be no compensation for the kindling of fire upon the altar. The accusation of the prophet, however, does not presuppose the covetousness of the priests, but merely states that such offerings would be of no avail, ineffective in their purpose to restore and strengthen the covenant relationship between God and his people.

This interpretation is also evident from the fact that God would have no pleasure in them. The Hebrew word *rāṣâ,* "to be pleased with," "to be favorable to," is a part of the offering terminology that denotes the effectiveness of the offerings.[62] Hosea, for instance, explicitly stated that the Lord is not "pleased" with the sacrifices offered to him (8:13; cf. Jer. 14:12; Ezek.

---

nothing." The Vulg. deletes *gam* and the negative *lō'* in the second clause: *Quis est in vobis, qui claudat ostia et incendat* [sing.] *altare meum.* The Targ. paraphrases "the doors" by explaining: "of the house of my sanctuary," and adds: "that you might not bring detestable sacrifices upon my altar." The Pesh. replaces the uncommon Hebrew word *tā'îrû* with a verb meaning "to bring."

60. See GKC, § 151a.

61. See GKC, § 153. Cf. C. J. Labuschagne, "The emphasizing particle 'gam' and its connotations," in *Studia Biblica et Semitica,* Fest. Th. C. Vriezen (Wageningen: H. Veenman, 1961), pp. 193–203.

62. Cf. R. Rendtorff, "Priestliche Kulttheologie und prophetische Kultpolemik," *TLZ* 51 (1956) 339–42; E. Würthwein, "Kultpolemik oder Kultbescheid?" in *Tradition und Situation,* Fest. A. Weiser, ed. E. Würthwein and O. Kaiser (Göttingen: Vandenhoeck & Ruprecht, 1963), pp. 115–31.

20:40, 41; 43:27). According to Malachi God will accept no offering from them. The Hebrew word *minḥâ* is used here and in v. 11 in the general sense of an offering as such, irrespective of its material (cf. Gen. 4:3–5, etc.).

The main emphasis throughout this passage lies upon the responsibility of the priests. Brandenburg rightly observes that this passage in general and this verse in particular do not substantiate the doctrine of the *character indelebilis* of the priesthood, according to which the effectiveness of the priestly act is in itself independent of the spiritual attitude and moral integrity of the priests. The Lord has no pleasure in either the priests or their offerings. The "Damascus Rule" of the Qumran community refers to this verse as a basis for rejecting the validity of the sacrificial system at Jerusalem.[63]

Laetsch rightly observed that the doors giving access to the altar were permanently shut when the Romans destroyed both Jerusalem and its temple.

11 This significant verse, which according to G. A. Smith is "perhaps the most original contribution which the Book of Malachi makes to the development of prophecy,"[64] is a direct antithesis of the preceding accusation and motivation. There the name of the Lord was not honored and feared, here it is great among the nations; there polluted "food," defective sacrifices, are being offered, here pure offerings are being brought in honor of the Lord's name. In vv. 6–10 the accusation was spelled out negatively, in v. 11 the positive realization of God's demands in the sphere of the temple service is emphasized. Verse 11, therefore, is the central theme of the prophet's discourse in this passage.

63. See G. Vermes, *The Dead Sea Scrolls in English* (London: Collins, 1962), p. 103: "None of those brought into the Covenant shall enter the Temple to light His altar in vain. They shall bar the door, forasmuch as God said, *Who among you will bar its door?* And: *You shall not light my altar in vain."*

64. G. A. Smith, II:647. See also my article, "Some Notes on Malachi 1:11," *Biblical Essays, OTWSA* 1966 (Potchefstroom: Pro Rege, 1967), pp. 163–72 (repr. in *NGTT* 21 [1980] 21–30); see also J. G. Baldwin, "Malachi 1:11 and the Worship of the Nations in the Old Testament," *Tyndale Bulletin* 23 (1972) 117–24; Th. Chary, *Les prophètes et le culte à partir de l'exil* (Paris: Desclée, 1955), pp. 179–86; R. Martin-Achard, *A Light to the Nations*, tr. J. P. Smith (Edinburgh and London: Oliver and Boyd, 1962), pp. 42–46; M. Rehm, "Das Opfer der Völker nach Mal. 1:11," *Lex tua Veritas*, Fest. H. Junker, ed. H. Gross and F. Mussner (Trier: Paulinus, 1961), pp. 193–208; J. Swetnam, "Malachi 1:11: An Interpretation," *CBQ* 31 (1969) 200–209; Th. C. Vriezen, "How to Understand Malachi 1:11?" in *Grace upon Grace*, Fest. Lester J. Kuyper, ed. J. I. Cook (Grand Rapids: Eerdmans, 1975), pp. 128–36; C. Stuhlmueller, "Sacrifice among the Nations," *TBT* 22 (1984) 223–25.

Scholarly opinion differs with regard to the text, the authenticity, and the exegesis of this verse.[65] There is, however, no need to alter the text or to disregard vv. 11–13 (14) as secondary. The proposed readings by both *BHK* and *BHS* are not supported by textual data, and Brockington justly asserts that vv. 11–14 are indeed "fully in keeping with the thought of the rest of the book."[66]

The exegesis of this verse is in general quite clear. It is introduced by the particle *kî,* which, as a matter of fact, has a varied application.[67] In this context scholars prefer the meaning "for," thus giving the particle a causal sense, in accordance with the ancient translations. Thus v. 11 is seen as a conclusion to the general statement of v. 10. The Lord has no need for the sacrifices of his priests in Jerusalem, because his name is great among the pagans. It is of course also possible to translate *kî* as a particle of assertion or asseveration: yes, indeed![68] In this connection it introduces a rather unexpected truth, a truth which transcends the comprehension of the local priests and the covenant people. In either case, v. 11 is closely connected with v. 10, and is an integral part of a significant argument.

The Lord is not going to allow the continual despising of his name and pollution of his altar any longer. He would rather have the doors leading up to the altar for burnt offerings be closed than receive from their hands unworthy sacrifices. He can easily dispense with the honor that is due to him from his sons and servants by way of their offerings in the newly erected temple. As a matter of fact, his name is great, that is, he is manifesting himself and is being acknowledged and honored far and wide beyond the boundaries of the promised land!

from the rising to the setting of the sun. This expression must not be understood temporally but as an indication of the vastness of this territory; it does not mean that the offerings, on account of their multitude, took the whole day to accomplish, but that they were brought in every place from east to west.[69] Thus the general scope of this unexpected magnifying of the name of the Lord is expressed in unmistakable terms: it reaches from the rising of the sun to its setting. The same comprehensive designation of the whole world, known and unknown, occurs in Ps. 50:1 and 113:3. In an Amarna Letter we read: "Behold, the king, my lord, has set his name at the rising of

65. Cf. F. Horst; K. Elliger, ATD. According to Rendtorff in *RGG,* IV:628, vv. 11–14 (along with 2:2) "is an addition: a parallel word to the people," etc. This point of view is endorsed by Elliger and Van der Woude.

66. Cf. H. Haag, *Bibellexikon* (Zürich: Benziger, 1956), s.v. "Malachias."

67. See Gemser, *Hebreeuse Spraakkuns,* § 220.

68. See De Moor, who considers *kî* to be an aposiopesis.

69. So, rightly, M. Rehm, op. cit., p. 196.

the sun and at the setting of the sun"—in this case, of course, a rather grave exaggeration.[70]

Another point of significance is that the name of the Lord is said to be great *among the nations (baggôyim).* The specific purport of this expression can only be ascertained in the context of the meaning of this verse as a whole. Does *baggôyim* mean concerning the nations, or in the midst of the nations? Does it presuppose the positive acknowledgment of the name of the Lord by the nations as such, or by smaller groups within the boundaries of the nations? At present we find it sufficient to say that the honor due to the name of the Lord is according to our text not confined to the temple in Jerusalem, to the centralized place of worship (Deut. 12), but that it is glorified among the heathen, far and wide beyond the boundaries of Palestine.

In a certain sense this would have been common knowledge to every Israelite, since they knew the history of revelation up till then. Everyone in Israel knew that God is a great king, Lord of every nation on the face of the earth. According to some scholars, this truth was attested in v. 5: "Your own eyes will see it, and you will say: Great is the Lord, beyond[71] the territory of Israel!" This, indeed, is the purport of v. 14: "for I am a great King, says the Lord of hosts, and my name is feared among the nations." This truth of the universal kingship of the Lord was evident, for it was written on every page of the history of revelation.

But the problem in connection with our text is that the wall of partition seems to be broken down at two very significant points: between Israel and the nations, and between the promised land and all the earth. The designation of Israel as "a kingdom of priests" (Exod. 19:6) is made to apply to the nations from east to west; and the centralized place of worship in the temple of Jerusalem (Deut. 12) is expanded and applied to every place across the face of the world. This, indeed, is the significance and the problem of our text.

incense is offered to my name, a pure offering. The translation and exegesis of these words *(muqṭār muggāš lišmî ûminḥâ ṭ^ehôrâ)* are not quite clear, and many attempts have been made to emend the text and to explain its construction. I am not going to enlarge upon all these problems, but find it

70. Cf. C. J. Mullo Weir, in *Documents from Old Testament Times,* ed. D. Winton Thomas (London: Nelson; New York: Harper & Row, 1958), pp. 43–44. A. Malamat drew my attention to some other parallels: in the Karatepe Inscription, II:2–3; Panammu, II:13 (nos. 26 and 215, respectively, in *KAI*); and in a letter from Mari published by G. Dossin, in *Studies in Old Testament Prophecy,* Fest. Th. H. Robinson, ed. H. H. Rowley (Edinburgh: T. & T. Clark, 1950, repr. 1957), pp. 103–107; discussed by Malamat in *Eretz Israel* 5 (1958) 68.

71. We prefer the translation "above"; see the commentary above on 1:5.

sufficient to say that a radical emendation of an OT text is seldom warranted, and that the meaning of this clause is not affected by the uncertainties of the text. I take *muqṭār* in the sense of a noun, *muggāš* as a predicate, and *minḥâ ṭᵉhôrâ* as a second subject: hence "incense is offered to my name, and a pure offering."[72] Both these words bear witness to the astonishing fact that real offerings are being brought in every place to the honor of the Lord. These offerings were exactly opposite to the unworthy sacrifices of the local priests.[73]

The concept *ṭᵉhôrâ,* "pure," must be understood in its OT context. An offering was pure when an animal conformed to the stipulations of the law (Lev. 11; Deut. 14:3–19), when the person on whose behalf it was brought was ceremonially clean, and when the circumstances under which an offering was being brought were in agreement with the law.[74] This last statement is of special importance. An offering was impure when it was brought on the soil of the heathen or on polluted altars. According to the law it would be impossible to bring pure offerings in the heathen countries because those countries were deemed impure on account of idolatry.[75] This text, then, presupposes a radical alteration in the circumstances, making those countries sacred places of worship. Principally this could only be obtained on the basis of the conversion of the heathen nations, the breaking through of the wall of partition. This is, exegetically, the content of this text. By way of emphasis it concludes with a repetition of the words *for my name is great among the nations, says the Lord Almighty.*

In the course of the history of its exegesis, this text has been explained mainly in four different ways. Three of these explanations maintain that the text should be understood in the light of the contemporary situation, because the pure offerings of our text were evidently compared with the unworthy and impure sacrifices of the local priests. On this basis the question arises, Who are the people who brought those pure offerings? In answer to this question three different explanations are given: (a) the heathen, (b) the Jews in dispersion, and (c) the proselytes.

(a) The theory that refers our text to the heathen worship of the nations was introduced by Ephraim Syrus, and particularly by Clement of Alexandria and Theodore of Mopsuestia. Especially the last-named maintained that God was acknowledged as supreme Ruler and Lord by all people.

72. Cf. LXX; RSV; König, *Syntax,* § 133; Brockelmann, *Syntax,* § 46; etc.
73. So, convincingly, Rehm, op. cit., pp. 195–96.
74. Cf. Nötscher, *Biblische Altertumskunde* (Bonn: Hanstein, 1940), pp. 334–41.
75. Cf. Nötscher, op. cit.

Even in serving the idols, they were, in fact, worshiping the true God.[76] In a modified form this point of view has become dominant among most modern scholars. According to G. A. Smith, "it is not the mere question of there being righteous people in every nation, well-pleasing to Jehovah because of their lives. The very sacrifices of the heathen are pure and acceptable to Him."[77] S. R. Driver suggests that the text seems to say that when "the heathen in his blindness bows down to wood and stone," his worship is "worship of the Lord, simply because it is worship in sincerity, though not in truth."[78] This concept finds poetical expression in the words of Pope:

Father of all, in every age,
In every clime adored,
By saint, by savage and by sage,
Jehovah, Jove or Lord![79]

A modification of this theory is that the reference is not to the pagan worship as such, but to the singularly pure monotheistic worship of the Persians. According to J. T. Marshall, there is no doubt that the early Persian kings were worshipers of one supreme God and that they despised idolatry. "From this evidence I am disposed to infer that the Jews and Persians recognised one another as worshippers in common of the God of heaven—as did also Abraham and Melchizedek. . . . The admission by the prophet that the monotheistic worship of the Persians was virtually the worship of Jehovah, is quite consistent with his abhorrence of the sensualistic idolatry of the Phoenicians, Ammonites and Philistines."[80]

To this point of view we may add the argument drawn from the name "God of heaven," which was being used in the Persian empire, in Phoenicia, in Syria, and in their subordinate countries.[81] With the exception of Gen. 24:3, 7, this name occurs only in the later OT books,[82] where it is found in the edicts of the Persian kings (2 Chr. 36:23; Ezra 1:2; 6:9, 10; 7:12, 21, 23;

76. Theodore of Mopsuestia in his commentary on Malachi; cf. also O. Procksch, *Theologie des Alten Testaments* (Gütersloh: Bertelsmann, 1949), p. 593; W. Eichrodt, *Theology of the Old Testament,* II:344.

77. G. A. Smith, p. 647.

78. S. R. Driver, Sermon III in *Christianity and other Religions: Three Short Sermons,* by S. R. Driver and W. Sanday (London: Longmans, Green, and Co., 1908), pp. 31–46 (summarized in *ExpTim* 20 [1909] 151–52).

79. A. Pope, quoted by S. R. Driver, op. cit.

80. Marshall, "The Theology of Malachi," *ExpTim* 7 (1895) 75.

81. Cf. O. Eissfeldt, "Baalsamen und Jahwe," *ZAW* 57 (1939) 1–31.

82. Its occurrence in Ps. 136:26 may be a later addition; most scholars date the books of Jonah and Daniel late. Cf. also Jdt. 5:8; 6:19; 9:12; 11:17; 2 Macc. 15:23; Tob. 1:18; 6:18; 7:12, 17; 8:15; 11:13; 13:9, 13, 17; 1 Esd. 4:46, 58.

Neh. 4:37), in the discourses between Israelites and foreigners (Ezra 5:11, 12; Dan. 2:37, 44; 5:23; Jon. 1:9), but also in the supplications and communications of the Israelites themselves (Neh. 1:4, 5; 2:4, 20; Dan. 2:18, 19; cf. Ps. 136:26). Thus it is evident that this name was preeminently used by the Jews of the dispersion, as is confirmed by the Aramaic papyri from Elephantine.[83] Grosheide, among others, attests to the fact that this name was used as a medium of communication between the Israelites and the heathen, especially the Persians.[84] According to him the application of this name is in harmony with the postexilic attitude, which emphasized the transcendence of God.

In discussing this almost universally accepted theory, I must confine myself to a few general remarks. The theory that the worship of the heathen as such is worship of the Lord simply because it is worship in sincerity, though not in truth, cannot be maintained in the face of the general teaching of the Bible, and is contradicted by the contents of Malachi's prophecy and the real content of this text. The pure sacrifices are being offered *lišmî,* "to my name," and this statement cannot be made applicable to the idolatry of the heathen. It was rightly observed that Malachi shares the theocratic exclusiveness of Ezra and Nehemiah, especially in their protestations against the mixed marriages (2:10–16) and the abuse of the priestly office (1:6–2:9).[85] His prophecy nowhere presupposes the erosion of the borders between the covenant people and the heathen nations, as is manifest in his word concerning Edom (1:2–5). He does not disregard the sacrificial system of worship in Israel as such, for in 3:4 he prophesies of a time when "the offerings of Judah and Jerusalem will be pleasing to the Lord as in the days of old."

We do not deny the universalistic teaching of the OT, but this is quite different from the intention of this theory. Von Bulmerincq pointed out that the way in which Malachi had expressed the idea of the universal worship of God presupposed full agreement on the part of his hearers, who made no objections; then he asked whether the postexilic community of Israel would have fostered the thought that all offerings of the heathen were in fact made to the honor of his name.[86] According to him this cannot be proven. On the contrary, J. T. Marshall rightly observes that the pious of that age had an

83. Cf. A. Cowley, *Aramaic Papyri of the Fifth Century B.C.* (Oxford: Clarendon, 1923), 30:2, 15; 32:3, 4; 38:(2), 3, 5; 40:1.

84. Grosheide, *De Terugkeer uit de Ballingschap,* Exegetica 2/4 (The Hague: Uitgeverij van Keulen, 1957), p. 37.

85. By J. T. Marshall, *ExpTim* 7 (1895) 18–19; cf. G. L. Robinson, pp. 157–69.

86. Von Bulmerincq, 2:122.

exceptional abhorrence of paganism, as is evident from the books of Ezra and Nehemiah.

Nowhere in OT prophecy do we have the idea that the sacrifices of the heathen are as such pleasing in the sight of the Lord. The worship of Yahweh by the heathen nations is an aspect of eschatology and not in accordance with a contemporary situation. The paganism of the days of the prophets was denounced as an abhorrence and as blind folly.[87] During the messianic age the heathen nations will indeed serve the Lord, but they will do that in the land of Israel and in Jerusalem.[88] There are only two exceptions to this rule, Isa. 19:18–25 and Zeph. 2:11 (cf. 3:10), but neither of these texts bears witness to the soundness of the said theory. In the Isaiah passage, the five cities in the land of Egypt which speak the language of Canaan and swear allegiance to the Lord Almighty, and the altar to the Lord in the midst of the land of Egypt, do not refer to the contemporary religion of the Egyptians but have an eschatological significance. The same applies to the important text in Zephaniah: "and to him shall bow down, each in its place, all the lands of the nations." Here we have the same idea as in our text, but then seen as a future reality. Other texts which are quoted in support of this theory (e.g., Ps. 65:3, 6 [Eng. 2, 5]; 145:18; Jon. 1:6; Deut. 4:19) do not substantiate the idea of heathen worship being as such well-pleasing to the Lord.[89]

This hypothesis is indeed foreign to the real universalistic concept of the relationship between the Lord and the people of the earth, and is opposed to the antithetical character of the OT teaching in connection with the pagan cult. This is evident from the Decalogue and the message of the prophets. Malachi, for instance, deemed it an abomination to marry "the daughter of a foreign god" (2:11). Therefore I agree with Rehm when he says: "In this context it is impossible to evaluate the heathen cult in a positive sense."[90]

The argument deduced from the monotheistic character of the religion of the Persians cannot be maintained. There is quite a difference between the Persian and the OT point of view. With the Persians the acknowledgment of one highest god does not exclude the existence of other deities, an idea which is contrary to the preaching of the prophets, including

87. Cf. Isa. 40:19–20; 41:7; 44:9ff.; 45:20; 46:1–2.

88. Cf. Isa. 2:2–4; 18:7; 25:6ff.; 45:14; 52:8; 56:7; 60:3, 11, 14; 66:23; Mic. 4:1–4; Zech. 8:20ff.; 14:16ff.

89. Cf. Von Bulmerincq, 2:124–25.

90. Rehm, op. cit., p. 201. Cf. also Van der Woude. According to him the emphasis is not on the heathen worship as such but on the awe and respect which the name of the Lord evoked among the nations. This point of view is shared by Snyman, "Antiteses in die boek Maleagi," pp. 105–106.

the message of Malachi.[91] König rightly observed that the universalism of the Yahweh religion has nothing to do with the monotheism of the religions of the heathen nations.[92]

The only argument of any importance is the one in connection with the name "God of heaven." But this medium of communication between Israel and the heathen nations does not imply that Israel, and especially the prophets of that time, gave way to religious syncretism.[93] Indeed, this idea is contrary to the theocratic character of Malachi's prophecy and the general trend of the history of revelation. This theory, therefore, must be rejected.

(b) The next point of view makes the text refer to the Jews in the dispersion. Justin Martyr mentioned that the Jews of his time adhered to this theory.[94] The pure offerings are understood as the prayers of the pious Jews. This point of view is reflected in the translation of the Targum and was advocated by Rashi. The modern version of this theory maintains that the Jews in the dispersion were allowed to bring incense and grain offerings[95] but not meat offerings, and subsequently it was substantiated with reference to the religious practices at the military colony of Elephantine.

The arguments against this theory amount to the following. The dispersion at the time of Malachi was not as extensive as is described in this text; the offerings of the text do not concern incense and grain offerings only but apply to offerings as such; the worship in the temple at Elephantine had a syncretistic character[96] and certainly could not have been called a "pure offering"; it cannot be proven that there were more temples like that of Elephantine in other parts of the dispersion, and those that are mentioned belong to a later period.[97]

Is this theory also to be rejected then? Perhaps not. One must not underrate the actual extent of the dispersion, even in Malachi's time. But

91. Cf. R. Mayer, "Monotheismus in Israel und in der Religion Zarathustras," *BZ* 1 (1957) 23–58.

92. E. König, *Geschichte der Alttestamentlichen Religion,* 4th ed. (Gütersloh: Bertelsmann, 1924), p. 454.

93. Cf. Rehm, op. cit., p. 202; Th. Chary, op. cit., pp. 182–86.

94. Justin Martyr, *Dialogue with Trypho,* 117. Cf. also Rashi, D. R. Jones.

95. Cf., e.g., W. Pressel, pp. 393ff.

96. According to S. J. Schwantes, *A Short History of the Ancient Near East* (Grand Rapids: Baker, 1965), p. 172, "It presents the sorry spectacle of colonists there worshipping Anath-El and Beth-El side by side with Jahweh, early in the sixth century B.C." After the temple was destroyed in 411 B.C. no more sacrifices were allowed.

97. E.g., in Leontopolis and in Arah el-Emir; cf. Von Bulmerincq, op. cit.; R. de Vaux, *Ancient Israel: Its Life and Institutions,* tr. J. McHugh (repr. New York: McGraw-Hill, 1965), pp. 340–42.

more relevant still is the fact that the prophets paid due attention to the Jews in the dispersion and favorably judged their religious devotion and zeal (cf. Isa. 19:16–25; 24:14–16a; 27:13). We have a pointer to the meaning of this text in the history of Pentecost, where the multitude who gathered in Jerusalem from east to west were indeed "both Jews and proselytes" (Acts 2:10). The element of truth in this explanation must not be overlooked and does not exclude the application of this prophecy in its more universalistic and Christian intent.

(c) The objections against the first-named theories induced some scholars to apply this text to the proselytes,[98] with the additional argument that all the nations were being presented by the individual believers of that time (Zech. 14:9; etc.). The main arguments against this theory are, first, that the religious practices of the proselytes do not comply with the terms of our text, and second, that the history of Malachi's time does not refer to groups of believers from the heathen.

In the meantime we must not exclude an element of truth even from this theory. The conversion of the Gentiles is an integral part of OT eschatology, and it is true that the firstfruits are being made to represent the full harvest—according to the idea of "corporate personality" (cf. Isa. 66:21; Zeph. 2:11). The emphasis on this possibility, namely, that the Jews in the dispersion along with the proselytes could have been the objects of the reference of this text, is deduced from the sound hermeneutical principle that the prophets are first of all concerned with the people and the circumstances of their own time.

(d) But then we must admit that the meaning of our text in all its fullness cannot be confined to the circumstances of the Jews in the dispersion and to the proselytes. This text, therefore, must also be applied to the situation of the messianic age, according to the general trend of the prophetical message. One should emphasize the word "also." This is not an exclusive point of view, contrary to the contemporary explanation. The eschatological application of this text is but a continuation of its first application to the Jews and the proselytes.[99] Therefore, we need not translate this verse to read: "For from the rising of the sun to its setting my name shall be great" (cf. AV). We maintain the present tense, for this is indeed its first meaning in the general scope of the context. But then, according to the character of the prophecy,

98. Cf. Ewald; Köhler, in *Real-Encyclopädie für protestantische Theologie und Kirche,* ed. J. J. Herzog; Von Orelli; E. König, *Die messianischen Weissagungen des Alten Testaments* (Stuttgart: Belser, 1923), p. 282. See also Blenkinsopp, *A History of Prophecy in Israel,* p. 241.

99. This is also the view of Reinke, op. cit., pp. 292ff.

the beginning and the end, the firstfruits and the full harvest, are being conceived as a whole.

This conclusion, namely, "that Malachi wanted to make an announcement concerning the messianic age," is not contrary to the literary sense of our text.[100] The bringing of the offerings is in accordance with the stipulations of the law, as is evident from the words *muqṭār, muggāš,* and *minḥâ ṭᵉhôrâ*. The OT dispensation is still in force. And the terms applied to describe the messianic age are fully in accordance with that dispensation. The forms of worship in the great future are those prescribed in the law.[101]

We know that our text transcends the general picture of the messianic age on two essential points: the persons who are offering to the Lord are not the priests in Jerusalem but the believers across the face of the earth, and the place where the offerings are being brought is not the temple in Jerusalem but everywhere. How shall we account for this? Rehm offers some good arguments. In olden times offerings were brought by members of a family, thus expressing the idea that the priestly function originally belonged to all members of the covenant people.[102] This office is accorded by Isaiah even to the Gentiles: "And some of them also I will take for priests and for Levites, says the Lord" (66:21). Exod. 20:24 offers the legitimate basis of the prophecy of Malachi: "An altar of earth you shall make for me and sacrifice on it your burnt offerings and your peace offerings, your sheep and your oxen; in every place[103] where I cause my name to be remembered I will come to you and bless you." In the light of these considerations it is quite possible to draw a continuous line connecting our text with Pentecost and the NT dispensation.

The significant character of our text is evident. All nations are concerned with the priestly function in bringing pure offerings to the Lord, and the whole earth is deemed worthy of being a sacred place of worship. The wall of partition is broken down in two essential ways: nationally and locally. The Jews in the dispersion and the proselytes form the bridgehead which leads to all the nations, and their religious zeal and devotion, their prayers and modes of worship, adapted to the circumstances of the Exile and the dispersion, are the connecting link between the OT forms of worship and that which Jesus Christ announced to the Samaritan woman (John 4:23–24). The inclusion of all the nations in the kingdom of God was an integral part of

100. So Rehm, op. cit., p. 205.

101. Cf. also Isa. 2:3; 42:4; 51:4; Jer. 3:17; Zech. 8:22.

102. See Judg. 6:26; 13:19; 1 Sam. 13:9; 2 Sam. 6:13, 17; 24:18–25.

103. In the sense of "alternatively"; cf. G. Ch. Aalders, *Oud-Testamentische Kanoniek* (Kampen: Kok, 1952), pp. 92–94.

prophecy, but the idea of the sanctification of the whole world to become one great Zion from the rising to the setting of the sun is found only in this text, and partly also in Isa. 19:19 and Zeph. 2:11. In the light of this prophetic perspective it is clear that the Lord is too great to be well pleased by unworthy offerings, a conclusion which has lost none of its significance even today.

12 By way of contrast to the positive worldwide compliance with the demands of the Lord in connection with the "pure offerings," the prophet now turns to the sacrifices offered by the priests in the restored temple of his time. The accusation of vv. 6b and 7 is repeated and directed strongly against the priests. *But you.* The contrast is obvious and is being stressed. Unlike what is happening and will happen "among the nations," they, the priests in Jerusalem, do not offer pure sacrifices, but they profane the Lord's name by saying or suggesting that the table of the Lord is defiled, and that its produce, its food, is contemptible.

profane it. The priests are habitually and continually profaning "it," that is, the name of the Lord. The Hebrew word *ḥālal* (here the Piel part.), "to profane," is synonymous with "to despise" *(bāzâ)* and "to defile" *(gā'al* II) in vv. 6 and 7. They have made common, of no consequence, that which is holy and profound. To deem the Lord's name insignificant and ordinary is the same as despising it. The suffix on *'ôṯô* refers to the name of the Lord, which was mentioned in v. 11. According to *BHK* the pronominal third person singular suffix is a correction made by the scribes for the first person singular, "me." This does not affect the meaning, because God's name is himself.

the table of the Lord is the altar, as in v. 7. *'ᵃḏōnāy* is used instead of *YHWH* to emphasize the lordship of God over against the priests as human beings, and to stress the fact of their desecrating of the Lord. The alternate use of the word "defile" (v. 12) and "despise" (v. 7) in connection with the table of the Lord is of no exegetical consequence: the defiling and the despising of the altar amount to the same thing.

The intimate relationship between altar and sacrifice is evident from the concluding sentence: *and that its produce, its food, is contemptible.* There is no need to delete *nîḇô:* "its produce," as a dittography of *niḇzeh,* or to attach to it the meaning of the revenue which was due to the priests (cf. Lev. 6:9 [Eng. 16]; Num. 18:31; etc.). Both the "produce" and the "food" of the altar are the offering itself (cf. v. 7). The Lord's assessment of the priests' intentions and attitudes is that they have no respect for the stipulations of the law concerning their sacrificial duties and have no reverence for the holiness of God's name.

13 The despising of the temple service is evident from something else. The priests are agreed that the ritual is in itself a burden. It is sheer *weariness,* "hardship." The Hebrew word *mattelā'â* is a compound consisting of the interrogative particle *mâ* and the substantive *telā'â,* meaning "what a weariness." They are bored with their duties. They have no fervency for or interest in performing the prescribed tasks. Because they are in the habit of despising the altar and defiling the offerings, of deeming it contemptible, they are experiencing their duties as something that causes weariness, as an unbearable burden. "The joy of restored worship at Jerusalem, experienced half a century ago, was gone" (Edgar). They *sniff at it,* that is, "look in contempt at it." The Hebrew expression *hippaḥtem 'ôṯô* may be translated "you blow against it" (i.e., consider it to be contemptible), or "you cause it to languish" (i.e., you deprive it of its meaning; cf. Job 31:39).

The despising of the altar is evident from the defective animals which were offered as sacrifices. The same categories of animals as in v. 8 are mentioned, except that the blind of v. 8 are here replaced by *stolen* (*gāzûl,* "that which is taken by force or fraud, which was torn from a larger group"). Some interpreters assume that *gāzûl* is an animal that has been taken by violence, that has been caught and mutilated by a wild animal. Mauled animals were considered unfit for sacrificial purposes, or even for human consumption, and were to be thrown to the dogs (Exod. 22:31; Lev. 17:15). This interpretation is indeed possible, because reference is also made in v. 14 to a "maimed" animal (so Van der Woude, Rudolph, et al.). However, the meaning "stolen" seems preferable (cf. Lev. 5:23; 6:4; 19:13; Judg. 9:25; etc.); even though the law nowhere explicitly forbade the offering of stolen animals, the prohibition was implied in the law's sanctions against theft and robbery. It was rightly observed that the offering of an animal would be meaningless if it did not belong to the man who brought it. There is no need to alter the Hebrew text. *Gāzûl* is without the definite article because it is introduced for the first time and represents a general category of stolen animals. The article with the other categories stresses the fact that they were already mentioned in v. 8. They are therefore the "known" categories: the crippled and diseased.

The accusation and motivation of v. 8 are thus repeated. These blemished animals were being brought as an offering. The Hebrew verb is the Hiphil form of *bô':* "to cause to come," "to bring," and then as a technical term for the act of offering. The repetition of the verb is to emphasize the fact of the sacrificial act. It suggests remarkable eagerness to comply with the responsibilities of the prescribed ritual. The mere and mechanical act of offering would be in itself appropriate, irrespective of their attitudes and the blemished sacrifices! The priests (and people) did not realize that "only when sacrifices represented penitence and faith had they any value to God or efficacy for man" (Baldwin). The Lord is not impressed by their burnt offerings, with their thousands of rams and ten thousand rivers of oil; what he requires is to do justice and to love mercy and to walk humbly with him (Mic. 6:6–8). In communion with his great predecessors Malachi poses the rhetorical question: *Shall I accept it (these offerings) with pleasure from you?* The Lord is not interested in religious activity which implies the defiling of his altar and the despising of his name.

14 From this verse it is evident that the people were also guilty of bringing unworthy sacrifices. There is no need to consider this "parallel word to the people" (Rendtorff) as secondary. We have already pointed out that both the priests and the people were responsible for the blemished sacrifices. The part of the people is now spelled out and illustrated by way of a particular example.

Cursed is the cheat. The Hebrew word *'ārûr,* a Qal passive participle, denotes the condition or attribute of being cursed.[104] The deception consists of a malpractice in paying to God the offering that was due to him on account of a voluntary vow. A male animal is specified for such a sacrifice (Lev. 22:19). Although the cheat had a male animal among his flock, he presented to God a mutilated animal. Some interpreters suggest vocalizing the Hebrew word *mošḥāṯ* as *mošḥaṯ* (i.e., *mošḥaṯṯ*ᵉ), a feminine form, thus referring to an unworthy female animal, in contrast to the required male animal. This seems to make sense. But the problem is that this feminine form of the Hebrew word does not occur elsewhere in the OT; in addition, female animals were not as a matter of course excluded from some offerings (Lev. 3:1–6) but were sometimes explicitly required (Lev. 4:28, 32; 5:6). Most interpreters explain the Hebrew word as the Hophal masculine participle of *šāḥaṯ,* in the sense of "polluted" (Prov. 25:26), "mutilated," "castrated."[105] Such an animal was not acceptable as a vow offering. The terms of the law were explicitly stated in Lev. 22:23: "You may . . . present as a freewill offering a specimen of your cattle or sheep that is deformed or stunted, but it will not be accepted in fulfillment of a vow" (cf. NIV). The deception of this cheat was that he wanted to pay his vows by presenting to God, contrary to the stipulations of the law, an unfit offering. This could not be permitted. God is not a person who can be deceived in such a fashion. Rather, he is *a great king.*[106] If a person would not dare to cheat his fellowman or his human

104. See GKC, § 116a.

105. See GKC, § 80bn.2.

106. The contention that the title "king" was applied to God, because Israel was at that time (after the Exile) without a king—so Dummelow—is hardly tenable. The idea of God's universal kingship occurs frequently; cf. Judg. 8:23; 1 Sam. 12:12; Isa. 6:5; 33:22; 43:15; 44:6; Jer. 8:19; 10:10; Zeph. 3:15; Ps. 10:16; 24:7–10; 84:3;

governor (v. 8), how much more detestable would be such an attempt to deceive God, whose name is feared among the nations.

The purport of the last-named reference is not the same as that of v. 11. In v. 11 the greatness of God's name among the nations was an expression of the way his name was *honored* among the nations. In v. 14 his name is *feared* among the nations, which does not imply that they were serving him or having faith in him. The difference between vv. 11 and 14 can be expressed in terms of a universalism in a pregnant sense (v. 11), over against a universalism in a general sense (v. 14).[107] God's name is great because he is honored and acknowledged (v. 11), and feared (v. 14) among the nations. In both instances they were illustrations of the fact that God is not satisfied with blemished sacrifices.

95:3. Cf. F. E. Deist and J. J. Burden, *'n ABC van Bybeluitleg* (Pretoria: J. L. van Schaik, 1980), p. 12, concerning the concept of the Great King.

107. Cf. P. J. N. Smal, *Die universalisme in die Psalms* (Kampen: Kok, 1979), pp. 210ff., 223ff., for a definition of both terms.

IV. THE PRIESTHOOD IN THE BALANCE (2:1–9)

1 *And now this command is for you, O priests.*
2 *If you do not listen, and do not set your heart to honor my name,*
says the Lord Almighty, I will send a curse upon you,
and I will curse your blessings.
Yes, I have already cursed them, because you have not taken it to heart.[1]
3 *I will rebuke your descendants,*
and I will spread dung on your faces, the dung from your feasts;
and you will be carried off to it.
4 *Then you would know that I have sent to you this command in order that my covenant with Levi might be maintained,*
says the Lord Almighty.
5 *My covenant with him was life and peace;*
I gave them to him,
reverence,
and he revered me
and stood in awe of my name.
6 *Reliable instruction in the law was in his mouth*
and nothing unjust was found on his lips.
He walked with me in peace and uprightness,
and he has turned many away from sin.
7 *Verily, the lips of a priest preserve knowledge,*
and from his mouth people are seeking instruction in the law,
because he is a messenger of the Lord Almighty.
8 *But you have deserted the way*
and by your teaching have caused many to stumble;
you have annulled the covenant with Levi, says the Lord Almighty.

1. Elliger and Van der Woude deem v. 2 to be an addition to the text, disrupting the sequence between vv. 1 and 3. According to Marti, Smith, Dentan, et al., only v. 2b is considered to be secondary. The problem with these scholars arises with their interpretation of *miṣwâ* as a decree of judgment.

9 *So I will cause you to be despised and humiliated by all the people,*
because you have not followed my ways,
and have shown partiality in the instruction of the law.

In conjunction with the prophet's rebuke of the priests and people because they offered blemished sacrifices (1:6–14), he now addressed the priesthood by way of threat. He pointed out their privileged position, reminded them of the gripping example of the classical or ideal priesthood, and admonished them for violating the priestly office.[2]

1 The prophet begins by reminding the priests that *this command* was especially applicable to them. With the introductory *we*ʿ*attâ,* "and now," the prophet recapitulates what was said in the preceding passage[3] and emphasizes the topic of his new discourse. The prophet's statement that *this command* (Heb. *miṣwâ*) is meant for the priests can be interpreted in two different ways. The first is to render *miṣwâ* according to its general sense, "order," "commandment" (both a particular commandment and the sum of all commandments), and to consider v. 1 as an introduction to the announcement of God's judgment in vv. 2 and 3. The "command" is thus a part of the judgment itself. According to this point of view *miṣwâ* is the "decree" (NEB, Botterweck), the "decision" (J. Ridderbos), the "announcement" (NBG), the "admonition" (Reinke, NIV) that God will send a curse upon the priests. "This command" implies "that there can be no mitigation of the punishment about to be pronounced."[4] According to the second point of view "this command" must not be considered a separate "decree" or "admonition" which in itself implies an act of judgment, but must be interpreted in terms of v. 4, according to which "this command" is identified with the "covenant of Levi" and its maintenance (so rightly D. R. Jones). Just as there is a *miṣwâ* for the king (1 Sam. 13:13) and for the prophet (1 K. 13:21), there is one for the priests. By "this command" the priestly office as a divine institution is meant.

2. Special studies on this pericope include A. Gelin, "Message aux prêtres (Mal. 2:1–9)," *Bible et Vie Chrétienne* 30 (1959) 14–20; U. Devescovi, "L'alleanza di Jahwe con Levi," *BeO* 4 (1962) 205–18. Following Rudolph and Van der Woude, Snyman in his thesis stresses the unity of 1:6–2:9 as a separate pericope, allowing only for a subdivision between 1:6–14 and 2:1–9. We agree with this point of view, but want to emphasize the distinction between the two subdivisions: the persons addressed and implied in 1:6–14 are the priests *and the people,* whereas 2:1–9 concern the priests only.

3. According to Van der Woude, et al., the preceding passage is 1:6–10, because 1:11–14 is deemed a secondary and parallel word to the people.

4. So Baldwin; cf. also Van der Woude.

The very essence of "this command" is the duty and the privilege of the priests to honor the name of the Lord (v. 2). Instead of being a mere introduction to vv. 2 and 3, it is the focus of the whole passage. God's "command" for the priests is synonymous with his covenant with Levi, his institution of the priestly office. The demonstrative pronoun *hazz'ōṯ,* "this," emphasizes the specific application of the "command" to the priests. It is also evident from the use of the vocative, *O priests,* here expressed by the article *(hakkōhanîm).*[5]

2 The priests' honorable position as the mediators between God and his people (Exod. 28:1–29:46) demanded a corresponding faithfulness in the performance of their duties (Laetsch). They were urged to listen to the Lord. If they were not going to listen, God would send a curse upon them. The pronounced judgment is conditional. *If you do not.* In Hebrew the sentence begins *'im-lō'*, "if not"; *'im* with an imperfect verb in the protasis and a perfect verb in the apodosis is used to express what is possible in the present or future if a condition is fulfilled.[6] The assumption is that the priests *did not (lō')* fulfill the condition. They have the opportunity to correct themselves, however; if they will listen and give wholehearted attention to the words of the Lord, the consequences of the threat of judgment may be averted. But then they must fulfill God's condition. That condition concurs with God's "command," is the very essence of the covenant with Levi, and consists in the giving *(lāṯēṯ)* of honor to the name of the Lord.

I will send a curse upon you. If they persist in not listening and not honoring the name of the Lord wholeheartedly, however, then they will have to bear the consequences.[7] In Hebrew the word *curse* has the definite article and thus represents a whole class of attributes or states expressed in the abstract word.[8] The curse is here presented as an objective entity, a power in itself, but one that is disposed by God, because he sends it. The curse is realized only after and because the priests have sinned. It is, therefore, not an "illegitimate curse,"[9] which, according to heathen conceptions, is self-determining, an active power that once spoken cannot be taken back.[10] The "legitimate curse," that which is sent and disposed of by God, is a destructive power. Everything and anyone that is being cursed by God is destined for annihilation. The "legitimate curse" is devastating in its effect because it is an instrument of God's wrath (cf. Gen. 3:14, 17; 5:29; Deut. 28:20; etc.).

5. See GKC, § 126e, f.
6. See GKC, § 159l, q.
7. See GKC, §§ 112ff, 159q, o, s.
8. See GKC, § 126n.
9. Cf. N. H. Ridderbos, *De Psalmen,* KV (Kampen: Kok, 1962), I:31.
10. Cf. Vriezen, *An Outline of Old Testament Theology,* rev. ed., p. 30.

If God so chooses he could turn the curse into a blessing (Deut. 23:6 [Eng. 5]; Judg. 17:2; Neh. 13:2). In this text it must be considered against the background of the "covenant with Levi" and of "the command" relating to the priests. The curse is the inevitable counterpart of the covenant blessing and comes into effect because the stipulations of the covenant were ignored.

The curse of God is directed against the priests' *blessings*. This expression has been interpreted in three different ways. First, most interpreters relate the "blessings" to the function of the priests to bless the people in the name of the Lord. According to Brockington, "the priestly blessing was a most solemn part of the service (see Num. 6:22–27) and ultimately came to be the only occasion on which the divine name was actually pronounced in Israel. To threaten that the blessing be turned into a curse was to undermine and overthrow the whole fabric of institutional religion in Israel."[11]

Second, some interpret "blessings" to mean the material benefits which were due to the priests and Levites in performing their duties.[12]

Third, and most convincing, others attribute to the "blessings" a comprehensive meaning. One should consider the "blessings," like the curse, as an essential aspect of the covenant with Levi. It concerns the priesthood as a divine and therefore blessed institution. Thus we agree with Jones: "The curse and the blessings have reference to Yahweh's original commission to the priesthood. The cursing of their blessings is the blight and withering of a fruitful tree." The curse, therefore, will affect the priests first of all in their status as a blessed generation (1 Sam. 2:28), who were privileged to "approach" God (Zech. 3:7) and were honored to be called "sons" and "servants" of the Lord (Mal. 1:6). Status and function are interrelated, however, and therefore the curse will also affect the performance of their duty, especially in pronouncing God's blessing upon the people and their sacrifices (Num. 6:22–27). Because transgression and punishment are connected, we may assume that the curse will also affect the sacrificial duties of the priests, which they deemed a "burden" (1:13) and something contemptible. In addition, the priestly office also includes material benefits. This is explicitly referred to as the *mišpāṭ* of the priests and the *miṣwōṯ* of the Levites (Deut. 18:3; 1 Sam. 2:13; Neh. 13:5) and described as "blessings" in Ezek. 44:29 and 30. In the time of Malachi the material benefits were a sensitive matter, because the people refrained from bringing the tithes and

11. See also Von Orelli, Keil, De Moor, J. Ridderbos, Botterweck (*BibLeb* 1 [1960] 28–38).

12. So, e.g., Hitzig-Steiner, Von Bulmerincq, Dentan, Rudolph. According to Van der Woude the blessings are meant for the whole of Israel, and nowhere in the OT do they concern the priests. This point of view is unacceptable, however, and can only be maintained by considering v. 2 as secondary.

offerings to the temple (Mal. 3:6–12). The extensiveness of this curse is suggested in the final indictment in v. 9: God will cause them to be despised and humiliated by all the people. The whole content of the priests' blessed existence and office will be turned into a curse.

The one comprehensive blessedness of the priests is broken into different branches, and that is why reference to it can be made in both the singular (*'ārôṯîhā,* lit. "I have cursed it") and the plural (*birḵôṯêḵem,* "your blessings"). Thus there is no need to change the plural into a singular in conjunction with the LXX (cf. *BHS*). The singular suffix of *'ārôṯîhā* may refer to the blessing as a whole or distributively to each separate blessing.

Yes, I have already cursed them. There is no need to regard this clause as secondary. The priests were reminded of what had already happened to them (2:13; 3:9), and that these adverse experiences were really an aspect of God's curse upon them. Simultaneously this reminder emphasizes the threat and actuality of the pronounced curse that will become effective in the near future. The Hebrew verb *'ārôṯîhā* is not a prophetic perfect[13] but a historic perfect, as is evident from the emphasizing particle *wᵉgam,* "and also," "and yes," and the following motivation introduced by the particle *kî,* "because."

because you have not taken it to heart. The nominal construction of this sentence stresses that it is characteristic of the priests not to take "this command" to heart.[14] They are in the habit of not doing it. Thus their waywardness has a history of its own. That is the reason why God has already cursed them in the past. The LXX's addition, "I will scatter your praise (blessing), and it will not be among you," is "a clear case of verbose expansion" (J. M. P. Smith).

3 In this verse the threat amounts to the following. The priests' descendants will be rebuked, that is, will be struck by the judgment, so that an end will be put to the priests' privileged position. The dung of the sacrificial animals which were slaughtered in connection with the annual feasts will be spread upon their faces, causing them to become unclean and therefore incapable of performing their official duties. Finally, they will be cast onto the dunghill, as an indication that their place is no longer in the sanctuary but with the refuse.

The word *descendants* translates Hebrew *zeraʿ* (lit. "seed"). Some interpreters, in conjunction with the rendering of the Syriac and Targum (cf. AV), explain this expression to mean a threatening of the priests' crops.

13. So Rudolph, Van der Woude; cf. König, *Syntax,* § 368h. This interpretation is probable but seems to disregard the continuity of the curse between the past, present, and future.

14. See GKC, § 152l, m.

According to Laetsch "God's rebuke keeps the seed from fulfilling its desire to sprout (cf. Hos. 2:21f.). He will forbid the seed to sprout and grow and bear fruit for such disobedient priests. And the seed, unlike the priests, will obey his command. The priests will be punished where these selfish belly servants are most vulnerable; they will have nothing to fill their bellies." The objection against this interpretation that the priests did not till the ground and that failure of the crops could not have been a curse to them disregards the fact that they were dependent upon the crops of the people for their own revenue (cf. Deut. 18:4; Neh. 12:44). More important, however, is the consideration that *zeraʿ* nowhere indicates fruit or crops.

We interpret *zeraʿ* to mean *descendants* (NIV), "offspring" (RSV, Berkeley). In Deut. 28:15–68 the curses for disobedience are enumerated, with the inclusion of "your sons and your daughters" (v. 32). The same applies to the second command of the Decalogue (Exod. 20:5), which pronounces punishment on the children for the sin of the fathers. When the priests' descendants are being cursed, it is obvious that they would be without descendants, and that would imply the annulment of the priesthood as such. This is the purport of the Hebrew word *gāʿar*, "shout," "rebuke," "scold," "threaten." The assumption is that the word of God will cause destruction. According to P. J. van Zijl "God's threat is the same as the outpouring of his wrath and the execution of his judgments," with reference to Deut. 28:20; Isa. 17:13; 30:17; 51:20; 54:9; Ps. 80:17 (Eng. 16).[15] The meaning of *gāʿar* here is similar to the sending of God's curse in v. 2.

Most interpreters prefer the reading of the LXX and Vulgate *zᵉrōaʿ*, "the arm," instead of *zeraʿ*, "seed," "descendants." "The arm" that is being threatened is the arm or hand of the priest which is held up high in benediction. According to this interpretation the threatening of the arm is a concrete explanation of the statement that God will curse the priests' blessings (v. 2). The problem with this interpretation is that it would be a mere repetition of the pronounced judgment of v. 2, and that the expression of "threatening the arm" is rather unusual. Other interpreters, therefore, suggest a reading *gāḏaʿ*, "to cut off," instead of *gāʿar*, "to threaten," "rebuke" (hence NEB: "I will cut off your arm"). We have a similar expression in 1 Sam. 2:31. The intention is that God will cut short Eli's strength. The strength of a family consists in the vital energy of its members, and shows itself in the fact that they reach a good old age. This strength was to vanish in Eli's house; no one

15. P. J. van Zijl, "A Discussion of the Root *gaʿar* (Rebuke)," in *Biblical Essays, OTWSA*, ed. A. H. van Zyl (Potchefstroom: Pro Rege, 1969), pp. 53–56; A. A. Macintosh, "A Consideration of Hebrew *gʿr*," *VT* 19 (1969) 471–79; S. C. Reif, "A Note on *gaʿar*," *VT* 21 (1971) 241–44; A. Caquot, in *TDOT*, III:49–53; G. Liedke, in *THAT*, I:429–31.

would ever again preserve his life to old age (Keil and Delitzsch). In Malachi the expression would indicate that the priests would not be able to perform their special duty of pronouncing the blessing of the Lord. They will be deprived of their function to act as mediators between God and his people.

This explanation is, indeed, tenable, but not preferable. It is based upon a very doubtful reading of the LXX. In this text the LXX reads "arm" instead of "seed," but in 1 Sam. 2:31 it substitutes "seed" for "arm." The main problem with the reading of the LXX is the accompanying verb, *aphorízō,* in the sense of "set apart," "separate." In the LXX this Greek verb is used as a translation of fifteen different Hebrew words, but never *gāḏaʿ*. The Greek translators obviously conjectured the meaning of the Hebrew text, and consequently provided an inconsistent translation. We maintain the reading of the Hebrew text.

I will spread dung on your faces. This is another aspect of the priests' punishment. According to Koehler *pereš* is the contents of the stomach, not that of the intestines. GB, Dentan, et al., define it as the "contents of the bowels of the slain sacrificial animals." The same definition is given by BDB, Lattey, et al.: "foecal matter found in intestines of victim." This word is also found in Exod. 29:14; Lev. 4:11; 8:17; 16:27; and Num. 19:5. In all these passages it refers to a part of the sacrificial animal, along with the bull's flesh and its hide (Exod. 29:14; Lev. 8:17; 16:27) and the blood (Num. 19:5), that should be burned outside the camp. In Lev. 4:11–12 the stipulation is spelled out extensively: "But the hide of the bull and all its flesh, as well as the head and legs, the inner parts and offal *[pereš]*—that is, all the rest of the bull—he must take outside the camp to a place ceremonially clean, where the ashes are thrown, and burn it in a wood fire on an ash pile" (NIV).

The interpretation according to which the priests would be denied not only the "shoulder" but also the "inner parts" *(haqqāḇâ)* as part of their share (Deut. 18:3) cannot be maintained. The *pereš* is not taken from them but is *spread (zārâ)* on their faces. The real point in this threat is not so much the humiliation that is caused by this symbolic act, because the priests have "humiliated" God by offering unfit sacrifices (1:6–14, esp. v. 9), but the main intention is to degrade the priests in such a manner that they would be unfit and unclean to perform their official duties. There is an aspect of permanence in the realization of God's judgment. This is substantiated by the concluding sentence.

and you will be carried off to it. This sentence is deemed a crux interpretum. Dentan voices the general opinion by saying: "Whatever the words mean, they are almost certainly no part of the original prophecy." *BHK* and *BHS* consider this clause as secondary, and *BHS* suggests as a probable reading: "And I will lift you up away from me," that is, "I will dispose of you," with reference to the Syriac and LXX. Although this emendation seems likely, there is really no need to alter the Hebrew text. The main problems concern the indication of the subject; the explanation of *nāśā'* in a transitive sense, the verb usually having an intransitive meaning; and the identification of the suffix "it" *('ēlāyw)*. We agree with Laetsch that the subject is impersonal or indefinite: "one," "someone," or "they," usually rendered by the passive. The expression *nāśā' 'el* is used in various contexts in the sense of "lifting up to, in the direction of." The suffix in *'ēlāyw* refers back to "dung," but then in the sense of the "dunghill," the place outside the camp where the ashes are thrown (Lev. 4:11). The intention is that the priests will be carried by "them" or "one" (even God) to that place outside the camp where the dung and other matter are deposited. That would imply a radical reversal of their elevated position: from the sanctuary to the dungheap! Two passages in Jeremiah are analogous to this degradation of the original privileged position. In 16:4 the judgment on the "day of disaster" would amount to the following: "They shall not be lamented, nor shall they be buried; they shall be as dung [*dōmen*, "manure"] on the surface of the ground." In 22:19 it is said: "With the burial of an ass he shall be buried, dragged and cast forth beyond the gates of Jerusalem." In Malachi it concerns the priests. "The invective of the eighth-century prophets against the cultus (Isa. 1:11–15; Hos. 4:6–10; Amos 4:4, 5; 5:21–23; Mic. 6:6–8) was polite by comparison" (Baldwin).

4 This verse has been variously interpreted. We have translated the initial *waw* not as a conjunction, "and," but as the introduction of an apodosis in a conditional sentence: *Then you would know*. There is a difference of opinion on the meaning of the Hebrew verb *yāḏa'*, "observe," "know," in this context. Some suggest that this knowledge presupposes the conversion of the priests, while others refer this knowledge to the judgment that the priests would experience. The correct interpretation of *yāḏa'* is dependent on the explanation of *lihyôṯ* in the second clause.[16] There are three possible interpretations. First, "this command" of the Lord will be his covenant with Levi; the subject of the sentence would be "the command." According to this interpretation the priests will become aware of the fact that from now on the Lord is not going to act in accordance with his covenant with Levi but in accordance with "this command," the expression of the judgment, which will replace the covenant of Levi. The pronounced judgment is thus continued in this verse. This interpretation should be rejected

16. See Van der Woude, pp. 108–109, for proposed emendations to the text. According to him such an emendation is unnecessary.

because according to our interpretation of v. 1, "this command" is not to be identified with God's pronounced judgment, and this explanation is contrary to the definition of the "covenant with Levi," which is given in v. 5.

The second possible interpretation explains the preposition *l^e^* in the sense of "while," "seeing that." On account of the realized judgment the priests will have to acknowledge that this serious admonition was directed to them, *seeing that* God has entered into a covenant with Levi. God's covenant with Levi is the very basis for the responsibility of the priesthood. Their awakening consciousness concerning the meaning of "this command" has a double motivation: the pronounced judgment of vv. 2 and 3, and the covenant with Levi (so J. M. P. Smith). This interpretation seems most likely, especially when we consider the covenant as being the basis and background of both maledictions and benedictions, curses and blessings.

We prefer the third interpretation, however, which takes the preposition *l^e^* in its primary meaning to denote direction or purpose.[17] Thus we may translate the clause: *in order that my covenant with Levi might be maintained.* The subject is "my covenant," and the intention is that "this command" was meant to lead to repentance and so make possible the continuation of the covenant with Levi (cf. Baldwin).

The formal act of establishing a covenant with Levi is nowhere mentioned in the OT. In Genesis the reference to the person and tribe of Levi is not very complimentary (cf. 29:34; 34:25, 26; 49:5–7). We may assume that the tribe obtained a certain prominence due to the fact that Moses and Aaron belonged to it (Exod. 2:1–10; 4:14). In Deut. 10:8, 9 Israel was reminded of the time at Horeb when God had "set apart" the tribe of Levi, "to stand before the Lord to minister to him and to bless in his name." The historic occasion was when "all the Levites" rallied to carry out Moses' orders after the incident of the golden calf (Exod. 32:26–29). Because they did what Moses commanded them to do, Moses told them: "You have been set apart to the Lord today" (v. 29, NIV). This "setting apart" of the tribe of Levi presupposes the covenant relationship, but at this stage it was not explicitly stated. In Num. 18:19 reference is made to "a covenant of salt for ever" in connection with the offerings for priests and Levites. This covenant is not identical with the "covenant with Levi" in Malachi, however. The same applies to the "covenant of peace" mentioned in Num. 25:11–13. This "covenant" was established with Phinehas, the son of Aaron, and not with the Levites as a whole. The earliest mention of a "covenant with Levi," in the context of other "covenants," is Jer. 33:20–21: "This is what the Lord says: 'If you can break my covenant with the day and my covenant with the night,

17. See GKC, § 114f, g.

so that day and night no longer come at their appointed time, then my covenant with David my servant—and my covenant with the Levites who are priests ministering before me—can be broken" (NIV). This mention of the "covenant with the Levites" presupposes that it was established during the early history of Israel. It is true that the blessing of Moses on the tribe of Levi (Deut. 33:8–11), according to which they were commissioned for the specific task of giving guidance through the Urim and Thummim and of teaching and officiating in worship, is not explicitly called a covenant. But sometime in the past and somewhere God did enter into a covenant with Levi, most probably in connection with the historic event mentioned in Exod. 32:26–29. This explanation seems preferable to that according to which the divine promise to Levi was eventually raised out of its private and limited context to be made yet another instance of the concern of the covenant God for his whole people.

In due course the Levites, including the priests, have "broken" (*pārar,* Ezek. 44:7) and "defiled" (*gā'al* II, Neh. 13:29) this specific covenant. The purport of Malachi's admonition is that "all evil priests had to repent or be swept away from the sanctuary in order that the covenant with Levi might stand" (Baldwin).

It is interesting to note that Malachi, like Ezekiel, does not mention the high priest, even though we may assume that a high priest was in office at that time (cf. Neh. 12:10–11). Another obvious fact is that our prophet does not distinguish between priests and Levites. He refers to the "covenant with Levi," and according to him the priests are "the sons of Levi" (3:3; cf. Deut. 21:5; 31:9). It is evident, however, that he addresses himself to the priesthood of his time (Mal. 1:6; 2:1, 7; 3:3, 4). An attempt to explain these problems will be made at the end of this section.

5–7 These verses describe the participants and the content of the "covenant with Levi." The participants are God and Levi, and the content is most significant. From God's side the covenant means life and peace, and from Levi's side the obligation presupposes unlimited subjection in reverence and the fear of the Lord. The priesthood in the time of Malachi could have pleaded human weakness as an excuse for their failure to comply with the stipulations of the covenant. Therefore the prophet reminds them of the example that was set by the priesthood in the classical period of Israel's history (vv. 5c–7; cf. Exod. 32:26–29; Num. 25:11–13; Ezek. 44:15). In contrast to this example the priests in the time of Malachi failed miserably (vv. 8, 9).

5 The relationship between the different clauses of v. 5 is a matter of dispute. Verse 5a is interpreted in three different ways. According to the first interpretation the words "life" and "peace" are in a genitive relationship to "covenant." The translation adopted by the LXX, Vulgate, and some modern versions like the RSV and Berkeley reads: "My covenant with him was a covenant of life and peace." This interpretation seems preferable. The second interpretation (closely related to the first) regards the words "life" and "peace" as a nearer definition of the "covenant," and renders the clause: "My covenant with him was life and peace." A third group of translators and interpreters consider v. 5a to be an independent sentence, with the purpose of establishing the fact and significance of the "covenant." According to the NEB, "My covenant was with him: I bestowed life and prosperity on him." The first two interpretations are interrelated and are preferable to the third one, because they identify more closely the covenant with its content, "life" and "peace."

The same structural problems occur in v. 5b. The Masoretes, followed by the LXX, Vulgate, Luther, Calvin, and most modern translations, combine the two clauses *wā'ettᵉnēm-lô môrā'*: "And I gave them to him, that he might fear" (RSV), or, with a minor emendation of the text: "I laid on him the duty of reverence" (NEB). But it seems preferable to interpret *môrā'* as a parallel to *(bᵉrîṯ) haḥayyîm wᵉhaššālôm,* just as *wayyîrā'ēnî* is a parallel of *wā'ettᵉnēm-lô*. The subject of both parallel clauses is "my covenant," the content being, on the one hand, "life and peace," and on the other hand, *môrā'*, "fear," "reverence." God's blessing to Levi consists of "life and peace." These he gave him. Levi's obligation was to comply with the *môrā'* aspect of the covenant.[18] That is exactly what he did: *and he revered me and stood in awe of my name* (so NIV).

It is important to note that the participants of this covenant were not on a par with one another. God is the main and real subject of the covenant. It was *his* covenant with Levi. Even the content bears witness to this fact. He is the author not only of the benefits of "life and peace," but also of the obligation "to fear." All these elements are aspects of God's covenant with Levi.

The aspect of *life* presupposes the institution of the priesthood, the power and ability to perform their official duties, the privilege of being priests in the service of the Lord. The aspect of *peace* characterizes the "life," the very existence of the priesthood, as wholesome, as harmonious and blessed. The third essential aspect of the covenant is fear, *reverence*. The priests have no option but to comply to this aspect of the covenant. This

18. So, rightly, also Van der Woude: *môrā'* is not part of the covenant blessing but an aspect of the covenant obligation. Cf. also Rudolph, contra E. Kutsch, *Verheissung und Gesetz,* BZAW 131 (Berlin: Töpelmann, 1973), p. 120. See also A. Renker, *Die Tora bei Maleachi,* pp. 117–21.

"fear of God" is expressed both in the attitude of reverence and in the meticulous performing of their duties in accordance with the stipulations of "this command."

he revered me and stood in awe of my name. Malachi asserts that the priesthood has on occasion revered the Lord and been awed by him. The Heb. *niḥaṯ* is a Niphal perfect of *ḥāṯaṯ* meaning "to be filled with terror," "to stand in awe." They have honored their obligation and have acted according to the content and purport of God's covenant with them.

6 The exemplary attitude and behavior of the classical (or ideal) priesthood is spelled out in more detail in this verse. In positive and negative statements the prophet stresses the fact that the earlier priests were reliable in their instruction of the law. Their general conduct was characterized by this reliable instruction, a devout life, and a zeal for the spiritual welfare of the covenant people. The prophet's emphasis on the function of the priest as a teacher is remarkable. This has led to the conclusion that "the function of a priest is primarily that of a teacher" (Dentan). We will deal with this point of view at the end of this pericope.

Reliable instruction in the law. The term *tôrâ,* from *yārâ,* "to point with the finger" (Prov. 6:13), is generally used in the sense of instruction or guidance, and is applicable to a single instruction or a whole complex of it. In regard to God it concerns the revelation of his will, through the medium of a prophet (Isa. 13:14), and generally by means of the priests. In our text *tôrâ* does not refer to the Mosaic law as such, but to the oral instruction of that law by the priests.

One of the main tasks of the priests was "to teach the people of Israel all the statutes which the Lord has spoken to them by Moses" (Lev. 10:11), and Israel was admonished "to do according to what they [the priests] declare to you. . . . be careful to do according to all that they direct you *[yôrûḵā]*, according to the instructions *[tôrâ]* which they give you *[yôrûḵā]*, and according to the decision which they pronounce to you" (Deut. 17:10–11). The tribe of Levi was set apart to teach God's precepts to Jacob and his law to Israel (Deut. 33:10). Their task was to hand down the content of the Mosaic law, to give instruction in it, to expound and apply the law according to the need and circumstances of the people. "They related the law to the changing circumstances of contemporary life" (Edgar).

The *instruction* of the earlier priests was characterized by *'ěmeṯ*. This word is a contracted form of *'ěmeneṯ,* from *'āman,* with the general meaning of "firmness," "trustworthiness," and then with a whole host of derived or related meanings. In Exod. 18:21 Jethro advises Moses to "choose able men *['anšê-ḥayil]* . . . such as fear God, men who are trustworthy *['anšê 'ěmeṯ]* and who hate a bribe." Neh. 7:2 describes Hananiah as "a man of integrity *['îš 'ĕmeṯ]* and feared God more than most men do" (NIV). In connection with words or oral instructions, as in Malachi, the Hebrew word *'ĕmeṯ* qualifies that instruction as reliable, trustworthy, genuine, fully in accordance with the intent and content of the law itself. In Ps. 119:142 God's righteousness is proclaimed as "everlasting" and his law *(tôrâ)* as true *('ĕmeṯ)*. God's regulations *(mišpāṭîm)* and laws *(tôrôṯ)* are in themselves just *(yešārîm)* and right *('ĕmeṯ)*, according to Neh. 9:13.

in his mouth. The people need not seek this kind of instruction in vain, for the priests had it in their mouths, that is, ready; they were capable and motivated to dispense their knowledge of the law in all circumstances and according to the needs of the people. The prophet does not itemize the content of the priests' instruction, but we may assume that it was directed among other things at the distinction between "the holy and the common, and between the unclean and the clean" (Lev. 10:10; cf. Ezek. 22:26), and that they related the law to the changing circumstances of contemporary life (Deut. 17:9; 31:9–13; 33:10; Ezek. 7:26; etc.).

and nothing unjust was found on his lips. This is the negative statement paralleling the previous positive assertion. The Hebrew word *ʿawlâ* has the sense of "unrighteousness," "wickedness," "deceit," "falseness," and in this context is exactly the opposite of *'ĕmeṯ,* that which is reliable, trustworthy, true, right.

Unjust instruction in the law may comply with the formal aspects of the law, but it is essentially contrary to its intent and therefore does not reflect the revealed will of God. This untrue, false representation of God's *tôrâ,* however, was not found on the lips of those priests. They were not intent upon material gain for themselves. They were true and faithful mediators of God's revealed will to the people, and therefore fully in accordance with their elevated position as priests in the service of the Lord.

He walked with me. The priests' exemplary behavior was also evident in their devout life. They had a constant communion with him. This presupposes a life fully in accordance with God's will, both personally and professionally. The expression "walking with God" denotes an even more intimate relationship than "following him" (Deut. 13:4; 2 K. 23:3). Early examples of people walking with God are Enoch and Noah (Gen. 5:22; 6:9). Israel was admonished to walk humbly with their God in Mic. 6:8.

The daily communion with God was *in peace and uprightness.* "Peace" refers to full harmony with the will of God, and it presupposed the blessed experience of wholesomeness and well-being in their personal and professional life. "Uprightness" refers to the moral integrity of their behavior and conduct. They were immune to any negative influence in their personal and official relationship to God.

he has turned many away from sin. The consequences could have been foreseen. A tree planted by streams of water could do nothing else but yield its fruit in season (Ps. 1:3). This also applied to the earlier priests. The way they performed their official duties as teachers of the people, and their devout life in humbly walking with their God, had as an inevitable effect that many were turned away from sin. It is important to emphasize two aspects in this regard. The repentance and conversion of *many* may be seen as the result of the priests' general conduct and moral integrity. They were reliable in their instruction in the law, and were exemplary in the devotion of their lives. It was inevitable that a tree like this should ever bear fruit. At the same time the priests were actively involved in the "evangelistic" program of turning the people away from sin. We may assume that they had a zeal for the spiritual welfare of the covenant people.[19]

turned away. They have caused people to do two things, to desist from sinning and to turn back to God. These were really two elements of the same act. Negatively they were persuading people not to sin anymore, and positively they prevailed on them to renew the covenant relationship with God. Both these aspects are included in the Hebrew word *hēšîḇ,* the causative form of *šûḇ,* "to turn back."

sin. The Hebrew word here is *ʿāwōn,* which means a conscious, intentional offense or transgression, with the derived meaning of guilt. Both elements of meaning are applicable to the situation of our text. The people (many of them!) had willfully transgressed God's commands and therefore were guilty because of it. Due to the priests' ministry their relationship with God was renewed.

7 Since Bohme many interpreters deem v. 7 as secondary on the following grounds. It truncates the contrast between vv. 6 and 7; it is *post festum* in the sense that everything it conveys was already said in v. 6; God is introduced in the third person, contrary to vv. 6 and 8, where he is spoken of in the first person, and the reference to the *mal'aḵ YHWH* in v. 7 is a foreign element in the prophecy of Malachi.[20] These considerations are not conclusive and have been rightly contradicted by J. M. P. Smith. He concludes: "Hence, the case against 2:7 seems too weak to carry conviction." In this verse it is stated that the earlier priesthood has acted according to what one might rightly expect of them.

Verily, the lips of a priest preserve knowledge. We prefer the mean-

19. The reference to the "many" as the covenant community for whom the priests were responsible is expounded in the Qumran mss. and in the Babylonian Talmud (Sanhedrin 7:8). Cf. Van der Woude, p. 110. See also Ps. 40:4 (Eng. 3); 71:7; 109:30; Dan. 9:27; 11:33, 39; 12:3; Est. 4:3; Josephus *BJ* 2.8.9 (145–49).

20. So also Van der Woude and most scholars.

ing of *kî* in the sense of an asseveration, "yes," "verily" (cf. also 1:11). Some scholars and translations render the imperfect *yišmᵉrû* as a potential imperfect denoting an obligation: "For the lips of a priest ought to preserve knowledge" (NIV, etc.). But this interpretation is contrary to the positive character of this pronouncement. The imperfect is here used rather in the sphere of the present time to express actions which may be repeated at any time, or are customarily repeated on a given occasion.[21] It is, therefore, customary for the lips of the priest to keep or preserve knowledge. The prophet is still referring to the classical or ideal priesthood.

The *lips* of the priest are represented as a storehouse of knowledge. At the same time the idea is suggested that the knowledge is at his disposal, that he can dispense it according to the required need or circumstances. This *daʿaṯ,* "knowledge," refers to God's revealed will, as it is reflected in his *tôrâ*. Because the priests, in the time of Hosea, had rejected knowledge *(haddaʿaṯ),* the people were destroyed from lack of knowledge (*haddaʿaṯ,* Hos. 4:6). The (ideal) priests, on the other hand, have not rejected the knowledge of God's revealed will, but have preserved it, were keeping it intact, and therefore their instruction, the dispensing of that knowledge, has been reliable. That is why the people, all of them in general, were seeking from the priests' mouths instruction in the law. The Hebrew word *yᵉḇaqšû* suggests the idea of seeking with the view of finding.[22] The people would not seek in vain. The result is assumed in the very act of seeking. What they were looking for is the *tôrâ,* again in the sense of the oral instruction in the law. The preeminence of the priest in this connection is based upon *(kî)* the fact that he is a *mal'aḵ YHWH-ṣᵉḇā'ôṯ,* a "messenger of the Lord Almighty." This expression, elsewhere applied to the prophet Haggai (Hag. 1:13), designates the priest as a messenger who mediates the message of God's *tôrâ* to his people. In this specific function the priest does not replace the prophet, as is alleged by some scholars. Malachi is not referring to the priests of his own time, but to those of the classical period, or otherwise to the ideal priesthood. He therefore does not suggest the demise of the prophetic office.[23] On the contrary, by describing the priest as "messenger" he allows for a certain similarity between the proclamation of a prophet and the teaching function of an (ideal!) priest, but at the same time realizing the difference between the mediator of the *dāḇār* and that of the *tôrâ*. This distinction, to which we will

21. See GKC, § 107f, g.

22. Cf. C. Westermann, "Die Begriffe für Fragen und Suchen im Alten Testament," *Kerygma und Dogma* 6 (1960) 2–30 (repr. in *Forschung am Alten Testament,* Theologisches Bücherei 55 [München: Chr. Kaiser, 1974], pp. 162–90).

23. Contra Van der Woude, p. 111: "our text originates from post-prophetic times."

again turn at the end of this section, is explicitly made by Jeremiah (18:18), Ezekiel (7:26), and Micah (3:11).

This verse, along with its direct context, represents a climax in the history of the divine revelation with respect to the teaching office of the priests. J. M. P. Smith described it in elevated terms: "This is a conception of the importance and dignity of the priesthood that is unsurpassed, if it be even equalled, elsewhere in the Old Testament," and according to Dentan, "this verse contains both the noblest statement of the function of priesthood to be found in the Old Testament and the highest estimate of its dignity."

8 In contrast to the exemplary behavior of the earlier priesthood, the priests in the time of Malachi failed miserably. They were just the opposite of their true predecessors. Verse 8a and b is antithetically parallel to v. 6c and d. According to v. 6c the true priests walked with God in peace and uprightness, and in regard to v. 8a the priests in the time of Malachi have deserted (turned away from) the "way" of God. According to v. 6d the earlier priests have turned many away from sin, but according to v. 8b the teaching of the contemporary priests has caused many to stumble. According to v. 4 God has sent the priests "this command" in order that his covenant with Levi might be maintained, but according to v. 8c the present priests have annulled that covenant. The antithesis between the two groups of priests is total and radical. The priests in the time of Malachi have annulled every one of the three aspects that characterize the attitude and conduct of the earlier priesthood: they have turned aside from the way, they have caused many to stumble by their instruction, and they have corrupted the covenant of Levi.

you have deserted the way. The Hebrew verb *sûr* combined with the preposition *min* means "to deviate from" a certain course, "to turn away from" something, with the additional idea of deliberateness: they have deliberately turned away, they have willfully deserted the way. This specific "way" (with the definite article) is that which was mentioned in vv. 6 and 7; it is the very essence of "this command" that God has given to the priests, involving both their attitudes and the performing of their duties. Part of the reason for this accusation is found in 1:6–14; additional motivation is that they have not listened and have not set their heart to honor the name of the Lord (2:2).

The picture of the priests' behavior in the time shortly after the return from exile is rather favorable. The great number of priests (4,289) and relatively few Levites (341) who had returned from exile (Ezra 2:36–58; 8:2; Neh. 7:39–60; 12:1–26) played an important role in erecting and dedicating the house of God (Ezra 6:16). They were installed in their divisions and groups for the service of God in Jerusalem (Ezra 6:18), and in order to be ceremonially clean they purified themselves (Ezra 6:20–22). They also were actively involved in Ezra's and Nehemiah's endeavors to reform the community and religious life of the people (Ezra 10:19; Neh. 3:1, 17; 8:7–9, 12, 14–19; 9:4–15, 38; 10:29, 30 [Eng. 28, 29]; 12:30; 13:22).

Although this picture of the priests (and Levites) was generally favorable, the contours of a negative behavior were becoming apparent. Some of them indulged in mixed marriages (Ezra 9:1; 10:18, 20–44; Neh. 13:4, 5). Especially in the time between Nehemiah's first and second visits to Palestine, thus in the time of Malachi as well, the conduct of some of the priests, even one of the sons of the high priest, was detestable. It caused Nehemiah to pray: "Remember them, O my God, because they have defiled *[gā'al]* the priesthood and the covenant of the priesthood and the Levites" (13:29).

The priests in Malachi's time have also *caused many to stumble* on account of their instruction in the law. The "many" in this verse parallels that in v. 6. The instruction of the earlier priests had been a blessing to a large number of people, but the teaching of the present priests was a curse to many. It caused people to *stumble (kāšal),* which, in this context, is just the opposite of turning them away from sin (v. 6). Hos. 4:6–9 reflects an analogous situation. The people of God are destroyed from lack of knowledge, because the priests have rejected that knowledge, that is, have corrupted it. The more the priests increased, the more they sinned against God. They "feed" on the sins of God's people, so that it will be "like people, like priests." Just as in the time of Ezekiel the priests in Malachi's time became "a stumbling block toward iniquity" *(lᵉmiḵšôl ʿāwōn)* (Ezek. 44:12). They have done that by (RSV) or with (NEB) their *tôrâ,* again in the sense of instruction, teaching.

you have annulled the covenant with Levi. This is the third aspect of the accusation. Here, as in vv. 4 and 5, *Levi (hallēwî)* is "a vivid personification of the priestly order" (Dentan). It must be noted that the expression "covenant with Levi" is literally "covenant of Levi" (vv. 4, 5). The genitive construction must, however, be interpreted as an objective genitive: that specific covenant which concerns Levi. In this sense it is a synonym of the covenant with Levi (vv. 4, 5). This covenant was *annulled,* corrupted, violated, spoiled, ruined. God wanted to maintain, to continue the covenant with Levi by reminding them of "this command" which was especially applicable to them (vv. 1, 4), but they did not take it to heart to honor and serve the Lord. Thereby they forfeited their privileged position as mediators between God and his people.

From God's side we must consider his faithfulness toward his own covenant with Levi, and that he, in a certain, higher sense, will uphold it, contrary to the failures of those priests. Although the accusation is put in absolute terms, the pronounced judgment is always conditional. We also have the perspective on the fulfillment of the priestly office in the person and work of the great priest-king (Zech. 6:12, 13; Ps. 110).

9 In its essence and according to its intent, the covenant relationship is unbreakable. But when one party does not live up to his obligations, the other party may take disciplinary steps. *So I* (*w^egam ʾ^anî,* lit. "and so I").[24] The priests have annulled or violated the covenant, so now God will approach them with the vengeance of the covenant. Instead of giving them "life and peace" (v. 5), he *will cause them to be despised and humiliated by all the people*. The perfect form of the Hebrew verb *nāṯattî* refers to a fact that has started in the past (v. 2b) but will continue in the present time.[25] It may be rendered either in the past ("So I, in my turn, have made you," NEB; cf. NIV) or in the present ("and so I make you," RSV). The idea is that the past judgment will continue to have its effect in the present time. The judgment corresponds with the way in which the priests have slighted the name of the Lord, the altar, and their sacrificial duties (1:6–14). God will cause them to be despised and humiliated by all the people, even by those whom they have caused to stumble by way of their unreliable instruction in the law. Instead of their privileged position (Deut. 33:11), they will be humiliated by all the people.

because you have not followed my ways. The reason for this judgment is introduced by the Hebrew expression *k^epî ʾ^ašer,* "according as," "because." The accusation of the whole passage is now summarized: you have not followed my ways; you have shown partiality in the instruction of the law.[26] The priests were literally nonexistent *(ʾên)* with regard to following (*šāmar,* lit. "keep, guard") God's ways. The *ways* of God are the stipulations of his law concerning the conduct and obligations of the priests. Contrary to 1:8, the expression *nōś^eʾîm pānîm* is taken in *malam partem,* "to show partiality."[27] Their instruction of the law was instigated by material gain and was based on bribery and corruption.

In this significant portion of Scripture the priests in the time of

24. For the translation "I in my turn," "from my side," see C. J. Labuschagne, "The emphasizing particle 'gam' and its connotations," in *Studia Biblica et Semitica,* Fest. Th. C. Vriezen (Wageningen: Veenman, 1961), pp. 193–203.

25. See GKC, § 106g. According to Rudolph, Van der Woude, et al., the perfect is a prophetic perfect, as in 2:3a: the judgment will occur in the (near) future.

26. The distinction that is being made between the written and oral law as the basis of the priests' instruction (so Van der Woude; A. Renker, op. cit., pp. 121–22n.25) seems to be arbitrary. Cf. the comments on the *tôrâ* in v. 6.

27. Cf. Deut. 1:17; 16:19; Prov. 24:23; Sir. 4:22; 35(32):13; 42:1.

Malachi were hanging in the balance. They were reminded of their privileged position (vv. 1, 4, 5), contrasted to the attitude and conduct of the classical (or ideal) priesthood (vv. 5c, 6, 7), accused of violating the covenant with Levi (v. 8), and judged because they have failed miserably in both their personal and professional life (v. 9).

1:6–2:9: SACRIFICE AND PRIESTHOOD ACCORDING TO MALACHI

This passage of Malachi focuses on three distinctive though related problems. The first is the remarkable emphasis in this prophecy on the sacrificial system as such. The second is the surprisingly clear statement in regard to the teaching function of the priesthood (2:1–9). The third is the vexing problem of the relationship between priests and Levites.

The perennial problem with respect to the relationship between the "cult theology of the priests and the cult polemic of the prophets" has led to the conclusion that Malachi's attitude toward the cult was inferior by far to that of his great predecessors.[1] The most radical statement in this respect was made by B. Duhm.[2] According to him the whole book of Malachi gives evidence that true religion consists of the sacrificial system as such. If Amos, Isaiah, Micah, Jeremiah, et al., were prophets, then Malachi could hardly be considered one.

We cannot accept Duhm's criticism for a number of reasons. First, it is based upon the fallacious assumption that the preexilic prophets rejected the sacrificial system as such and in principle.[3] Many scholars have rightly criticized this point of view, stressing the fact that the preexilic prophets denounced the *opus operatum* idea in connection with the temple worship, but were not against the sacrificial system as a matter of principle.[4] If this is true, then Duhm has no basis for his comparison between Malachi and the preexilic prophets, and the attitude of the preexilic prophets could not be considered radically different from that of Malachi. All the OT prophets presupposed and maintained the cult as an essential part of Israel's religion.

1. Cf. R. Rendtorff, *TLZ* 51 (1956) 339–42.

2. B. Duhm, *Die Theologie der Propheten,* p. 320.

3. E.g., R. Hentschke, *Die Stellung der vorexilischen Schriftpropheten zum Kultus* (Berlin: Töpelmann, 1957).

4. So, rightly, H. H. Rowley, "The Meaning of Sacrifice in the Old Testament," *BJRL* 33 (1950) 79–96 (repr. in *From Moses to Qumran: Studies in the Old Testament* [New York: Association, 1963], pp. 67–107).

Second, it is not true that Malachi simply equated Israel's religion with the sacrificial system. His reference to the cultic aspect of Israel's religion forms only a part of the entire book (1:6–2:9; 3:1–4, 6–12). In addition, it is evident that the temple worship is evaluated from the point of view of the honor and the fear of the Lord (1:6, 11, 14; 2:1–5; 3:16, 20 [Eng. 4:2]). G. A. Smith has rightly characterized Malachi's attitude toward the cult in terms of "prophecy within the law," thereby acknowledging Malachi's prophetical emphasis.

Other scholars, while recognizing the fact that Malachi was a true prophet even in his attitude toward the cult,[5] nevertheless assume a difference in the reason for criticizing the sacrificial practices between Malachi and his predecessors. According to Botterweck the preexilic prophets criticized the cult because of the unwarranted trust that the people had put upon it, and because Israel regarded it as a substitute for their religious and moral life.[6] According to him Malachi's criticism, on the other hand, was directed against the negligence and sluggishness of both priests and people in bringing their offerings, and their lack of reverence for the altar. After the purging occasioned by the eschatological judgment, they will bring offerings that will be well pleasing to the Lord (3:3, 4). G. A. Smith endorses this view, and suggests that the changing attitude toward the cult was due to the growing influence of the law on the spirit of prophecy. From Ezekiel onward, he remarks, the prophets became more ecclesiastical and legal.[7]

Our solution to this problem is as follows. The presupposed or assumed differences in emphases and attitude between Malachi and his predecessors must not be conceived of as a radical contrast. The general attitude toward the cult was basically the same. If we have to allow for a difference in emphasis, then that must be assessed in the context of the various historical situations. This is rightly done by scholars like Rendtorff, Haag, et al. Rendtorff asserts that the strong interest in the cult and a revived eschatological expectation were characteristic of the postexilic times. J. Bright wrote extensively about the holy commonwealth and the apocalyptic kingdom as the two focal points of Israel's religion during this period.[8]

According to Procksch the postexilic priesthood was rooted in the temple of Jerusalem, and the temple worship itself found the legal basis for its central position in the edict of the Persian king, while the erection of the

5. Cf. G. Quell, *Wahre und falsche Propheten* (Gütersloh: Bertelsmann, 1952), p. 12; Adamson, p. 764; etc.

6. Botterweck, *BibLeb* 1 (1960) 104.

7. G. A. Smith, p. 646.

8. J. Bright, *The Kingdom of God*, pp. 156–86.

temple was inaugurated by the labors of the prophets Haggai and Zechariah.[9] In the time of Malachi the priests and people failed miserably in their responsibility to honor and fear the Lord in performing their sacrificial duties, and therefore the message of the prophet was directed at the abuses with respect to the cult. The cult itself was not rejected. Such an attitude would have been contrary to the message of Haggai and Zechariah, to the reform conducted by Ezra and Nehemiah, and to Malachi's own expectations of offerings that again will be acceptable to the Lord (3:3, 4).

The surprising manner in which Malachi stresses the importance of the teaching function of the priesthood has not failed to draw the attention of scholars. They all agree that with Malachi the message of the OT in this respect reaches its climax. The concept of the importance and dignity of the priesthood presented in Mal. 2:5c–7 is unsurpassed elsewhere in the OT. But this aspect also raises two problems: what is the relationship between the two functions of the priests, viz., to officiate at the altar and to communicate the *tôrâ,* and how must we distinguish between priest and prophet, both of whom are called "messenger of the Lord"?

The relationship between the twofold office of the priesthood is generally solved by attributing preeminence to the teaching function of the priest. Dentan expresses the opinion of most scholars when he asserts that "the function of the priest is primarily that of a teacher."[10] Acccording to Jones the teaching function of the priest is fundamental. Usually people think of the priests as specialists in bringing sacrifices, and indeed, that does appear to have been their characteristic function in the time long after the return from exile. Nevertheless, the OT ideal of the priesthood was different. The teaching function precedes the sacrificial function in Deut. 33:8–10 and 2 Chr. 15:3.[11]

We agree that the teaching function of the priest was of great importance. De Vaux rightly pointed out that the *tôrâ* belonged to the priests, just as the verdict *(mišpāṭ)* belonged to the king, the counsel *(ʿēṣâ)* to the wise man, and the word *(dāḇār)* or vision *(ḥōzeh)* belonged to the prophet (see Mic. 3:11; Jer. 18:18; Ezek. 7:26).[12] In addition he observed that the teaching function after the Exile was no longer monopolized by the priests, because it was gradually exercised by the Levites, and even later by the scribes. In the interpretation of Mal. 1:6–2:9, however, it is important to note that the two functions of the priests are not opposed to one another. As mediators be-

9. O. Procksch, p. 345.
10. Dentan, p. 1132.
11. D. R. Jones, p. 192.
12. De Vaux, *Ancient Israel,* pp. 353–54.

tween God and his people the priests offered sacrifices acceptable to the Lord on behalf of the people, and through their instruction in the law they represented the will of God to the people. Both functions are mentioned and stressed in our prophecy. After the eschatological purge of priests and people, the offering of Judah and Jerusalem will again be acceptable to the Lord as in the days of old (3:4), and in this the priests would have a major part (3:3). The fact that the teaching function is mentioned first in Deut. 33:10 does not mean that it was the primary or more important one. The sequence in Deut. 33:10 must be seen in the light of v. 9, where it is said of Levi: "he watched over your word and guarded your covenant" (NIV). The context suggests the maintenance of the Sinaitic covenant, with its stress on the obligation to listen to the word of the Lord (Exod. 19:5) and to do all that the Lord had spoken (Exod. 24:7). The two functions of the priests are basically in harmony with one another.

The same conclusion applies to the problem of the distinction between priest and prophet, since both are called "messengers of the Lord." According to some scholars this function was previously exercised by the prophets, but at a later stage it was taken over by the priests.[13] Thus it is simply a matter of succession. When the prophets were silenced the priests became the proclaimers of the divine revelation. This point of view is not convincing. The reference to the priest as messenger of the Lord is found only in Mal. 2:7 (cf. Eccl. 5:5), but the same applies to the prophets, who are called that only in Hag. 1:13. Both these references are postexilic. In addition it is important to note that the reference in Mal. 2:7 was applicable to the earlier (or ideal) priesthood, and not to that in the time of the prophet. This consideration is contrary to the argument of succession.

The difference must rather be sought in the manner in which priest and prophet both received and dispensed the revelation. The prophet is the man of the *dāḇār,* which was given him in a direct and personal manner by way of special revelation. The priest, on the other hand, is the man of the *tôrâ,* which was handed down to him either in written or in oral form, and which he communicated by means of instruction in the context of his priestly function (cf. Hag. 2:10–14).[14]

The third issue, viz., the relationship between priests and Levites, has rightly been called "one of the thorny problems of Old Testament re-

13. Cf. Botterweck, op. cit., p. 109; Dentan, p. 1133; Van der Woude, p. 111.

14. According to E. Jacob, *Theology of the Old Testament,* tr. A. W. Heathcote and P. J. Allcock (London: Hodder & Stoughton; New York: Harper and Brothers, 1958), p. 248n.1, the *daʿaṯ* of the priest is "a mediated knowledge," that of a prophet "a direct knowledge."

ligion."[15] According to Hubbard the last word on this "puzzling problem" has not yet been spoken.[16]

Wellhausen and his school reinterpreted the scriptural data in such a manner that their conclusion led to a definition of this relationship that is contrary to the prima facie evidence of the biblical narrative. Wellhausen's point of view is as follows.[17] In his reconstruction of the scriptural data he gave primary consideration to a new interpretation of Ezek. 44:6–16. In this passage he found the origin of the distinction between priests as sons of Zadok on the one hand, and Levites as priests who originally had served at the altars on the high places on the other hand. A second basic consideration is that the facts mentioned in Deut. 18:6–7 and in 2 K. 23:8–9 must be conceived of as related. According to Deut. 18, after the centralization of the public worship, the Levites, who had priestly functions in the country places, were allowed to return to Jerusalem and to exercise their priestly office at the temple. Wellhausen's contention is that these Levites were to be identified with the priests who had served at the altars on the high places. King Josiah, however, would not allow them to fulfill this office at the temple, probably because of the hostile attitude of the sons of Zadok toward them. The consequence was that these priests from the high places were degraded to become assistants of the Zadokite priests in Jerusalem. According to Wellhausen, this is the way in which the distinction between priests and Levites originated.

In the so-called Priestly Code (often simply called P) this distinction is spelled out more plainly, with the proviso, however, that the priests no longer were called sons of Zadok but sons of Aaron, thereby relating the origin of the priesthood to the classical beginning of Israel's history. This point of view, advocated by Wellhausen and his school, represents the modern critical position, though in a modified form.[18]

According to Gispen it is of no avail trying to refute Wellhausen's arguments. Nothing less than the authority of Scripture is involved here. Wellhausen's radical, although persistent, point of view is based upon an arbitrary reconstruction of the scriptural data. Passages like Exod. 19:22;

15. So D. A. Hubbard, in *NBD,* 2nd ed., p. 1028.

16. Ibid., p. 1034.

17. An outline of Wellhausen's theory is given by Hubbard, op. cit., pp. 1031–33; and W. H. Gispen, *Numbers,* COT (Kampen: Kok, 1959), p. 45.

18. Cf. R. de Vaux, op. cit., pp. 345–405; Th. C. Vriezen, *An Outline of Old Testament Theology,* rev. ed., pp. 236–42. See also A. Cody, *A History of Old Testament Priesthood* (Rome: Pontifical Biblical Institute, 1969); A. H. J. Gunneweg, *Leviten und Priester* (Göttingen: Vandenhoeck & Ruprecht, 1965); R. Abba, "Priests and Levites in Ezekiel," *VT* 28 (1978) 1–9.

32:29; and 1 K. 8:4 do not fit his pattern of thought and are therefore considered to be secondary.

With regard to the exegesis of Malachi the problem concerns the presupposed "tradition" which was followed by the prophet. It is a remarkable fact that Malachi nowhere refers to the high priest. According to Neh. 12:10–11 high priests were functioning throughout the whole of the fifth century B.C. The omission by Malachi is the more remarkable, because the high priestly function became of great importance after the Exile, especially in the absence of a national leader. The reason for this omission is not clear. Perhaps it was due to the fact that Malachi addressed himself to the tribe of Levi in a comprehensive fashion, thus including all the members of this tribe.

The same probable solution is also applicable to the fact that Malachi apparently does not distinguish between priests and Levites. He refers to "the priests" (1:6; 2:1), "the covenant with [2:4, 5; or of, 2:8] Levi," and speaks of "the sons of Levi" (3:3). According to some scholars this lack of explicit differentiation was due to an early date for Malachi. He must have been unaware of the distinction, which was the result of King Josiah's reform, and which was expressed in Ezek. 44 and especially in the Priestly Code. According to Dentan, for instance, "the reference to *Levi* as the ancestor of the priestly order gives one of the chief clues to the date of the book."

The argument deduced from the dating of the so-called sources does not solve our problem, however. If Malachi's lack of distinction between priests and Levites had been due to the fact that he was unaware of the historical situation in which that distinction originated, then he antedated both Josiah and Ezekiel, and this is highly improbable. Other scholars maintain that Malachi must have known the material of P.

Most scholars are of the opinion that Malachi has followed the terminology of Deuteronomy in not distinguishing between priests and Levites. It is true that "priest" and "Levite" are often used as synonyms in Deuteronomy (17:18; 18:1; 21:5; 24:8; 27:9; 31:9), but this usage is not confined to Deuteronomy (cf. Jer. 33:21; Ezek. 43:19 with v. 24; 1 K. 8:3, 4; 2 Chr. 5:4–14; 23:6, 7, 8, 18; 30:27; Neh. 12:23). In Malachi, however, we do not find the typical expression "levitical priests" which is used in Deuteronomy (17:9, 18; 18:1; 24:8; 27:9) and elsewhere (cf. Josh. 3:3; 8:33; Ezek. 43:19; 44:15; etc.).

The solution to this problem must not be looked for in terms of the various "sources," but rather in terms of the circumstances which occasioned a more specific or a more general way of expressing or defining the concepts. The broader usage of the terms "priests" and "Levites" in Deuteronomy must be related to the character of this book's content as a general survey in retrospect of the Mosaic law. In the same corporate, generalizing manner Malachi expressed himself in connection with the priests.[19] "Jacob" (1:2–5; 2:12) represents "Israel," and in the same sense "Levi" is the eponym of the priesthood as such (2:4–8; 3:3). For Malachi the most important aspect of his prophecy concerns the covenant, not only with Israel (1:2–5; 2:10–16; 3:1, 16–18, 22–24), but also with the priestly tribe of Levi (1:6; 2:4, 5, 8; 3:3, 22).

19. "Because Malachi referred back to the Mosaic period (cf. Deut. 33:8–11), it was not necessary to distinguish between the priests as the *clerus maior* and the Levites as the *clerus minor*. This distinction was not known in the time of Moses" (Van der Woude, p. 109). We agree with the first statement, but disagree with the point of view that the distinction between priests and Levites was not known in the time of Moses. For a thorough discussion of the history of the priesthood, see K. Mino, "Die Heiligheidswet (Levitikus 17–26): 'n Historiese en teologiese beoordeling," Th.D. thesis, University of Stellenbosch, 1984, pp. 230–35.

V. GOD'S CONCERN WITH THE MARRIAGES OF HIS PEOPLE (2:10–16)

10 *Have we not all one Father?*
Has not one God created us?
Why then are we faithless to one another,
profaning the covenant of our fathers?
11 *Judah has broken faith;*
a detestable thing has been committed in Israel and in Jerusalem:
Judah has desecrated the sanctuary of the Lord, which he loves,
by marrying the daughter of a foreign god.
12 *May the Lord cut off from the tents of Jacob that man,*
whoever he may be, even though he brings offerings to the Lord Almighty.[1]
13 *Another thing*[2] *you do: You cover the Lord's altar with tears, with weeping and wailing,*[3]
because he no longer pays attention to the offerings
or accepts them with pleasure from your hands.
14 *You ask, "Why?"*
It is because the Lord acted as witness between you
and the wife of your youth, to whom you have been faithless,
though she was your partner and your legal wife.
15 *No one with a residue of spirit would act that way.*
What does the one do?
He is seeking godly offspring.

1. There is no textual evidence for the proposition to delete v. 12 as the work of a glossator, contra Van der Woude, et al.

2. Lit. "a second time" or "secondly." The LXX reads "which I detest"; cf. v. 16. For the use of the demonstrative pronoun *zō't,* "this," see GKC, § 136b. Van der Woude explains it incorrectly as a substantive with the meaning "disgrace," a "scandalous deed," with reference to Ps. 7:4; 44:18; 74:18; Job 17:8; and, e.g., M. Dahood, *Psalms I,* AB (Garden City: Doubleday, 1966), p. 42.

3. For this circumstantial clause, see GKC, § 156c.

So take heed to yourselves,[4]
and let none be faithless to the wife of his youth.
16 *I hate divorce, says the Lord God of Israel,*
even the one who covers his garment with (the marks of) violence,
says the Lord Almighty.
So take heed to yourselves,
and do not be unfaithful.

This pericope is regarded as the most difficult in the book of Malachi.[5] It poses many and various problems with regard to the translation and interpretation of its contents, and in connection with questions pertaining to the *Sitz im Leben,* the context, and the general theme of this prophetical discourse. We need not enter into every detail of the scholarly discussion, because, with a few exceptions, scholars are agreed on the general purport of Malachi's message here.

When the spiritual and religious leaders of God's people do not comply with the elevated demands of their calling, a moral decline takes place, generally manifesting itself in, among other things, various malpractices concerning the marriage life of the people. It is, therefore, not without significance that the prophet's judgment, mainly upon the priests (1:6–2:9), is now directed to the people's malpractices in the realm of marriage.

The occasion of this prophecy might have been a feast of penance (cf. Zech. 7:5; 8:19), because of the failure of crops due to locusts and drought (cf. 3:10–12). Its connection with the preceding prophecy is accidental, although the purport of its message is the same: to mention another aspect in which Israel denied and insulted the love of God for them.

We do not agree with the "consensus of critical opinion" (voiced by Curt Kuhl, et al.)[6] that the dicta on mixed marriages (2:11, 12) are later interpolations, because the arguments in favor of this "opinion" are uncon-

4. The meaning of the Hebrew text of v. 15 is uncertain. The JPSV reads: "Did not the One make (all) so that all remaining life-breath is his? And what does that One seek but godly folk? So be careful of your life-breath." See the commentary below and other modern translations.

5. Special literature on this pericope includes M. Adinolfi, "Il ripudio secondo Mal. 2:14–16," *BeO* 12 (1970) 247–56; R. Althann, "Malachi 2:13–14 and UT 125, 12–13," *Bib* 58 (1977) 418–21; A. de Nicola, "La moglie della tua giovinezza," *BeO* 12 (1970) 153–83; A. Renker, *Die Tora bei Maleachi,* pp. 86–90; S. Schreiner, "Mischehen—Ehebruch—Echtscheidung. Betrachtungen zu Mal. 2:10–16," *ZAW* 91 (1979) 207–28 (and W. Rudolph's response: "Zu Mal. 2:10–16," *ZAW* 93 [1981] 85–90); A. Tosato, "Il ripudio: delitto e pena (Mal. 2:10–16)," *Bib* 59 (1978) 548–53.

6. So also G. A. Smith, Marti, Sellin, Elliger, Renker (op. cit., p. 90).

vincing. Malachi's reference to the "daughter of a foreign god" (v. 11) is not contrary to his "sympathetic" allusions to the heathen nations (1:11), and there is no reason to consider the dual message of this pericope as unoriginal.[7]

Since the time of Jerome interpreters have conceded that this pericope, in its present form, is concerned with two interrelated malpractices: mixed marriages (vv. 10–12) and divorce (vv. 13–16). It is important to note that the typical dialogue style of Malachi presupposes the unity of this pericope: the initial question in v. 10 is not repeated in v. 13, but it has a bearing upon the whole passage.

We may analyze the structure of both sections of this pericope in the following way.

Sentences 1 and 2 (v. 10a and b) are parallel and convey the deepest motivation for the accusation that follows.

Sentences 3–7 pronounce the accusation, first in general terms (sentences 3–6, vv. 10c–11c), and then with a specific application (sentence 7). The "broken faith" and "desecration" of sentences 3–6 are specified in sentence 7 as marriages between the covenant people and the daughters of heathen nations, who are adherents of the religion of foreign gods.

In sentence 8 (v. 12) the judgment is pronounced upon two related categories of people: those who have contracted mixed marriages, and those (being the same people) who notwithstanding their transgression indulged in offering to the Lord.

The inner structure of this passage is as follows. Because the covenant people are attached to one another through faith in the one and only God, the introduction of a "foreign" element is a fundamental violation of this intimate bond, and therefore the transgressor himself must be detached from this bond and eliminated from "the tents of Jacob."

The second passage, sentences 9–22 (vv. 13–16), concerns divorce. Sentences 9–13 (vv. 13–14) introduce, in the well-known pattern of statement-question-answer, the accusation of being unfaithful toward the legal wife.

Sentences 14–16 (v. 15a–c) suggest, in an elliptical manner, the very foundation of marriage fidelity and therefore of the prohibition of divorce. This motivation is essentially similar to that in section A. It consists in the intimate bond between God and the marriage couple, and between the couple themselves, and in the deep concern for the kingdom of God.

7. Van der Woude is adamant that divorce is not explicitly mentioned in 2:10–16, because the reference to "divorce" is incorrectly based upon an unwarranted interpretation of v. 16. In order to endorse his point of view, he deems it necessary to delete *šēnîṯ*, "another thing," in v. 13.

Sentences 17–22 (vv. 15d–16) conclude with an admonition to "guard their spirits" and not to break faith with the wife of their youth. The reason for this admonishment is God's displeasure with two related transgressions of his people: divorce and violence. The generally accepted interpretation of these "transgressions" is that they concern both the seventh and sixth commandments of the Decalogue. According to our structural analysis, however, this prophecy reflects a situation similar to the former one (2:10–12). In both cases we have one central transgression, in each case with the same aggravating circumstance, viz., that the transgressor is simultaneously indulging in religious activity. The divorcee is the same man who "covers his clothing with violence," that is, who is so zealously concerned with the slaughter of sacrificial animals that his clothes were spattered by their blood. This combination of professed piety and profound transgression is detestable before God (v. 11), an act and attitude which he hates (v. 16).

10 In accordance with his characteristic style (cf. 1:2, 6; etc.), the prophet addresses himself mainly to the people and begins with a general verdict which forms the basis of the following admonitions. He reminds them of their common origin. *Have we not all one Father?* The specific form of the question, *h^a^lô'*, presupposes an affirmative answer: "Yes, indeed" (cf. 1:2). The interpretation of *'āḇ 'eḥāḏ* as referring to an earthly father is old and widespread. Some scholars think of Adam (Tarnov), the majority favors Abraham, because it is, according to them, required by the context, with the possible inclusion of Jacob. According to Baldwin "mention of *the covenant of our fathers* indicates that the *one father* could well be one of the patriarchs, either Abraham or Jacob (Israel)." She correctly refers to the scriptural precedent for "Abraham your father" (Isa. 51:2), and to the fact that Malachi frequently mentions Jacob (1:2; 2:12; 3:6), from whom the twelve tribes (fathers) descended. This interpretation is, indeed, feasible. On the basis of this interpretation some ancient versions and church fathers have interchanged the first two sentences to give preference to God as Creator above (?) the earthly father.

But we share the opinion of Van der Woude that the *one Father* is indeed a reference to God. This interpretation is determined by the synthetic parallelism of the first two sentences, and by the antithetical reference to *the daughter of a foreign god* (v. 11). The scriptural precedent for God as Father of his people is found within the prophecy of Malachi (1:6), and elsewhere in the OT and NT (cf. Exod. 4:22, 23; Deut. 32:6, 18; Isa. 63:16; 64:7 [Eng. 8]; Jer. 2:27; 3:4, 19; 31:9; and the Lord's Prayer, Matt. 6:9). In the fatherhood of God his particular relationship to Israel is stressed not in a natural sense but in the spiritual sense of adoption and on the basis of his covenant. We reject the notion that Malachi was thinking in terms of "the universal brotherhood of man,"[8] and agree with Baldwin, et al., that his concern was rather for evidence of brotherly loyalty within the nation of Israel. "Have *we* not all one Father?" Malachi's point of reference is indisputably his fellow Jews.

Has not one God created us? The idea of God as Creator of his people is attested by Deut. 32:6, where Israel was confronted with the question: "Is he [God] not your Father, your Creator, who made you and formed you?" (NIV), and also by Isa. 64:8, where this truth is confirmed: "Yet, O Lord, thou art our Father; we are the clay, and thou art our potter; we are all the work of thy hand." The idea of God as Creator of Israel is intimately connected with the concepts of "redemption" (Isa. 43:1; 44:2; 63:16), God's "kingship" (Isa. 43:15), and his future concern for his people (Isa. 45:11).

It is important to note how Malachi has formulated his question. He deliberately uses the word *bārā'*, "to create," because he wants to stress the exceptional character of Israel's origin as God's covenant people. At the same time he endorses the intimate relationship between the members of that people by stressing the oneness of the God who created them. Westermann rightly asserts that the oneness of God determines the oneness of Israel and the continuity of the history between God and his people.[9] Malachi again identifies himself with his people by deliberately using the word *us*. There is no need to exclude him, as the LXX reading *you* does.

Against the background of the undeniable fact that God is Israel's Father and Creator, that they have one origin and therefore are intimately related to one another, it is inconceivable that the members of this people should break the faith among themselves. *Why then are we faithless to one another?* Why do we not honor the exceptional and spiritual unity which binds us together as members of God's covenant people? This question does not imply "a general tendency to disregard promises and agreements of all kinds, in business, marriage or social affairs generally (Isa. 24:16)" (Baldwin, et al.). The semantic domain of this question is not "the universal brotherhood of man," the general tendency of all people to be faithless toward their fellow human beings. The context presupposes "the brotherly loyalty within the nation of Israel."[10] It concerns the communion with God

8. Van der Woude rightly pointed out that "Father" does not refer to God being "Father of all mankind," but to the Creator of the people of Israel, with reference to Isa. 43:1, 15; 44:7; Ps. 102:19; etc. *Bārā'* in this context denotes the election of Israel as the children of God; cf. Exod. 4:22; Hos. 11:1; Isa. 1:2; 30:9.

9. Westermann, *Elements of Old Testament Theology*, tr. D. W. Stott (Atlanta: John Knox, 1982), p. 32.

10. According to S. Schreiner, op. cit., pp. 218n.1, 223–24, the question in v. 10a really was voiced by the people, justifying their mixed marriages with reference to the fact that one God had created us, i.e., both us and them! This explanation

and the intimate relationship of the members of the covenant people. *Bāgad* signifies "to cover or cloak *[beged]* things over, and so to act falsely, perfidiously, to break faith." The present form and vocalization of *nibgad* is the Qal first person plural imperfect,[11] "Why are *we* faithless?" The faithlessness is mutual (reciprocal). It is "a man against his brother."[12] This expression emphasizes the intimate character of the relationship that is being affected by the people's unfaithfulness. The prophet completely identifies himself with his people, and thereby accepts the solidarity of guilt. If one member sins all are affected.

profaning the covenant of our fathers. The cause and effect of the people's conduct are expressly stated. By acting faithless to one another, they have in fact "loosened," "degraded," "desecrated," "made common" (Laetsch), profaned the covenant. The semantic domain of this expression is essentially religious, being defined by the covenant relationship and the reference in v. 11 to "the sanctuary of the Lord, which he loves." We therefore do not agree with the opinion that the desecrated covenant must be conceived of as an annulling of the general obligation to act loyally to one another, or even that it concerns "the matrimonial regulations in the law."[13] *the covenant of our fathers* refers to the covenant that God made with "the fathers" at Sinai, the very act which constituted Israel's becoming "the treasured possession" of God (Exod. 19:5, 6; 24:8).[14] We agree, especially with the second part of Jones's statement, that "*the covenant of our fathers* echoes the language of Deuteronomy . . . and refers to the total divine dispensation which brought Israel into existence as God's people."[15]

11 The two key words *bāgad* and *ḥillēl* of v. 10 are repeated in v. 11, with Judah as subject in both instances. The accusation is still in general terms. Judah has acted faithlessly and has desecrated the sanctuary of the Lord. It is significant to note that "Judah" is construed with both a feminine *(bāgᵉdâ)* and a masculine *(ḥillēl)* form of the verb. There is no need for an alternative reading of *bāgad* (contra *BHS*). Because of the faithlessness of its inhabitants the country of Judah (grammatically feminine) has itself become faithless. We have a similar identification in Deut. 21:23; 24:4;

---

is incompatible with the context, esp. with the accusation against marriage with the daughter of a foreign god.

11. The vocalization of *nibgad* as a Qal imperfect is also possible; cf. Bauer and Leander, *Historische Grammatik,* § 40g; and Schreiner, op. cit., pp. 208–209.

12. See GKC, § 139e.

13. So J. Lindblom, *Prophecy in Ancient Israel,* p. 405.

14. See G. Ch. Aalders, *Het Verbond Gods* (Kampen: Kok, 1939), pp. 95–96.

15. Jones, p. 194. There is no reason to doubt the authenticity of v. 10, as is done by, e.g., G. A. Smith, Nowack, Sellin, Horst, Elliger.

Jer. 2:7; 3:2; Ezek. 36:17, 18. The same applies to "Edom" in Mal. 1:4. The country and the people are united in the solidarity of guilt. Thus the emphasis is placed upon the general and serious character of the atrocity which has been committed.

Judah's broken faith is more precisely defined as *a detestable thing*. The Hebrew word *tôʿēḇâ* signifies things and acts which are abominable in the sight of God, such as idolatry, impurity, etc. In Deut. 18:9–13 Israel is admonished, when entering the promised land, "do not learn to imitate the detestable ways *[tôʿᵃḇōṯ]* of the nations there" (NIV). These "ways" or "things" concerned the sacrificing of children in the fire and various mantic practices. By using this significant word Malachi equates Judah's faithlessness with the defection into paganism. The idea of "idolatry" (cf. Deut. 12:31; 13:1–18; 16:21–17:7) is just below the surface of Judah's breach of faith.

The universal occurrence of this atrocity is expressed in the words that it *has been committed in Israel and in Jerusalem*. The suggestion to delete either "in Israel" (*BHK*, Wellhausen, et al.)[16] or "in Jerusalem" (Jones, et al.)[17] or both *(BHS)* is without textual grounds. We agree with Baldwin that the use of the names *Judah* and *Israel* indicates that the prophet sees the repatriates in Judah as the contemporary heirs of the ancient promises, and, with Jones, that *Israel* is here a parallel description of *Judah* as the true people of God and does not refer to the northern kingdom. *Jerusalem* is the capital city and the religious center of God's people, the place of which it is said: "My name shall be there" (1 K. 8:29). The scope of reference is not only spatial but also, and essentially, religious. The people who have committed this atrocity are the covenant people of God, and the place where it was done is the promised land and the holy city. This "Israel" has committed a detestable thing even in this "Jerusalem."

desecrated the sanctuary of the Lord, which he loves. The atrocity is interpreted *(kî)* as being a desecration of the Lord's beloved sanctuary. Generally the "sanctuary of the Lord" (Heb. *qōḏeš*, lit. "holiness") refers to the temple.[18] But the context suggests a reference to "Israel" as the chosen and holy nation.[19] They are the "holy seed" (Isa. 6:13; Ezra 9:2), the Lord's portion (Deut. 32:9). God has chosen them out of all nations to be his "treasured possession" (Exod. 19:5–6; cf. Deut. 7:6; 14:2; Isa. 62:12; 63:18;

16. See also Sellin, Deissler, Chary, Nowack, Marti, Deden, Horst, Elliger, Rudolph.

17. According to Van der Woude Jerusalem is nowhere mentioned in the authentic text of Malachi, with reference also to Zech. 2:2 (Eng. 1:18).

18. So G. A. Smith, Marti, Dentan, et al. According to Schreiner, op. cit., p. 210, the reference is to the holiness of the Lord.

19. So also Von Orelli, Sellin, Van der Woude, et al.

Jer. 2:3; Dan. 12:7; Ps. 114:2). This interpretation is reflected in the translation of the Targum: "Because the house of Judah desecrated themselves, who have been sanctified by the Lord, and whom he loves." The accusation is couched in general terms. It provides the background of the real transgression. As such it is of the utmost significance. Malachi reminds his people of what is implied in connection with their breach of faith. They are violating and desecrating the intimate bond with God as their Father and Creator, as well as desecrating themselves, since they are the sanctuary of the Lord. What a deep and striking exposure of the nature and effect of the covenant people's breach of faith. All are involved in the transgression of one, and every relation is detrimentally affected thereby.

Narrowing now from the general to the particular, the prophet turns to the real point of his accusation. *by marrying the daughter of a foreign god.* There is no need to regard this phrase as secondary, because of its so-called prosaic nature (Botterweck). We are more interested in the rendering of some of the ancient versions. According to the LXX, Judah "has gone after other gods," and thus has committed idolatry. The reason for this variant reading is presumably to avoid mentioning mixed marriages, which were "normal" among Hellenistic Jews. The renderings of the Vetus Latina and of the Peshitta correspond basically with that of the LXX, and must have been dependent upon it. In their translations these versions have focused their attention on "a foreign god," omitting in the process the reference to "the daughter of," and having misunderstood the meaning of the Hebrew word *bāʿal* ("own, rule over," "take possession of a woman as bride or wife," "marry"; Deut. 21:13; 24:1; Isa. 62:5). The Vulgate renders: *et habuit filiam dei alieni,* in accordance with the MT. The Targum again paraphrases: "They had pleasure in marrying daughters of heathen nations," thereby reflecting the historical situation. The reading of the Hebrew text is well attested, and must be given preference to that of the LXX, Vetus Latina, and Peshitta.

The peculiar form in which this verdict is molded has called forth various opinions as to its exact meaning. According to some interpreters it is a figurative indication of idolatry in general. Others are of the opinion that it refers to an unholy alliance with heathen nations through intermarriage. But it seems most likely that the prophet is here alluding to mixed marriages. He has just called God the Father of the covenant people, and now he refers to the daughter of a foreign god. The marriages were therefore concluded with gentile girls who still remained pagan! They were still devoted to the service of their respective idols.[20] Such a marriage is referred to as *a detestable*

20. So, correctly, Botterweck (*BibLeb* 1 [1960] 179–85), Schumpp, Van der Woude, et al.

thing, because it assumed a compromise between the God and Father of Israel and a pagan idol. Through these marriages Judah has brought their Father and Creator into the "family" of pagan gods. Through this breach of faith Judah has committed idolatry! At the same time the mixed marriages were a desecration of the "sanctuary of God," a violation of Israel's spiritual existence as covenant people. Through these marriages the frontiers between covenant people and heathen, between church and world were obliterated.[21]

Israel was forbidden to marry the sons or daughters of the Canaanites (Exod. 34:16; Deut. 7:3), but it is evident from the reason which was explicitly stated that all marriages with people still adhering to an idolatrous religion were contrary to God's intentions with his covenant people. Baldwin rightly points out that it had been proved in Israel's experience that in practice the less demanding standards prevailed (1 K. 11:1–8; 16:31; Neh. 13:23–27), and apostasy quickly became the fashion. We know from the history of Ezra and Nehemiah that there were a great number of such marriages, even among priests and Levites, despite Ezra's initial reforms (cf. Ezra 9 and 10; Neh. 9:2; 10:31 [Eng. 30]; 13:1–3, 23–29).

12 Malachi prays that the Lord will excommunicate the guilty members from the communion of the people of God. They have violated the intimate relationship of the covenant people, and therefore they must be eliminated from the tents of Jacob. The prophet initially identified himself with the guilt of the people. Now he acted as mediator in beseeching God to eradicate (Heb. *yak̲rēt̲,* Hiphil jussive of *kārat̲,* "may he [God] cut off") the evildoers. His yearning signifies the application of chastisement in its extreme degree. *that man* (Heb. *lā'îš,* lit. "to the man"). The preposition *l*ᵉ is used to denote the accusative.[22] With the article the "man" in question is emphasized: the guilty man, the man who has committed the atrocity. This "man" represents every member of the covenant people who has acted accordingly. The prophet's zeal to eradicate this evil corresponds with that of Ezra (9:3) and Nehemiah (13:25–29).

whoever he may be. The Hebrew expression (lit. "he who calls and he who answers") is an idiom which has been variously explained. The

21. Procksch rightly stresses the point of view that the accusation does not so much concern the national identity of Israel but its religious existence as the covenant people of God (*Theologie*, p. 359).

22. See GKC, § 117n. According to Van der Woude the curse of v. 12a corresponds formally with pronouncements of judgment in 1 K. 14:10; 21:21; 2 K. 9:8; Isa. 14:22; and Jer. 47:4; thus the preposition *l*ᵉ in *lā'îš* must be explained as *dativus incommodi:* "against the man." The emphasis, however, is rather on the identification of the guilty person.

Peshitta and Targum render it as "son and grandson," presumably in connection with the Hebrew expression *nîn wāneḵeḏ,* "offspring, descendant" (Gen. 21:23; Isa. 14:22; Job 18:19; Sir. 41:5; 47:22). This interpretation, followed by a number of modern scholars, is used in the sense of every descendant. The Vulgate, followed by Luther, the AV, et al., has "the master and the pupil," the first being the man with authority, who issues commands, the second being compelled to obey them. Another explanation, reflected in the RV "him that waketh and him that answereth," envisages a nomadic custom of keeping watch round the tents at night (cf. Baldwin).

In trying to solve this exegetical problem, the point of departure must be the Hebrew text. According to Kruse-Blinkenberg "there are no weighty arguments against literal translation and understanding of the M.T."[23] It is evident that this idiomatic expression is used to denote totality by means of two opposite categories. A similar kind of expression is *ʿāṣûr weʿāzûḇ,* "slave or free" (Deut. 32:36; cf. 1 K. 21:21; 2 K. 9:8; 14:26; Zech. 9:8; etc.). Arabic has a similar expression, "There is not a caller or one who answers in the city," and this means that no living person remains. In our text we have the same idea: "any to witness or answer" means irrespective of the person, whoever he may be.[24]

Every guilty man must be cut off *from the tents of Jacob* (cf. 2 Sam. 20:1; 1 K. 12:16), i.e., from the midst of the covenant people. The excommunication from the body elect is radical. It presupposes an exclusion from the messianic community (Botterweck).

even though he brings offerings to the Lord Almighty. The meaning of this expression may be to include those who want to offer on behalf of the transgressors,[25] but it is more in accordance with the context to identify these persons with the guilty ones themselves. The detestable thing was to act piously while at the same time desecrating the sanctuary of the Lord. This cancer in the body of the people of God must be cut out and totally removed. Here no extenuating circumstances are applicable. The discipline must be

23. Kruse-Blinkenberg, *ST* 20 (1966) 101.

24. Our knowledge of Hebrew, according to Van der Woude, is too scanty to interpret this expression. He associates it with similar expressions like "name and survivors, offspring and descendants" (Isa. 14:22), "both head and tail" (Isa. 9:14), "all who come and go" (Ezek. 34:7), "slave or free" (1 K. 14:10; 21:21; 2 K. 9:8), and explains it to mean the man with his whole family. So also JPSV, "no descendants." This aspect of the "curse" may surely be included in the general meaning of the text. Our emphasis, however, is on the identification of the guilty person. "Whoever he may be," therefore, is not a translation out of embarrassment, contra Van der Woude.

25. The NIV refers in a note to this possibility: "May the Lord cut off from the tents of Jacob anyone who gives testimony on behalf of the man who does this."

applied in its severest form, irrespective of the persons concerned. God is asked to do this, but it does not exclude the cooperation of the responsible individuals. The history of Ezra and Nehemiah shows that these leaders really acted powerfully against this evil and that the heathen women were sent away.

The seriousness of the religiously defined mixed marriages is accentuated in this passage. It is defined as a breach of faith to one another, as a defiling of the Sinaitic covenant, as a detestable thing, by means of which the sanctuary of the Lord is desecrated. Through "mixed marriages" the way is opened for apostasy and idolatry. We agree with Baldwin: since apostasy had been responsible for the Exile it was unthinkable that the "whole community should be put at risk again."[26]

13–16 In these verses Malachi draws attention to another blatant example of unfaithfulness: divorce. It is typical of the prophet's style to maintain the tension in his discourse. The factual remark in sentence 9 (v. 13a) is his point of departure for a statement expressed in sentences 10 and 11 (v. 13b), followed by the inevitable question (sentence 12, v. 14a) and answer (sentence 13, v. 14b). The prophet's accusation concerns an act of faithlessness against the first and legal wife. This is followed, in sentences 14–16 (v. 15a, b), by a motivation for marriage fidelity and against divorce, with a concluding admonition against the breach of faith (sentences 17–22, vv. 15d–16).

Another thing you do. The point of reference is not the sins of the priests, mentioned in 1:6–14 (according to some rabbis), but the previously mentioned atrocity of mixed marriages. The meaning of *šēnîṯ* here is logical and not chronological. It specifies another example of unfaithfulness, and does not denote the same transgression committed "a second time" (cf. Gen. 22:15). The rendering of the LXX, "that which I hate," is an inappropriate interpretation of the Hebrew word.

Before mentioning his accusation, the prophet comments on the effect that the people's transgression has for their religious activities. *You cover the Lord's altar with tears, with weeping and wailing*. The fact that lay people had no access to the altar does not exclude the comprehensive purport of the prophet's statement. Generally speaking both people and priests were concerned with the sacrificial activities. All of them, therefore, were included in this general sorrow. The whole nation was involved. They all shared the same guilt and its consequences. The inference of the Targum, followed by Jerome and other ancient and modern interpreters, that it was the deserted wives who were weeping is possible but not preferable. The

26. Baldwin, p. 238.

compound Hebrew word *mē'ên* can denote either cause or effect, either "so that there is not," or "because there is not."[27] The second alternative is favored by the context. God has turned himself away from the offerings and does not accept them with pleasure from their hands. The infinitives *p^enôṯ* and *lāqaḥaṯ* are both dependent on *mē'ên,* with "the Lord" as assumed subject. The Hebrew expression *pānâ 'el* means "to turn yourself with pleasure, eagerly, toward someone or something" (cf. Num. 16:15). According to Malachi the Lord will no longer *(ʿôḏ)* be eager to turn himself to the people's offerings, and when they present their offerings he again will not accept them *with pleasure* from their hands. The Hebrew word *rāṣôn,* "(with) pleasure," is an accusative referring to the condition, the attitude, and the manner in which the offerings were being accepted. This, of course, is of great significance. The *pleasure* of the Lord is the very raison d'être of every offering. When an offering is not accepted with pleasure it fails in its intention to restore or affirm the communion with God.

This attitude of God toward the people's offerings now was probably not caused by that which happened at the altar, for instance, the weeping of the deserted wives. On the contrary, the people wept because God no longer paid attention to their offerings. They came to the painful realization that their religious fervor and activities were in vain. We cannot be certain how the people became aware of the broken communion with God. We must remember that the deepest relationship between the people and God is here the object of prophetic revelation. Yet there is reason to believe that the tears had at least a partial basis in the people's concrete experiences.

They must have become conscious of God's displeasure, because they experienced failure of crops (3:10–12), and their prayers apparently were not heard. In all probability the feeling that their sacrifices were futile, as well as the realization that their religious activities were undue trouble (1:13), also contributed in pressing on their mind that something concerning the altar was radically wrong. Their religious activities amounted to nothing. The communication with the Lord was broken. That is why they now cover the altar with tears, with weeping and wailing. We have every reason to believe that this sorrow did not come from a broken spirit and a contrite heart. It was not a "godly sorrow" that brings repentance and leads to salvation (2 Cor. 7:10; cf. Hos. 7:14), but rather a "worldly sorrow," such as that of Cain (Gen. 4:13, 14).

14 The statement of the prophet took the people by surprise. They could not understand why God should not accept their offerings with pleasure. What was wrong with their endeavors to please God with their sacri-

27. See GKC, § 152y.

fices? They ask, Why *(ʿal-mâ)* does the Lord no longer pay attention to our offerings? The prophet provides the answer: The sinful divorces which they had considered a private affair had not escaped the notice of the Lord. *It is because the Lord acted as witness.* We are not sure whether a religious ceremony was attached to the contracting of a marriage in Israel. According to De Vaux marriages in the ancient Near East, and also in Israel, were civil affairs, without any religious confirmation.[28] In a few texts the marriage is called a "covenant" (Prov. 2:17; Ezek. 16:8), but De Vaux interprets them as referring to the marriage contract. We agree with Koole that the marriage could be denoted as "a covenant of God"[29] because it is contracted in submission to the revealed will of God (Exod. 20:14) and with the expectation of his blessing (Gen. 1:28). According to Mal. 2:14 God acted as witness. In a certain sense he was present when the marriage was contracted. His name was proclaimed in the blessings of the family (cf. Ruth 4:11). But even more than that, the Lord is the witness, guarantor, and protector of every legal transaction, and this includes the marriage "contract" (cf. Gen. 31:48-54). The context suggests that God's being a witness also implies that he eventually would be witness for the crown and prosecutor![30] This is apparent from the fact that he hates divorce (v. 16).

between you and the wife of your youth. The prophet is pointing with his finger. He uses the second person singular to identify the guilty person. In reality he accuses the people as such, since they are represented by all the persons who have committed this sin. The emphasis is both on the solidarity of the communal guilt and on the extensiveness of the occurrence of the transgression. The expression *the wife of your youth . . . your legal wife* (lit. "your covenant wife," or as the NEB translates it, "your wife by solemn covenant," i.e., the one to whom you have promised faithfulness and support, to whom you legally attached yourself) refers to the first love and to the wholehearted commitment to one another at the time of their marriage. In the ancient Near East the marriage was contracted at an early age. According to the Talmud a young man was cursed if he was not married by the age of twenty (cf. Isa. 54:6; Prov. 2:17; 5:18; Joel 1:8).

28. De Vaux, *Ancient Israel,* p. 33.

29. The fact that marriage is nowhere else in the OT called a "covenant" does not imply that it could not have this meaning here, contra Rudolph, Van der Woude, Sellin, et al. The covenant of the Lord with Israel is implied but not explicitly mentioned in this context.

30. The meaning "act as judge" is not explicit but implied, contra Van der Woude. His interpretation is conditioned by his rendering of *zōʾṯ* as "a scandalous deed," and by his contention that the second atrocity is not divorce as such but the perfidious actions against their legal wives.

to whom you have been faithless. The assumption is that the marriage was dissolved and the wife divorced, as is apparent from v. 16. The accusation is molded in such a manner that it included an appeal to the conscience of the transgressors. Various motives are suggested to explain why so many Israelites at that time divorced themselves from their legal wives. The wives had become unattractive at a later stage of marriage (life). They were no longer the wives of their youth. A more probable reason relates the two malpractices of Mal. 2:10–16. The Israelite wife was deserted because a mixed marriage was contracted. To be sure, a man was allowed to have more than one wife. But it was customary in a polygamous marriage to allot the place of honor to the first wife. In this case it would have been the Israelite woman. But it surely would have been against the wishes of the influential parents of the gentile daughters to occupy a second place in such a polygamous marriage.[31] We may assume that the gentile parents prompted the Israelite husbands to desert their legal wives in favor of the gentile daughters.

It is also possible that the consideration of the Israelite husbands was inspired by a meritorious motive. We may assume that the monogamous marriage was becoming the rule at that time. In that case the divorces had a quasi-theological basis: the husbands concerned did not want to relinquish the significant custom of a monogamous marriage, and therefore they sent their first wives away, in order to marry "a daughter of a foreign god." This motive would explain their surprise that the Lord would not accept their offerings with pleasure. Whatever the reasons for the divorces might have been, the fact remains that it was the reason why the communion with God was broken.

15 We agree with Baldwin, et al., that it is impossible to make sense of the Hebrew as it stands, especially in v. 15a (sentences 14-16). The wording of this text is grammatically and syntactically incomplete. None of the ancient versions has an appropriate rendering. Endeavors to emend the text are numerous, but none can be considered an absolute and objective solution to the various problems of v. 15. Despite the problems, it is possible to deduce the general purport of this text from the scanty material, and especially from the context. Baldwin rightly asserts that one guide to the interpretation is that it must agree with the clear intention of Malachi, expressed at the end of the verse, to encourage husbands to remain true to their first wife. Somehow v. 15 conveys the deepest motive for being faithful in marriage life, and for the prohibition of mixed marriages and divorce.

31. For the influential position taken by foreigners like Sanballat, Tobiah, Geshem, etc. in the Jewish community of that time, cf. Neh. 2:10, 19; 4:1–23; 6:1–14; 13:23–28.

No one. The first two words pose "the most difficult problem" (Smith). The Hebrew words *lō'-'eḥāḏ* may be rendered "not one" or "nobody." The word "one" again can be taken as subject, presupposing God (so RSV, NEB, NIV), or it may be the object of the verb, the subject (God) being understood: "did he not make one?" An additional complication is that it is not clear whether the Hebrew words are meant as a question or as a statement. The Vulgate and Peshitta, followed by the RSV and NIV among others, render it as a question: "And did he not make one?" (RSV). In the text itself we have no indication of a question. The LXX's rendering is an example of *Fehlerkonsequenz,* because one error leads to a following one. It has "and nobody else."

with a residue. The meaning of these three words is also not clear. The Heb. *ûšᵉ'ār rûaḥ lô* means literally "he has a residue of spirit." The problem is to understand the meaning of "spirit" in this context. There are three possible explanations. It may refer to the Spirit of God (RSV), the breath of life (the same as *nᵉšāmâ* in Gen. 2:7), or intelligence, sound judgment. The problem with the first alternative is how to explain *šᵉ'ār*. According to Heaton it means "to remain or be left over from a larger number or quantity which has in some way been disposed of."[32] The OT does not have an analogy for the idea of "the remnant of the Spirit," unless one refers to Num. 11:25, where the Lord took "some of the Spirit" from Moses and put it upon the seventy elders. But it remains a problem what that expression could have meant. The second interpretation, of "spirit" as "breath of life," is found elsewhere in the OT, and indeed makes sense in this context. The idea is that God made Adam and Eve one flesh, although he had enough breath of life (cf. Gen. 2:7) left so that he could have made Adam more wives. The third possibility, to interpret "spirit" as "sound judgment" (cf. Num. 27:18; Deut. 34:9; Josh. 5:1; 1 K. 10:5; Isa. 19:3), will be discussed further below.

What does the one do? Various interpretations have also been offered for this clause (Heb. *ûmâ hā'eḥāḏ,* lit. "and what the one?"). The LXX renders "and you say: What other?" The Vulgate has *et quid unus . . . nisi,* "which one . . . except." Some modern translations separate this clause from the following verb, for instance, NIV: "And why one?" Others, like NBG, translate: "Because what does the one seek?" The first rendering seems preferable, however.

If one takes all the scanty data into consideration, the following three possible interpretations might be deemed feasible. According to the first one

32. E. W. Heaton, "The Root *š'r* and the Doctrine of the Remnant," *JTS* 3 (1952) 28.

God is subject, and "one" is understood as "one flesh." The idea is that God gave Adam only one wife, although he had "spirit" (Calvin: "overflowing power") left and if need be could have given him more wives. God, however, made two human beings one with the specific purpose of giving them godly offspring. This purpose is contrary to both divorce and mixed marriages. It is contrary to divorce because it does not rest with the husband to act faithlessly with his legal wife. God has made them one. It is also contrary to mixed marriages because such a marriage cannot yield godly offspring. This interpretation is indeed feasible and in accordance with the context. In v. 10 God is called Father and Creator of Israel, and in v. 14 he is referred to as "witness." In 2:15 the point of reference is Adam and Eve, but the application concerns all marriages, especially of the covenant people. The "law" of marriage as a divine institution precedes the "law" concerning divorce!

A second possibility, favored by Jewish interpreters, is that "the one" refers to Abraham, who, some protested, married Hagar and so set a precedent for taking a second wife.[33] The prophet would then have replied that Abraham did it for a different reason: he sought a godly offspring, while you indulge in your own lusts and desires! Against this interpretation, which is also found in the Targum, G. A. Smith rightly argues that Abraham did not send away "the wife of his youth." Another disadvantage of this interpretation is that it does not provide the prophet with a strong case for his main argument (Baldwin).

Thus the third possible explanation seems preferable. One can paraphrase v. 15a as follows: "But no one does it (as a rule) in whom there is a remnant of spirit (intelligence, sound judgment). Yet what does the one (do)? He is seeking godly offspring." In other words the person who seeks a godly offspring has spiritual insight and does not violate the marriage as a divine institution. Such a person will not send his legal wife away in order to marry a heathen girl, because he has consideration for the elevated character and purpose of marriage. His marriage is one within "the covenant with the fathers" (v. 10), and serves to procreate citizens not only for the kingdom of Israel but above all for the kingdom of God. This significant purpose is frustrated when the wives of their youth are being divorced in favor of mixed marriages. Therefore Malachi urged his people to take heed to themselves and not to be faithless to the wives of their youth.[34]

33. See Baldwin, p. 240n.1.

34. The proposed solutions to the problem in the commentaries of Rudolph and Van der Woude are interesting, but they are unacceptable because both commentators based their explanations on the emendation of the text and by giving words a different meaning. Rudolph's reconstructed text reads: "He has not created a single

16 A second compelling factor is the negative consideration of God's grave displeasure directed against two related facts: divorce and violence. The Hebrew word *kî* introducing the admonition is rendered by the LXX, Targum, and some modern versions in a conditional sense: "*if* a man divorces or puts away his spouse." Most modern interpreters and versions prefer the causal sense, *For, because,* or they do not translate it (cf. NIV). Verse 16 does not convey a new problem, but represents the very reason for the problems which were mentioned earlier: why he no longer accepts the people's offerings with pleasure (v. 13), why he was described as being a witness and eventually a prosecutor with regard to their marriages (v. 14), and why they were admonished not to be faithless to the wives of their youth (v. 15).

I hate divorce. The Masoretic punctuation of the Hebrew word for *hate* is that of the perfect third person masculine singular: *he hated.* Laetsch justifies this reading: "the prophet states a fact and then claims divine authority for this fact." The third person singular, with God as subject, is, however, contrary to the direct speech, according to which God is introduced in the first person: *says the Lord.* The alternative is to suggest an impersonal subject and to translate: "If one sends away out of hate," or: "If one hates, (let him) send away."[35] The assumption is based upon the LXX and Targum, both of which justify divorce when a man hates his wife.

We agree with Baldwin that such a reading undermines all that the prophet is seeking to convey. Therefore, we prefer the reading according to which God is the subject, and only the Masoretic punctuation is altered to provide a participle with a suppressed personal pronoun: "I hate, I am hating."[36] The participle suggests continuity. The Lord continually and habitually hates. The object of his hate is denoted in terms of a Piel infinitive construct, *šallaḥ,* "to send away."[37] In Isa. 50:1 the Hebrew verb has the

---

person *[Einzelwesen],* but flesh from his flesh as supplementary to him." Following the LXX, Van der Woude has: "A foreigner [reading *'aḥēr* = LXX *állos,* instead of MT *'eḥaḏ*] will not do that, as long as he has a residue of mind. For how is the foreigner? He is one who seeks a family of god *[godsfamilie].*" According to Van der Woude the glossator reminded his people of the exemplary attitude of the heathen nations, just as in 1:11.

35. So Van Hoonacker; Junker; Nötscher; Chary; Schreiner, op. cit., pp. 213–14.

36. So Rudolph. See GKC, § 116s.

37. Van der Woude is alone in his interpretation of *šālaḥ* in the sense of *šālaḥ yaḏ,* "the outstretching of the hand," implying a morally detestable act, with reference to 2 Sam. 6:6; Obad. 13. He thus eliminates the idea of divorce altogether. This, of course, is unacceptable.

meaning of divorce, in connection with the "certificate of divorce." The same applies to Deut. 22:19, where *šallaḥ* is used in the sense of divorce. Malachi's intention with regard to the people's breach of faith against the wives of their youth now becomes clear: these wives were sent away.

the Lord God of Israel. There is no need to delete this name, which occurs only here in Malachi. The Hebrew text is supported by the ancient versions, and the name is appropriate because the subject concerns the future of the chosen nation. Verse 16 provides a parallel statement concerning God's hate, but at the same time poses some interesting problems. Is the parallelism antithetic or synthetic? Our interpretation of v. 16a assumes the latter.

and (or *even*) *the one who covers his garment with violence.* The Hebrew verb is a Piel perfect of *kāsâ,* with the preposition *ʿal,* meaning: "to cover something or somebody with something else." According to some scholars *kissâ* must be conceived of as a second object next to *šallaḥ,* in which case *kissâ* must be punctuated as an infinitive construct (*kassēh;* cf. *BHS*). In this case God hates both the sending away and the covering up. The Masoretic vocalization is preferable, however, because of the suffix on *lᵉḇûšô,* "his garment."

The exegetical cruces are the interpretation of the word *ḥāmās,* "violence," and *lᵉḇûš,* "garment." According to the LXX, Vulgate, and many interpreters, *ḥāmās* is the subject of the verb, and thus the clause should be translated: "and violence covers his garment." This is then interpreted as a figurative expression for all kinds of gross injustice which, like the blood of a murdered victim, leave their mark for all to see (so Baldwin, et al.). The rendering of the Peshitta and Targum seems preferable, however, taking *ḥāmās* as accusative: "and who covers his garment with violence." This interpretation depends upon the meaning of *lᵉḇûš,* "garment." It is occasionally taken as a figurative expression for obtaining a wife, which is sometimes done by covering her with one's garment (cf. Deut. 22:30 [Eng. 23:1]; Ruth 3:9; Ezek. 16:8). According to others *lᵉḇûš* is a metaphor for a wife, with reference to the Arabic word *libasun.* In the Koran it is stated that the wife is the "garment" of the man and vice versa (Sura 2:183). The assumption is that God hates those husbands who are sending away their legal wives in order to blemish themselves with frivolous marriages. But the problem is that nowhere in the OT does *lᵉḇûš* have such a meaning, or even a similar one, not even in Ps. 65:14 (Eng. 13).

Another possible interpretation is that the severity of God's hate is illustrated with reference to something else that he hates just as much: that one should cover his garment with violence. The second object of his hate is then deemed in apposition to the first one and serves only to emphasize the intensity of God's hate for divorce. Although this explanation seems feasible, we must depend upon the structural analysis to provide the key to the understanding of our text. It is of significance that the verb *kāsâ* is used twice in this pericope. In v. 13 the semantic domain is predominantly cultic. Despite the fact that the people were accused of divorcing their wives, they indulged in sacrificial activities. The altar was covered with tears. The situation is clear: we have here a repetition of what happened in vv. 10–12. Transgression and humiliation, the desecration of the Lord's sanctuary and of offerings, went hand in hand. Therefore it seems appropriate to combine these two elements also in sentences 19–20 (v. 16a, b). The covering of the garment with violence would then denote a cultic activity. Notwithstanding their sins of divorcing their legal wives, the people were at the same time fervently indulging in offering sacrifices. In their eagerness to serve the Lord they brought "thousands of rams" (Mic. 6:7), they splashed the blood of the sacrificial animals on their garments, and in the process committed violence to these animals. The scope of reference is the same in all three cases, in vv. 12, 13, and 16. This interpretation emphasizes the aggravated circumstance of sinning combined with religious activity.

Scholars are generally agreed that nowhere else in the OT do we find such an elevated view of marriage as in Mal. 2:10–16. Nowhere else is divorce condemned in such explicit terms. We know that divorce actually occurred during the OT dispensation, that it was the sole right of the husband to issue a "certificate of divorce," that it was forbidden under two circumstances, namely, when a man unjustly accused his newly wedded wife of premarital intercourse (Deut. 22:13–19), and when a man seduced an unmarried girl (Deut. 22:28, 29). In Deut. 24:1–4 the practice of divorce is more precisely defined, and rightly in this sense that the husband was compelled to provide his wife with a certificate of divorce. The further stipulations are that if the divorced wife should marry another man, the first husband is not allowed to remarry her. The purport of this law is clear: the frequent and manifold divorces had to be checked according to set regulations. Yet divorces themselves were not forbidden. In the postexilic period stricter demands were made on the marriage bond, apparently in connection with the prohibition of marriages with Canaanites and heathen people in general (Exod. 34:16; Deut. 7:4). The prophecy of Malachi endorses these stricter stipulations, and provides in this respect the ultimate in the OT revelation. Koole rightly pointed out that Christ appealed to the "Law" (Gen. 2:24) when he responded to the question of some Pharisees whether it is lawful for a man to divorce his wife for any and every reason (Matt. 19:3). He did it because the Jews regarded the "Law" as more authoritative than the

"Prophets." Christ's answer, however, is already stated in Mal. 2:14–16: I hate divorce, says the Lord.

The marriage is principally meant to be unbreakable. Scripture offers two exceptions: the dissolving of mixed marriages, with the NT version that the initiative must be taken by the unbeliever (1 Cor. 7:15), and "marital unfaithfulness" (Matt. 19:9). But it is important to stress that the marriage as a divine institution is meant to be for life. The so-called "reasons for divorce" (cf. Matt. 5:32; 19:9; Mark 10:11–12; Luke 16:18) do not alter the fundamental point of view that the marriage bond ought not to be broken. This point of view is expressed by Paul, who gave this command to the married couple: "the wife should not separate from her husband . . . and that the husband should not divorce his wife" (1 Cor. 7:10, 11). A significant scope of reference is given to marriage in Eph. 5:22–33, where Paul talks about the "profound mystery" of marriage, with reference to Christ and the Church (v. 32).

VI. THE DAY OF JUDGMENT (2:17–3:5)

2:17 *You weary the Lord with your words.*
Yet you ask: "How have we wearied him?"
By saying: "All who do evil are good in the eyes of the Lord, and he is pleased with them,"[1] *or else:*
"Where is the God of justice?"
3:1 *Behold, I will send my messenger;*
he will prepare the way before me.
Then suddenly he will come to his temple,
the Lord you are seeking,
the Angel of the covenant, in whom you delight.
Behold, he comes, says the Lord Almighty.
2 *Who can endure the day of his coming?*
Who can remain upright when he appears?
He,[2] *indeed, is like a refiner's fire,*
He is like[3] *a launderer's soap.*
3 *He sits like a refiner and purifier of silver;*
he will purify the Levites,
he will refine them like gold and silver.
Then they will present right offerings to the Lord.
4 *The offerings of Judah and Jerusalem will be pleasing to the Lord,*
as in days gone by,
as in former years.
5 *I will draw near to you for judgment;*
I will be quick to testify against sorcerers, adulterers, and perjurers, against those who defraud laborers of their wages, who oppress the widows and the fatherless, who

1. Heb. *bāhem* refers back to the collective *ʿōśēh rāʿ*, "who do evil"; cf. GKC, § 135p; König, *Syntax*, § 346p.

2. It is also possible to explain *hûʾ* in this context as referring to the *day* of the Lord's coming (so Duhm, Van der Woude). The emphasis, however, is on what the Lord himself will do, in response to the words of 2:17. The purport is parallel to that of Joel 2:11.

3. For the implied comparative particle *kᵉ*, "as," "like," see GKC, § 118r.

thrust aside the sojourners; (against those) who do not fear me, says the Lord Almighty.

Since Ibn Ezra scholars have rightly regarded v. 17 as the beginning of a new pericope and of the second main part of the prophecy of Malachi. There is no direct connection with the preceding pericope (against the Berkeley Version, note m), and it does not form a separate unit unto itself (against Pressel, Lange, et al.), but is an integral part of 3:1–5, as the structure indicates.[4]

By way of the statement-question-answer schema the prophet focuses attention on the twofold reproach of the people against the Lord in sentences 1–3 (2:17). They said (a) God approves of evil, and they asked (b) where is the God of justice? The answer to this twofold reproach is given in sentences 4–18 (3:1–5).

First we have an answer in general terms:

(a) Sentences 4–5 (3:1a, b): A messenger of the Lord will prepare his way.

(b) Sentences 6–9 (vv. 1c–2b): The Lord will arrive suddenly (sentences 6–7), and his arrival will be unpleasant (sentences 8–9).

In sentences 10–16 (vv. 2c–4) the answer is given to the people's first reproach, viz., that God approves of evil. The answer is that he does not approve of evil. He is going to purify his people like a refiner's fire and like a launderer's soap!

Sentences 17–18 (v. 5) provide the answer to the second reproach: "Where is the God of justice?" He is not dead or far away. On the contrary, he will draw near to them for judgment, he will be in a hurry to testify against them. It is important to note that the *mišpāṭ* of the people's reproach (2:17) figures prominently in the answer (sentence 17, v. 5a).

The interpretation of this pericope hinges on the question of the identification of the people to whom the prophet addressed himself. Whether the day of the Lord's coming will be a day of judgment or of salvation depends on the answer to this question.

In agreement with the general trend of Malachi's prophecy, namely,

4. Cf. K. Elliger, "Maleachi und die kirchliche Tradition," in *Tradition und Situation,* Fest. A. Weiser, ed. E. Würthwein and O. Kaiser (Göttingen: Vandenhoeck & Ruprecht, 1963), pp. 43–48; Van der Woude; et al. The unity and authenticity of this pericope are endorsed by, e.g., J. M. P. Smith, Van Hoonacker, Smit, J. Ridderbos, Frey, Nötscher, and Baldwin, but disputed by most scholars, with a considerable variation of opinion with regard to the secondary elements. They are all agreed, however, that 2:17 and 3:1a, 5 are original. The disputed elements are more or less 3:1b–4 (Van der Woude, endorsed by Snyman) or parts thereof. Cf. Sellin, Nowack (3:1c, 4), Elliger, Rudolph (3:1c, 3–4), Deissler (3:4), Chary (3:1c, 3), Horst (3:1c). However, see our structural analysis of this passage.

to address the people as a whole and to hold them responsible even when the sin is committed by individuals or groups, we may assume that the present addressees were the temple community, the covenant people as such. This point of view was advocated by Jerome and subsequently by a number of modern interpreters (e.g., Van der Woude). We therefore do not agree with other points of view according to which the addressees were the frivolous section of the people (Pressel), the skeptics (Sellin, Procksch), the people lacking in faith (Nowack), the freethinkers (Torrey), a separate group in between the godless (3:15, 18) and the pious (3:16) (Marti), and especially the pious among the people (Wellhausen, Von Hoonacker, J. Ridderbos, et al.). We admit that the covenant people at that time were divided into different groups or factions.[5] We also admit that the general scope of reference in 2:17 is defined more precisely in 3:3–4 as "the Levites" and as "Judah and Jerusalem." In 2:17, however, just as in 3:5 and 3:13, the addressees are the people as a whole. The opinion of J. Ridderbos and others that the prophet is here addressing the pious among Israel meets with so many exegetical problems that it deserves no recommendation.

The historical and theological background of the people's reproach is to be found in their experiences. They had returned from exile quite a while ago. In the beginning the external circumstances seemed to justify their messianic expectations: the return was regarded as a miracle from God (Ps. 127:1–3); Zerubbabel was chosen to be God's signet ring (Hag. 2:23); the erection of the second temple and the renewal of the sacrifices caused the people to rejoice (Ezra 3:10–13; Hag. 2:9; Zech. 2:10); the people had reconfirmed the covenant with their God (Neh. 8–10). The later course of events had been disappointing, however. The messianic age had not yet arrived. The people were still subject to Persian rule (1:8). The promised land did not become a paradise, but instead crops failed due to locusts and drought (3:11). Religious activities were becoming burdensome (1:13) and without spiritual effect (2:13). Priests and people alike were violating the covenants of the fathers (2:8, 10).

As a result the question had arisen whether it still made sense to adhere to the promise of the coming of the Messiah. At any rate the expectation appears to have had no concrete meaning. The evildoers apparently had their way, without fear of punishment. It made no difference whether a person did good or evil, because the rule of retribution, which would be especially applicable on the Day of the Lord, seemed to be ineffective (cf. Job 9:24; Zeph. 1:12). And so the words of these speakers were marked by

5. See H. H. Grosheide, *Israel na de Babylonische ballingschap, Religieuze Stromingen in de eerste eeuwen na de ballingschap* (Kampen: Kok, 1979).

biting irony and reckless exaggeration. The fact that evildoers in general were not immediately punished is interpreted to mean that the Lord endorsed evil and was pleased with the evildoers. With audacity they proposed an alternative conclusion: Or, if this is not the case, where is the God of judgment? Why does he not reveal himself as judge to punish all the evil that is done?

2:17 The reproach of the people must not be interpreted in a positive sense. The contents of their *words* were different from that of Asaph (Ps. 73), Habakkuk (1:2–4, 12–17), or "the souls of those who had been slain for the word of God and for the witness they had borne" (Rev. 6:9, 10). Their "words" were not intended to remind the Lord of his promises (Isa. 62:6, 7). They lack the character of true piety and devotion.

The comment of the prophet is susceptible to no misunderstanding. These thoughts and words *weary the Lord,* they put his patience to the test. The Hiphil of *yāgaʿ*, "make weary," is also found in Isa. 43:23–24, where it is parallel to the Hiphil of *ʿāḇaḏ,* "compel to labor as a slave," "cause to serve," "burden someone with something": "You have *burdened [ʿdb]* me with your sins and *wearied [ygʿ]* me with your offenses" (v. 24). Here the perfect tense has the meaning of a present tense, and indicates that the conduct of the people was not only a fact of history but continued until the present day.[6] The LXX expressed the idea of continuity by rendering the Hebrew word with a participle.

Yet you ask. But (*waw*-adversative) the people respond to the prophet's accusation with amazement: *How have we wearied him?* Could you please specify more accurately in what manner we have caused the Lord to become weary? The object ("him") is not mentioned in Hebrew, but the assumption is evident, and therefore it is rightly supplied by the ancient versions. The prophet responds by drawing the people's attention to two aspects of their wearying words. They say (a) all who do evil are good in the eyes of the Lord, and he is pleased with them; and they ask (b) where is the God of justice? According to the general opinion God approves of evil, and he is not interested in dispensing justice.

All who do evil. The Hebrew construction suggests the idea of distribution, that is, everyone.[7] The reference is concrete but also comprehensive; it is directed to the individual but includes all the evildoers. In the parallel clause the comprehensive idea is stressed by *bāhem,* "in (or with) *them.*"

Who are the evildoers? Various groups of people have been sug-

6. See Gemser, *Hebreeuse Spraakkuns,* § 248; GKC, § 106g.
7. See GKC, § 127b.

gested: the priests (Cyrillus), the priests and leaders of the nation (Van Til), the sinners in Israel (Köhler), the unbelieving mass of the people (Deden), the pagans (Umbreit, Keil), especially those who are Israel's enemies (Venema), the neighboring nations, including the people of Babylon (Jerome), the Persians (Reinke), the Samaritans (Von Bulmerincq). According to Goddard "the reference is to profane Jews as well as to the heathen."

In trying to solve this exegetical problem, we must assume an *innerjudische* (Wellhausen) situation, which will exclude any reference to people outside of Israel. This is evident from the prophet's answer in 3:1–5. Furthermore, it must be deemed likely that the reproach against the Lord originally started with "the sinners in Israel," "the unbelieving mass of the people," "the profane Jews." This distinction was gradually erased, however, and the reproach became the cliché of the people as such.

According to these speakers everyone who does evil is good in the eyes of the Lord. This is exactly the opposite of what God has admonished his people to do. They were emphatically prohibited to do evil in the eyes of the Lord and to provoke him to anger (Deut. 4:25; 9:18); they were charged to do what is right and good in the Lord's sight (Deut. 6:18; 12:28). On the basis of their own "experiences" the speakers have come to the blasphemous conclusion that God now has contradicted his own injunction: in his eyes, that is, according to his perception and evaluation, it is good to do evil!

The people's reproach is elaborated in the parallel clause: *and he is pleased with them.* The emphasis is placed upon *bāhem,* "with them," the evildoers. He not only endorses their evil conduct, but he delights therein. God is pleased not with their offerings (1:6–14; 2:12, 13, 16) but with the evildoers. Then the people asked with astonishment: How have our words wearied him?

The alternative of their blasphemous reproach is a conclusion in the form of a question: *or else: "Where is the God of justice?"* The Hebrew conjunction *'ô* is not used here as an exclamation "Oh!" (L. de Dieu) or a copulative "and" (Sellin, Nowack), but in the sense of "or," as in Job 16:3 and 22:11.[8] The interrogative particle *'ayyēh,* "where?" introduces a direct question, usually concerning God (2 K. 18:34; Isa. 36:19; Jer. 2:28). The assumption was not to deny the existence of the Lord (Calvin, Baldwin, et al.), but the way he acts. *the God of justice,* who acts justly.[9] The same

8. See GKC, § 104c. Cf. E. König, *Die messianischen Weissagungen des Alten Testaments* (Stuttgart: Belser, 1925), p. 284.

9. Van der Woude rightly assumes a double aspect in this expression: he is Lord of the order of salvation and God of judgment. Cf. also H. W. Hertzberg, "Die Entwicklung des Begriffs *mišpāṭ* im AT," *ZAW* 40 (1922) 256–87; 41 (1923) 16–76.

expression (without the definite article) occurs in Isa. 30:18: "For the Lord is a God of justice." He who, through Moses, charged the judges of Israel to judge fairly, not to show partiality in judging (Deut. 1:16, 17), not to pervert justice (Deut. 16:18, 19), is himself the very embodiment of justice. Therefore it is sheer audacity even to suggest the denial of this fact. The expectation that God will dispense justice at the day of his coming is an integral part of the covenant relationship between him and his people, and of Israel's eschatology. The people's question suggests a denial of this truth, because their experiences seem to confirm the notion that the law of retribution was not functioning anymore. Their reproach has a formal resemblance with that of the psalmists (Pss. 37, 49, 73) and of Job, but it lacks true piety. The unspiritual character of their words and question is evident from the prophet's answer in 3:1–5.

3:1 Because of the seriousness and importance of the people's accusation, the Lord himself responds, first in general terms (sentences 4–9, 3:1–2b), and then answering their twofold reproach. *Behold, I will send my messenger*. Hebrew *hinnēh* with the participle *šōlēaḥ* does not refer to the present (contra Elliger), but, like 2:3, to the future.[10] In connection with the people's reproach in 2:17, the emphasis is on the certainty and imminence of the messenger's coming. The assumed subject of *šōlēaḥ*, "send," is the Lord, as is evident from the direct speech: *says the Lord Almighty*. The interpretation of the subject as being the triune God (Cappellus, à Lapide) or Christ (Jerome, Calvin) is more a dogmatic than an exegetical conclusion. The notion that the great day of the Lord will be preceded by a "forerunner" is found only here and in 3:23, 24 (Eng. 4:5, 6). In a somewhat different context the idea of the preparation of the way of the Lord is also found in Isa. 40:3 (cf. Isa. 57:14; 62:10). The notion rests upon an eastern custom of sending messengers ahead of a visiting king to inform the inhabitants of his coming and to pave the way, to make it passable, literally to remove all the obstacles. In the Piel the Hebrew verb *pānâ*, with *dereḵ*, "way," means "to make clear, to prepare a way," "to turn aside, to remove (the obstacles)."

my messenger. The identity of the *mal'āḵ*, "messenger," is a point of dispute among scholars. According to the various points of view, he is a heavenly messenger (e.g., the angel of death—Rashi, Kimchi; the Messiah ben Joseph, who would precede the Messiah ben David—Ibn Ezra; a human being, e.g., the prophets in general—Eichhorn, Hengstenberg; an ideal figure—Driver; or the prophet Malachi—Von Orelli, Elliger). Most inter-

10. Cf. GKC, § 116p; König, *Syntax*, § 237g; Driver, *A Treatise on the Use of Tenses in Hebrew* (Oxford: Clarendon, 1874), § 135 (p. 168): "It asserts forcibly and suggestively the certainty of its approach."

preters agree that the "messenger" would be a human being.[11] They also identify him with Elijah, whom the Lord will send before the coming of his day and who then would reconcile fathers and sons, according to 3:23, 24 (Eng. 4:5, 6). The fact that the messenger of 3:1 is sent indicates that he may not be identified with the priests who are also called "messengers of the Lord" in 2:7 (Keil). Since Ephraim Syrus many interpreters, following the NT application (Matt. 11:10; Mark 1:2; Luke 1:76; 7:27), think of John the Baptist. Perhaps it is more likely to construct a pyramid of "forerunners," which eventually has its pinnacle in John the Baptist (cf. Gen. 22:18 with Gal. 3:16; Hos. 11:1 with Matt. 2:15; etc.).

The harbinger is closely followed by the king.

Then suddenly he will come to his temple, the Lord you are seeking, the Angel of the covenant, in whom you delight. Behold, he comes.

Structurally sentences 6 and 7 represent a complete chiasm.

He will come suddenly . . . the Lord you are seeking.
The messenger . . . in whom you delight. . . . Behold, he comes.

The emphases are placed upon the fact and certainty of the coming and upon the identity of the one who is about to arrive. In a general way this is part of the response to the people's reproach: *Where is the God of justice?* The answer is: You will be surprised. Suddenly, unexpectedly, surprisingly he will come. The Hebrew word *piṯ'ōm* here has not the meaning of *statim* (Vulg.), "immediately," "at once," but rather *subito,* "unexpectedly," "surprisingly" (cf. Num. 6:9; 12:4; Isa. 30:13; 47:11; Jer. 4:20; Prov. 6:15; 24:22). In spite of the preparation effected by the forerunner, the King's arrival will be unexpected (cf. Luke 18:8; 1 Thess. 5:2).

The identity of this "King" is obvious. He is *the Lord* to whom the respect of the people was due (1:6), the One who has dominion over all, who is the most powerful One (cf. Zech. 4:14; 6:5). That God is hereby indicated is apparent from the knowledge that he is returning to *his temple* or palace, and from the relative sentences *whom you are seeking and in whom you delight,* which refer back to the question in 2:17.[12] Duhm thinks of a separate

11. Van der Woude favors a heavenly messenger but not an ordinary angel; rather, the highest representative of the heavenly King. According to Blenkinsopp, *A History of Prophecy in Israel,* p. 241, the closest parallel to the promise of this emissary occurs in Exod. 23:20. He deems the identity of this mysterious emissary patient of more than one interpretation. According to an earlier prophetic tradition (Hos. 12:13) it was Moses himself in the guise of prophet. The author of Mal. 3:1 seems to have taken up this tradition and interpreted it in an eschatological sense.

12. For the problems relating to the identification of the different "figures" in 3:1, see also Rudolph and Van der Woude. The JPSV (note) regards the "messenger" in 3:1a "as Israel's tutelary (guarding) angel." See also Bruce V. Malchow,

figure, the "Lord of the temple," distinguishable from the Lord himself, but unjustly so. From v. 5 it is clear that God himself is also meant in v. 1. We therefore do not agree with the interpretation according to which *hā'āḏôn,* "the Lord," must be identified either with the Messiah or with the "messenger" of 3:1a. The parallel clause, which some scholars consider secondary (*BHS,* Elliger), mentions *the Angel* or messenger *of the covenant.* It is apparent from the parallelism and chiastic structure of the two sentences that "the Angel" is associated or identified with "the Lord." "The Angel" is therefore not to be identified with the forerunner. The relationship between "the Angel" and "the Lord" is clearly the same as elsewhere in the OT where "the angel of the Lord" is both identified with and distinguished from God (cf. Gen. 16:7–14; 21:17–21; 22:1–18; Exod. 3:2–22; etc.).

The specific name *Angel of the covenant,* which appears only here, indicates that he was of special significance to the covenant. The covenant is apparently the one which God made with Israel and in which the relationship between God and his people found its fundamental expression.[13] The "Angel of the covenant" was destined to dispense both the covenant blessing and the covenant vengeance.

The question as to which of the two functions of the Angel is stressed depends upon whether the prophecy is to be interpreted as conveying a promise of blessing or a threat of judgment. The context favors the idea of judgment. The fact that the speakers of 2:17 are represented as longing for the coming of the Lord must be interpreted in the same sense in which Israel, in the days of Amos, longed for the day of the Lord (5:18–20). They really thought that the day of the Lord must inevitably be a day of light and blessing

---

"The Messenger of the Covenant in Mal. 3:1," *JBL* 103 (1984) 252-55; and esp. R. T. France, *Jesus and the Old Testament: His Application of Old Testament Passages to Himself and His Mission* (repr. Grand Rapids: Baker, 1982), p. 91n.31. According to him, all three figures are in fact different descriptions of the same messenger of Yahweh.

13. According to R. Kraetzschmar, *Die Bundesvoorstellung im Alten Testament in ihrer geschichtlichen Entwicklung* (Marburg: N. G. Elwert, 1896), pp. 237ff., the "angel of the covenant" must be identified with the guardian (tutelary) angel of the congregation of Israel. The "covenant," therefore, does not so much refer to the Sinaitic covenant but to the covenant community of Israel. Van der Woude endorses this point of view, with reference to Dan. 11:28, 30, 32; Ps. 74:20a; and the application of this term in the Dead Sea Scrolls. Cf. A. S. Kapelrud, "Der Bund in den Qumranschriften," *Bibel und Qumran,* Fest. H. Bardtke, ed. S. Wagner (Berlin: Evangelische Haupt-Bibelgesellschaft, 1968), pp. 137–49. See also A. Skrinjar, "Angelus Testamenti," *Verbum Domini* 14 (1934) 40–48; M. P. Heigel, *Mal'ak Habbᵉrit: De Angelo Foederis dissertatio ex Malach. III:1ff.,* ed. J. Frischmuth (Jena: Krebs, 1660).

for the people of God. This was Israel's great and abiding error. Their conclusion, drawn from a legitimate theological premise, was at fault. God's relationship with them was not automatic and mechanical. Because of their sins the people in reality became the object of the covenant vengeance.

The aspect of the near expectation which is expressed in the words *Behold, he comes, says the Lord Almighty,* is characteristic of the prophetic preaching. Thereby a heavy emphasis is laid upon the certainty of the fulfillment. In the light of the history of the fulfillment, it is obvious that the prophecy unites the facts of the first and second comings of Christ, but then in such a manner that the aspect of judgment is stressed in both instances. That this is the purport of the Lord's response is especially evident from vv. 2–5.

2 With increasing emphasis and by way of perceptive questions the prophet conveys the thought that it is not a trifling matter to long for the coming of the Lord. His coming would not only be unexpected but also unpleasant. *Who can endure the day of his coming? Who can remain upright when he appears?* Note the parallel structure of these two sentences. The interrogative pronoun which is repeated for the sake of emphasis refers to people and therefore alludes to the speakers of 2:17. The rhetorical questions suggest a negative answer: Nobody![14] No one will be able literally to "grasp, take in, endure" the day of his coming, no one will be able to remain standing, to uphold and assert himself when he becomes visible, when he appears. His *coming* and *appearing* are synonymous.[15]

In the following sentences the prophet provides the answer to the twofold reproach of the people. First, that God approves of evil: when he comes, quite unexpectedly, they would experience just the opposite. He will be *like a refiner's fire, he is like a launderer's soap* to remove all impurities and unclean elements from his people. It is evident that the coming of the Lord will serve to purify and refine the covenant people from within, as an *innerjudische* concern. The ungodly and the ungodliness will be removed, as the slugs are removed from the metal and the stains from the garment (cf. Isa. 4:4; Ezek. 22:18; Ps. 66:10; Luke 3:16; 21:22).

3 In v. 3 the rhetoric is continued, but it is modified in that the Lord is now compared not with the fire of the refiner but with the refiner himself. *He sits like a refiner and purifier of silver.* The silver- and goldsmiths of that time sat bending forward over their small melting furnaces to ascertain from the color of the metal whether it was pure (cf. Ps. 12:7 [Eng. 6]; Prov. 17:3; 1 Pet. 1:7). In the Jordan Valley and in the Negeb are some structures that

14. Cf. GKC, § 151a; König, *Syntax,* § 352a.
15. The suffixes in both verbs refer to the Lord/Angel in the previous verse.

may have been ancient foundries.[16] The purport of this text is that the Lord will refine his people just as peacefully and expertly as a silversmith. The participles *m^eṣārēp*, "refiner," and *m^eṭāhēr,* "purifier," describe the quality of his sitting, namely, as one who melts and purifies silver.

The objects of this refining process are, remarkably, the sons of Levi, or better, *the Levites.* In the prophecy of Malachi (see 1:6–2:9) they represent the priests who attend to the service in the temple, precisely that temple which the Lord will suddenly visit! They are called by name because they were the mediators between God and his people, and were therefore also responsible for the religious decline of the people. Thus the purification of the people has to start with them. The fact that the people themselves were also included in this act of purification is evident from v. 4.

The result is expressed in materially parallel sentences:

They will present right offerings to the Lord.
The offerings of Judah and Jerusalem will be pleasing to the Lord.

Scholars disagree about the interpretation of the first sentence. Von Bulmerincq, for instance, translates this phrase in conjunction with the ancient versions: "Then the Lord will bring them (the Levites) as an offering in righteousness." But this interpretation and rendering are unacceptable. The emphasis is on the purification of the Levites, with the inclusion of the priests, and the result will be that they will again perform their duties in accordance with the stipulations of the law.

Then (Heb. *w^ehāyû,* "and they will be"). The perfect with *waw*-consecutive describes that which would follow, the result of the purifying process. *they will present right offerings to the Lord* (lit. "to the Lord those who bring an offering in righteousness"). The offering presented to the Lord is qualified as being an offering in righteousness. This does not refer to the right spirit *(pio animo),* but to the right manner (Jerome: *iusta sacrificia;* Calvin: *iusta sacrificia sicuti Deus in lege sua praescripserat;* J. M. P. Smith: "in accordance with all the requirements of the ritual"; etc.). The offerings would be in perfect accord with the demands of the law, and therefore would be fundamentally different from those that were brought by the priests before (Mal. 1:8, 13).

Roman Catholic interpreters unjustly consider this text a witness to the doctrine of the Mass. The Hebrew word *minḥâ* is here, as in 1:10–12 and 2:12, the general term for an offering as such. In 1:6–14 it included sacrificial animals. This is at variance with the idea of an unbloody offering. The

16. Cf. N. Glueck, *The River Jordan* (Philadelphia: Westminster, 1946), pp. 145–47.

Hebrew construction of *hāyâ* with the participle *maggîšê* denotes a continuous action.[17] The right offerings will be brought continually, habitually.

4 This verse completes the picture by declaring that the purifying process will be to the advantage of the whole people. In Hebrew the word order emphasizes the fact that the offerings *(minḥâ)* will be *pleasing* (*ʿāreḇâ* III, Jer. 6:20; Hos. 9:4; etc.) *to the Lord.* With this qualification the offerings obtained their real purpose. This is the norm that determines the true character and meaning of every offering. *Judah and Jerusalem,* the state and the capital of the postexilic community, indicate and represent Israel as a whole (cf. 1:1). In contrast to the universal purport of the sacrifices in 1:11, the pure *(ṭehôrâ)* and right *(ṣeḏāqâ)* offerings are now being brought by the covenant people.

In explaining the particularistic character of this prophecy the historical situation must be taken into account. Malachi was very much concerned with unworthy sacrifices (1:6–14); his prophecy was directed against the covenant people at that time; even when prophesying about the messianic future he always spoke in terms of the old dispensation with its reference to a glorified Israelite theocracy. In its direct sense the sacrificial service of the purified community still refers to the economy of the OT dispensation, as is evident from the fact that it is compared with that of days gone by, of former years. Only in its deeper sense was the prophecy also fulfilled in the facts of the new dispensation.

as in days gone by, as in former years. Scholars disagree about the scope of reference in both expressions. They are usually applied to two periods in the history of Israel: the time of Moses, especially of the Exodus (cf. Isa. 63:9, 11; Hos. 2:17 [Eng. 2:14]; Mic. 7:14, 15), and that of David (cf. Amos 9:11). Granting the importance of these periods in the scope of prophetical reference, we need not restrict Malachi's comparison to either of them. God's love for his people extended way back to the period of the patriarchs (Mal. 1:2–5). The true instruction of the former priests may refer to the time of Moses (2:4–7), but it was not restricted to that time (cf. Ezek. 44). Mal. 2:10 may be best explained in terms of the Mosaic period, but 3:7 refers to a more comprehensive period, including the pre- and post-Mosaic period. In 3:22–24 (Eng. 4:4–6) reference is made to both the time of Moses and the time of Elijah. Malachi's references in 3:4 must therefore not be unduly restricted, because different periods could be taken into account: the period of the patriarchs (1:2–5) and of the former priests (2:4–7), that of Joshua (Josh. 5:7–12), Samuel (1 Sam. 7:3–17), Hezekiah (2 Chr. 30–33), and Josiah (2 Chr. 34, 35). We reject the opinion that Malachi's reference

17. See GKC, § 116v; König, *Syntax*, § 239b; Ewald, *Syntax*, § 168c.

must be understood in terms of "the good old days," without any basis in historical fact (cf. Wellhausen, Marti, Smith, Edelkoort, et al.). This point of view coincides with the critical opinion that Malachi's emphasis on the importance of the ritual contrasts sharply with the criticism that the preexilic prophets directed against the cult as such (cf. the discussion in connection with 1:6–2:9). This presumed tension between Malachi and the preexilic prophets is specifically of critical origin!

5 Malachi now turns his attention to the second reproach of the people, their question, Where is the God of justice? The Lord is having the word again, just as in v. 1. *I will draw near to you for judgment*. The word *mišpāṭ* constitutes a key to the understanding of the context. Verse 5 must not be isolated from vv. 1–4 (contra Van der Woude, et al.); it represents another aspect of God's answer to the people's reproach in 2:17. It is again directed to the speakers in general and constitutes a broader scope of reference than in the case of v. 3. At the same time the response of the Lord in v. 5 precedes the result of his judgment according to vv. 1–4. The connecting *waw* was not translated in order to emphasize that v. 5 must be considered by itself. The perfect with *waw*-consecutive denotes a future action: *I will draw near*. The subject is not the Messiah (Cappellus) but the Lord Almighty.

In sentence 18 (v. 5b) the reality and seriousness of God's judgment are expounded in connection with several categories of sinners. *I will be quick to testify against* (lit. "I will be a swift witness"). The Lord will come unexpectedly (3:1) as a "swift witness," as one who is going to testify against the evildoers, but who will be at the same time prosecutor and judge (cf. 2:14; so also Van der Woude). In this function as "God of justice" he will be "swift," both with the trial of the case and with the execution of the sentence.

The sins which are here enumerated were of a serious nature and in specific cases punishable by death. Under the influence of the heathen nations at that time *sorcerers* thrived with their witchcraft and were strictly forbidden in Israel (Exod. 7:11; 22:17; Deut. 18:10; etc.). *adulterers* are those who have sexual intercourse with the wife or fiancée of another man. This was expressly forbidden (Exod. 20:14; Deut. 5:18). Both the adulterer and the adulteress must be put to death (Lev. 20:10; Deut. 22:22; Ezek. 16:40; John 8:5). In the law it was deemed a great sin to be a *perjurer,* one who swore falsely in the name of God (Exod. 20:7, 16; Lev. 19:12; Jer. 29:23; Zech. 5:3, 4). In certain qualified circumstances this sin could be atoned for (Lev. 5:4–6; 6:1–7).

The Lord will also testify against and judge *those who defraud laborers of their wages*. The oppression or holding back of a hireling's wages was rightly punished by the law, because the hireling was altogether dependent on his wages for his livelihood (Lev. 19:13; Deut. 24:14). *the widows and the fatherless* were often the victims of social injustice, because they had nobody, no husband or parent, who could promote their case (Exod. 22:22–24; Ezek. 22:7; Zech. 7:10).[18] In the law special provision was made for their sustenance (Deut. 10:18; 14:29; 16:11, 14; 26:12; Ps. 68:6 [Eng. 5]). The *sojourner* was a man of foreign nationality who lived in Israel and was dependent on the Israelites' goodwill (Exod. 22:21; 23:12; etc.). They were being *thrust aside,* deprived of those things to which they were entitled (Exod. 22:21; 23:12; Lev. 19:10; 23:22; Deut. 14:29; 24:17; 27:19; Jer. 7:6; 22:3; Ezek. 22:7). It is remarkable that Malachi, who accused the people of contracting mixed marriages (2:11), took up the case of the sojourners.

The summary of the various categories of sinners is concluded with a reference to the deepest cause of the people's sinfulness: they do not fear God. They are not a separate category from the already mentioned groups (cf. LXX and Vulg.). By way of a circumstantial clause[19] all these groups were identified as people who do not fear the Lord. Baldwin rightly concludes: "All who ride roughshod over other people reveal that they *do not fear* the Lord of hosts, but when he 'draws near for judgment' the question 'Where is the God of justice?' will be answered."

The prophecy in 2:17–3:5 offers a lesson in eschatology. The covenant people were expecting the Day of the Lord. Their experiences since their return from exile disillusioned them. Internationally they were still subjected to the Persian rule. They did not experience the independence and glorification of the promised messianic age. Internally the law of retribution seems not to have come into effect. The injunction to "follow justice and justice alone, so that you may live and possess the land the Lord your God is giving you" (Deut. 16:20, NIV) was no longer applied. Indeed, it seemed that the Lord himself did not show any concern about it. If they were living in the messianic age, it surely would be a major concern of the Lord and his Messiah to do and promote justice (Isa. 9:6 [Eng. 7]; 11:3–5).

According to Scripture, there is a correct and legitimate way to question the divine dispensation and God's dealings with his people. Asaph (Ps. 73) and Habakkuk (1:2–4, 12–17) knew about it. Even our Savior was prompted to ask: "My God, why have you forsaken me?" (Matt. 27:46). When these lamentations arise from a deep longing for God, from a need to

18. Cf. F. C. Fensham, "Widow, Orphan and the Poor in Ancient Near Eastern Legal and Wisdom Literature," *JNES* 21 (1962) 130–31; L. M. Muntingh, "The Social and Legal Status of a Free Ugaritic Female," *JNES* 26 (1967) 102–12.

19. See GKC, § 156f, g.

have communion with him, to understand his way with the life of his people, and to know his way through history, there is nothing wrong with it. As in the case of Job, this is a struggle against God for the sake of God, and as such a spiritual movement toward and a communion with him.

The speakers of Mal. 2:17, however, do not belong to the company of Asaph and others like him. It was not spiritual motives that inspired them to utter these "words." In reality they wanted to make God subservient to the secularized interests of their own existence, to have prosperity for the sake of prosperity, and even the coming of the Messiah had to serve their own political interests. Even in their eschatological expectations they were taking the covenant relationship between God and themselves for granted; they thought that he was bound to bless them if they served him in a mechanical way, in spite of all their sins which the prophet enumerated in 1:6–14; 2:1–9, 10–16; 3:5; cf. 3:7–12.

The lesson of this pericope is that such words and such an attitude weary the Lord. Their disillusioned expectations were really false expectations. They were drawing the wrong conclusions from a formally correct premise. The Lord will come on his day, not automatically to bless them but to purge them. His coming will be unexpected and unpleasant (cf. Amos 5:18–20). The question is not whether God approves of evildoers, but whether the priests are offering according to the stipulations of the law (3:3; cf. 1:6–14) and whether the people fear the Lord (3:5).

From this pericope it is evident that the people were expecting the Day of the Lord. An interesting aspect of their expectation is that God's judgment on that day will also be directed against the evildoers within the covenant people. This is a remarkable new trend in the popular eschatology.

According to our interpretation the judgment on the Day of the Lord will be an *innerjudische* concern, and it will include an aspect both of purifying and of judgment. These emphases are typical of Malachi. The Day of the Lord will cause a crisis within the covenant people, a point of view which is especially stressed in 3:13–21 (Eng. 4:3). An additional characteristic of Malachi's "lesson" in eschatology is that the coming of the Lord will be preceded by a "forerunner," who will pave his way. A point of view which Malachi shares with his predecessors is the so-called *Naherwartung:* the Day of the Lord is imminent, it comes surely and unexpectedly.

With regard to the fulfillment of this prophecy we agree with both N. H. and J. Ridderbos that the different components will be realized successively. The final fulfillment will concur with the second coming of Christ, the central fulfillment was realized in his first coming, and temporary fulfillments accompany God's dealings with his people, in both the OT and NT dispensations.

The references to the "forerunner" and to "the Angel of the covenant" (3:1) suggest the realities of Christ's first coming. He was preceded by John the Baptist, and his appearance caused a crisis within the covenant people, with the result that only a remnant was purified and incorporated within the church as members of the new people of God (cf. Luke 2:34; John 9:39; 2 Cor. 2:16). This new and true Israel (Rom. 9:6–9) were called and sanctified to present their bodies as living sacrifices that would be holy and acceptable to God (Rom. 12:1).

We may assume that the prophecy's final fulfillment will coincide with the coming of the great Day of the Lord at the second coming of Christ. It is true that the components of this prophecy do not include the universal, cosmological, and absolute characteristics of Israel's eschatology, especially according to Joel and Zephaniah. According to Malachi the judgment on that day will be confined to Israel, first as a refining process, but then also as a judgment. In the dispensation between the first and second comings of Christ, the herald of the day of consummation is essentially the Church through the Word and Spirit of God.

VII. ROBBING GOD (3:6–12)

6 *Truly, I the Lord have not changed,*
Therefore you, descendants of Jacob, are not destroyed.
7 *Ever since the time of your forefathers you have turned away from my decrees;*
you have not kept them.
Return to me, and I will return to you, says the Lord Almighty.
But you ask: Why do we have to return?
8 *Will a man rob God?*[1]
Yet you rob me.
But you ask: How do we rob you?
In tithes and offerings.
9 *You are greatly cursed (with a curse),*
yet you are robbing me: the whole nation.
10 *Bring the whole tithe into the storehouse, that there may be food in my house.*
And test me in this, says the Lord Almighty, if I will not[2] *open the windows of heaven for you and pour out for you an overflowing blessing.*
11 *I will destroy the devouring locusts for you, so that they will not ruin the crops of the land, and the vines in your fields shall not fail to bear, says the Lord Almighty.*
12 *Then all the nations will call you blessed, for yours will be a delightful land, says the Lord Almighty.*

The pervasive theme of this pericope is the relationship between God and people. The first statement in connection with this relationship is found in

1. The imperfect is explained in various ways: as a limitative or restrictive imperfect, "is it correct that" (Luther, Keil, et al.); as a potential imperfect, "is one able to" (Pressel), "may a man rob" (cf. GKC, § 107t); or as a fact of experience, "Is it according to custom that" (cf. GKC, § 107g; Driver, *Tenses*, § 33b). With Van der Woude we prefer the last alternative.

2. Heb. *'im lō'* is explained either as an introduction to a direct question, "if not" (cf. GKC, § 150i), or as an (abbreviated) oath formula, "(I swear that I may be cursed) if not," "(I swear that I) verily"; cf. GKC, § 149b; M. R. Lehmann, "Biblical Oaths," *ZAW* 81 (1969) 74–92.

sentences 1–4 (vv. 6–7b). God has not changed, as is evidenced by the continuing existence of the people (sentences 1–2, v. 6). But the history of the people is one of a perpetual disregarding of God's decrees (sentences 3–4, v. 7a, b). Sentence 5 (v. 7c) is the key to the evaluation of this relationship. It is remarkably structured. The parallelism of the twofold *return to (šûḇ 'el)* is chiastically arranged with regard to the personal suffixes: *you-I-I-you*. The very essence of the relationship between God and people consists in a turning to one another.

Sentences 5–12 (vv. 7c–9) are structured according to Malachi's typical style: statement-question-answer. Statement (sentence 5): *Return to me, and I will return to you.* Question (sentence 6): *Why do we have to return?* Answer (sentences 7–12, vv. 8–9). This answer is again formed in the same manner: statement (sentences 7–8, v. 8a, b), question (sentence 9, v. 8c), answer (sentences 10–12, vv. 8d–9).

In sentences 13–16 (vv. 10–12) the renewal of the relationship between God and people in terms of sentence 5 is expounded in a concrete manner. The people must *return* to the Lord by bringing the whole tithe into the storehouse (sentence 13), and God will *turn* to his people by restoring to them material blessings (sentences 14–16).

Scholarly opinions differ with regard to the problem of context. According to some interpreters v. 6 concludes the preceding pericope (Reinke, Hengstenberg, Hitzig, Keil, J. M. P. Smith, Laetsch, et al.); according to others v. 6 figures only as a connecting link between the two pericopes (Pressel, J. Miklik);[3] while still others maintain that v. 6 belongs to the following pericope. Although the first alternative surely makes good sense, the structural analysis favors the third possibility: v. 6 introduces the central theme of the relationship between God and people.

Another contextual problem concerns the relationship of this pericope with both the preceding and following pericopes. It is obvious that this pericope forms a kind of parenthesis between two prophecies concerning God's judgment (2:17–3:5 and 3:13–21 [Eng. 4:3]). The semantic domain of this pericope is not eschatology but cult: it concerns the compulsory contributions for the support of the temple staff. The contention that this pericope was originally connected either with 1:6–2:9 (Elliger, et al.) or with 1:2–5 (Haller, Sellin, et al.) is too hypothetical to be taken seriously. We also do not know whether the different pericopes reflect a chronological order, or whether they were uttered on separate occasions. The data to deny

3. J. Miklik, "Textkritische und exegetische Bemerkungen zu Mal. 3:6," *BZ* 17 (1925/26) 225–37. We agree with Van der Woude and others that Mal. 3:6–12 forms a separate pericope distinctly different from both the preceding and following pericopes.

or confirm these assumptions are lacking. At the same time it is possible to ascertain a kind of connection between this pericope and what has gone before. In this pericope the question of 2:17 is answered in another and concrete manner: the cause of Israel's present adversity and future judgment must be seen in the people's habit of turning away from the decrees of God. The link with the following pericope is especially the idea of "testing" *(bāḥan)* the Lord (3:10, 15).

6 This verse begins with the connecting particle *kî*. Some of the ancient versions (LXX, Peshitta, Targ.) and modern interpreters render it with *for, because,* with the assumption that v. 6 is an explanation of the pronounced judgment of 2:17–3:5. It is questionable, however, that the prophet would postpone giving his reason for vv. 2–5 (Laetsch) until now. Assuming that v. 6 is the beginning of a separate pericope, we render *kî* as a particle of asseveration: *Truly*.[4] The Vulgate has *enim,* which may be translated "truly," "naturally," but also "for." Some Hebrew manuscripts have *hinnēh,* "behold," instead of *kî*. This interpretation is in accordance with the solemn assurance given in v. 6a that the Lord has not changed. There is no need to delete *kî* "as an artificial connective introduced by an editor" (Dentan, et al.; cf. NIV).

Truly, I the Lord. The Vulgate, followed by some interpreters (e.g., Hengstenberg), has "I am the Lord," rendering "the Lord" as the predicate of "I." This translation is not favored by the context. The two halves of the sentence balance one another, "I the Lord" being parallel to "you, descendants of Jacob." The specific construction serves to emphasize the subjects concerned.

have not changed. As in most Semitic languages *šnh* means "to repeat" (Sir. 7:8, 14; 33:6), "to change" (cf. Ps. 77:11 [Eng. 10]; Prov. 24:21 [see RSV, note]; Lam. 4:1 [RSV]; Est. 1:7; 3:8). The solemn assurance that the Lord had not changed presupposes a frame of mind which sincerely doubts the truth of this statement, in connection with either God's dispensing of his justice (2:17) or the profession of his love (1:2–5). According to Malachi, however, there is no shadow of doubt. The perfect tense stresses this truth as a fact of history but also as significant for the present. The Lord had not changed in the past and this is also applicable in the present time.

The unchangeableness of God (cf. 1 Sam. 15:29; Jer. 4:28; 15:6; 20:16; Ezek. 24:14; Hos. 13:14; Zech. 8:14 in connection with his judgment;

4. Following the LXX *(dióti)*, Pesh. *(mšl'd)*, and Targ. *('ry)*, many scholars translate *kî* in its causal sense: "because" (so Keil, Pressel, Laetsch: "v. 6 states the reason for vv. 2–5"). But we agree with most commentators that *kî* must be understood in the sense of "verily," "indeed" (cf. 1:11; see Gemser, *Hebreeuse Spraakkuns,* § 220a; GKC, §§ 148d, 159ee).

and Ps. 110:4; Hos. 11:8, 9; Jas. 1:17 in regard to his love) is balanced by what is said of *the descendants of Jacob*. The problem is the translation of *k^e-lîṯem*.[5] Two possible translations in this context have been suggested. The one is "to cease," "to come to an end," and the other "to be destroyed," "to be consumed." In connection with the first translation the meaning of the sentence may be interpreted in two ways. First, the Israelites have not ceased to be sons of Jacob, that is, they are unchangeable in their sinfulness. Second, the sons of Jacob have not yet come to the end of their sins, or, according to the LXX, "have not departed from the unrighteousness of your fathers." According to both these interpretations the point of reference is the unchangeableness both of the Lord and of the descendants of Jacob. This interpretation is feasible. According to Baldwin it is a fact that "neither God nor Israel had changed," with the observation: "The antithetic parallelism accentuates God's goodness."

The other translation, which seems preferable, stresses the fact of God's unchangeableness as the reason for Israel's continued existence. Because the Lord had not changed in his love for his people (1:2–5), the descendants of Jacob are not *destroyed* (cf. Jer. 30:11). This is Malachi's opening statement. Israel's continued existence is due to God's unchangeable love. The real cause of their predicament (2:17; 3:10, 11) must be sought elsewhere. This will be pointed out in v. 7. In v. 6 the people are confronted with the gospel (cf. 1:2).

7 The people's reproach that the God of justice approves of evildoers (2:17) is flatly denied. He does not change, especially not in his awareness of sin. *Ever since the time of your forefathers you have turned away from my decrees; you have not kept them.* God was fully conscious of the total history of their waywardness. The construction of the prepositions *l^e* and *min* with *yôm* denotes the terminus a quo: "from the days of (and onward)."[6] This expression is also found in Judg. 19:30; 2 Sam. 7:6; Isa. 7:17; 1 Chr. 17:10. *your forefathers* is literally "your fathers." The scope of this concept embraces the whole history of the covenant people, and therefore need not be restricted to a specific period in Israel's history (contra many interpreters, e.g., J. M. P. Smith, who restricts it to the contemporary generation; Von Bulmerincq, to the time of the settlement in Canaan, with the exclusion of the classical Mosaic period; Duhm, Marti, Procksch, and

5. According to Van der Woude both *lō' šānîṯî* and *lō' ḵ^elîṯem*, are circumstantial phrases with an adverbial meaning: "I am Yahweh, unchanging, and you are sons of Jacob, unceasing," with reference to GKC, § 156d-g. See my commentary in COT for a variety of views. Snyman, "Antiteses," pp. 160–61, endorses this point of view.

6. See GKC, § 119c.

esp. Jacob, to the era of the patriarchs, with reference to v. 6 and the variant reading "your father"; others are convinced that Malachi was referring to the generation prior to the Exile, in connection with Zech. 1:2–6; 7:7–14). The point of reference is that Israel's waywardness was a pervasive theme through their entire history. They have sinned habitually and continually.

you have turned away from my decrees. This expression is only found here, but a similar idea is expressed in 2 Sam. 22:23 (par. Ps. 18:23 [Eng. 22]), where David asserts: "All his laws are before me; I have not turned away from his decrees" (NIV; cf. also Deut. 5:31–33; Ps. 119:102; Dan. 9:5). The *decrees* (Heb. *ḥūqqîm,* from the verb *ḥāqaq,* "engrave, inscribe," "enact, decree") denote something that is prescribed, a rule, regulation, decree, given by God or man. When it is given by God it is synonymous with *mišpāṭ,* "decision, judgment, justice," and *miṣwâ,* "order, commandment" (cf. Deut. 5:31; 6:1; 7:11; 26:17; 1 K. 8:58; 2 K. 17:37).

The positive assertion is followed by a negative one: *you have not kept them.* The connection between *sûr,* "to turn away," and *lō' šāmar,* "not to keep," is also found in Mal. 2:8; Deut. 17:19, 20; 2 K. 18:6. It is characteristic of Deuteronomy to combine *šāmar* and *ḥūqqîm* (6:17; 7:11; 12:1; 16:12; 17:19). Because *šᵉmartem* is without an object, various suggestions are made to supply it. *BHK* and *BHS* suggest the insertion of *mišmartî:* "What is to be observed in regard to me" (cf. KB, Sievers, Elliger). Wellhausen, et al., alter the Masoretic vocalization to read: *šᵉmartûm,* "You have not kept *them.*" This suggestion seems preferable, because it accords with the implied meaning of the text. The people of God have turned away from the decrees of God, and that turning away consisted in their not keeping them.

Because of their sins the people have turned their back to God. It is essential for the covenant relationship that God and people should again turn to one another. This is the key note of sentence 5 (v. 7c): *Return to me, and I will return to you.* According to W. L. Holladay the Hebrew verb may have the opposite meanings of "to repent" and "to become apostate."[7] Here it is the former, because the act of turning is *to me ('ēlay).* H. W. Wolff pointed out that the call to repentance in the prophecies is usually accompanied by a *Heilswort,* a word of salvation.[8] This applies also to our text. The call to repent is followed by a promise. Similar phraseology is found in Zech. 1:3 and 2 Chr. 30:6 (cf. Jer. 31:18; Lam. 5:21). If the people return to God, then

7. W. L. Holladay, *The Root šûbh in the Old Testament* (Leiden: Brill, 1958).

8. Wolff, "Das Thema 'Umkehr' in der alttestamentlichen Prophetie," *ZTK* 48 (1951) 129–48.

he will surely return to them. This aspect of promise is expressed in the syntactical structure. The cohortative with *waw*-copulative is dependent on the preceding imperative and denotes a consequence: "in order that I may turn to you," or "then I will turn to you."[9] The transgressions of the people were the cause of God's turning away from them, the reason why he was no longer pleased with them (1:8, 10; 2:13). If they repent, he is eager to confirm by his own turning to them that he still loves them and that he has not changed in his covenant relationship to them (v. 6).

In the customary objection the people expressed their surprise at the necessity of repentance. *But you ask: Why do we have to return?* They are not aware of any shortcoming on their side. In what respect, with reference to what must we repent? This appeal to ignorance concerning their misbehavior characterizes the very nature of the people's waywardness and reveals a lack of guilt consciousness. They had no sense of sin (Jones). Von Orelli justly connects the self-righteousness of the people to that of the Pharisees in NT times.

8 The people's reaction obliged the prophet to explain the content of the concept *šûḇ* in connection with both the people (vv. 8–10a) and God (vv. 10b–12). The first part of the prophet's answer is again structured in terms of statement-question-answer (sentences 7–12, vv. 8–9).

First a general truth is propounded by way of a rhetorical question: *Will a man rob God?* The answer is obviously in the negative. Between God and man there is always an infinite distance; therefore it is unthinkable that a man could rob God. This antithesis between God and man is characteristic of Malachi's discourse (cf. 1:6, 8; 2:10, 17). The Hebrew verb *qāḇaʿ*, also found in Prov. 22:23, is connected with an Arabic word meaning "seize," "take away." In Prov. 22:22–23 it is synonymous with "plunder" *(gāzal)*. Jewish interpreters and some of the ancient versions (Aquila, Symmachus, and Theodotion) maintain the meaning "to rob." The LXX, however, renders the Hebrew word persistently with *pternízō*, in the sense of "to deceive." Instead of *qāḇaʿ* the LXX reading presupposes *ʿāqaḇ*, which would be a pun on the name of Jacob. Modern scholars and some modern versions are inclined to follow the reading of the LXX,[10] but we agree with other

9. See GKC, § 108d.

10. See JB, "Can a man cheat God?"; NEB, "May a man defraud God?" See also Wellhausen, Nowack, Marti, Sellin, Deissler, Chary. Aquila, Theodotion, and Symmachus, however, render with *aposterein*. The Vulg.'s *affigere* (cf. *configere* in Prov. 22:23) assumes the Aramaic sense of the word (cf. J. Levy, *Chaldäisches Wörterbuch über die Talmudim und Midraschim,* 3rd ed. [Leipzig: G. Engel, 1866], s.v. *qbʿ*). In this sense ("secure," "attack") Jerome relates the text to the death of Christ on the cross: "Can a man secure a God (on the cross)?"

interpreters that the Hebrew, supported by the Vulgate, "has the advantage of a bluntness that rings true, and should be retained" (Baldwin).

The general truth is applied to the attitude and conduct of the people. The accusation is direct and personal: *Yet you rob me*. What one would not have expected in general had become a reality in the life of the covenant people. We prefer the adversative meaning of the particle *kî*, "yet" (cf. Isa. 8:23; 28:28; Ps. 141:8; also RSV, NIV).[11] The antithesis in the general statement between "man" and "God" has now become *you* and *me*. The participle *qōḇeʿîm* denotes continuity: They were continuously robbing God.[12]

But you ask: How do we rob you? This demand for a reason or motivation is apparently not meant as sheer rhetoric, but suggests a frame of mind which reveals a shocking unawareness of the transgressions. The background of this "ignorance" is apparently the failure of the priests to give true instruction in the law (2:6, 8), and therefore the people are destroyed from lack of knowledge (Hos. 4:6).

The answer of the Lord is also specific and concrete: *In tithes and offerings*. In Hebrew both terms have the definite article, which emphasizes the fact that the people's robbing concerns the specific tithes and offerings which were prescribed by the law. They were the compulsory contributions. Our translation is dependent on the preposition *bᵉ*, "in," in the preceding question. The ancient versions substituted the words "which are with you," because of the elliptical style.

tithes. The Hebrew word *maʿaśēr* means a tenth part (cf. Ezek. 45:11, 14).[13] The practice of giving a tenth part of one's possessions for the maintenance of both cult and government is ancient and widespread. We find it with numerous neighboring nations, such as the Canaanites, Phoenicians, Arabs, Carthaginians, and Lydians, as well as with the Greeks and Romans. In the OT the first occurrence of this custom is found in connection with the history of Abraham (Gen. 14:20) and Jacob (Gen. 28:22), and in both cases it is presented as a common practice. In the Mosaic law it was given the status of a compulsory contribution. It was decreed that a tenth of all produce was "holy to the Lord" (Lev. 27:30) and was intended for the Levites (Num. 18:28). From the legislation in Deuteronomy it is clear that the recipients of the tithes were the people themselves. Israel was admonished to bring the

11. Cf. German *doch, trotzdem* (so GB). Other alternatives are to give *kî* a causal sense, "because" (so LXX *dióti;* Vulg. *quia;* Calvin; et al.); or a consecutive sense, "that" (cf. GKC, §§ 107u, 166b; König, *Syntax,* § 395; NEB; etc.).

12. See GKC, § 116a.

13. See H. A. Brongers, *Die Sehnzahl in der Bibel und in ihrer Umwelt* (Wageningen: Veenman, 1966), pp. 30–45.

tithe and everything that God has commanded to the sanctuary "to eat it before the Lord" (Deut. 12:4–19; 14:22–29). A further distinction is drawn between the annual tithe (Deut. 14:22–27), and a triennial tithe (Deut. 14:28–29). At the end of every three years the tithes were destined to feed the needy as well as the Levites (cf. Deut. 26:12).

The data in the relevant books of the Law (Leviticus, Numbers, and Deuteronomy) pose the problem of the exact number of tithes that were required of the people. Conservative theologians are inclined to endorse the traditional Jewish interpretation in accepting two different kinds of tithes: one for the Levites and the other one for the prescribed eucharistic meal. The third tithe, also called the tithe of the poor (Deut. 14:28, 29; 26:12), apparently refers to the special use that was made of the second tithe in the third year. In addition to the data in the Mosaic law mention is also made of tithes in 1 Sam. 8:15, 17; 2 Chr. 31:5, 6, 12; Neh. 10:37, 38; 12:44; 13:5, 12; Amos 4:4; Mal. 3:8, 10.

With reference to the dating of Malachi it is important to know that during Nehemiah's absence from Palestine the people neglected the compulsory contributions for the support of the temple staff, so that these people were obliged to abandon the temple service in order to support themselves (Neh. 13:10). On his return to Palestine Nehemiah saw to it that the tithes were again brought (Neh. 13:12). The period between Nehemiah's first and second visit to Palestine must be considered the historical background of Malachi's complaint that the people are robbing God, because they neglected the compulsory contributions, consisting of tithes and offerings. After the time of Nehemiah and Malachi the paying of tithes remained in force (cf. Sir. 7:31; 35:11–13; 1 Macc. 3:49; Tob. 1:6–8; Jdt. 11:13; Josephus *Vita* 12, 15 [62–63, 80]; *Ant.* 20.8.8 [179–81]; 9.2 [204–207]; Matt. 23:23; Luke 11:42; 18:12). It seems, however, that the recipients progressively became the priests, rather than the Levites, according to Josephus (*Ant.* 11.5.8 [181–82]; *CAp* 1.22 [187]; cf. Heb. 7:5). In the time of Christ the high priests (e.g., Annas!) demanded the tithes for themselves, thus causing many priests to die of want (Josephus *Ant.* 20.8.8 [179–81]; 9.2 [204–207]).

offerings (Heb. *tᵉrûmâ*) were contributions which were set aside from a larger quantity for a holy purpose. The word itself has both a specific and a general application. As a specific term it is distinguished from other kinds of contributions (cf. Exod. 25:1–7; 29:27, 28; 30:11–16; 35:4–36:7; Lev. 7:14, 32, 34; 10:12–15; Num. 6:20; 31:25–54; Deut. 12:6, 17; 2 Chr. 31:12; Ezra 8:25). As a general term it includes all the offerings and contributions required for the sanctuary (but not for the altar!), such as firstlings, holy offerings, etc. (cf. Lev. 22:2, 3, 12, 15; Num. 5:9; 15:17–21; 18:8–20). It consists of every kind of possession (cf. Exod. 25:3–7; 30:11–16; Lev.

7:14; Num. 31:25–54; etc.). It was contributed for the erection and maintenance of the tabernacle (Exod. 25:1–7), and later also for the second temple (Ezra 8:25), but its purpose was mainly to provide for the need of the priests (Exod. 29:27, 28; Lev. 7:32, 34; 10:14; 22:12; Num. 5:9; 6:20; 15:17–21; 18:8, 11, 19; etc.). It was partly a voluntary and partly a compulsory contribution. It could have an accidental application (Exod. 25:1–7; etc.), but usually it had a perpetual application (Exod. 29:27, 28; Num. 18:19; etc.). The *t^erûmâ* was not taken from the cereal offering, or from the sin offerings, these being most sacred, but from the peace offerings and other sacred gifts, in the form of the breast of the wave offering, the thigh of the ram of ordination (Exod. 29:27, 28; etc.), cakes of leavened bread, etc. (Lev. 7:14). It was one of the chief sources of the priests' livelihood.

The accusation of Malachi therefore refers to the compulsory contributions which were prescribed by the law for the maintenance of the temple staff. J. M. P. Smith rightly emphasizes that the tithes and offerings "together constituted a large element in the maintenance of the temple staff of priests and Levites." Israel's robbing of God therefore coincides with the conditions alluded to in 2 Chr. 31 and Neh. 13:10.

9 The seriousness of the collective transgression of the whole nation is evident from the fact that they persist in robbing God despite the curse which rested upon them. The Hebrew syntax stresses the seriousness of the prevailing curse. The substantive with *b^e*-instrumentalis, *bamm^e'ērâ,* "with a curse," is used in the sense of an adverb: *you are greatly cursed.*[14] (For the meaning of *curse* see the commentary above on 1:14 and 2:2.) The different translation of the LXX, "And you surely look off from me," is due to the fact that the Greek translators did not seem to grasp the meaning of *'rr,* "to curse" in the Niphal, which occurs only here.[15] The use of the participle here in the sense of a present perfect denotes an action which began in the past but whose effect still remains in the present.[16]

From vv. 10b and 11 it is evident that the curse consists in the failure of crops (cf. Hag. 1:4–11), which in turn again was the result of drought and locusts. The people were spiritually unable to recognize the religious significance of this judgment. Instead of repenting, they found an additional excuse in the economic conditions not to give the Lord what was rightfully his. By neglecting the compulsory contributions they were in fact robbing God. In Hebrew the emphasis is on *me.* The temple service concerned the Lord, and therefore what the people did was a sin against God. *yet* (*waw*-adversa-

14. See GKC, § 119o, q.
15. Kruse-Blinkenberg, *ST* 20 (1966) 112n.94.
16. See GKC, § 106g; Driver, *Tenses,* § 8.

tive) *you are robbing me*. Again the participle expresses continuity.[17] This habitual and continual robbing of God was done by *the whole nation*. The Hebrew word *kol* is used in an absolute sense,[18] the nation in its "entirety." In Isa. 9:8 (Eng. 9) we have the same expression, "All the people," where *ʿām* instead of *gôy* is used. The reference to Israel as *gôy* conveys a suggestion of paganism. In many instances this word is used to describe Israel as "a nation void of counsel" (Deut. 32:28), a "sinful nation" (Isa. 1:4), "a godless nation" (Isa. 10:6), a nation who has "transgressed my covenant" (Judg. 2:20), "the nation that did not obey the voice of the Lord" (Jer. 7:28), "a nation of rebels" (Ezek. 2:3). The apposition of *gôy* with *ʾattem*, "you," emphasizes the collective character of the guilt.

10 The renewal of the relationship between God and people with reference to sentence 5 (v. 7) is now stated in concrete terms. The people must return to the Lord by bringing the compulsory contributions to the storehouse (sentence 13, v. 10a), and then God will return to them by providing them with material blessings (sentences 14–16, vv. 10b–12).

Bring the whole tithe into the storehouse. The Hebrew verb is an imperative, thus expressing a command. The people are not allowed to treat the compulsory contributions as they deem fit. Most ancient versions support the Hebrew reading, with the exception of the LXX, which renders the verb in the perfect tense: "And you have brought. . . ." The people must *bring* (Hiphil of *bôʾ*) the tithes. This is the general term that is used in connection with tithes (cf. Deut. 12:6, 11; Amos 4:4; Neh. 10:38; 2 Chr. 31:5, 6, 12). In Num. 18:24, 26, 28–30 the Hiphil of *rûm* is used, but in connection with the tithes as *terûmâ*, "offering."

the whole tithe. When Heb. *kol* (which is deleted by the Pesh.) is followed by a determinate genitive, it means the entirety, i.e., all, the whole.[19] The supposition is either that a part of the tithes were kept back, or that not all the people have fulfilled their obligation in this respect. The first alternative is preferable, because in v. 9 *the whole nation* was accused of robbing the Lord. We may assume that the people's negligence especially concerned the contributions for maintaining the temple staff of priests and Levites. This is evident from the admonition to bring the tithes *into the storehouse*. The Hebrew expression means literally "the house of supplies," from a verb *ʾāṣar*, "store up." This "storehouse" may refer to a special building somewhere on the temple square, or to one of the additional buildings of the temple complex that was specially adapted for this purpose (cf.

17. See GKC, § 107d.
18. See GKC, § 117c.
19. See GKC, § 127b.

2 Chr. 31:11; Neh. 10:39 [Eng. 38]; 12:44; 13:5, 12; 1 Macc. 4:38). The command to bring the contributions to the storehouse is in accordance with the postexilic custom (Neh. 10:38 [Eng. 37]; 12:44; 13:5, 12), although it was also done by Hezekiah (2 Chr. 31:11).

The absence of these contributions means a scarcity of *food,* literally "that which was torn off as prey." Here it signifies the "food" which served as maintenance for the Levites and priests (cf. Ezek. 44:29–31). *my house* (LXX "his house") is the same as "the house of the Lord," which is the temple (cf. Isa. 56:5, 7; Jer. 23:11; Hag. 1:9; Zech. 1:16; 3:7).

The Lord then invites his people to take a risk with him and his commandment. *And test me in this.* If they will repent and turn to him, he will again turn to them (sentence 5, v. 7). The idea that the Lord subjects himself to testing thereby to confirm the authenticity of his promises is also found in Exod. 4:1–9; Judg. 6:36–40; 1 K. 18:22–46; Isa. 7:10–17; Jer. 28:16–17. The subject of *bāḥan,* "to examine, try," is usually God (Jer. 11:20; 17:10; Zech. 13:9; Ps. 7:10 [Eng. 9]; 11:4, 5; 17:3; 66:10; 139:23). In this text, as in 3:15 and Ps. 95:9, God is being put to the test by human beings. In the last two texts the testing is expressive of humankind's arrogance against God, but in our text it is due to God's invitation.

The Hebrew particle *nā'* is probably not meant to emphasize the command but to soften it: "Please, put me to the test."[20] Do it *in this,* in the way you are fulfilling your obligations.

Some scholars find it strange that the test refers to the material contributions for the temple service; they infer that Malachi's conception concerning the nature of religion is less ethical and spiritual than that of his great predecessors, like Amos, Hosea, Isaiah, and Jeremiah. "It is inconceivable that they could have represented Yahweh as contented with the performance of any single act, least of all one in the sphere of ritual" (J. M. P. Smith).[21] This judgment is subjective, however, and rests unjustly on the assumption that the cult and law in Israel were principally rejected by the preexilic prophets, and that they were eliminated from the covenant of the living God.[22] Malachi's appreciation of the cult is nowhere abstracted from the covenant relationship of the people, and is therefore strictly religious and also prophetically legitimate! The testing of God is an aspect of their return to him.

20. See Gemser, *Hebreeuse Spraakkuns,* § 226.

21. Cf. E. Würthwein, in *TDNT,* IV:980–89.

22. See G. Berkouwer, *Sin,* tr. P. C. Holtrop (Grand Rapids: Eerdmans, 1971), pp. 197–98; H. N. Ridderbos, *The Coming of the Kingdom,* tr. H. de Jongste, ed. R. O. Zorn (Philadelphia: Presbyterian and Reformed, 1962), pp. 313–14.

In v. 7 (sentence 5) the Lord anticipated his return to the repentant people. Here the thought is concretely elaborated. In anticipation of the people's obedience, the Lord *will open the windows of heaven for you and pour out for you an overflowing blessing.* On their behalf God will *pour out,* "make empty," the abundance of his blessing, through the open "windows of heaven," as it was done in the time of the flood (Gen. 7:11). The promised "blessing" is evidently a figurative indication of rain. A similar combination of "blessing" and "rain" occurs in the doubtful text of Ezek. 34:26, 27, but also in Deut. 11:14; Joel 2:23, 24; Zech. 10:1; 14:17.[23] This blessing will be *overflowing,* literally "until there is no more want," that is, "boundless" (cf. Lev. 25:26; Obad. 5; Nah. 2:13; Prov. 25:16). Some interpreters combine *b^elî* and *dāy* to make it one concept, "lack," in the sense of "lack of room" (e.g., NIV: "I will . . . pour out so much blessing that you will not have room enough for it"). An analogous expression is "without limit" (Isa. 5:14).

We agree with Von Bulmerincq that the terms of the promise include an eschatological aspect in addition to the concrete element.[24] The same relationship between abundance of rain and the future fertility of the promised land is found in Isa. 30:23; 44:3; Joel 2:23; Zech. 10:1; along with a rich harvest in Isa. 30:23–26; Joel 2:26–27; 3:18 (Eng. 4:18); Amos 9:13; Hag. 2:18, 19; Zech. 8:12.

11 In this verse the blessing concerns the fruits of the soil. In his turning to his people, God will do two things in connection with the harvests: he will destroy the devouring locusts and he will prevent crop failure in the case of the vines.

I will destroy the devouring locusts for you, so that they will not ruin the crops of the land. In Hebrew *gāʿar b^e,* "rebuke, restrain, make of none effect" (Lattey), is used to denote God's threat, which is the same as the outpouring of his wrath and the execution of his judgment (cf. 2:3). When God "rebukes" the "devouring locusts" (lit. "the devourer") he actually destroys them. The Hebrew word *'ōḵēl,* "he that eats," "the eater," may denote all kinds of pests (NEB, NIV), but is more specifically applied to locusts in general (cf. Josh. 1:4). This application is supported by the context. They are described as "things" which destroy the fruit of the land. And, interestingly, they usually accompany drought (cf. Joel 1:19). During a prolonged dry spell the eggs of the locusts remain (and accumulate!) in the dry sand, until the first rains. Then, suddenly, the locusts appear and devour

23. For the opposite, see Lev. 26:19; Deut. 11:17.

24. So also Smit and Elliger, contra Rudolph and Van der Woude, who deny this aspect.

everything they can get to eat.[25] The consequence of God's "rebuke" will be that the devourer will no longer destroy the crops or fruit (Gen. 4:3) of the land.[26]

the vines in your fields will not fail to bear. The second thing that God will do is to prevent the vines from being or becoming (lit.) "childless." The vines in the field, a very important representative of the fruit trees in the promised land, will not fail to bear grapes (RSV, Berkeley), "will not cast their fruit" (NIV) (cf. Hag. 2:16; 2 K. 2:19).

J. M. P. Smith again draws attention to the fact that the blessing, which is promised as a token of the Lord's favor toward his people, has a material character, just as in Amos 9:11–15. His explanation for the fact that the moral content is missing here is that the prophet meets the people on their own level: material prosperity is to them the proof of the favor of God, and therefore such blessings are also promised here.

We do not agree with this interpretation, however. The old dispensation is still in vogue, with both its demands (compulsory contributions) and its blessings (material prosperity). Under this dispensation earthly blessings were legitimate expressions of God's pleasure within the covenant relationship with his people.[27] In addition we must allow for an eschatological aspect as an integral part of the promise: locusts and vine are elements of the eschatological perspective (cf. Joel 2:11, 22; Hos. 14:8; Amos 9:13–15; Hag. 2:20; Zech. 3:10; 8:12).

12 As a result of God's blessings *all the nations will call you blessed*. Israel will then once again take up its central and unique position as "the favored people" (Gen. 12:3; Isa. 61:9; Zech. 8:13). The expression *all the nations,* that is, the nations in their "entirety" (cf. v. 10), is sometimes used in a hyperbolic sense to denote Israel's neighboring countries. The same nations who have ridiculed and oppressed the returning exiles will be obliged to proclaim them a nation which is being blessed by God.

The reason for this *(kî)* is because *yours will be a delightful land*. The emphasis is placed upon the personal pronoun "yours" (Heb. *'attem*). The covenant people are included in the promise. Some interpreters and versions favor the present tense: "For you are . . . ," but the context demands a future tense.

The Hebrew expression *'ereṣ ḥēpeṣ*, "delightful land," denotes a

25. See A. D. Imms, *A General Textbook of Entomology* (London: Chapman and Hall, 1957), § 331k.

26. For a negative final clause with *wᵉlō'*, see Gemser, *Hebreeuse Spraakkuns,* § 312b; GKC, § 109g; Driver, *Tenses,* § 62.

27. See G. Ch. Aalders, *Het Verbond Gods,* pp. 179–88.

land in which one has delight, which is very much desired. Scholars differ in their interpretation of the subject. According to some it is God (Rashi, Ewald, Reinke, Schumpp, et al.); according to others it is the nations (Pressel, et al.). We agree with the point of view which includes both God and nations as the subject of the delight. God will again have pleasure in the promised land, and the nations will be obliged to acknowledge the blessed state of that country (cf. N. Ridderbos, et al.). This will be exactly the opposite of the ridicule and abuse of the nations (Ezek. 36:15). A similar evaluation of the land is stressed elsewhere in different terms. It is called "the pride of Jacob" (Ps. 47:5 [Eng. 4]), "Beulah" (the married one, Isa. 62:4), "a desirable land, the most beautiful inheritance of any nation" (Jer. 3:19, NIV), "the most glorious of all lands" (Ezek. 20:6, 15), "the glorious land" (Dan. 8:9; 11:16, 41), "the pleasant land" (Zech. 7:14). The "land of divine and human delight" and the "covenant people" are both aspects of the eschatological perspective (cf. Ezek. 34:28). Brandenburg rightly compares the content of v. 12 with the *Weihnachtschoral* of the heavenly host praising God and saying: "Glory to God in the highest, and on earth peace to men on whom his favor rests" (Luke 2:14, NIV).

In this pericope the continuous waywardness of the people (v. 7a) is more specifically defined as a general and sinful neglect of the compulsory contributions for the maintenance of the temple staff (vv. 8, 9). The call to repentance also includes the obligation to bring the whole tithe to the storehouse (v. 10a). When they, in obedience, will risk it with God (v. 10b), he will turn to them in his favor and pour out rich blessings upon them (vv. 10c–11) as a confirmation of his unchangeableness (v. 6). Then they will be called blessed by all nations as a country of divine and human delight (v. 12).

This emphasis on the high importance of the ritual does not imply that Malachi's conception of the nature of religion is less ethical and spiritual than that of his great predecessors. The emphasis on the demands in connection with the cult does not exclude the significance of the covenant relationship with the living God, as far as Malachi is concerned. His appreciation of the cult is essentially religious and therefore prophetically justified. Lattey rightly concedes that Malachi was "possessed with an especial zeal for the seemly worship of God," but, he adds, "this does not of course imply any obscuring of the moral and religious issue, as is clear throughout this prophecy itself, where the main emphasis remains always upon the honor due to Jehovah in itself."

An important consideration in connection with this pericope is whether the demands and the promises are also applicable in the NT dispensation, as they were under the OT dispensation. Our answer must be "Yes" and "No."[28] Yes, because there is continuity in connection with both our obligation to fulfill our stewardship and the promises of God's blessing in our lives. This cannot be denied. At the same time our answer must be "No," because we also have a discontinuity pertaining to the specific relationship between the OT and the NT and the relative dispensations. The discontinuity consists especially in the outward scheme of things, regarding both the obligations and the promises.

In connection with "tithing" it must be clear that it belonged, in conjunction with the whole system of giving and offering, to the dispensation of shadows, and that it therefore has lost its significance as an obligation of giving under the new dispensation. The continuity consists in the principle of giving, in the continued obligation to be worthy stewards of our possessions, but the discontinuity in the manner in which we fulfill our obligations. "It is admitted universally that the payment of tithes or the tenths of possessions for sacred purposes did not find a place within the Christian Church during the age covered by the apostles and their immediate successors."[29] Greathouse, who favored the bringing of tithes even in the new dispensation, states: "Material prosperity and physical health do not invariably accompany faithfulness to God. But spiritual health and prosperity do."

In his commentary on the Minor Prophets, Hans Brandenburg rightly reminds us, with regard to the *Zehntengebot,* that the stipulations of the ceremonial law are only a shadow of what was to come in Christ (Col. 2:17; cf. Heb. 10:1). The law, he says, is in every respect a pointer to and a prophecy of the new order of life, which only Christ can inaugurate. The law declares one day out of seven to be holy unto the Lord, the Spirit sanctifies all seven of them. The law sets apart one tribe out of twelve to be priests, the Spirit declares that the whole congregation has to fulfill the priestly office (1 Pet. 2:9). The law demands a tenth part of his people's possessions, the Spirit translates us to become God's possession with all that we have. Everything belongs to him. We are but stewards who will have to give account of all we possess.

28. See my article, "Die gee van tiendes" ("The giving of tithes"), *NGTT* 21 (1980) 31–42; idem, "Tithing—A Hermeneutical Consideration," in *The Law and the Prophets,* Fest. O. T. Allis, ed. J. H. Skilton, et al. (Philadelphia: Presbyterian and Reformed, 1974), pp. 115–27. See also J. Jagersma, "The Tithes in the Old Testament," in *Remembering All the Way . . . , OTS* 21 (Leiden: Brill, 1981), pp. 116ff.

29. J. R. Willis, in *Dictionary of the Apostolic Church,* ed. J. Hastings, 2 vols. (New York: Scribner's, 1916–1918), s.v. "Tithes."

VIII. ANTITHESIS BETWEEN RIGHTEOUS AND WICKED (3:13–21 [Eng. 4:3])

13 *You have used harsh words against me, says the Lord.*
Yet you ask, What have we spoken among ourselves against you?
14 *You have said, It is futile to serve God. What do we gain by observing his charges and by going about in mourning before the Lord Almighty?*
15 *Henceforth we deem the arrogant blessed; evildoers not only prosper, but they put God to the test and get away with it.*
16 *Then those who feared the Lord spoke to one another;*
the Lord heeded and listened.
A book of remembrance was written before him concerning those who feared the Lord and kept his name in mind.
17 *They will be mine, my treasured possession, says the Lord Almighty, on the day that I will make.*
I will spare them just as a man spares his son who serves him.
18 *Then again you will see the distinction between the righteous and the wicked, between those who serve God and those who do not.*
19 (4:1) *For surely the day is coming; it will burn like a furnace.*
All the arrogant and every evildoer will be like stubble, and the day that is coming will consume them, says the Lord Almighty.
I will leave them neither root nor branch.
20 (2) *But for you who revere my name, the sun of righteousness will shine forth,*
and there will be healing in its wings.
And you will go out and leap like calves (released) from the stall.
21 (3) *Then you will trample down the wicked, for they will be ashes under the soles of your feet on the day that I will make, says the Lord Almighty.*

Scholars differ in their opinion concerning the relationship between this and the preceding pericopes, especially with regard to the identity of the addressees in vv. 13–15 and 16–17.

3:13–21 [Eng. 4:3] ANTITHESIS BETWEEN RIGHTEOUS AND WICKED

We agree with most interpreters that the prophet in this pericope returns to the subject of the judgment on the Day of the Lord which was expounded in 2:17–3:5, but this time on a more profound level. The links with the immediately preceding pericope (3:6–12) are formal and arbitrary, concerning the seeming antithesis between the promised state of blessedness in 3:6–12 and the categorical assertion in 3:13–15 that it is futile to serve the Lord (so Brandenburg). Although we may concede such an antithetical connection between the two pericopes, even in its distinction between the twofold "testing" of God (vv. 10 and 15), it is evident that this relationship is purely casual. Formally and according to its content 3:13–21 (Eng. 4:3) is parallel to 2:17–3:5, with a few profound differences. According to 2:17–3:5 the judgment on the Day of the Lord will be primarily an act of purification; in 3:13–21 (Eng. 4:3) the emphasis is on the final judgment. Another difference concerns the addressees in both pericopes. In 2:17–3:5 the "speakers" are the covenant people without any distinction; according to 3:13–21 (Eng. 4:3) it is evident that in Malachi's time there were also "seven thousand" (1 K. 19:18) who did not agree with the "harsh words" of their contemporaries and compatriots.[1]

The identification of the addressees depends upon the conclusion concerning the relationship between the pericopes 2:17–3:5 and 3:13–21 (Eng. 4:3). Those who stress the similarity are inclined to equate the "speakers" of both 2:17 and 3:13–15. The interpreters who emphasize the dissimilarity between the two pericopes have no other option but to distinguish between the "speakers" in both cases. We agree with the first-mentioned alternative and regard the "speakers" of 3:13–15 to be the same as those of 2:17.[2]

An additional problem is the identification of the "speakers" in 3:16–17. There are two probable interpretations, one in conjunction with and the other in antithesis to vv. 13–15. According to the first alternative the "speakers" of 3:13–15 and those of 3:16–17 are the same. The second alternative seems preferable, however, assuming an antithetical relationship between the relative "speakers": those of vv. 16 and 17 are the real pious ones in Israel, and they deliberately oppose the sinful arrogance in the words of the speakers of vv. 13–15.

Structurally this pericope may be divided into three subsections. The

1. For the relationship between this pericope and 2:17–3:5, see esp. Botterweck (*BibLeb* 1 [1960] 253–60), Elliger, and Van der Woude.

2. Contra Van der Woude, J. Ridderbos, Snyman ("Antiteses"), et al., who identify the "speakers" with the pious, although frustrated, section of the people. According to Von Bulmerincq, Elliger, Botterweck, et al., the distinction is drawn between the temple community and the Samaritans.

first cluster of sentences is 1–3 (vv. 13–15), of which 1 and 2 are chiastically structured:

against me—your words—says the Lord
say you—our conversation—against you.

The well-known scheme of statement-question-answer results in the distinction between the futility of religion and the prosperity of the wicked. It is to be noted that the whole pericope is dominated by the antithesis between the righteous and the wicked, those who serve God and those who do not.

The second cluster of sentences is 4–9 (vv. 16–17) and consists of two parallel sections: (a) sentences 4–6 (v. 16a–c) and (b) sentences 7–9 (vv. 16d–17b). In this section the relationship between God and the righteous is expounded:

Sentence 4: Those who feared the Lord spoke to one another.

Sentences 5–6: God takes heed of them.

Sentence 7: Those who feared the Lord kept his name in mind.

Sentences 8–9: God will spare them as his treasured possession.

The third cluster of sentences is 10–17 (vv. 18–21 [Eng. 4:3]), which again can be subdivided into four sections.

Sentence 10 (v. 18), with an internal parallelism, emphasizes the real antithesis between the righteous and the wicked, quite contrary to the presupposed distinction of the popular opinion (sentence 3, v. 15). This antithesis reveals itself in the following manner:

Sentences 11–13: The wicked will be destroyed on the day of the Lord.

Sentences 14–16: For those who fear the Lord the sun of righteousness will shine forth.

Sentence 17: The righteous will eventually overcome the wicked on the day which God will create.

13 Because of the seriousness of the accusation, the Lord himself is speaking in the first person. The people are again rebelling against him. They were talking among themselves, and their words were "strong, arrogant, harsh" against the Lord. The accusation is similar to that of 2:17. There the words of the people "wearied" the Lord; here the tenor is more antagonistic and aggressive.[3] The Hebrew verb *ḥāzaq* with the preposition

3. Van der Woude favors the translation: "your words rest heavily on me." Cf. also N. M. Waldman, "Some Notes on Malachi 3:6, 3:13 and Ps. 42:11," *JBL* 93 (1974) 543–45.

ʿ*al* in connection with *dāḇār,* "word," is also found in 2 Sam. 24:4 and 1 Chr. 21:4, in both texts in the sense of "overruling." These words were not only multiplied with regard to the Lord (against Pressel), but had their own weight and quality, "hard, strong, arrogant." The people are using offensive language against the Lord. Just as in 2:17 the perfect here has the meaning of a present perfect: the people's harsh words were uttered some time ago but are still in effect today.[4]

The prophet retains his form of dialogue and lets the people deny the charge by way of a question: *What have we spoken among ourselves against you?* The ancient versions neglected the reciprocal sense of the Niphal (*niḏbarnû,* "have we spoken ourselves"), but this is evidently the meaning here, as it is in 3:16; Ps. 119:23; Ezek. 33:30.[5] The people were busy with malicious gossip, which was directed against the Lord. The content of this gossip is reflected in the prophet's answer to their question in vv. 14 and 15.

14 The prophet resumes the discourse and defines the accusation. The people have said *It is futile to serve God,* because (a) the righteous are not rewarded (v. 14), and (b) the wicked are not punished (v. 15).

Serving the Lord does not make sense. It is *futile,* in vain. The Hebrew word *šāw'* denotes that which is without substance or content, which is in itself worthless. The word is used as a synonym of "to lie," Heb. *kāzaḇ* (Ezek. 13:6–9; 21:34), "to deceive," Heb. *šāqar* (Ps. 144:8, 11), and "deceit," "treachery," Heb. *mirmâ* (Job 31:5). Contrary to the reality of salvation, the word *šāw'* denotes "disaster" (Zech. 10:2; Ps. 41:7 [Eng. 6]), and contrary to the reality of consequence it means "futility," "unavailing" (Ps. 127:1, 2; Jer. 2:30; 4:30; 6:29; 46:11).

The notion that it is futile to serve God is expounded in v. 14b in a notable way. The *šāw'* of the first phrase is paralleled by *beṣaʿ* in this one, and the idea of serving God is elaborated by two separate phrases, both introduced by *kî.* The Hebrew verb *bāṣaʿ* is a technical expression of the weaver denoting the portion of the thread that is "cut off from the woof." The extended meaning of the word *beṣaʿ* is "gain," "profit," that which is to be regarded as the result of the weaver's work. In this text the very idea of profit in connection with the service of the Lord is harshly questioned: *What do we gain by observing his charges?* What benefit do we derive from it? What does it avail to keep his commandments, to walk in his ways? Just as in Gen. 37:26 and Ps. 30:10 (Eng. 9) the question presupposes a negative answer.[6] The futility of the service of God is explicated in two parallel phrases:

4. See GKC, § 106g.
5. See Gemser, *Hebreeuse Spraakkuns,* § 97n.1; GKC, § 51d.
6. See GKC, § 150d; König, *Syntax,* § 352a-o.

(a) that we observe what is to be observed in regard to God, and (b) that we go about in black, as an indication of mourning. In both instances it is of no avail to serve the Lord. The righteous ones are not rewarded.

The paronomastic expression *šāmar mišmeret*, "to observe what is to be observed," is occasionally used to indicate the specific service of the temple staff, be it of the Levites (Ezek. 44:8), the priests (Lev. 8:35; 22:9; Ezek. 44:15, 16; 48:11), or the high priest (Zech. 3:7). In connection with the priestly service it is used to denote the correct observation of the separate cultic ordinances (Lev. 8:35; 22:9), or of all the functions of the Levites (Ezek. 44:8), priests (Ezek. 44:1), and high priests (Zech. 3:7). This expression is also used in connection with the people, as in this text, to denote the observation of separate ordinances (Lev. 18:30; Num. 9:19, 23) or of all the requirements of the Lord with regard to the temple service (2 Chr. 13:11). The ancient versions have the plural *mišmārôt*.

According to our dating of Malachi in the period between the two visits of Nehemiah to Palestine, these harsh words of the speakers reveal a state of mind which no longer rejoices in the service of the Lord. The renewal of the covenant with God and the joyful acceptance of its obligations (Neh. 8–10) were past history as far as these people were concerned. According to their experiences and common regard there was no benefit in serving the Lord.

The same is true for another act of devotion and penitence, in regard to the temple service. *What do we gain by . . . going about in mourning before the Lord Almighty?* The specific form of the Hebrew word *qᵉdōrannît* is found only here, but the expression is similar to *qōdēr hālak* in Ps. 42:10 (Eng. 9), "to go about mourning" (cf. Ps. 38:7 [Eng. 6]; 43:2; Job 30:28).[7] The word *qādar* means "to be dark," "to be dirty, unattended, in mourning attire." It is sometimes used as a synonym of "grieve," "mourn" (cf. Jer. 4:28; 14:2; Ezek. 31:15; Isa. 50:3). Both meanings, to go in darkness and to mourn, are combined in the mourning customs and attire, and found their expression in the words of the psalmists ("I wore sackcloth . . . in mourning," Ps. 35:13, 14; "all the day I go about mourning," lit. "in dark," Ps. 38:7 [Eng. 6]) and of Job ("I go about blackened," Job 30:28).

This "proof" of the people's righteousness to appear in mourning was done *before*, on account of, on behalf of *(mippᵉnê)* the Lord Almighty.[8]

7. Cf. D. Winton Thomas, "The Root *ṣnʿ* in Hebrew and the Meaning of *qdrnyt* in Malachi 3:14," *JJS* 1 (1948/49) 182–88. He relates the Hebrew word to the Arabic *qadara*, "to measure," and interprets it to mean "to decide, to measure."

8. Or on account of the wrath of the Lord; cf. Ps. 21:10 (Eng. 9). See also Van der Woude, in *THAT*, II:452.

They have voluntarily submitted themselves to the rites in connection with mourning and penitence to please the Lord, but according to them it all was of no avail. Their experience contradicted the law of retribution, and they arrogantly came to the conclusion that it does not pay to be righteous.

The same attitude toward God and his service is also found in 1:2–5 and 2:17. J. M. P. Smith is of the opinion that it was characteristic of that time to see righteousness as something that one had to pay. If the Lord is served with gifts, offerings, and obedience, then he must also reward it in the form of material blessings, political influence, and domination. He observes that Malachi apparently made this criterion for the appreciation of religion his own, because he does not attempt to replace it with any other.

This interpretation is not fair either to the speakers or to the prophet. The fundamental error in the expectation of the speakers was not so much that their religious practices seemed to be in vain, but that they believed that the external performance of their duty belonged of itself to the very nature of religion. The law of recompense was a legitimate component of Israel's religion, as is also apparent from 3:10–12. The problem, however, was that the people were satisfied not only with defective service to God (cf. 1:6–14; 2:8–9; 3:3–5; 3:6–12), but also with a purely external form of service. This is evident, for example, from the surprise with which they time and again reacted to the prophet's accusations. Smith's criticism of the prophet's attitude is unwarranted. The prophet did not accommodate himself to the people's purely external conception of religion; his criticism was specifically directed at the heathen notion that there is a mechanical and magical connection between religion and prosperity. Malachi's emphasis throughout is on the people's obligation to love, revere, and honor God (1:6; 2:5; 3:3, 4, 16).

15 The futility of religion as a serving of God is apparent from something else. The wicked seemed to benefit from it. The experiences of the people were radically opposite to the prosperity promised in 3:10–12. It does not pay to be righteous. In these circumstances *(wᵉʿattâ),* the arrogant are deemed blessed. The people who are referring to themselves as *we,* Heb. *ʾᵃnaḥnû,* are not the hypocrites (De Moor) or the pious minority in Israel (Smit, N. and H. Ridderbos, Edelkoort, et al.), but the people as such, the same as in 2:17 and 3:13. In the Hebrew this "we" is emphasized: "we ourselves" (NEB), "even we" (Lattey). The assumption is that they have up till now tried to act as pious people, but they deem the wicked, arrogant people blessed. The Hebrew participle *mᵉʾaššᵉrîm,* "to pronounce happy," "call blessed," has the meaning of a *futurum instans,*[9] denoting what the

9. See GKC, § 116p.

people have determined to do from now on and in the future. *Henceforth we deem blessed.* They have made up their mind.

the arrogant. The meaning of Heb. *zēḏîm* is "to boil over in anger, pride, or cruelty" (cf. Exod. 18:11; 21:14; Deut. 1:43; Neh. 9:16, 29). People so characterized are insolent, presumptuous, arrogant. They are twins of the *ʿārîṣîm,* "the ruthless," "tyrannical people" (cf. Ps. 86:14; Isa. 13:11). The hearts of the arrogant are "callous and unfeeling" with regard to the precepts of the Lord (Ps. 119:69, 70), they do not believe the word of God (Jer. 43:2) but stray from his commands (Ps. 119:21) and act contrary to his law (Ps. 119:85); they are inclined to mock the righteous (Ps. 119:51, 69, 78, 122). In Isa. 13:11 the "arrogant" are the heathen nations, but in Jer. 43:2 they are compatriots of the prophet. A number of ancient and modern interpreters are of the opinion that Malachi is here referring to heathen nations, either in general (Hengstenberg,[10] Keil) or specifically to the Persians (Reinke) or to the neighboring nations (Jerome, Cyrillus). Others, like Von Bulmerincq, Elliger, Botterweck, et al., think of the Samaritans.

We cannot agree with this point of view, however. The words and acts of the heathen nations could not have been a problem of faith for Israel. In addition it would be hardly possible for them to put God to the test and get away with it (v. 15c). The *zēḏîm* of v. 15a are characterized in v. 15b as "evildoers," and in v. 19 these categories are identified as one and the same. It is evident from Malachi's prophecy concerning the Day of the Lord (3:1–5; 3:19) that it presupposes an *innerjudische* situation. The "arrogant" therefore were either the covenant people as such, or else those members of the nation who had already inwardly and publicly broken with the faith of the fathers, the agnostics, and the skeptics.

The reason why these people are deemed to be blessed is given in two parallel phrases, both introduced by the particle *gam*. The parallelism of both statements does not favor a different rendering of the two *gam*'s, as is done by the Vulgate: *siquidem . . . et.* We also do not favor the copulative translation of both the LXX and Peshitta; rather, the disjunctive rendering seems preferable: *The evildoers not only prosper, but they put God to the test and get away with it.*

The *ʿōśê riš*ʿ*â,* "evildoers" (RSV, NIV), are the same as those whom the prophet signifies as *zēḏîm,* "the arrogant" (v. 15a), *rāšāʿ*, "the wicked" (v. 18), and *rᵉšāʿîm,* "the wicked" (v. 21 [Eng. 4:3]). They are characterized as those who do not serve the Lord (v. 18), and who will be consumed by fire

10. E. W. Hengstenberg, *Christology of the Old Testament,* tr. T. Meyer and J. Martin, 4 vols. (repr. Grand Rapids: Kregel's, 1956), IV:183.

on the day of judgment (v. 19). Two things are said about them. They will literally "be built," that is, they will prosper, and even when they defiantly put God to the test, they will have nothing to fear and will get away unscathed. Especially in this "testing of God" we have perhaps "an intentional contrast" with 3:10 (so Lattey). Laetsch rightly calls this "a blasphemous perversion of God's challenge." Their testing of God is presumptuous and does not evolve from the fear of the Lord. In spite of their arrogant words and behavior, the assumption is that they will escape the judgment of God. The Hebrew *yimmālēṭû* (Niphal imperfect of *mālaṭ*), "they escape," "they get away with it," is often used in a technical sense to denote those who have survived a crushing defeat in war or another form of total calamity. Thus the prophet's initial accusation that the people were using strong, harsh words against the Lord (v. 13) was substantiated by his answer in vv. 14 and 15.

16 Scholars differ in their interpretation of this verse. The crux of the problem concerns (a) the relationship between v. 16 on the one hand and vv. 13–15 on the other hand, (b) the meaning of the Hebrew particle *'āz,* and (c) the content of the deliberations in v. 16.

According to many scholars v. 16 is an integral part of the context of vv. 13–15, as is evident from the significant Niphal forms of *dāḇar* in both vv. 13 and 16. This means that the speakers in both instances were the same, even if we have to allow for a smaller group in v. 16 (Budde, N. Ridderbos, et al.). This point of view has a bearing upon the interpretation of the remaining two aspects of the crux: *'āz* is then to be interpreted in the sense of the LXX's rendering, *taúta,* "this," "these things," or "so," and the content of the deliberations in v. 16 is accordingly to be found in vv. 14–15 (cf. J. Ridderbos, Horst, Deden, et al.).

We prefer the point of view according to which *'āz* is taken in its ordinary meaning of "then," supported by the Vulgate, LXX, and most of the modern translations (RSV, Berkeley, NEB, TEV, NIV, etc.). This rendering of *'āz,* "then," poses an antithesis between v. 16 and the preceding verses. Thus *those who feared the Lord* (v. 16) were not the same as the "arrogant" and "evildoers" of v. 15. For the first time it became evident that a remnant of true believers was prepared to testify against the malicious gossip of the people at large. We do not have to differentiate further between the different groups of people in Israel at that time. The Day of the Lord will disclose the existence of two groups only: those who fear and serve the Lord and those who do not. The point of reference introduced by *'āz,* "then," is not the past (Venema) or future, but the present. The testimony of the faithful group is a direct reaction to and contradiction of the presumptuous statements of the evildoers.

The only problem in our interpretation is to define the exact words spoken by those who feared the Lord. There are two possibilities. The one is that the words were not indicated. Verse 16 depicts only the situation in which the faithful exerted themselves, without mentioning what they have spoken (so Jewish interpreters, the Vulg., Jerome, Calvin, et al.). The second possibility is that the content of their words is to be found in v. 16b, with the introducing copulative taken in the sense of *namely* or rendered with a colon: *Then those who feared the Lord spoke to one another: The Lord has heeded and he has listened* (so Luther, S. van Til, J. Marck, Drusius, Michaelis, Stier, et al.). In a resounding testimony they denied the current accusation of the evildoers: the Lord is certainly not an idle spectator of the things which happened in Israel. He takes note of everything, and so far be it from him not to trouble himself with the righteous that he even has written a book of remembrance on behalf of those who fear him.

The expression *those who feared the Lord* (Heb. *yirʾê YHWH*) does not refer to the proselytes of the postexilic (and NT) times, but to the spiritual remnant, the true Israel (Rom. 9:6–9), whose lives and testimony are in full accord with a living realization of the holiness and majesty of God, their Father and Lord (1:6).[11]

They have spoken to one another (Heb. *niḏbᵉrû*), and the content of their testimony was that the Lord has heeded, has given attention (Heb. *yaqšēḇ*), and has listened (Heb. *yišmāʿ*).[12]

A book of remembrance was written before him. The Niphal form of the verb *kāṯaḇ,* "was written," suggests the idea that the Lord as king has his own official who is responsible for the entries in the "book of remembrance." The Hebrew word *zikkārôn,* "remembrance," does not merely refer to things in the past which have to be called to mind. It also suggests the idea of actual performance in connection with the remembrance. Botterweck rightly asserts: "Gottes Gedenken ist immer schöpferisches Ereignis und wirkmächtige Vergegenwärtigung" ("God's remembrance is always a creative event and an active actualization"). In God's "book of remembrance" these things are written which he wanted to be "reminded" of, and concerning which he wanted to do something.

The expression *book of remembrance* (Heb. *sēper zikkārôn*) is found only here. But the idea of God having a special "book" in which entries are made is also found elsewhere in the Bible (cf. Exod. 32:32; Ps. 139:16; Isa.

11. For the identification of "those who feared the Lord," see Ps. 22:24, 26 (Eng. 23, 25); 25:14; 31:20 (Eng. 19); 33:18; 34:8, 10 (Eng. 7, 9); 66:16; 103:17; 119:74, 79; etc.

12. The verbs are characteristic of the individual and collective psalms of lament; see Ps. 5:3–4 (Eng. 2–3); 17:1; 55:3 (Eng. 2); 61:2 (Eng. 1); 66:19; 86:6; 142:7; Jer. 18:19; Dan. 9:19.

4:3; 65:6; Ezek. 13:9; Rev. 20:12). It was a known custom of ancient Near Eastern kings to have a record written of the most important events at their court and in their kingdom (cf. Est. 6:1; Dan. 7:10; Acts 10:4). In the OT this "book" served as a register in which the names of the pious were written (Exod. 32:32; Ps. 69:29 [Eng. 28]; 87:6; Ezek. 13:9). In this connection it is sometimes called "the book of life" (Ps. 69:29 [Eng. 28]), which excludes the names of the wicked (Exod. 32:33). Elsewhere the entries in this "book" concern the good and bad acts of people (Isa. 65:6; Neh. 13:14), or the fortunes and experiences of the righteous and the wicked (Ps. 139:16; Dan. 10:21; 12:1).[13] In our text the entries in this "book" are all-inclusive. It was written *concerning*, or better still, *on behalf of*,[14] *those who feared the Lord.* This may imply the entry of their names, but the scope of reference is rather the concrete situation created by the antithetical relationship between the righteous and the wicked. The people in general wearied the Lord by asking "Where is the God of justice" (2:17), and maintaining that it is "futile to serve God" (3:14). The book of remembrance will include all those harsh words and arrogant acts and attitudes. In a special sense, however, the entries in this book will be on behalf of those who feared the Lord. They will be singled out in a special manner, according to vv. 17 and 18. This "book of remembrance" is *before* the Lord, not so much in the sense of "in his presence," but in front of him, in order to remind him of the righteous ones and what they have done (cf. Isa. 62:6, 7).

17 It may be worthwhile to refer again to the structural analysis of vv. 16 and 17 (sentences 4–9). Verse 16a and d (sentences 4 and 7) are parallel: those who feared the Lord spoke to one another (sentence 4), and those who feared the Lord kept his name in mind (sentence 7). The key expression in both phrases is "those who feared the Lord." We have a similar parallel construction between v. 16b and c (sentences 5 and 6) and v. 17 (sentences 8 and 9): God takes heed of them (sentences 5 and 6), and God will spare them as his treasured possession (sentences 8 and 9). Both of these sections are again internally parallel: God takes heed and he listens (sentences 5 and 6), and they will be his treasured possession and he will spare them (sentences 8 and 9).

The identity of the pious ones and their future experiences will be fully revealed on the day that God will make. *Indeed, they will be mine.* The copulative in v. 17 is either explicative, "namely," or emphatic, "indeed."[15]

13. Cf. W. Herrmann, "Das Buch des Lebens," *Das Altertum* 20 (1974) 3–10.

14. The *l*ᵉ denotes a *dativus commodi.*

15. See Driver, *Tenses,* § 141; König, *Syntax,* § 370l.

The subject is "those who feared the Lord" (v. 16). The significance of this statement is explained by the Hebrew word *s^e^gullâ*, "treasured possession." There is no need to regard this word, because of its peculiar position at the end of the sentence, as a later addition to the text (so J. M. P. Smith, et al.). The reading is supported by the ancient versions, and it would be unthinkable that a glossator should have disregarded the rules of syntax by adding the word in its present position.

To be the Lord's is to be his treasured possession. In its profane usage *s^e^gullâ* means "property" (Lat. *peculium,* "that which is accumulated by thrift"). In Eccl. 2:8 it is used of the treasures which Qohelet has amassed in the course of time (cf. 1 K. 10; 2 Chr. 1:14–17; 9:1–28). In 1 Chr. 29:3 it denotes the "personal treasures" of David. In the religious sense the word is used to denote the special position of Israel in its relationship to God as his elect people (Deut. 7:6; 14:2; Ps. 135:4). The parallelism of election and possession in connection with Israel is significantly expressed in Ps. 135:4: "For the Lord has chosen Jacob to be his own, Israel to be his treasured possession."

This elevation of Israel to be God's *s^e^gullâ* is an essential aspect of the Sinaitic covenant (Exod. 19:5, 6), with its later renewal in the territory of Moab, where the Lord declared, "that you [Israel] are his people, his treasured possession as he promised. . . . He has declared that he will set you in praise, fame and honor high above all the nations he has made and that you will be a people holy to the Lord your God, as he promised" (Deut. 26:18, 19, NIV). The word *s^e^gullâ* sometimes occurs in the phrase *ʿam s^e^gullâ*, "peculiar people" (Deut. 7:6; 14:2; 26:18), as a parallel expression to *ʿam qāḏôš,* "holy people" (Deut. 7:6; 14:2; 26:19), or *gôy qāḏôš,* "holy nation" (Exod. 19:6). The rendering of the LXX, *peripoíēsin,* "to save something," "that which remains," "profit," and then "(acquired) possession," forms the basis of the NT's usage of the term (cf. Eph. 1:14; 2 Thess. 2:14; Tit. 2:14; 1 Pet. 2:9). The term *s^e^gullâ*, usually applied to Israel as people (Exod. 19:5, 6), is here used to denote the pious remnant in an eschatological context. They represent the true Israel (Rom. 9:6–9), "a remnant, chosen by grace" (Rom. 11:5).

The promise to those who feared the Lord to be or become his treasured possession will be fulfilled *on the day that I will make*. The Hebrew relative *ʾ^a^šer* is not taken as an accusative of time (Vulg., Calvin, et al.), but as an accusative of the object (LXX, Luther, et al.), in the sense of "the day that I will create." This "day" is the "time" of the Lord's unexpected appearance (3:1, 5), when he will purge his people (3:2–5), consume the wicked (3:19), and bless the righteous (3:20, 21 [Eng. 4:2, 3]).

I will spare them, just as a man spares his son who serves him. The fact that the pious will be the *s^e^gullâ* of the Lord entails that he will spare them. The Hebrew verb *ḥāmal* means "have compassion on," with the extended meaning "spare." Amid the tribulations of the day of judgment God will bestow his compassion on the pious by delivering, sparing them from the ordeal (cf. Jer. 50:14; Ezek. 8:18; Joel 2:18; etc.).[16] The comparison with the behavior of a father toward a diligent and faithful son refers to 1:6 and stresses the significance of the relationship between God and those who truly belong to him. In addition it serves as an answer to the arrogant supposition that it is futile to serve the Lord (v. 14). The truly righteous ones will be revealed on the day of God's judgment as those who are justified by the Lord himself. This is especially apparent from v. 18.

18 In this verse the prophet addresses the speakers of 3:13–15. The third person plural is now replaced by the second person plural (cf. v. 17). On the Day of the Lord the real distinction between the righteous and the wicked will become apparent. The "speakers" will then know how the truly righteous are dealt with and how they ought to regard themselves. *Then again you will see the distinction.* Some scholars consider *w^e^šaḇtem* to be an independent verb with the meaning "to turn about," either in the religious sense of "conversion" (Jerome, Calvin), or in the sense of changing one's opinion (Pocock, Drusius, Cappellus, Wellhausen, Driver, et al.). This interpretation corresponds with the rendering of the LXX, Peshitta, and Vulgate, but is contrary to the purport of the context. The speakers are not urged to convert themselves or to mend their ways, but they are told what will become apparent to them on the Day of the Lord.

They will *again* see. The verb *šûḇ* is used in the sense of an adverb.[17] This does not mean that they may have had that insight before, and have lost it in the meantime. The "again" rather refers to the fact that God has tried throughout their history in various ways to impress the distinction between the righteous and the wicked upon their minds. They will again see that which they have refused to observe, that the Lord has proclaimed the difference through the message of his prophets and the facts of his judgments in the course of their history (Exod. 11:7; Isa. 26:8, 9). In the past they could have seen it, but on the Day of the Lord they surely will see the difference. The expression *rā'â bên . . . l^e^*, "to see between . . . with regard to," has the meaning "to see the difference between."[18]

The distinction will be made between two categories of people: the

16. See KB, p. 310, s.v. *ḥml*, no. 3.

17. See GKC, § 120d; König, *Syntax*, §§ 361m, 369q; most interpreters and modern versions agree.

18. See KB, s.v. *r'h*, no. 18 (p. 863).

ṣaddîq and the *rāšā*ʿ (Targ. and Pesh. have both words in the plural). They are described as *those who serve God and those who do not*. This distinction must of course be viewed in a religious and spiritual perspective. It does not refer to a merely formal way of serving the Lord. The semantic domain of this reference is the fundamental covenant relationship between God and his treasured possession. Judicially the righteous and the wicked represent the two opposite positions in the judge's verdict: the one is found not guilty, the other is found guilty. Religiously and ethically the life of the righteous corresponds with the obligations concerning the covenant relationship with God; the conduct of the wicked is just the opposite. It is typical of Malachi's representation of the Day of the Lord that it will be essentially a *crisis* (from *krínein*, "to divide") within the covenant people itself. This thought is further and more strikingly expounded in vv. 19–21 (Eng. 4:1–3).

19 (4:1) There is no reason whatsoever why the LXX, Vulgate, and all modern versions should start a new chapter at this point. Verses 19–21 (modern versions 4:1–3) are an integral part of the discourse in vv. 18–21, and also of the pericope in vv. 13–21.

The antithesis between the righteous and the wicked (v. 18) will be the consequence of the Lord's Day. The fact of v. 18 will be the effect following that which will happen according to v. 19. *For surely the day is coming*. The Hebrew expression *hinnēh . . . bā*', "behold (the day) is coming," is used in the sense of a *futurum instans* (cf. 2:3; 3:1), something that is imminent; "behold," or "surely," the coming of the day can be expected any time.

the day (Heb. *hayyôm*) is the well-known "day of the Lord," which nobody would be able to endure (3:2), which the Lord will make or create (3:17), and which is characterized as "the great and terrible day" (3:23 [Eng. 4:5]). This notion of "the day of the Lord" is supported by the LXX, Vulgate, and Targum, but incidentally not by the Peshitta, which renders the Heb. *hayyôm* with the plural "days," which probably indicates that the translators were not familiar with the concept of *yôm YHWH*.[19]

Interpreters differ concerning the identity of this "day." According to Calvin it refers to the first coming of Christ, while many others think of his second coming, especially as the day of judgment (Cyrillus, Cornelius à Lapide, et al.). Hengstenberg,[20] De Moor, et al., have a comprehensive interpretation including all God's judgments until the last day. Von Bulmerincq's view is that Malachi is here referring to an imminent catastrophe, which his contemporaries would themselves experience.

19. See Kruse-Blinkenberg, *ST* 20 (1966) 105.
20. Hengstenberg, *Christology of the Old Testament*, IV:188.

None of these explanations is exclusively correct. It is true that the coming of that day is represented as near at hand, and would serve as God's answer to the harsh words of the speakers with which they have wearied him (2:17; 3:13–15). The semantic domain of this representation, however, is the typical *Naherwartung* as an aspect of OT eschatology. The same combination of the participle *bā'*, "is coming," and *yôm*, "day," is found in Joel 2:1; 3:4 (Eng. 2:31); Zech. 14:1. The representation of the "day" as imminent serves to stress the fact and certainty of its coming. Another feature of the prophetic literature is that various facts of the future are focused into a single datum. The specific application of a prophecy can only be discerned in the various stages of its fulfillment. The first application generally concerns the facts and events with regard to the covenant people within the old dispensation. In this respect Von Bulmerincq's point of view has an element of truth. The actions taken by Nehemiah (and also by Ezra) were in a certain sense the application of God's judgment on his people. It had the effect of distinguishing more clearly between those who really serve the Lord and those who do not. But this would be just one aspect of the prophecy's application. Apart from all the intervening judgments in the course of the history of God's people, the central fulfillment is to be related to the first coming of Christ, just as the final fulfillment must be seen in connection with his coming again, the day of the final judgment.

That the coming day will be a day of judgment is apparent from the accusative of condition: *bōʿēr kattannûr*, "burn like an oven" (or "furnace"). The notion that the Day of the Lord will "burn" is only found here. But the word is used in connection with human (Est. 1:12) and divine anger (Isa. 30:27; Jer. 4:4; 21:12; Ps. 2:12; 89:47 [Eng. 46]). An oven or furnace was well known throughout Israel's history (cf. Gen. 15:17; Exod. 7:28; Lev. 2:4; 7:9; 11:35; 25:26; Isa. 31:9; etc.).

This day of judgment concerns *All the arrogant and every evildoer*. The reference is not to two separate categories of people, but is simply a twofold description (cf. v. 15) of all those who do not fear the Lord. For all the ungodly in Israel the "day" will burn like a furnace. In this "oven" nobody and nothing connected with unrighteousness will be spared. All the people who wearied the Lord (2:17) with their harsh words (3:13–15), all the sorcerers, adulterers, and perjurers, all those who defraud laborers of their wages, who oppress the widows and the fatherless, who thrust aside the sojourners (3:5), they will all be judged on that day. This time the judgment will not be to refine and to purify (3:2) but to consume.

All these categories of evildoers *will be like stubble*. The Hebrew word *qaš* may denote three things: stubble, straw, chaff. In this text the distinction is not important. The point of reference is the flammability of the substance, which is true of every one of the possible definitions. The image of stubble that is burned by fire is also found in Exod. 15:7; Isa. 5:24; 47:14; Joel 2:5; Obad. 18; Nah. 1:10. The "evildoers" will not be able to "escape," "to get away with it" (v. 15) on the day of judgment. They will be set on fire, *consumed,* on the day that is coming. The Hebrew verb *lihaṭ,* "devour," "scorch," is in this connection a synonym of *'āḵal,* "eat," and metaphorically "devour," "consume" by fire (cf. Deut. 32:22; Joel 1:19; 2:3). The expression that the coming day will cause a fire to consume the evildoers is found only here in the OT, but it also occurs occasionally in the Jewish literature of later times.[21] An analogous expression is found in Jer. 47:4: "because of the day that is coming to destroy *[šāḏaḏ]* . . . to cut off [Hiphil of *kāraṯ*]." In the original of our text the emphasis is placed upon the objects *('ōṯām):* "them the coming day will consume." The evildoers will not be able to disguise themselves; there will be no doubt whatsoever in connection with the identity of the objects of the judgment on the Day of the Lord.

They will be consumed, they will be totally annihilated because that day (or the Lord Almighty) *will leave them neither root nor branch.* The prophet is using another metaphor, but with the same intent. An interesting commentary on what happens to a man who is without "root or branch" is given by Bildad in Job 18:16–21: "His roots dry up below and his branches wither above. The memory of him perishes from the earth; he has no name in the land" (NIV). The expression "root and branch" is found only in our text. The Hebrew text is supported by the LXX and Vulgate. The Targum has "son and grandson." An analogous expression with a similar meaning is found in Amos 2:9: "I destroyed his fruit above, and his roots beneath." In 2 K. 19:30 and Isa. 37:31 (NIV) it is said that Judah's remnant "will take root below and bear fruit above," which is a metaphor for the blessing of total renewal. A tree with "roots and branches" (Ps. 80:10, 11 [Eng. 9, 10]) suggests growth and prosperity. When neither "root nor branch" is left, then the tree itself perishes and succumbs. This will happen with every evildoer in Israel on the day that comes. Contrary to the public suggestion that evildoers prosper, that they put God to the test and get away with it (3:15), they will all perish on that day!

This is the one side of the Day of the Lord. On that day God will react against all the arrogant words and unrighteous deeds. The seriousness of the

21. Cf. P. Volz, *Die Eschatologie der jüdischen Gemeinde im Neutestamentlichen Zeitalter* (Tübingen: Mohr, 1934); M. A. Beek, *Inleiding in de Joodse Apokalyptiek van het Oud- en Nieuw-Testamentische Tijdvak* (Haarlem: Bohn, 1950); D. S. Russell, *The Method and Message of Jewish Apocalyptic,* OTL (London: SCM; Philadelphia: Westminster, 1964).

day of judgment will not only be the unexpectedness of its coming, but also the surprising manner in which it will expose every reckless word and faithless deed. All the resentment of the "speakers" will be wiped away, and all the insolent questions—Wherein? Whereby? In what manner?—will finally be answered. From the books of Ezra and Nehemiah it appears that many in Israel repented and renewed the covenant with God. On the other hand there were those who rejected the call for repentance and who persisted in their waywardness. To those evildoers the prophecy of Mal. 3:19 (Eng. 4:1) was directed.

20 (2) The Day of the Lord will be "the ultimate stroke of judgment" for the evildoers (v. 19 [Eng. 4:1]), but at the same time "the crown of salvation" for those who revere the name of God (vv. 20, 21 [4:2, 3]).[22] On the one hand his judgment will burn like a furnace, but on the other hand his righteousness will shine forth like the sun. On this "day" the distinction between the righteous and the wicked (v. 18) will reach its climax.

This verse is one of the most significant texts in the prophecy of Malachi. At the same time it represents an exegetical labyrinth for the interpreter.

The direct speech (*lāḵem*, "for you") probably refers to v. 16. The addressees are "those who feared the Lord." The initial *waw* is interpreted either as "then" or as "but." We prefer, along with most interpreters and nearly all modern versions, the adversative meaning: *But for you who revere my name*. The crux of the interpretation is what the shining forth of *the sun of righteousness* really means.

This problem has a number of aspects. First, the specific relationship between the words *sun* and *righteousness*. There are several possibilities. The word "sun" can be seen as an accusative of condition, explicating the manner in which the righteousness will shine forth, namely "like a sun."[23] This interpretation, incidentally, will in a way explain the inconsistency between the masculine "sun" and the feminine verb, "shine forth." The second possible interpretation is to explain the relationship between the two words as a *genitivus epexegeticus* or *appositionis*.[24] "Righteousness" is here the subject and "sun" the nearer definition. If one wants to appreciate the "righteousness" one will have to visualize the "shining sun."

The rendering of the ancient versions assumes a genitive relation-

22. So T. B. Kilpatrick, in *Encyclopedia of Religion and Ethics*, ed. J. Hastings (repr. New York: Scribner's, 1959), I:478; and Verhoef, *Die Dag van die Here*, Exegetica (The Hague: Uitgeverij van Keulen, 1956).

23. See GKC, § 118n-r; König, *Syntax*, § 332l.

24. See GKC, § 128k-q.

ship: "the sun *of* righteousness." The LXX has *hḗlios dikaiosýnēs,* and the Vulgate *sol iustitiae*. A number of scholars agree with this interpretation but differ in their explanation of this genitive. According to Calvin, et al., it is a genitive of quality: the sun that consists of righteousness. Cocceius, et al., consider the genitive to be a genitive of working: the sun that produces righteousness. A third explanation regards the genitive as one of definition: the sun which is righteousness. In all these explanations the emphasis is on the sun, with "righteousness" as a nearer description of it.

We prefer the point of view according to which *righteousness* must be regarded as the key word, and *sun* to be its nearer definition. On the Day of the Lord righteousness will become apparent just like the shining sun in all its brightness and blessedness. The same idea is found in Ps. 37:6: "He will make your righteousness shine like the dawn, the justice of your cause like the noonday sun" (NIV). In Isa. 58:8 we read: "Then your light will break forth like the dawn, and your healing will quickly appear; then your righteousness will go before you, and the glory of the Lord will be your rear guard" (NIV).

Interpreters again differ concerning whether *righteousness* is to be explained in the sense of a person or of matter. According to most ancient interpreters the "righteousness" here represents the Messiah, either as Christ incarnate or in his function as Judge of the world, or as both. The second interpretation, which was introduced by Theodore of Mopsuestia, has become the generally accepted one. That which those who fear the Lord will acquire on his day is *righteousness* as a blazing sun. In this OT key word everything worthwhile will become the possession of those who revere God's name.

The literature concerning "righteousness" as a key concept in the OT is extensive.[25] In this specific form *ṣᵉḏāqâ* occurs 155 times in the OT. In the history of its interpretation we have two main definitions. The fundamental idea of the word suggests, on the one hand, the conformation with a specific norm, and on the other hand, the conformation with a certain relationship. According to the first interpretation "righteousness" means to act rightly in terms of the norm that is set by a specific community, while the second definition emphasizes the importance of the relationship within the community; in this case "righteousness" is the performing of the obligations of that relationship.

In trying to establish the semantic domain of this concept we must

25. Cf. my article "Sol Iustitiae Illustra Nos," in *Sol Iustitiae*, ed. P. A. Verhoef, D. W. de Villiers, and J. L. de Villiers (Cape Town: N. G. Kerk Uitgewers, n.d.), pp. 1–23, with extensive literature.

not confine it to one or another aspect. *ṣᵉḏāqâ* is primarily a forensic term, but this does not exclude its religious and ethical meaning. These distinctions are more Western than biblical. We agree with the statement that "the covenant idea is the 'emotive force' (H. Sperber) or the 'predominant thought-trend' (J. Schwietering) which provided the dynamic for the semantic expansion and development of the word."[26] In our text "righteousness" is an aspect of the coming day, and as such a gift of God to the pious ones. Thus it is primarily something positive, in the sense of restoring justice and bringing about salvation. We agree with Vriezen that "righteousness" in this positive sense "aims at restoring the law that has been infringed first of all by saving the one who had suffered by the violation of the law and on the other side by punishing the one who had made somebody else suffer."[27] Both aspects of the ambivalent meaning of "righteousness" are implied in our text, but the emphasis is now on the positive aspect of deliverance and salvation in the most comprehensive sense of these words. This "righteousness" on the Day of the Lord will not merely be "external" (Hitzig), or "objective," denoting the "right" of God (De Moor), but will be fully experienced in all its significance and consequences, including the full scope of God's salvation on behalf of his pious remnant.

To appreciate the real meaning of this promise, we must consider three components of the context. The first is the simile of the *sun*. The thrust of the comparison is not that it will become fully day for the righteous, but rather that the light of the sun is representing the fullness of God's salvation for them. In this metaphor we have two emphases: on the comprehensiveness and on the nature of God's righteousness for those who fear him. It will shine forth not like a little candle in the night, but as the sun in its blazing fullness; furthermore, it will not bring darkness but shining light, in the sense of salvation and deliverance.

The last-named aspect of the promise is confirmed in the second component of the context. *there will be healing*. The Hebrew word *marpē'* can be translated as "peace" or "healing" (Jer. 14:19; 33:6; Prov. 4:22; 12:18; 13:17; 16:24; 29:1; 2 Chr. 21:18; 36:16). The latter is the meaning in our text. The rendering of the LXX is *íasis*, "healing," and of the Vulgate *sanitas*. The semantic domain of this word is comprehensive. It is not only the opposite of "disease" (2 Chr. 21:18, 19) but also of "disaster" (Prov. 6:15) and "trouble" (Prov. 13:17). A synonym for "healing" is the Hebrew word

26. D. Hill, *Greek Words and Hebrew Meanings: Studies in the Semantics of Soteriological Terms*, Society for NT Studies Monograph Series 5 (Cambridge: Cambridge University Press, 1967), p. 97.

27. Vriezen, *An Outline of Old Testament Theology*, 2nd ed., pp. 388–89; cf. pp. 307ff.

'ᵃrûḵâ, meaning that new flesh has been growing on a wounded spot, that the wound has been healed (Isa. 55:8; Jer. 8:22; 30:17; 33:6). "Healing" is also parallel to "abundant peace" (Jer. 33:6, NIV) and "life" (Prov. 4:22). In Jer. 17:14 the prophet's prayer is: "Heal me, O Lord, and I shall be healed; save me and I shall be saved." The same relationship between repentance and healing is found in Hos. 6:1: "Come, let us return to the Lord; for he has torn, that he may heal us; he has stricken and he will bind us up." In Ps. 6:3 (Eng. 2) David besought the Lord: "Be gracious to me," and "heal me." That which Israel's leaders neglected to do (Jer. 6:14; Zech. 11:16) will be done by the Servant of the Lord: in preaching the good news to the poor he will bind up the brokenhearted and proclaim freedom for the captives and release for the prisoners (Isa. 61:1). Through his vicarious suffering the Servant of the Lord will reconcile his people: "by his wounds we are healed" (Isa. 53:5). "In this pregnant saying OT religion transcends itself and reaches its climax."[28]

In the eschatological context of Mal. 3:20 (Eng. 4:2) it will not be overloading the meaning of the word "healing" to suggest that all or most of the above-named elements must be incorporated in its interpretation. The righteousness of God for his pious ones will cause their "healing" in the most comprehensive sense of the word. The thousand wounds that were inflicted upon them by the evildoers will be covered by new flesh; the "disaster" and "trouble" that were caused by their sins will be removed, and they will be reconciled; their whole existence will be radically changed and will be characterized by "abundant peace" and real "life." This "healing" ultimately will be the consequence of the vicarious suffering of the Servant of the Lord.

in its wings. Most interpreters combine the figurative use of the wings of a bird with the rays of the sun, while attaching to it alternative meanings, for instance, as symbol of protection with reference to a hen and her chickens (Luther), or of rapid movement (Reinke), while the majority of interpreters follow Wellhausen in his reference to the comparable motif of the sun depicted as a winged disk in Near Eastern religion and culture.[29] The

28. A. Oepke, in *TDNT*, III:203.

29. According to Van der Woude the "wings" do not denote the rays of the winged sun disk but the rain clouds which would cover the skies, with reference to R. Hillmann, "Wasser und Berg," diss. Halle/Saale, 1965, pp. 52ff. For other literature concerning the winged disk, see B. Pering, "Die geflügelte Scheibe," *AfO* 8 (1932/33) 281–96; O. Eissfeldt, "Die Flügelsonne als Künstlerisches Motiv und als religiöses Symbol," *Kleine Schriften* (Tübingen: Mohr, 1963), II:416–19; O. Keel, *Die Welt der altorientalischen Bildsymbolik und das Alte Testaments* (Neukirchen-Vluyn: Benziger, 1977), p. 22; for pictures related to this disk, see *ANEP*, nos. 351, 531, 532, 536.

similarity between the "wings" of the sun-righteousness and the winged disk of Israel's *Umwelt* is indeed remarkable. In the astral religions of the ancient Near East the sun did play a major role. The sun-god Shamash was the god of righteousness and the protector of the poor. The possibility of such an association in the metaphor of our text with similar notions in the religion and culture of that time cannot be ignored. Nevertheless, there is an aspect that we must not forget. The sun disk of the Assyrians and Persians was a symbol of dominion and therefore a sign of violence and destruction. Under the wings of Malachi's sun no violence or destruction will be found, but healing, redemption, everlasting life, and peace.

An interesting explanation is offered by C. van Gelderen in his commentary on Hos. 4:19. According to him the figurative meaning of "wings" is not derived from birds but from a common practice among the Jews.[30] A person's "wing" was also the fold in his garment, in which money or other precious things were stored (cf. Num. 15:38; 1 Sam. 15:27; 24:5, 6, 12; Jer. 2:34; Ezek. 5:3; Hos. 4:19; Hag. 2:12; Zech. 8:23; cf. also JPSV note). According to this interpretation the shining sun of righteousness has a precious article in the fold of his garment, namely, healing in the all-inclusive sense of the word.

An additional component of the context is that the pious ones will rejoice exceedingly. *And you will go out and leap like calves released from the stall.* Interpreters have tried to establish both the terminus a quo and the terminus ad quem of this going out of the addressees. The alternative points of departure which were suggested are "this world" (*de hoc saeculo,* Jerome), "the burial places" (Cappellus), the *durae angustiae,* "the experienced catastrophes" (Calvin, Halevy, with reference to Ps. 107:28), "the hideouts of the people" (Driver), "out of their bondage" (Hitzig). The answers to the second question, "Whereto?", usually correspond to those of the separate alternatives in connection with the first question, "Wherefrom?" Ibn Ezra's view is "to the light of the sun." Von Bulmerincq suggests "to meet her," that is, the righteousness.

The problem with all these and similar interpretations is that the point of reference in connection with the "movement" is not so much that of the pious ones but that of the *calves.* Those who feared the Lord will be similar to fattened and therefore lively calves that are released from the stall and are leaping and tramping about in overriding joy. The point of comparison is not the going out of the calves but their expression of joy. The meaning of the Hebrew verb *pôš* is "playfully paw the ground" (cf. Jer. 50:11; Hab. 1:8). The expression "calves from the stall" in this form is also found in Jer. 46:21,

30. C. van Gelderen, *Het Boek Hosea,* COT (Kampen: Kok, 1953).

where it is rendered "fattened calves" (NIV). The righteousness as a shining sun on the Day of the Lord will also cause the pious ones to rejoice exuberantly.

21 (3) In this verse another component is added to the new and renewed situation for the pious ones on the coming day: the generally acquired roles will be reversed. Instead of being the troubled and downtrodden, the pious will henceforth be the victors. *Then you will trample down the wicked.* This notion, differently expressed, is a typical motif in the prophetic perspective on the Day of the Lord. The restored remnant will possess the remnant of Edom (Amos 9:1), subject the surrounding nations (Isa. 11:14), plunder them (Zeph. 2:9); they will be given honor and praise among all the peoples of the earth (Zeph. 3:19–20) and a double-edged sword to inflict vengeance on the nations and to carry out the sentence written against them (Ps. 149:7). In our text, however, the antithesis is not between the restored covenant people and the nations, but within the covenant people between the righteous and the wicked. The "wicked," Heb. *r^e^šāʿîm,* are the "arrogant" and "evildoers" of vv. 15 and 19 (Eng. 4:1). They will be *trampled down,* according to the custom in times of war that the victor put his foot on the neck of the victim (cf. Josh. 10:24; Isa. 51:23; Ps. 110:1).

In this text the reason is *for [kî] they will be ashes under the soles of your feet on the day that I will make*. The Hebrew word *'ēp̱er* is usually translated "dust," but the context here favors the rendering *ashes* (so LXX *spodós;* Vulg. *cinis;* RSV, NEB, NIV). The coming day will burn like a furnace (v. 19 [Eng. 4:1]), and that will cause the wicked to become *ashes,* on which the righteous will trample. The same metaphor is found in Ezek. 28:18. Malachi is not proclaiming the theology of revolution, the "gospel of violence," but describes in terms of a metaphor what will happen when "the God of justice" (2:17) performs the ultimate stroke of judgment on the day which he creates. The expression "under the soles of your feet" is also found in 1 K. 5:17 (Eng. 3).

In 3:13–21 (Eng. 4:3) the same situation as in 2:17–3:5 is represented, but with the difference that the key question concerning the distinction between the righteous and the wicked is answered in a most convincing way. In 2:17 it was stated that it is all the same to God whether a person is righteous or wicked. The same assumption is reflected in the harsh words uttered by the same people in 3:13. According to them it is futile to serve the Lord (3:14). It is better to be wicked than righteous (3:15). A new dimension in this prophecy became evident when a separate group of believers exerted themselves (3:16) and contradicted the assumption that God does not care. On the contrary, he has noticed everything that occurred in Israel and had it written down in a book of remembrance on behalf of the real believers as his treasured possession (3:16, 17). The real distinction between the righteous and the wicked will radically and finally be revealed on his coming day (3:18). This "day" will be both the ultimate stroke of judgment to the wicked (3:19 [Eng. 4:1]) and the crown of salvation for the righteous (3:20, 21 [Eng. 4:2, 3]). The wicked will be "consumed" like stubble in a burning furnace, and the pious ones will experience the wholesome gift of God's merciful righteousness, which will burst forth like a blazing sun, with healing, redemption, and salvation in its wake. On that day the roles will be reversed. The righteous will overcome and dominate the wicked (3:21 [Eng. 4:3]).

The description of the blessedness that the believers will experience on the Day of the Lord is cast in terms of the OT dispensation. The NT teaches us that this blessedness surpasses all human understanding. We may assume, however, that the love of the merciful God, of which Malachi has also spoken (1:2–5), will then be an astonishing reality. On the Day of the Lord nobody who loves him will have reason to doubt it.

Malachi's references to *the day of the Lord* (3:17, 19, 21, 23 [Eng. 4:1, 3, 5]) coincide with an essential motif in OT eschatology. The term itself occurs 16 times in the OT (Isa. 13:6, 9; Ezek. 13:5; Joel 1:15; 2:1, 11; 3:4 [Eng. 2:31]; 4:14 [Eng. 3:14]; Amos 5:18 [bis], 20; Obad. v. 15; Zeph. 1:7, 14 [bis]; Mal. 3:23 [Eng. 4:5]). The other expressions for the Day of the Lord are *yôm leYHWH* (Isa. 2:12; Ezek. 30:3, and Zech. 14:1), *yôm ʿeḇraṯ YHWH* (Ezek. 7:19; Zeph. 1:18), *yôm ʾap-YHWH* (Zeph. 2:2, 3; Lam. 2:22), *yôm zeḇaḥ YHWH* (Zeph. 1:8), *laʾḏōnāy YHWH . . . yôm neqāmâ* (Jer. 46:10; cf. Isa. 34:8), *yôm rāṣôn YHWH* (Isa. 58:5), and finally *yôm mehûmâ . . . laʾḏōnāy YHWH* (Isa. 22:5). Apart from the terminology, the motif of this day may be found in every absolute and final element of each prophecy concerning the future.

The following main solutions have been proposed with regard to the question of the original purport and motif-content of the Day of the Lord. According to H. Gressmann, who was the first to discuss this problem, the origin must not be seen in the context of history but of eschatology.[31] He distinguishes three stages in its development: (a) the mythological stage, where Israel relied upon the representations of the Babylonians and Canaanites; (b) the stage of the people's eschatology; and (c) the reaction of the prophets to this popular conception, with the emphasis on the aspect of

31. Gressmann, *Der Ursprüng der israelitisch-jüdischen Eschatologie* (Göttingen: Vandenhoeck & Ruprecht, 1905), pp. 141ff.; idem, *Der Messias* (Göttingen: Vandenhoeck & Ruprecht, 1929), pp. 77ff. For a foreign (Iranian) origin of this concept, see also T. H. Gaster, *Myth, Legend, and Custom in the Old Testament* (New York: Harper & Row, 1969), p. 688.

judgment for Israel itself. In Mowinckel's view the day of Yahweh was essentially a cultic conception.[32] It was originally an annual commemoration of Yahweh's ascension to the throne, celebrated at the New Year Festival. G. von Rad is of the opinion that the concept had its roots in the sacral institution of the holy war.[33] The origin of this concept is not the cult or eschatology but history. With the prophets it became eschatological, in the sense that they projected the idea of the holy war into the near or more distant future. F. C. Fensham regards the stipulations of the covenant, especially with regard to the sanctions pertaining to salvation and judgment, as the origin of the concept.[34]

There is no need to derive this concept from Babylonian or Canaanite mythology, or to connect it with "the elaborate and lurid eschatology of the Iranians."[35] Von Rad rightly criticized Mowinckel's point of view as contrary to the exegesis of the relevant passages. His own theory and that of Fensham may be taken into account as two ways in which God has dealt with his people. The specific manifestation of his dealings, however, must not be identified with the origin of his dynamic and living intercourse with his people. Since the origin of all communication between God and people rests with him and manifested itself by way of revelation, it seems appropriate to look for the origin of this concept in the history of God's special revelation.

A significant aspect of this "history" is that God eventually will exert himself in a special manner, that he will appear on the day which he will create (Mal. 3:17, 21 [Eng. 4:3]), for ultimate salvation and judgment. According to S. Herrmann "the concept *day* describes the eventful and historic character of a powerful happening and its effects."[36] This is especially applicable on the Day of the Lord. We agree in this respect with M. Weiss that "the day of the Lord *per se* signifies the action of the Lord, his might- and power-potential. Those 'who desire the day of the Lord' are desiring the unfolding of his might and power, or in other words are anticipating an actual theophany in all its concrete incisiveness."[37]

32. S. Mowinckel, "Jahves Dag," *Norsk teologisk Tidskrift* (1958) 1–56; L. Cerny, *The Day of Yahweh and Some Relevant Problems* (Prague: University of Karlova, 1948).

33. Von Rad, "The Origin of the Concept of the Day of Yahweh," *JSS* 4 (1959) 97–108; idem, *Old Testament Theology,* II:119–25.

34. Fensham, "A Possible Origin of the Concept of the Day of the Lord," *Biblical Essays, OTWSA* (Potchefstroom: Pro Rege, 1966), pp. 90–97.

35. Gaster, op. cit., p. 688.

36. Herrmann, *A History of Israel in Old Testament Times,* tr. J. Bowden (London: SCM; Philadelphia: Fortress, 1975).

37. Weiss, *HUCA* 37 (1966) 47.

Many motifs are associated with the Day of the Lord. Seth Erlandsson enumerates the following six major motifs: wrath (Isa. 13:9, 13 with parallels in Zeph. 1:18; 2:2; 3:8), slaughter (Isa. 34; Zeph. 1:7, 8; etc.), devastation (Isa. 13:9; etc.), lamentation (Isa. 13:6; Ezek. 30:3; Joel 1:15), calamity and terror (Isa. 13:7; etc.), and cosmic changes (Isa. 13:10; Joel 2:2; Zeph. 1:15; etc.).[38]

We are especially interested in Malachi's representation of the Day of the Lord. It is characterized as follows. Malachi differentiates between a judgment of purification (3:2, 3) and the final judgment (3:19, 23 [Eng. 4:1, 5]). Roman Catholic interpreters are inclined to overemphasize the importance of this distinction. According to them both aspects of the judgment eventually pass via the intertestamental literature and the NT into the theological distinction between purgatory and the final judgment. According to our point of view the judgment of purification is an essential aspect of the judgment on the Day of the Lord. In the one the call for repentance is emphasized, but the implication is that the final judgment will become applicable when the people do not repent.

We maintain that Malachi restricted his announcement of the coming day exclusively to the covenant people. In this respect his presentation differs from the universal and cosmic motifs of other prophets (esp. Joel, Zephaniah, and Zechariah). The Day of the Lord will cause a crisis within the covenant people. On that "day" the difference between those who fear and serve God and those who do not will be apparent.

It is noteworthy that the people in the time of Malachi, just as in the days of Amos (5:18–20), expected the coming of the day (2:17; 3:1). We therefore disagree with some scholars according to whom there was a deep religious difference between the "popular" and the "prophetic" expectation. The real difference was not so much the expectation as such, but the application thereof on the people themselves and the conclusions that were drawn from it.

A significant aspect of Malachi's representation of the Day of the Lord is the notion that that day will be preceded by a "forerunner" (3:1, 23 [Eng. 4:5]). The coming of that day is God's answer to all the people's reproaches, and that is why it is represented as near at hand (3:1, 5, 19 [Eng. 4:1]). This characteristic trend in the prophetic eschatology must not be "dated," but concerns the dynamic character of its coming and emphasizes its seriousness and certainty. The coming of the Day of the Lord is real and

38. Erlandsson, *The Burden of Babylon: A Study of Isaiah 13:2–14:23*, Coniectanea Biblica, OT 4 (Lund: Gleerup, 1970), pp. 143–45.

timely in the concrete situation of the people's reproaches and sins, although the central and final fulfillments will occur respectively at the first and second comings of Christ. The universal and cosmic motif of Malachi's representation is found only in the notion of the annihilation of the wicked (3:19 [Eng. 4:1]) and the definition of the day as "the great and terrible day of the Lord" (3:23 [Eng. 4:5]; cf. Joel 2:11, 3:4 [Eng. 2:31]).

IX. MOSES AND ELIJAH (3:22–24 [Eng. 4:4–6])

22 (4) *Remember the law of my servant Moses, the decrees and ordinances that I commanded him at Horeb for all Israel.*
23 (5) *Behold, I will send you the prophet Elijah before the great and terrible day of the Lord comes.*
24 (6) *He will turn the hearts of the fathers to their children, and the hearts of the children to their fathers; or else I will come and strike the land with the ban.*

In this more or less independent addition to his prophecy Malachi focused attention on Moses, the lawgiver, and on Elijah, the representative of prophecy.

Scholarly opinions differ in connection with the authenticity and the inner relationship of these verses.[1] According to some interpreters v. 22 (Eng. 4:4) is considered to be a later addition by a Jew versed in the law, and vv. 23 and 24 (Eng. 4:5, 6) are regarded as secondary. Some of the reasons for regarding vv. 22–24 (Eng. 4:4–6) as secondary are the lack of continuity with the preceding prophecy, the absence of Malachi's dialogue style, and

1. The authenticity of this passage is endorsed by Von Bulmerincq, J. Ridderbos, Junker, Frey, Baldwin, and denied by Elliger, Deissler, Van der Woude. According to Nowack, Sellin, Smit, Deden, the only original verse is 3:22 (Eng. 4:4).

Van der Woude considers this passage the work of a representative of the Levitical Deuteronomistic movement, whose origin can be dated in the time of the Judges. This movement expressed itself also in Chronicles, and its subsequent history can be detected in the "synagogue of the pious people" *(hasidim),* the predecessors of the early Pharisees and the community of Essenes.

Scholars differ on whether this passage must be regarded as an epilogue to the book of Malachi (Smith, Horst, Elliger, Chary, Van der Woude), a postscript to the twelve Minor Prophets (Jones, Deissler; cf. also Haller), or a postscript to the canon of the Prophets, consisting of Joshua-Malachi (so Rudolph; cf. Marti). See also Snyman, "Antiteses," p. 208; D. G. Clark, "Elijah as Eschatological High Priest: An Examination of the Elijah Tradition in Mal. 3:22–24," Ph.D. diss., Notre Dame, 1975, p. 16.

especially the assumed dependence of these verses upon the diction of Deuteronomy. These and similar arguments are inconclusive, however. The content of these verses is fully in agreement with the general scope of Malachi's prophecy. As a matter of fact, in these verses the prophet appropriately focused attention on the two most significant themes of his message: the law and the prophecy, the covenant and the Day of the Lord. In the exegesis below we will return to some of the arguments.

22 (4) To survive the coming judgment the people must *remember the law of my servant Moses*. This is imperative! The Hebrew word *zāḵar* has an ambivalent meaning. It is not only to be reminded of something but also to act accordingly.[2] To "remember" something is to "do" *(ʿāśâ)* it (Num. 15:39, 40; Ps. 103:18), to "keep" *(šāmar)* it (Ps. 119:55), to "observe" *(nāṣar)* it (Ps. 119:56). At the same time to "remember" is "not to turn away" (*lōʾ nāṭâ,* Ps. 119:51), and "not to forget" (*lōʾ šāḵaḥ,* Ps. 119:61; Deut. 9:7).

The object of this imperative to remember is *the law of my servant Moses*. The extent of this "law" *(tôrâ)* is differently assessed. It is considered to be the Pentateuch (Marti, et al.), Deuteronomy (Wellhausen, et al.), the "lawbook" of Ezra (Von Bulmerincq). We agree with the tentative consideration of Horst, Deden, and others that the precise scope of this "law" is unknown. The reference to the law "of Moses" has, of course, its context in the Sinaitic covenant, with "all the Lord's words and ordinances" which Moses had written down (Exod. 24:3, 4). Reference to "the law of Moses" is also made in Dan. 9:11, 13 (cf. Isa. 63:11, 12; Jer. 15:1; Mic. 6:4).

The "law of Moses" is further defined in the phrase *that I commanded him at Horeb*. According to the Vulgate and some interpreters the antecedent of *ʾašer* is "the law of Moses," according to others it is "my servant Moses." Both are grammatically possible. Whatever our choice might be, it does not alter the meaning of the statement. In both cases the reference is to the "law" that has been revealed to Moses at Horeb. We need not enter into a detailed discussion concerning the so-called Deuteronomic phraseology that Malachi has adopted here.[3] Briefly, the argument is that the name of the mountain on which the law was given is predominantly *Horeb* in Deuteronomy (cf. 1:2, 6, 19; 4:10, 15; 5:2; 9:8; 18:16; 28:69 [Eng. 29:1]) and *Sinai* in P, the so-called priestly source (cf. Exod. 16:1; 24:16; 31:18; 34:29, 32; Lev. 7:38; 25:1; 26:46; 27:34; Num. 3:1; 28:6). But the alternative names

2. Cf. W. Schottroff, *"Gedenken" im Alten Orient und im Alten Testament,* WMANT 15 (Neukirchen-Vluyn: Neukirchener, 1964), pp. 156–57.

3. Van der Woude's conclusion is that 3:22 (Eng. 4:4) is not decisively Deuteronomic, but rather in accordance with the later Chronistic literature. This whole exercise is irrelevant for the understanding of the text.

are not confined to the two separate sources. The name *Sinai* also occurs in Deut. 33:2, and in passages usually attributed to the so-called E (Elohistic) and J (J/Yahwistic) sources (cf. Exod. 19:2, 23; 34:2, 4), and *Horeb* is also found in the E and J sources (cf. Exod. 3:1; 17:6; 33:6), and even in 2 Chr. 5:10 (cf. 1 K. 8:9; 19:8; Ps. 106:19). Both names occur in a parallel context in Sir. 48:7. We may grant the obvious fact that the name *Horeb* is mainly being used in the so-called Deuteronomistic (D) sources. But this need not imply that Malachi was exclusively dependent on "D" for his phraseology.

The fact remains that the Lord gave his law to Moses at Horeb. The reference is obviously to the Sinaitic covenant, which God made with his people on the basis of "all the Lord's words and ordinances," and which Moses had written down in "the book of the covenant" (Exod. 24:3–8; cf. 19:5, 6; 31:18; Deut. 4:10, 15; 5:2; 28:69 [Eng. 29:1]; 2 Chr. 5:10). This "law" was on behalf of *all Israel.* Some scholars suggest the deletion of this phrase because it is not used elsewhere in Malachi. The prophet indeed refers to Israel (1:1, 5; 2:16), and mentions "all the people" (2:9) and "the whole nation" (3:9). "Israel" and "all Israel" are often parallel terms (cf. Deut. 5:1; 6:3,4; 17:20; 18:1; etc.). The "all" in our text may refer to the entire nation, with the inclusion of their descendants, or to the nation in all its different groups or strata of people (cf. Deut. 29:1 with vv. 9, 10 [Eng. 2, 10, 11]). Both possibilities are appropriate for the meaning of "all Israel" in our text. The way in which God's law affected the different groups is expressed in Neh. 10:1–30 (Eng. 9:38–10:29). On the other hand "all Israel" has a technical meaning denoting the entire nation that was present at Horeb when God entered into a covenant relationship with them (Exod. 19–24; cf. 19:5, 6; 24:3–8). This covenant was continually renewed with "all Israel" (alternatively with "all Judah"): in the territory of Moab (Deut. 28:69 [Eng. 29:1]), in the times of Joshua (Josh. 24:25), Asa (2 Chr. 15:12), the high priest Jehoiada (2 K. 11:17), Hezekiah (2 Chr. 29:10), Josiah (2 K. 23:2, 3), and Ezra (10:3; cf. Jer. 23:8–22).

The "law" that was given to Moses consisted of *decrees and ordinances* (Heb. *ḥūqqîm ûmišpāṭîm.* This is obviously a reference to "the words" in Exod. 19:6 and all the Lord's words and ordinances (Heb. *hammišpāṭîm*) in Exod. 24:3. These were the stipulations of the covenant and the content of God's "Law." "In accordance *[ʿal]* with all these words" the Sinaitic covenant was made (Exod. 24:8). Those "words and ordinances" were written in "the book of the covenant," comprising Exod. 21:1–23:33, with the inclusion of the Decalogue (Exod. 20:1–17), and in a broader sense all the "laws" that were written in the Pentateuch.[4] Within the context of the

4. See G. Ch. Aalders, *Het Verbond Gods,* pp. 79–111.

Sinaitic covenant there is no need to distinguish between the *ḥūqqîm,* "decrees," and the *mišpāṭîm,* "ordinances." They are parallel terms expressive of the stipulations of the Sinaitic covenant. Malachi urges the people of his time to "remember" these stipulations and to observe them in all aspects of their covenant life. This will be one condition for their religious perseverance in the centuries to come. The second condition will be the perspective on the coming of Elijah.

23 (5) *Behold, I will send you the prophet Elijah.* The people's attention is drawn to this significant fact. God *will send.* Just as in 3:1, the *hinnēh* with the participle of *šālaḥ* is used here in the sense of a *futurum instans;* the sending is imminent! It will be *for you* (Heb. *lāḵem*), on your behalf. This is also evident from the purpose of this sending and the nature of the prophet's conduct. He is designated with name and function as *the prophet Elijah.* The LXX adds *tón Thesbítēn,* "the Tishbite" (cf. 1 K. 17:1). The description of Elijah as "the prophet" is also found in 1 K. 18:36 and 2 Chr. 21:12.

Interpreters differ about two problems concerning this Elijah. The first is whether he is the same as "the messenger" of 3:1. In the history of exegesis many interpreters distinguished between the two figures, "the messenger" of 3:1 being the forerunner of the first coming of Christ (John the Baptist), and "Elijah" being the forerunner of Christ's second coming. This interpretation was generally accepted by Roman Catholic scholars. Jewish exegetes like Kimchi and Ibn Ezra also distinguished between two persons, the one being Elijah (3:23) and the other (3:1) an angel (Kimchi) or the Messiah ben Joseph (Ibn Ezra). The majority of ancient and modern Protestant interpreters maintain that the two figures are in fact identical. The use of an appellative (3:1) and a proper name (3:23) to denote the "forerunner" is indeed strange, but not without precedent. A parallel situation concerns the reference to Cyrus (Kôreš) first in vague terms (Isa. 41:2, "one that is stirred up from the east"; and v. 25, "from the north"), and then by mentioning his name (Isa. 44:28). Compare also the reference to the Messiah as "David their king" (Jer. 30:9) and "my servant David" (Ezek. 34:23, 24; 37:24; Hos. 3:5). In both Mal. 3:1 and 3:23 (Eng. 4:5) the "figure" is *sent* by God to serve as a kind of "forerunner." The semantic domain of both presentations is the contracting nature of prophecy, according to which the different stages of the fulfillment are conceived of as one whole.

The second problem concerns the identity of "Elijah." In the history of exegesis many Jewish and Christian interpreters maintained that the historical prophet Elijah will return in person. This was apparently also the point of view of the LXX and of the Jews in the time of Christ (Matt. 17:10,

11), probably because of Elijah's ascension to heaven (2 K. 2:1–11) and the subsequent expectation of his coming again.

In the NT the proposed work of this "Elijah" was applied to John the Baptist (Luke 1:17). Jesus' answer to the question of the disciples, "Why then do the teachers of the law say that Elijah must come first?" is: "To be sure, Elijah comes and will restore all things. But I tell you, Elijah has already come" (Matt. 17:10–13 par. Mark 9:11–13, NIV); and: "If you are willing to accept it, he [John the Baptist] is Elijah who is to come" (Matt. 11:14).

In the light of the NT application it is not necessary to expect the coming again in person of the historical prophet Elijah. He was introduced in our text as a typical representative of the OT prophets. What was said about the historical Elijah who has proclaimed the divine judgment on a wicked dynasty and an apostate nation, but at the same time has called them to repentance (1 K. 18:20-46), has been applied to the Elijah of our text. He will go before the Lord "in the spirit and power of Elijah" (Luke 1:17).[5]

With the remark that he will be sent *before the great and terrible day of the Lord comes,* this Elijah is characterized as the paver of the way for the coming of the Lord. His function will therefore be the same as that of the "messenger" in 3:1. The expression "the great and terrible day of the Lord" is also found in Joel 3:4b (Eng. 2:31b), and by way of explanation in Joel 2:11. This "day" is also called "great" in Jer. 30:7; Zeph. 1:14 (cf. Hos. 2:2). The descriptive words "great" and "terrible" or "dreadful" are commonly used in the OT (cf. Deut. 1:19; 7:21; 8:15; 10:21; 2 Sam. 7:23; Ps. 99:3; Dan. 9:4; Neh. 1:5; 4:8; 9:32; 1 Chr. 17:21). Both these words do occur elsewhere in Malachi in the same verse (1:14). There is no need to regard v. 23b as being a gloss taken from Joel 3:4b (Eng. 2:31b), with the assumption that v. 24 was directly preceded by v. 23a (so Sellin, Deden, et al.). The notion of the day that comes as the Day of the Lord is well established in Malachi's prophecy concerning the imminent judgment (3:1, 5, 17, 19, 21 [Eng. 4:1, 3]).

24 (6) The purpose and seriousness of Elijah's coming is now described. *He will turn the hearts of the fathers to their children, and the hearts of the children to their fathers.* In connection with the rendering of the Peshitta and Vulgate *(convertet)* many interpreters consider the Hebrew verb *hēšîḇ* (from *šûḇ;* cf. 2:6) to mean "turn toward," "turn about," *faire re-*

5. We may grant the correctness of Van der Woude's observation that the text itself does not visualize a person other than the historical Elijah, with reference to D. G. Clark, op. cit. An essential aspect of the interpretation of a prophecy is the consideration of its fulfillment in the context of the canon. To exclude this element from the exegesis is to deprive such a prophecy of its ultimate meaning.

tourner (Halevy), *convertira* (Ostervald), "to convert" (Luther, Pressel, et al.). This interpretation is determined by the rendering of *ʿal* in connection with the LXX *prós* and the Vulgate *ad* in the sense of *ʾel,* "to" (cf. Jer. 11:10; Prov. 26:11; Job 34:15; Eccl. 12:7; 2 Chr. 30:9). According to this translation Elijah will turn the hearts of the fathers to their children, and the children's hearts to their fathers. There are differences of opinion concerning what this really means, however. Many interpreters are of the opinion that Elijah will again pacify the family quarrels that were caused by the mixed marriages and divorces mentioned in 2:10–16. The main purpose of Elijah's coming will therefore be to establish a new social order. This point of view is, according to Jeremias, et al., supported by ancient Near Eastern eschatology. A significant trend in this eschatology is the expectation of a renewed social order. The social disorder would be the characteristic of the time of curse.[6]

This interpretation seems feasible, especially when viewed in a synchronistic sense. At a given time Elijah would mend the broken family ties and would restore the *šālôm,* "the peace," within Israel's social order.[7]

But we favor the point of view according to which the semantic domain of this *hēšîḇ,* "turning back," is not so much the projected social order but the covenant relationship as such. When Elijah comes he will restore the covenant relationship. In this process he will turn about the hearts of the wicked posterity to the hearts of them with whom God has entered into a covenant at Horeb. We agree with Josef Scharbert that the solidarity between fathers and children must be determined from the covenant relationship.[8] The present order must be reconciled with the previous state of things when God has entered into a covenant relationship with the "fathers." We have an interesting parallel in Isa. 63:16. The "Israel" in the time of the prophet laments because their actual communication with Abraham and Jacob seems to have been broken: "Abraham does not know us and Israel [i.e., Jacob] does not acknowledge us." The fathers are of no significance any more when the "children" become apostate. That relationship can only be restored by way of the renewal of the covenant. This point of view is in accordance with Malachi's idiom. He compares the priesthood of his day

6. See A. Jeremias, *Babylonisches im Neuen Testament* (Leipzig: Hinrichs, 1905), pp. 97–98; idem, *The Old Testament in the Light of the Ancient East,* 2 vols., tr. C. L. Beaumont, ed. C. H. W. Johns (New York: Putnam's Sons, 1911), 2:312.

7. Rudolph considers the reason for this prophecy to be the fact that the hellenizing process during the centuries before the Christian era caused the younger generation to estrange themselves from the religious tradition of the fathers.

8. Scharbert, *Solidarität in Segen und Fluch im AT und in seiner Umwelt, I: Väterfluch und Vätersegen,* Bonner biblische Beiträge 14 (Bonn: Hanstein, 1958).

with that of the classical times (2:1–9), and the offerings of Judah and Jerusalem in his time with that "in days gone by, (and) in former years" (3:4). The present generation has through mixed marriages profaned the covenant entered into with their fathers (2:10), with the verdict that they will be cut off "from the tents of Jacob" (2:12).

This interpretation does not imply that the fathers themselves have not, on occasion, broken the covenant. In Mal. 3:7 it is stated explicitly. On occasion the Lord's wrath was poured out on the fathers, but when they repented of their sins, he was willing to accept them again (cf. Isa. 14:1; 29:22; 58:14; 65:9; Zech. 1:2–4). The acknowledgment of their own and their fathers' sins is an inherent aspect of true confession (Lev. 26:40; Isa. 64:1–11; Dan. 9:8, 16). In our text Malachi is expecting such a turnabout of the attitude, not as an initiative taken by the people themselves but as an act of God, who will send his prophet "Elijah" to perform it. By way of conversion (3:7, 10–12), the remembering and obeying of "the law of Moses" (3:22 [Eng. 4]), and the work of Elijah (3:23, 24 [Eng. 5, 6]), the solidarity of sins and curses will be broken and will be replaced by the solidarity of "peace" and blessings in the context of the covenant. Fathers and children will not meet one another on the temporary or personal plane, because the hearts of the fathers will then not be able to be turned to the children. The point of reference, the scope of the encounter, in this process of turning to one another is the covenant relationship, which transcends the many periods of apostasy, and which forms the real basis for the restored communion with God, their Father and Creator (1:6; 2:10), and with one another, stretching across the centuries of their history (1:2, 5; 2:4–7, 10; 3:3–4, 7, 10–12).

The seriousness of Elijah's mission must be conceived of in the light of the possibility that he might not succeed. The consequences are introduced by the "conjunction of rejection," Heb. *pen*, "lest," "otherwise."[9] It is important to understand that it is not "the coming" of the Lord that is to be prevented but his "striking" of the land. The Hebrew conjunction *pen* therefore must not be translated "lest I come" (NEB; cf. LXX and Vulg.), because the coming of the Lord is certain. Thus we prefer the rendering "or else," "otherwise" (NIV). If Elijah's mission will not attain its object, the Lord's coming will have a serious effect. *and strike the land with the ban.* The Hebrew verb *hikkêṯî* (Hiphil of *nāḵâ*) has a double accusative: "land" and "ban." The second accusative can be interpreted as an inner object, "as or like a ban,"[10] or as an instrumental accusative, "with or through the ban" (Köhler, Pressel, et al.). Both translations and interpretations are possible.

9. See Driver, *Tenses,* § 41; GKC, § 107q.
10. See König, *Syntax,* § 329h.

We prefer the second alternative because "ban," Heb. *ḥērem,* is here taken in the sense of utter destruction. That which God will strike is *hā'āreṣ,* not in the sense of "earth" (contra Luther, AV, et al.), but of "land," the territory of the fathers and children, the "delightful land" of 3:12 (cf. NEB, RSV, NIV, etc.). The "land" includes metonymically all its people (cf. Judg. 18:30; Isa. 66:8; etc.). The threat therefore is comprehensive; it is directed to the promised land, with the inclusion of the treasured possession of the Lord (3:17).

The threat is described in terms of the *ḥērem* (Vulg. *anathema*). The semantic domain of this term is a thing or person secluded from society and life and devoted either for destruction or for sacred use. According to R. de Vaux this term later became part of the general vocabulary of the cult (cf. Num. 18:14; Lev. 27:21, 28; Ezek. 44:29), but it belonged originally to the ritual language of the holy war.[11] De Vaux's diachronic delineation of *ḥērem*'s meaning may be questioned, but not its usage in the different spheres. Irrespective of its general use (cf. Jer. 50:21, 26; 51:3; Mic. 4:13), the term *ḥērem* is used in the prophetic literature as a metaphor for total destruction (cf. Isa. 43:28 [and NIV's footnote!]; Jer. 25:9). In Isa. 34 the meaning of *ḥērem* is defined in parallel terms: "to slaughter" (v. 2), "to descend in judgment" (v. 5), as the execution of God's wrath (v. 2). In our text, just as in Isa. 34:2 and Zech. 14:11, *ḥērem* is used in an eschatological context (so, rightly, Von Bulmerincq).

The prophecy of Malachi began by reminding the people of God of his irrevocable love (1:2–5), and it ends with the probable perspective on their utter destruction. God's judgment cannot be separated from his grace. "If any one has no love for the Lord, let him be accursed" (1 Cor. 16:22).

In the synagogue Mal. 3:4–24 forms the *haphtara,* the prophetic passage, to be read on the "great sabbath." The instruction to the reader of this pericope is, just as in the case of Isaiah, Lamentations, and Ecclesiastes, to repeat the next-to-last verse, because of the serious content of the last one (cf. JPSV). It is probably the reason why the LXX has transposed the verses to end the pericope with v. 22.

In the concluding section, vv. 22–24 (Eng. 4:4–6), the two main foci of Malachi's prophecy are again emphasized. The admonition to remember and obey "the law of Moses" is closely connected with the stipulations of the Sinaitic covenant (Exod. 19:5, 6, 8; 24:3–8). This covenant relationship is one of the pervasive motifs of Malachi's prophecy (cf. 1:2–5; 2:4–7, 10–12; 3:4). The second focus or motif concerns the coming of the Day of the Lord (2:17–3:5; 3:13–21 [Eng. 4:3]). That day will be a judgment

11. De Vaux, *Ancient Israel,* p. 260.

of purification (3:2–5), but at the same time a day that will reveal the real antithesis between the righteous and the wicked (3:13–21 [Eng. 4:3]). Before the coming of this great and terrible day Elijah will appear to rejoin ancestors and posterity in the benefits and blessings of the covenant relationship (3:23, 24a [Eng. 4:5, 6a]). If the covenant people will not allow Elijah to unite them in the fear of the Lord, they will be crushed with the ban of utter destruction (3:24b [Eng. 4:6b]).

The "last words" in Malachi's prophecy therefore serve a double purpose. They emphasize a life in accordance with the "law of Moses," that is, the word of God, and they focus attention again on the coming of the great and terrible day. These two motifs would also be of decisive significance for the covenant people in the centuries to come. The subsequent history reveals that the maintenance of the law soon degenerated into legalism and observantism, and that in spite of their messianic expectations the people in general were unable to recognize Jesus as their Messiah.[12]

With regard to the fulfillment of vv. 23–24 (Eng. 4:5–6), we have the problem that the reference to the great and dreadful day suggests Christ's coming again, while the NT recognized John the Baptist as being the promised Elijah (Luke 1:17; Matt. 11:10; 17:10–13; Mark 9:19–13). We have already pointed out that it belongs to the nature of prophecy to project separate future events into one eschatological "picture." In addition it is important to note that one fulfillment does not exclude the possibility of further fulfillments in the course of history. This is especially applicable to the first and second comings of Christ. That means that an aspect of the prophecy concerning Elijah and the coming of the Day of the Lord has a first and central fulfillment in the time of Christ's first coming, and that the final and ultimate fulfillment will be when he comes again. At the same time we may allow for various provisional fulfillments in the course of the Church's history.

The eschatological role that Malachi attributed to the person of Elijah became the biblical point of departure for later Jewish eschatology. The general view is that Elijah would be the forerunner of the Messiah. This expectation is also reflected among the Jews in the time of the NT (cf. Matt. 11:14; 17:10; Mark 9:11; Luke 1:17; John 1:21, 25). When Elijah arrives one or three days before the coming of the son of David, it will be his obligation to renew Israel both externally and internally. The external renewal will be to settle problems pertaining to family registers. Internally Elijah's task will be

12. See my *Messiasverwagting tussen die Ou en die Nuwe Testament* (Cape Town: N. G. Kerk Uitgewers, 1959), pp. 15–18; R. H. Charles, *Religious Development between the Old and the New Testaments* (London: Williams & Norgate, 1945), pp. 77–78; etc.

to put aside all juridical and religious quarrels among the people. He will also share in the resurrection of the dead and the anointing of the Messiah.

According to some talmudic traditions Elijah will also be a high priest. This argument links up with three texts in the prophecy of Malachi. The Elijah of 3:23 (Eng. 4:5) is the same as "the messenger (angel) of the covenant" (3:1), and this covenant is the one which God had entered into with the tribe of Levi (2:4). Therefore Elijah is regarded as a descendant of Levi.[13]

A new perspective on Elijah is opened when Mal. 2:4 is linked up with the "covenant of peace" that was made with Phinehas (Num. 25:11–13). According to this tradition Elijah and Phinehas will be one and the same.[14] In talmudic circles this high priestly figure is merely a forerunner of the Messiah. Among the priestly sect of Qumran he will be the high priestly Messiah.[15] This explains the problem concerning John the Baptist's denial that he is the Elijah that would come (John 1:21). John was addressing people in the neighborhood of the Qumran sect, and they regarded Elijah as the most significant messianic figure.

According to the church fathers Elijah would be one of the witnesses mentioned in Rev. 11:3–12.

13. See H. Strack and P. Billerbeck, *Kommentar zum Neuen Testament aus Talmud und Midrasch* (München: Beck, 1924), IV:462–63. Additional literature on Elijah in the Jewish tradition includes E. Schürer, *The History of the Jewish People in the Age of Jesus Christ,* rev. ed., ed. G. Vermes, et al. (Edinburgh: T. & T. Clark, 1979), II:515–16; J. Jeremias, in *TDNT,* II:931–33; A. de Guzlielmo, *Dissertatio exegetica de reditu Eliae* (Jerusalem: 1938); J. Kroon, "De wederkomst van Elias," *Studiën* 131 (1939) 1–11; J. Klausner, *The Messianic Idea in Israel,* tr. W. F. Stinespring (New York: Macmillan, 1955), pp. 451–57; Walter J. Michel, "I will send you Elijah," *TBT* 22 (1984) 217–22; Dale C. Allison, Jr., "Elijah Must Come First," *JBL* 103 (1984) 256–58.

In some Jewish circles the "Angel of the covenant" is conceived of as a forerunner of the Lord, and identified with Melchizedek/Michael, who would fulfill Elijah's duty to restore the diaspora and atone for the sins of the children of light. Cf. A. S. Van der Woude, "Melchizedek als himmlische Erlösergestalt in den neugefundenen eschatologischen Midraschim aus Qumran Höhle XI," *OTS* 14 (1965) 354–73.

14. See A. S. van der Woude, *Die messianischen Vorstellungen der Gemeinde von Qumran,* Studia semitica neerlandica 3 (1957), p. 228.

15. See Van der Woude, op. cit., p. 88; W. H. Brownlee, "John the Baptist in the New Light of Ancient Scrolls," in *The Scrolls and the New Testament,* ed. K. Stendahl (London: SCM, 1958), pp. 33–53.

INDEXES

I. CHIEF SUBJECTS

II. AUTHORS

Aalders, G.Ch. 12, 164, 231, 267, 309, 339
Ackroyd, P.R. 5, 6, 9, 10, 11, 59, 71, 106, 110, 113, 119, 120
Adamson, J.T.H. 157, 198
Albright, W.F. 6, 12, 26, 29, 30, 31, 160
Alt, A. 32, 219
Amsler, S. 83, 113, 118, 125
Andersen, F.I. 59, 130
André, T. 4, 5, 6, 8, 14, 67, 72, 73, 106, 112, 115, 125, 133
Augustine 153

Baldwin, J.G. 6, 7, 12, 16, 18, 25, 28, 30, 31, 32, 33, 50, 51, 52, 56, 57, 59, 62, 74, 83, 87, 88, 92, 94, 97, 99, 102, 104, 114, 116, 122, 129, 130, 132, 145, 163, 164, 166, 180, 181, 188, 198, 215, 222, 233–34, 237, 243, 265, 272, 275, 277, 278, 283, 286, 300, 303, 337
Balla, E. 165, 166
Beek, M.A. 326
Begrich, J. 85, 115, 116
Bentzen A. 17, 159
Berkhof, H. 137
Berkouwer, G. C. 201, 307
Beuken, W.A.M. 3, 6, 7, 9, 10, 11, 12, 14, 25, 40, 45, 46, 47, 48, 50, 51, 53, 54, 56, 57, 60, 64, 67, 69, 70, 71, 73, 76, 80, 81, 83, 85, 86, 89, 91, 93, 98, 106, 115, 119, 120, 121, 123, 126, 129, 132, 141, 142, 145, 147
Beyse, K.-M. 3, 5, 6, 7, 8, 11, 25, 26, 27, 28, 29, 30, 31, 40, 138, 140, 142, 145, 146, 148
Blenkinsopp, J. 8, 25, 32, 120, 149, 158, 230, 288
Bloomhardt, P.F. 11, 118
Boecker, H.J. 164, 197
Böhme, W. 14, 15, 83
Botterweck, G.J. 179, 198, 217, 239, 256, 258, 269, 271, 313, 318, 320
Brandenburg, H. 81, 89, 198, 210, 220, 222, 310, 311, 313
Bright, J.G. 6, 11, 25, 26, 27, 29, 36, 37, 38, 158, 160, 219, 256
Brockelmann, C. 44, 55, 60, 69, 72, 99, 117, 209, 225
Brockington, L.H. 200, 239
Budde, K. 44, 51, 67, 72, 73, 89, 91, 100, 110, 125, 133, 319
von Bulmerincq, A., 195, 227, 228, 229, 239, 286, 291, 308, 313, 318, 324, 325, 331, 337, 338, 344

Calvin, J. 82, 85, 87, 104, 105, 106, 119, 201, 211, 246, 277, 286, 287, 291, 303, 320, 323, 324, 328, 331
Cappellus, L. 203, 287, 293, 323, 331
Caquot, A. 241
Cerny, L. 334
Charles, R.H. 345
Chary, T. 32, 37, 38, 53, 63, 69, 72, 73, 75, 100, 113, 119, 222, 268, 278, 283, 302, 337
Clark, D.J. 111, 114, 121, 125, 126, 127, 128, 130, 131, 132, 133, 134, 337, 341
Clement of Alexandria 225
Cody, A. 259
Cyrillus 61, 70, 286, 318, 324

Dahood, M. 73, 74, 262
Dalman, G. 70, 76, 126, 127
de Boer, P.A.H. 187
Deden, D. 9, 16, 47, 63, 71, 73, 91, 112, 204, 268, 286, 319, 337, 338, 341

III. SCRIPTURE REFERENCES

IV. NONBIBLICAL TEXTS

V. HEBREW WORDS